Napoleone Perini

An Italian conversation grammar : comprising the most important rules of Italian grammar, with numerous examples and exercises thereon, English-Italian dialogues, hints on Italian versification, and extracts in Italian poetry

Napoleone Perini

An Italian conversation grammar : comprising the most important rules of Italian grammar, with numerous examples and exercises thereon, English-Italian dialogues, hints on Italian versification, and extracts in Italian poetry

ISBN/EAN: 9783337156909

Printed in Europe, USA, Canada, Australia, Japan

Cover: Foto ©Paul-Georg Meister /pixelio.de

More available books at **www.hansebooks.com**

AN ITALIAN
CONVERSATION GRAMMAR

COMPRISING THE MOST IMPORTANT RULES OF ITALIAN GRAMMAR, WITH
NUMEROUS EXAMPLES AND EXERCISES THEREON, ENGLISH-ITALIAN
DIALOGUES, HINTS ON ITALIAN VERSIFICATION, AND EXTRACTS
IN ITALIAN POETRY,

FOLLOWED BY

A SHORT GUIDE TO ITALIAN COMPOSITION.

ALSO AN ENGLISH-ITALIAN AND ITALIAN-ENGLISH VOCABULARY.

Throughout this Grammar the tonic accent on words is marked in darker
type, and the proper pronunciations of the letters "E," "O," "S,"
and "Z," are indicated.

By N. PERINI, F.R.A.S.,

Professor of Italian at King's College, London, and at the Royal College of Music, and at University College, Bristol, and Italian Examiner to the University of London, the Victoria University, Manchester, the Civil Service Commissioners, the Staff College, the Royal Military Academy, Woolwich, and the Society of Arts.

FOURTH EDITION—CAREFULLY REVISED.

LIBRAIRIE HACHETTE & CIE.

LONDON: 18, KING WILLIAM STREET, CHARING CROSS, W.C.
PARIS: 79, BOULEVARD SAINT-GERMAIN.
BOSTON, U.S.: CARL SCHOENHOF.

1895.
[ALL RIGHTS RESERVED.]

DEDICATED, BY PERMISSION, TO

LORD TENNYSON, POET LAUREATE.

D.C.L., F.R.S., &c.

PREFACE.

In bringing before the public this grammar, which is arranged in a way different from that generally adopted, I feel it incumbent on me to offer a few words of explanation.

I have throughout adhered to the deductive method, that is, I do not set any exercise before the student, except on points previously explained. I have always regarded as mischievous the system of setting exercises beyond the knowledge of the student, and in which one-half of the words are translated; these may be called exercises in writing, rather than exercises on grammar, and in doing them the student often loses sight of the very points the grammarian wishes to elucidate.

I have made the verb the framework of the whole grammar, as it is impossible to form a sentence without it. I have also discarded the usual method of separating Accidence from Syntax, for it seems to me that such a separation has no existence in reality; I have combined the two parts, and gradually introduced the Syntax as I thought its knowledge would be required by the student.

Being convinced, as most people now are, that the best way of learning a foreign language is to translate into it from one's own language, I have added to this grammar a Short Guide to Italian Composition, comprising extracts in English prose, with notes to facilitate their translation into Italian. I have also given some hints on Italian versification, and extracts in Italian Poetry, so that the student may, at an early stage, learn how to read, and, if so disposed, commit to memory some of the finest verses in the Italian language, and thus acquire a correct Italian accent. I have supplemented the whole with Vocabularies, which will enable the student not only to dispense with any other book for the first lessons, but to find without loss of time the word he wants.

The meaning of the letters in darker type, which will be found in many Italian words throughout this grammar, and the directions for the proper pronunciations of the letters "E," "O," "S," and "Z," which is a very important feature in my book, are given in rules 5, 9, 48, 53, and 63.

I hope that the improvements I have made in my book will increase the favour I have already received from my colleagues and from the public, and for which I am very grateful.

N. PERINI.

KING'S COLLEGE, LONDON.
    November, 1895.

TABLE OF CONTENTS.

	PAGE
INTRODUCTION	1

The Alphabet. Pronunciation of the Vowels. Pronunciation of the Consonants. Rules for Dividing Words into Syllables. On the Pronunciation of Words. The Written Accent. The Apostrophe. Use of Capital Letters. On Reading and Speaking Italian. Reading Exercises.

LESSON

I.	On the Definite Article	13
	On the Prepositions, "Di," "A," "Da"	14
II.	On the Verb, "Avere," *to have*	16
III.	On the Modes of Addressing People in Italian	19
	On the Interrogative and Negative Forms of Verbs	20
IV.	On the Partitive Article	22
	On the Indefinite Article	23
V.	On the Verb "Essere," *to be*	25
	On the Verb "Essere," with "Ci," and "Vi"	27
VI.	On the Verbs	28
	On the First Conjugation in "Are"	29
VII.	On the Personal Pronouns	34
	On the Conjunctive Personal Pronouns	35
	On the Disjunctive Personal Pronouns	38
VIII.	On the Double Conjunctive Pronouns	40
IX.	On the Words, "Ci," "Vi," and "Ne"	43
X.	On the Second Conjugation in "Ere"	46
XI.	On the Third Conjugation in "Ire"	50
XII.	On Verbs conjugated Passively	54
XIII.	On the Neuter Verbs	56
XIV.	On the Reflective and Reciprocal Verbs	59
XV.	On the Impersonal Verbs	62
XVI.	On the Impersonal Verbs expressive of the State of the Weather	65
XVII.	On the Irregular Verbs	66
XVIII.	On the Use of the Definite and Partitive Articles	93
XIX.	On the Use of the Indefinite Article	97
XX.	On the Gender and Number of Nouns	99
XXI.	On the Compound Nouns	109
XXII.	On the Italian Suffixes	111
	On the Collective Nouns	113

CONTENTS.

LESSON		PAGE
XXIII.	On Qualitative Adjectives	115
	On "Bello," "Grande," "Buono," "Santo," "Tutto," "Mezzo," "Ogni," "Altro," "Molto," "Tanto," &c.	117
XXIV.	On the Formation of Adverbs	122
	On the Degrees of Comparison	123
XXV.	On the Numeral Adjectives	128
XXVI.	On the Possessive Adjectives	132
	On the Possessive Pronouns	136
XXVII.	On the Demonstrative Adjectives	138
	On the Demonstrative Pronouns	140
	On the Demonstrative Personal Pronouns	141
XXVIII.	On the Relative Pronouns	143
XXIX.	On the Indefinite Pronouns	147
	On "Niente," "Nulla," "Quanto," and "Per Quanto"	152
XXX.	On the Infinitive Mood	154
XXXI.	On the Indicative Mood	156
XXXII.	On the Subjunctive Mood, and "Se"	161
XXXIII.	On the Form and Use of Passive Verbs	168
XXXIV.	On "Volere," "Dovere," "Potere," and "Sapere"	171
XXXV.	On the Negation	173
XXXVI.	On the Past Participle	176
XXXVII.	On the Verbs "Avere," "Essere," "Andare," "Dare," "Fare," "Stare," "Sapere," "Tenere," "Volere," and "Venire" used idiomatically	179
XXXVIII.	On the Adverbs	190
	On the Words "Onde," "Bene," and "Pure"	196
XXXIX.	On the Prepositions	198
XL.	On the Complements of Verbs	205
XLI.	On the Conjunctions and Interjections	209
	Transposition of Words in Italian Sentences	212
	Italian Idioms and Sayings	213
	Italian Proverbs	215
	English-Italian Dialogues	216
	Titles and Expressions used in Italian Letters	222
	A Guide to Italian Composition	224
	Italian Poetry	235
	English-Italian Vocabulary	246
	Italian-English Vocabulary	259

ITALIAN GRAMMAR.

INTRODUCTION.

ON THE PRONUNCIATION AND SPELLING OF THE ITALIAN LANGUAGE.

THE ALPHABET.

1. The Italian Alphabet consists of the following twenty-one letters:—

A, B, C, D, E, F, G, H, I, L, M, N, O, P, Q, R, S, T, U, V, Z. *

A, E, I, O, U, are vowels, and the other letters are consonants.

2. The Italian language is very nearly pronounced as it is written. There are no *real* diphthongs in Italian.

PRONUNCIATION OF THE VOWELS.

3. A is pronounced like the *a*, in *artist*. Ex. "amara," *bitter*.

4. E has two different sounds; one like that of the *e* in the English word *emigrant*. Ex. "pena," *punishment*, "fedele," *faithful*; the other a broad sound, like that of the *a* in the English word *gate*. Ex. "balestra," *cross-bow*, "bella," *beautiful*.

5. Throughout this grammar a dot is placed under the letter *e*, thus ẹ, when it has the broad sound of the *a* in the English word *gate*.

---

6. * The Letters, K, W, X, Y, are not made use of in spelling Italian words. The letter J was formerly used in spelling many Italian words, but it is now generally discarded; the letter *i*, which has very nearly the same sound as *j* (see rule 7), being used instead.

7. I is pronounced like the *ee*, in *eel*. Ex. " vita " *life*.

8. O has two different sounds ; one like that of the *o*, in the English word *vote;* as "fiore," *flower*, "colpo," *blow*, "molto," *much;* the other like that of the *o* in the English word *orphan*. Ex. " ọro,"* *gold*, "cọrpo," *body*, "tọsto," *soon*.

9. Throughout this grammar a dot is placed under the letter *o*, thus ọ, when it has the broad sound of the *v* in the English word *orphan*.

10. U is pronounced like the *oo*, in the English word *moon*. Ex. " uno," *one*, "universo," *universe*, " volume," *volume*.

PRONUNCIATION OF THE CONSONANTS.

11. The consonants B, D, F,† L, M, N, P, R,‡ T,§ and V, are pronounced in the same manner as in English.

Pronunciation of the letter C.

C, followed by A, O, or U, has a hard sound.

12. CA is pronounced like the *ca*, in *cart*. Ex. " capo," *head*.
13. CO is pronounced like the *co*, in *comet*. Ex. "colombo," *dove*.
14. CU is pronounced like the *cu*, in *cuckoo*. Ex. " cura," *cure*.

C, followed by E or I, has a soft sound.

15. CE is pronounced like the *cha*, in *chase*. Ex. " cena," *supper*.
16. CI is pronounced like the *chi*, in *chip*. Ex. " cibo," *food*.

H hardens the sound of C before E and I.

17. CHE is pronounced like the *ca*, in *cake*. Ex. " cheto," *quiet*.
18. CHI is pronounced like the *kee*, in *keep*. Ex. " chiave," *key*.

Pronunciation of SCE, and SCI.

19. SCE is pronounced like the *sha*, in *shape*. Ex. " scẹna," *scene*.
20. SCI is pronounced like the *shee*, in *sheep*. Ex. " sciame," *swarm*.

---

21. * When there are two or three o's in a word, the second and third always have the same sound as the first. Ex. " ọrọ," *gold*, " crọnọlọgia," *chronology*.

22. † The Italians always substitute *f* for *ph*, in words derived from the Greek. Ex. " filosofia," *philosophy*.

23. ‡ Notice that the " r," is pronounced much more emphatically in Italian than in English. Ex. " burro," *butter*.

24. § Notice that in Italian the vowel *u* is never pronounced like the *u* in the English word *union*, but always like the two o's, in the English word *moon*.

Pronunciation of the Letter G.

G, followed by A, O, or U, is pronounced hard.

25. GA is pronounced like the *ga*, in *garden*.   Ex. "gabbia," *cage*.
26. GO is pronounced like the *go*, in *goblet*.   Ex. "gola," *throat*.
27. GU is pronounced like the *goo*, in *goose*.   Ex. "gufo," *owl*.

G, followed by E or I, has a soft sound.

28. GE is pronounced like the *ge*, in *gem*.   Ex. "gente," *people*.
29. GI* is pronounced like the *gi*, in *gin*.   Ex. "giro," *turn*.

H, hardens the sound of G before E and I.

30. GHE is pronounced like the *ga*, in *gate*.   Ex. "leghe," *leagues*.
31. GHI is pronounced like the *gi*, in *gimlet*.   Ex. "laghi," *lakes*.

Pronunciation of GLI.

32. GLI is pronounced like the *illi*, in *postillion*.   Ex. "giglio," *lily*.

33. Notice, however, that "gli" is pronounced like the *gli*, in *glimmer*, in the words "Anglia," *England*, "anglicano," *Anglican*, "geroglifico," *hieroglyphic, hieroglyphical*, "negligenza," *negligence*, and in the verb "negligere," *to neglect*.

Pronunciation of GN.

34. GN is pronounced like the *gn*, in *design*.   Ex. "agnello," *lamb*.

On the Letter H.

35. H has no sound by itself, and may be considered as an auxiliary letter.

36. The principal use of the letter H in Italian is, as already explained in rules 17, 18, 30, 31, to give to the letters *c* and *g* a hard sound, when they are followed by *e* or *i*.

37. H is also used at the beginning of the words "ho," *I have*, "hai," *thou hast*, "ha," *he has*, and "hanno," *they have;* in which words the *h* is retained only to distinguish them from "o," meaning *or*, "ai," *to the*, "a," *to* or *at*, and "anno" *year*. The *h* is further used in the interjections "ah!" "oh!" "ahi!" "ehi!"

---

38. * The student should pay great attention to the pronunciation of the letters *c* and *g*, and to bear well in mind that the *i* serves only to soften the sound of *c*, and *g*, in the syllables "cia," "cio," "ciu," "gia," "gio," and "giu," which must be pronounced as *one*, and *not as two* syllables. Ex. "ciarlare" *to chat*, "ciotto," *pebble*, "ciuffo," *lock of hair*, "giallo," *yellow*, "giorno," *day*, "maggiore," *greater*, "giusto," *just*.

Pronunciation of QUA, QUE, QUI, and QUO.

39. QUA* is pronounced like the *qua*, in *quality*. Ex." quadro," *picture*.
40. QUE is pronounced like the *que*, in *question*. Ex. "questo," *this*.
41. QUI is pronounced like the *qui*, in *quick*. Ex. "quinto," *fifth*.
42. QUO is pronounced like the *quo*, in *quotation*. Ex. "quọta," *share*.

Pronunciation of the Letter S.

43. S has two different sounds; a sharp hissing sound, and a soft one.

44. S, at the beginning of a word, and followed by a vowel, has a hard sound, like the *s* in the English word *spirit*. Ex. "sito," *site*.

45. S, at the beginning of a word, and followed by one of the consonants *c, f, p, q, t*, has a hard sound, like the *s* in the English word *spirit*. Ex. "scanno," *bench*, "sforzo," *effort*, "spia," *spy*, "squadrone," *squadron*, "storpio," *lame*.

46. S, at the beginning of a word, and followed by one of the consonants *b, d, g, l, m, n, r, v*, has a soft sound, like the *s* in the English word *rose*. Ex. "ṣbaglio," *mistake*, "ṣdegno," *disdain*, "ṣgabello," *stool*, "ṣleale," *disloyal*, "ṣmalto," *enamel*, "ṣnello," *nimble*, "ṣregolato," *disorderly*, "ṣvelare," *to unveil*.

47. S, between two vowels, has, as a rule, the soft sound of the *s* in the English word *rose*. Ex. "spoṣo," *bridegroom*, "chieṣa," *church*; but this rule has numerous exceptions.

48. Throughout this grammar a dot is placed under the *s*, thus ṣ, when it has the soft sound of the *s* in the English word *rose*.

49. When the *s* is doubled it always has a hard, hissing sound. Ex. "rarissimo," *very rare*.

Pronunciation of the Letters Z and ZZ.

50. Z has two sounds; one sharp, like that of the *ts* in the English word *wits*. Ex. "zampa," *paw*, "zio," *uncle*, "amicizia," *friendship*, "prudẹnza," *prudence;* the other sound like that of the letter *z* in the English word *zeal*. Ex. "ẓelo," *zeal*, "garẓone," *youth, waiter*.

---

51. * Notice that the letter *q*, in Italian, is always followed by *u*.

52. ZZ have two different sounds; one like that of the *ts* in the English word *wits*. Ex. "piazza," *square*, "bellezza," *beauty*, "prezzo," *price*, "nozze," *wedding*, "mezzo," *over-ripe*; the other sound like that of the *zz* in the English word *muzzle*. Ex. "dozzina," *dozen*, "orizzonte," *horizon*, "gazza," *magpie*, "gazzetta," *gazette*, "mezzo,"* *middle, means, half.*

53. Throughout this grammar a dot is placed under the *z*, thus ẓ, when it has the soft sound of the *z* in the English word *zeal;* and dots are placed under the two *zz*, thus ẓẓ, when they have the soft sound of the *zz* in the English word *muzzle*.

RULES FOR DIVIDING WORDS INTO SYLLABLES.

54. (i) One or two consonants at the beginning of a word, followed by one, two, or even three vowels, form a syllable. Ex. "ve-de-re," *to see*, "pre-ga-re," *to pray*, "fie-le," *gall*, "quie-to," *quiet*, "scuo-la," *school*. Except when the stress of the voice, or what is called the "Tonic Accent," falls upon one of the vowels; in that case that vowel marks the end of the syllable. Ex. "Di-o," *God*, "mi-o," *my*.

55. (ii) A consonant between two vowels makes a syllable with the second vowel. Ex. "a-mi-co," *friend*, "o-no-re," *honour*.

56. (iii) When two consonants are in the middle of a word, one of them makes a syllable with the preceding, and the other with the following vowel. Ex. "al-ber-go," *inn*, "ac-cen-to," *accent*. But if the second of the two consonants is either *l, m, n*, or *r*, the two consonants are united to the following vowel. Ex. "mi-glio," *mile*, "sti-gma," *stigma*, "cam-pa-gna," *country*, "ve-dre-mo," *we shall see*.

57. (iv) When there are three consonants in the middle of a word, the first of them makes a syllable with the preceding, and the two others with the following vowel. Ex. "om-bra," *shade, shadow*, "sem-pre," *always*.

58. (v) The consonant *s*, with any other consonants which may follow it, always form a syllable with the following vowel. Ex. "que-sto," *this*, "a-spet-to," *aspect*, "vo-stro," *your*. Except in compound words. Ex. "dis-a-gio," *discomfort*, "dis-giun-ge-re," *to unconnect*, &c.

---

* Notice that the sound of the *e* in "mezzo," meaning *middle, means, half*, is broad.

ON THE PRONUNCIATION OF WORDS.

"Parole Piane," *flat words.*

59. In pronouncing most Italian words the stress of the voice, or what is called the "Tonic Accent" falls upon the penultimate, or last syllable but one. Ex. "prato," (the stress on the *a*) *meadow*, "felice," (the stress on the *i*) *happy*, "parlare," (the stress on the second *a*) *to speak*, "finivamo," (the stress on the *a*) *we were finishing*, "castello," (the stress on the *e* and the first *l*) *castle*. These words are called "parole piane," *flat words.*

"Parole Sdrucciole," *slippery words.*

60. In some words (perhaps one out of every eighteen) the tonic accent falls on the ante-penultimate, that is to say, on the last syllable but two. Ex. "tavola," *table*, "carcere," *prison*, "docile," *docile*, "vendere," *to sell*, "compravano," *they were buying*, "altissimo," *very high*. These words are called "parole sdrucciole," *slippery words.*

"Parole Bisdrucciole," *very slippery words.*

61. In about eighty words (third persons plural of verbs of the first conjugation, see rule 176) the tonic accent falls upon the last syllable but three. Ex. "terminano," *they end*, "rotolano," (21) *they roll*. These words are called "parole bisdrucciole," *very slippery words.**

"Parole Tronche," *curtailed words.*

62. There are besides the "parole piane," "sdrucciole," and "bisdrucciole," some words which have lost the final syllable, and are therefore called "parole tronche," *curtailed words*. The tonic accent in these words falls upon the last vowel, which is always marked by the grave accent (``), and is strongly pronounced. Ex. "carità" (caritade), *charity*, "credè" (credeo), *he believed*, "finì" (finio), *he finished*, "parlò" (parloe), *he spoke*, "virtù" (virtude), *virtue.*

Very Important Rule.

63. The way adopted to indicate the "Tonic Accent," throughout this grammar is this: In all the "Parole Sdrucciole" and "Bisdrucciole," the Letter or Letters upon which the Stress of the Voice should fall are Printed in Darker Type. No difference is made in the type on "parole piane," and "tronche."

---

64. * It is to be observed that the tonic accent in verbs never changes its place when a pronoun, or pronouns are joined to it, so that a "parola piana," by taking a pronoun after it, becomes "sdrucciola," and when two pronouns are joined to it, it becomes "bisdrucciola." Ex. "vendete," *sell*, "vendetelo," *sell it*, "vendetemelo," *sell it to me.*

THE WRITTEN ACCENT.

65. There is only one written accent in Italian orthography, namely the grave accent, marked thus (`), and which is written on the final vowel of the " parole tronche " (curtailed words), which have been explained in rule 62, such as " carità,"* *charity*, " credè," *he believed*, " finì," *he finished*, " parlò," *he spoke*, " virtù," *virtue*.

66. The grave accent is also written on the words " più," *more*, " può," *he* or *she can*, " già," *already, of course*, " giù," *down, below*, to prevent them being mispronounced.

67. Notice that there is no need of writing the accent on monosyllabic words, such as " re," *king*, " fu," (*he*) *was*, " su," *on* or *upon*; except however on the following monosyllables, to distinguish them from others spelt in the same manner, but written without accent, and which have a different meaning.

È* means (*he*) *is*,
DÀ means (*he*) *gives*,
DÌ means *day*,
LÀ means *there*,
LÌ means *there*,
NÈ means *neither* and *nor*,
SÈ means *one's self*, (conj. pron.)
SÌ (short for così) means *yes*,
TÈ means *tea*,

E means *and*.
DA means *from, by*, &c.
DI means *of*. *Di'* means *say* (*thou*.)
LA means *the*, (art.), and *her, it*, (pron.)
LI means *them*, (conj. pron.)
NE means *of it, us, to us*, (pron.)
SE means *if*.
SI means *one's self*, (conj. pron.)
TE means *thee*, (conj. pron.)

68. The grave accent is also used in the following words and a few others to indicate where the stress of the voice should be laid in pronouncing them:—

ÀNCORA means *anchor*,
BÀLIA, (f.), means *nurse*,
CÀNONE, means *canon, rule*,
CÙPIDO, means *greedy*,
TÈNDINE means *tendon*,

ANCÒRA means *again, still, yet*.
BALÌA, (m.), means *magistrate, power*.
CANÒNE, means *big dog*.
CUPÌDO, means *Cupid*.
TENDÌNE means *curtains*.

---

69. * The vowels over which the grave accent is placed must be pronounced with a broad, emphatic sound.

THE APOSTROPHE.

70. The apostrophe (') in Italian takes the place of a final vowel, preceding a word beginning with another vowel. Ex. "l'albero," instead of "lo albero," *the tree*, "l'anima," instead of "la anima," *the soul*, "gl'insetti," instead of "gli insetti," *the insects*, una "bell' opera," instead of una "bella opera," *a fine work*, un "grand'uomo," instead of un "grande uomo," *a great man*.

71. In a few words the apostrophe takes the place of a syllable. Ex. "un po'," instead of "un poco," *a little*, "me'," instead of "meglio," *better*, "vo'," instead of "voglio," *I will*, "to'," instead of "togli," *take*, "di'," instead of "dici," *say*.

72. It is to be observed that in poetry the apostrophe is sometimes placed before a consonant, in the place of a vowel which has been left out. Ex.

"E'l sospirar dell' aura infra le fronde."
        instead of
"E il sospirar della aura infra le fronde."
        (Petrarca.)
} *And the sighing of the breeze among the trees.*

73. All Italian words except "il," *the*, "un," *a* or *an*, "in," *in*, "per," *for*, *through*, "con," *with*, "non," *not*, end with one of the vowels *a, e, i, o, u*, and this vowel indicates the gender, number, and verbal inflection of words.*

USE OF CAPITAL LETTERS.

74. In Italian the names of the months, the names of the days of the week, and adjectives begin with a small letter, when not at the commencement of a sentence. Ex.

Mi mandò la grammatica francese lunedì.   He sent me the French grammar on Monday.

---

75. * Besides the words given above (in rule 73), which always end with a consonant, the Italians suppress the last vowel, or syllable, in many words, to avoid the monotony which would be produced by the use of too many ending vowels, so that they use "bel," instead of "bello," *beautiful*, "gran," instead of "grande," *great, tall, large*, "san," instead of "santo," *saint, holy*, "buon," instead of "buono," *good*. They also suppress the final vowel in many words, especially in the infinitive of verbs. Ex. "Aver avuto," instead of "Avere avuto," *to have had*, "Parlar francese," instead of "Parlare francese," *to speak French*. There is no rule for these curtailments; the judgment and ear decide.

ON READING AND SPEAKING ITALIAN.

76. Now that the student is in possession of the rules for the pronunciation of Italian words, he should read aloud to his teacher, and by himself. As far as reading goes, the Italian language is most attractive; it offers no serious difficulty to the English student, who, under the guidance of an able teacher can, after two or three hours' practice, read it far better than an Italian could possibly know how to read English after as many weeks' or months' practice.

77. In reading and speaking Italian, great care must be taken to UTTER THE DOUBLE CONSONANTS *bb*, *cc*, *dd*, &c., DISTINCTLY; after having pronounced the first of the two consonants, the voice is kept lingering for a short while, and then the other consonant, with its accompanying vowel, is pronounced. Ex. "avreb...be," *he would have*, "ec...citare," *to excite* (the *cc* sound like the *chi*, in *chicory*, because the *cc* are followed by *i*), "zoc...colo," *sandal* (the *cc* sound like *kk*, because the *cc* are followed by *o*), "ad...dio," *good-bye*, "ef...ficace," *efficacious*, "corag...gio," *courage*, "bel...lo," *beautiful*, "fum...mo," *we were*, "saran...no," *they will be*, "cop...pa," *nape of the neck*, "tor...re," *tower*, "bonis...simo," *very good*, "dot...to," *learned*, "bev...vi," *I drank*, "delicatez...za," *delicacy*.

78. The student must also be very careful NOT TO PRONOUNCE THE WORDS SEPARATELY, but RATHER TO LET THEM RUN INTO ONE ANOTHER, except, of course, when they are divided by punctuation.

79. The student must also remember that, although the ending vowels indicate the gender, number, and verbal inflection of Italian words, yet, IN READING AND SPEAKING, THE LAST SYLLABLE OF WORDS MUST BE PRONOUNCED SOFTLY, LOWERING THE VOICE, EXCEPT WHEN THE LAST VOWEL IS ACCENTED; in this latter case all the stress of the voice must be laid on the accented vowel, without however leaving any pause between it and the word which follows. Ex. "Parlerò a Carlo, e gli (32) dirò la verità," *I shall speak to Charles, and will tell him the truth*. Which must be pronounced as if it were written thus: "*ParleròaCarlo, eglidiròlaverità*."

80. It is characteristic of the Italians to express a great deal more emphasis than the English in pronouncing phrases in the interrogative and exclamative forms. Ex.

Ha Carlo portato il mio libro?*   Has Charles brought my book?
Che bel cavallo!†   What a beautiful horse!

---

* The voice must be gradually raised from the first to the last word in this phrase.

† The emphasis must be increased from the first to the last word in this phrase.

READING EXERCISES.

EXERCISE I. (on *CA*, *CO*, and *CU*.)

Carlo (12) ha (35) trovato il libro nella (77) mia camera (63).
Charles has found the book in my room.
Ho sempre (5) creduto che fosse italiano. È (69) vestito come (13)
I always thought that he was an Italian. He is dressed like
mio nipote. Vostro (9) padre non ha cura (14) della sua salute.
my nephew. Your father does not take care of his health.
La sua tema di mostrarmi il suo tema è ridicola. Ci sono quasi
His fear of showing me his exercise is ridiculous. There are nearly
venti nomi di diversi venti. Hanno fatto un foro nella porta del
twenty names of different winds. They have made a hole in the door of the
Foro. Quando diede il suo voto il Senato era quasi voto (21).
Forum. When he gave his vote the Senate was almost empty.

EXERCISE II. (on *CE* and *CI*.)

Tua sorella* ha una bella voce (15) di soprano. Sì, tu dici (16)
Your sister has a fine soprano voice. Yes, you say
la verità (69). Il fanciullo era nascosto (21) nell' armadio. Enrico
the truth. The child was hidden in the cupboard. Henry
è un uomo† di buona natura. Hanno portato la mia cena ? (80)
is a good-natured man. Have they brought my supper?
No, non ancora. Ora il cielo è sereno. Mi piace tanto respirare
No, not yet. Now the sky is bright. I am very fond of breathing
l'aria della mattina. Nell' autunno (2) l'aurora non è mai molto
the morning air. In autumn the dawn is never very
lucente. Ella cominciò (79) a parlare con una certa autorità.
bright. She began to speak with a certain authority.

EXERCISE III. (on *CHE*, *CHI*, *SCE* and *SCI*.)

Che (17) bel libro ! (80) Di chi (18) è ? Veramente non saprei
What a fine book! Whose is it? Really I cannot
dirlo; ma credo che sia di Odoardo. Le antiche cronache
say; but I believe it belongs to Edward. Ancient chronicles give
istruiscono molto. Il vostro fanciullo non ha più (69) paura del
much instruction. Your child is no longer afraid of
mio cane. Dov' è la chiave (18) della mia camera ? Il facchino
my dog. Where is the key of my room? The porter
l'ha attaccata al chiodo. Mio fratello ha veduto tutte le principali
has hung it on the nail. My brother has seen all the principal
città dell' Europa. La Maria ha scelto (19) un bel colore. Antonio
cities of Europe. Mary has chosen a beautiful colour. Anthony
sciupa (20) tutti i suoi abiti. C'erano cento uomini nella miseria.
spoils all his clothes. There were a hundred men in poverty.

---

* Notice that, in nouns and qualificative adjectives, the *e* followed by two *ll* (*ello*, *ella*, *elli*, *elle*), has always the broad sound of *a* in the word *gate*.

† Notice that the *o* preceded by a *u* has always the broad sound of *o* in the word *orphan*.

READING EXERCISES.

EXERCISE IV. (ON *GA, GO, GU, GE, GI, GHE, GHI* AND *GLI*.)

Il gatto (25) guarda (27) sempre la gabbia dell' uccello. Io ho
_{The cat is always looking at the bird's cage. I have}
male alla gola (26). Il generale (28) è un uomo giusto (29);
_{a sore throat. The general is a just man; he}
comprò le ghette (30), e le pagò una ghinea (31). La geografia
_{bought the gaiters and paid a guinea for them. Geography}
e la cronologia (21) sono gli (32) occhi della storia. Guglielmo è
_{and chronology are the eyes of history. William is}
andato nel giardino a cogliere dei fiori. Che bel giglio ! (80).
_{gone into the garden to gather flowers. What a beautiful lily !}
Ciò accadde al tempo degli dei falsi e bugiardi. Il Lago Maggiore.
_{That happened at the time of the false and lying gods. Lago Maggiore.}

EXERCISE V. (ON *GN, QUA, QUE, QUI,* AND *QUO*.)

I miei fratelli hanno viaggiato in Italia e in Francia durante i
_{My brothers travelled in Italy and France during the months}
mesi di maggio, giugno (34) e luglio. Il postiglione fu molto
_{of May, June and July. The postilion was}
negligente (33) verso la mia famiglia. Chi può sciogliere il
_{very negligent towards my family. Who can untie the}
nodo? (80). Io; ecco l'ho già sciolto. Voglio del caffè di buona
_{knot? I; see I have already untied it. I want some coffee of a good}
qualità (39). Giuseppe ed io siamo stati alla campagna ; abbiamo
_{quality. Joseph and I have been in the country; we walked}
camminato tre leghe (30). Questa (40) è la quinta (41) questione
_{three leagues. This is the fifth quarrel that my}
che i miei fratelli hanno avuta insieme. Un sogno di buon augurio.
_{brothers have had together. A dream of good omen.}

EXERCISE VI. (ON THE LETTER *S*.)

Questa signora (44) ha molto spirito. Abbiamo udito uno
_{This lady is very witty. We have heard}
squillo (45) di tromba. Allo sbocco (40) del fiume l'acqua è molto
_{a trumpet peal. At the outlet of the river the water is very}
turbata. Suo suocero ha mostrato troppo sdegno (46); ciò è uno
_{muddy. Your father-in-law has shown too much anger ; that is a}
sbaglio (46). Il prato era smaltato (46) di fiori. Questo giovinotto*
_{mistake. This meadow was full of flowers. This young man is}
è svelto (46). È venuto a dirmi che ha disegnato il suo quadro.
_{active. He came to tell me that he has drawn his picture.}
Non è lecito di susurrare in compagnia. Tutto l'edificio risonava†
_{It is not proper to whisper in company. The whole building resounded}
di applausi. Stefano ha disigillato† la mia lettera.
_{with applause. Stephen has unsealed my letter.}

---

* Notice that an *o* followed by two *tt* (*otto, otta, otti, otte*), has always the broad sound of *o* in the word *orphan.*

† Notice that an *s* preceded by *ri*, meaning *again*, and *di*, meaning *un*, has the hard sound of *s* in the word *spirit.*

EXERCISE VII. (on THE S, SHARP.)

Che cosa c'è? La casa del pievano è incendiata. Il riso rallegra.
What is it? The parson's house is on fire. Laughter cheers.
Mi piace il riso. Ho desiderio di vederlo. Non è così facile di
I like rice. I wish to see him. It is not so easy to punish
punirlo. La Giovanna portava una vesta di raso. Egli è molto
him. Joan wore a satin dress. He is very
geloso.* La sua gelosia* gli sarà fatale. Questo Inglese† ha
jealous. His jealousy will be fatal to him. This Englishman has
sposato una Francese.† Abbiamo fatte molte spese.‡
married a Frenchwoman. We have incurred a great deal of expense.

EXERCISE VIII. (on THE Z, and ZZ, SHARP.)

Vo altiero della sua amicizia (50, 53) per me. La bellezza (52, 53)
I am proud of his friendship for me. The beauty
della natura. Non vanno mai in carrozza. Ho comprato quattro
of nature. They never go in a carriage. I have bought four
fazzoletti da naso. Ammiro la sua presenza di spirito e la sua
pocket-handkerchiefs. I admire his presence of mind and
costanza. Ho incontrato mio zio nella piazza di San Marco; mi
constancy. I met my uncle in the Square of Saint Mark; he
ha dato quattro biglietti per le "Nozze di Figaro." Cameriere,
gave me four tickets for the "Nozze di Figaro." Waiter,
portatemi una tazza di caffè nero, la zuccheriera, e una scatola di
bring me a cup of black coffee, the sugar-basin, and a box of
zolfanelli. Che scherzo! Non voglio questa pera perchè è mezza.
matches. What a joke! I will not have this pear because it is over-ripe.

EXERCISE IX. (on THE Z, and ZZ, SOFT.)

La Signorina Bianchini ha una bellissima voce di mezzo-soprano.
Miss Bianchini has a beautiful light soprano voice.
"Nel mezzo (53) del cammin di nostra vita" (*Dante*). La rappre-
Midway the journey of our life. The repre-
sentazione dell' opera "La Gazza Ladra" del Rossini durò due ore
sentation of the opera "La Gazza Ladra" of Rossini, lasted two hours and
e mezzo. "I Promessi Sposi" del Manzoni (53) è un bellissimo
a-half. "The Betrothed," of Manzoni is a very beautiful
romanzo. Egli ha scelto una magnifica statua di bronzo.
novel. He has chosen a magnificent bronze statue.
Quest' uomo è molto bizzarro e rozzo; non ha il menomo zelo per il
This man is very eccentric and rude; he has not the slightest zeal for
suo lavoro. L'orizzonte era del colore azzurro del più puro zaffiro.
his work. The horizon was of the azure colour of the purest sapphire.

---

* Notice that the *s* in adjectives ending in *oso*, and words derived from them, is sharp, like the *s* in the word *spirit*.

† Notice that the *s* in adjectives indicating nationality, ending in *ese*, is sharp, like the *s* in the word *spirit*, except in "Francese," *French*, and "Lucchese," *Lucchese*.

‡ Notice that the *s* in nouns ending in *esa, ese,* is sharp, like the *s* in the word *spirit*, except in the words "chiesa," *church*, "Agnese," *Agnes*, and a few others.

LESSON I.

§ 1. ON THE DEFINITE ARTICLE.

81. The definite article *The* is translated into Italian by "il" in the singular, and "i" in the plural, before masculine nouns beginning with a consonant. Ex.

"Il libro,"* the book,   "i libri, the books.

82. *The* is translated by "lo" in the singular, and "gli" in the plural, before masculine nouns† beginning with an *s* followed by another consonant, or with a *z*. Ex.

Lo sperone,‡ the spur,   gli speroni, the spurs.
Lo zingaro, the gipsy,   gli zingari, the gipsies.

83. *The* is translated by "lo,"§ or rather "l'" in the singular, and "gli"‖ in the plural, before masculine nouns† beginning with a vowel; the "i" of "gli" may be replaced by an apostrophe before a noun† beginning with an "i." Ex.

L'albero,¶   the tree,   gli alberi,   the trees.
L'idolo,   the idol,   gl' idoli,   the idols.

84. *The* is translated by "la" in the singular, and "le" in the plural, before feminine nouns† beginning with a consonant. If the feminine noun† begins with a vowel, the *a* in "la" is suppressed and replaced by an apostrophe; the *e* in "le" may be replaced by an apostrophe before a noun† beginning with *e*. Ex.

La penna,**   the pen,   le penne,   the pens.
L' anima,   the soul,   le anime,   the souls.
L' ẹlegia††   the elegy,   l'ẹlegie,   the elegies.

---

85. * There are only two genders in Italian, masculine and feminine. Nearly all nouns ending in *o* are masculine, and form their plural by changing *o* into *i*.

† Also before adjectives; as it is a question of euphony.

86. ‡ Nouns ending in *e* are of both genders, and form their plural by changing *e* into *i*.

87. § The only words before which "lo" is used for the sake of euphony instead of "il" are "più" and "meno," in the expressions "per lo più," *for the most part*, and "per lo meno," *at least*.

88. ‖ The only word before which "gli," "degli," "agli," &c., are used for the sake of euphony instead of "i," "dei," "ai," &c., is "dei," *gods*. Ex.

"Al tempo degli dei falsi e bugiardi."—(Dante).
During the time of the false and lying gods.

¶ See rule 63, to understand the meaning of the letters in the darker type.

89. ** Most nouns ending in *a* are feminine, and form their plural by changing the *a* into *e*.

†† An *e*, dotted thus ẹ, has a broad sound, like the *a* in *gate*.

§ 2. ON THE PREPOSITIONS "DI," "A," "DA."

THE PREPOSITION "DI."

90. The preposition " di " corresponds to the preposition *of*. Ex.

Il padrone di questa casa.   The master of this house.
Il regno di Spagna.   The kingdom of Spain.
Il duomo di Milano.   The cathedral of Milan.

91. " D'," instead of " di," is used before words beginning with an *i*; when the word begins with any other vowel either " di " or " d' " may be used. Ex.

Il regno d' Italia.   The kingdom of Italy.

92. The English possessive case, expressed by *'s*, as *Peter's book*, is rendered in Italian by inverting the position of the two words, and placing the preposition " di," between them. Ex.

" Il libro di Piętro."   " Peter's book."

THE PREPOSITION "A."

93. The preposition " a " corresponds to the prepositions *to* and *at*. Ex.

Vado a Parigi.   I am going to Paris.
Ho parlato a Carlo.   I have spoken to Charles.
Mio padre è a casa.   My father is at home.

94. " Ad " may be used instead of " a," before a word beginning with a vowel, especially before an *a*. Ex.

Sono stato ad Atene.   I have been to Athens.

THE PREPOSITION "DA."

95. The preposition " da " is used in the sense of *from*. Ex.

Vengo da Firenze.   I come from Florence.

96. The *a* of " da " is never replaced by an apostrophe in Italian prose. Ex.

È partito da Edimburgo.   He has left Edinburgh.

97. The preposition " da " is also used in the sense of *by*, when preceded by a past participle. Ex.

Egli è stimato da tutti.   He is esteemed by everybody.

98. The preposition " da " is also used in the sense of *fit for*, *like a*.* Ex.

Carta da scrivere.   Writing paper.
Egli combattè (69) da eroe.   He fought like a hero.

---

* The preposition "da" has also other meanings which the student will find explained further on, pages 201 and 202.

ON THE PREPOSITIONS "DI," "A," "DA," ETC.

99. When "di," "a," "da," and the prepositions "in," *in*, "con," *with*, "per," *for*, "su," *on*, and "fra" or "tra," *among, between*, are followed by the articles "il," "lo," "la," "l'," "i," "gli," "le," the two words are contracted as shown in the subjoined table :—

100. Di il	into	del,	and	di i	into	dei,*	of the.
A il	„	al,	„	a i	„	ai,	to the.
Da il	„	dal,	„	da i	„	dai,	{ from / by } the.
In il	„	nel,	„	in i	„	nei,	in the.
Con il	„	col,	„	con i	„	coi,	with the.
Per il	„	pel,	„	per i	„	pei,	for the.
Su il	„	sul,	„	su i	„	sui,	on the.
Fra il	„	fral,	„	fra i	„	frai,	among the.
101. Di lo	„	dello,	„	di gli	„	degli,	of the.
A lo	„	allo,	„	a gli	„	agli,	to the.
Da lo	„	dallo,	„	da gli	„	dagli,	{ from / by } the.
In lo	„	nello,	„	in gli	„	negli,	in the, &c.
102. Di la	„	della,	„	di le	„	delle,	of the.
A la	„	alla,	„	a le	„	alle,	to the.
In la	„	nella,	„	in le	„	nelle,	in the, &c.
103. Di l'	„	dell,'	„	di gli	„	degli,	of the.
A l'	„	all,'	„	a gli	„	agli,	to the, &c.

VOCABULARY.

Il libro,	the book.	Il giardino,	the garden.
Il tema,†	the exercise.	L'albero,	the tree.
La tavola,	the table.	Il ramo,	the branch.
La donna,	the woman.	Il pane,	the bread.
Il ragazzo,	the boy.	L'uccello,	the bird.
La ragazza,	the girl.	La gabbia,	the cage.

EXERCISE I.‡

The boy's (92) book. The girl's exercise. The branch of the tree. The woman in the garden. The bird in the cage. The woman with the bread. The book on the table. The birds (85) among the branches of the trees. In the boys' gardens

---

* Instead of "dei," "ai," "dai," &c., "de'," "a'," "da'," are often used.

104. † There are only a few nouns masculine ending in *a*; they form their plural in *i*. See rule 397.

‡ For the numeral adjectives see page 128.

LESSON II.

ON THE VERB "AVERE," *TO HAVE.*

INFINITIVE MOOD.

PRESENT.	PAST.
Avere, *to have.*	Avere avuto, *to have had.*

GERUND.*	PAST PARTICIPLE.	PAST GERUND.
Avendo,† *having.*	Avuto, *had.*	Avendo avuto, *having had.*

INDICATIVE MOOD.

PRESENT.		IMPERFECT.		PAST DEFINITE.	
Io ho,‡	⎫	Avevo, ‖	⎫	Ebbi,	⎫
Tu hai,	⎬	Avevi,	⎬	Avesti,	⎬
Egli, *or* esso, ⎫ ha;		Aveva;¶	*I had, &c.*	Ebbe;	*I had, &c.*
Ella, *or* essa,§ ⎭	*I have, &c.*				
Noi abbiamo,		Avevamo,		Avemmo,	
Voi avete,		Avevate,		Aveste,	
Eglino, *or* essi, ⎫ hanno.		Avevano.¶		Ebbero.	
Elleno, *or* esse, ⎭					

---

105 * The Gerund in Italian always remains invariable. Besides a Gerund, most Italian verbs have a Present Participle, ending in "ente," and "enti," or in "ante," and "anti." Ex. "Una finestra avente carta, invece di vetri" (Pellico). *A window which had paper, instead of glass.* But as this form of the verb is seldom used, it is not given in the verbal paradigms, in this grammar.

† The *e*, dotted thus ẹ, has a broad sound, like the *a* in *gate*.

106. ‡ As the termination of the verb is sufficient to indicate the person and number of the subject in the sentence, the personal pronouns, used as subjects, are not expressed in Italian, except (*a*)—to avoid ambiguity, (*b*)—when two or more pronouns (used as subjects), are employed in the same sentence, (*c*)—when a particular stress is to be laid on the pronoun; so the Italian for "I have the book," is simply "Ho il libro."

107. § "Egli," "ella," "eglino," "elleno," are used only in speaking of persons, whilst "esso," "essa," "essi," "esse," are employed with reference to persons, animals and things. "Eglino" and "elleno" are becoming obsolete; "essi" and "esse" being used instead of them.

108 ‖ Both the first and the third persons singular of the Imperfect Indicative, of all verbs, *formerly* ended in *a*, but now the general tendency of Italian writers is to make the termination of the first person in *o*, and that of the third in *a*; by this means it is easier to mark the distinction between the first, and the third person singular, without the aid of the personal pronouns.

109. ¶ The letter *v* in the third persons of the Imperfect Indicative of all verbs, except those of the first conjugation, is often omitted. Ex. "avea," "aveano."

ON THE VERB "AVERE."

Past Indefinite.	Pluperfect.	Past Anterior.
Ho avuto,-a-i-e, &c.*	Avevo avuto, &c.	Ebbi avuto, &c.
I have had, &c.	*I had had, &c.*	*I had had, &c.*

Future.	Conditional.	IMPERATIVE MOOD.
Avrò,	Avrei,	*No first person.*
Avrai,	Avresti,	Abbi,
Avrà;	Avrebbe;	Abbia;
Avremo,	Avremmo,	Abbiamo,
Avrete,	Avreste,	Abbiate,
Avranno.	Avrebbero.†	Abbiano.

I shall have, &c. — *I should have, &c.* — *Have (thou), &c.*

Future Anterior.	Conditional Past.	
Avrò avuto, &c.	Avrei avuto, &c.	*The Past of the Imperative is seldom used.*
I shall have had, &c.	*I should have had, &c.*	

SUBJUNCTIVE MOOD.

Present.	Imperfect.
Che io abbia,	Che *or* se‡ io avessi,
Che tu abbia,	Che *or* se tu avessi,
Che { egli / ella } abbia;	Che { *or* se egli / *or* se ella } avesse;
Che abbiamo,	Che *or* se avessimo,
Che abbiate,	Che *or* se aveste,
Che { essi / esse } abbiano.	Che *or* se { essi / esse } avessero.

That I may have, &c. — *That or if I might have, &c.*

Past.	Pluperfect.
Che io abbia avuto, &c.	Che *or* se io avessi avuto, &c.
That I may have had, &c.	*That or if I might have had, &c.*

110. * The Past Participle in Italian is variable; it ends in *o*, when it is used in connection with a noun masculine singular; in *a* for the feminine singular; in *i* for the masculine plural; and in *e* for the feminine plural. The rules for the Past Participle are given further on. For the present the student had better to leave it invariable, in *o*.

111. † In poetry "avrìa" is often used instead of "avrei" and "avrebbe," and "avrìano" instead of "avrebbero."

112. ‡ The Italian conditional conjunction "se," *if*, when it precedes a verb used in the present or past tense, is followed by the Imperfect Subjunctive (followed by the Conditional Present), or by the Pluperfect Subjunctive (followed by the Conditional Past). Ex.

| Se io avessi del denaro, avrei degli amici. | If I had money, I should have friends. |
| Se io avessi avuto del danaro, avrei avuto degli amici. | If I had had money, I should have had friends. |

VOCABULARY.

Carlo,	Charles.	Maria,*	Mary.
Elisabetta,	Elizabeth.	Guglielmo,†	William.
Enrico,	Henry.	Giovanni,‡	John.

La lezione,	the lesson.	Il dizionario,	the dictionary.
La penna,	the pen.	La grammatica,	the grammar.
La matita,§	the pencil.	Lo (82) scrittoio,	the writing-desk.
La lettera,‖	the letter.	Il pennello,	the paint-brush.
La carta,	the paper.	L' uomo,	the man.
Il calamaio,	the ink-stand.	Gli uomini,	the men.
La lavagna,	the slate.	La chiave,	the key.
Il temperino,	the penknife.	La casa,	the house.

E,	and.	Oggi,	to-day.	Sotto,	under.
Anche,	also.	Ieri,	yesterday.	Vicino a,	near to.
Già,	already.	Domani,	to-morrow.	Accanto a,	by the side of.

EXERCISE II.

I (106) have the dictionary. Charles has the paper. Mary had (Imp. Ind.) the pen; she had also the grammar. We had Henry's (92) writing-desk. William and John have the ink-stand. Yesterday Elizabeth had (Imp. Ind.) the letter and¶ the penknife; she had already had (Pluperf. Ind.) the books.** I shall have the lesson to-morrow. William and Charles will have the slate and†† ink-stand. The man has the key of the (102) house. The men have had (Past Ind.) the books from (95, 96) Henry. We have John's paint-brushes in the (101) writing-desk, under the table.**

---

113. * In speaking of women the Italians often put the definite article before their names. Ex. "La Maria."

† An *e*, dotted thus ẹ, has the broad sound of the *a* in the word *gate*.

‡ An *o*, dotted thus ọ, has the broad sound of the *o* in the word *orphan*.

§ Another word frequently used in Italian for *pencil* is "lapis" (the *s* pronounced), written the same in the singular as in the plural.

‖ See rule 63, to understand the meaning of the letters in the darker type.

114. ¶ *Ed*, instead of *e*, may be used before a word beginning with a vowel, for the sake of euphony. Ex. "Carlo ed io." *Charles and I*.

** This word was given in the previous Vocabulary, and, with all the words which occur in the exercises, is contained in the General Vocabulary at the end of this grammar.

115. †† In Italian the definite article must be repeated before each noun.

LESSON III.

§ 1. ON THE MODES OF ADDRESSING PEOPLE IN ITALIAN.

116. The Italians have three ways of addressing one another; they employ the second person singular, "Tu," *thou*, or the second person plural, "Voi," *you*, or the third person singular, feminine, "Ella," *she*.

117. The second person singular, "tu," is used by parents when they speak to their children, and when husband and wife, brothers and sisters speak to one another. This form is used also when speaking to very intimate friends. Ex.

Amo la tua conversazione.   I like your (thy) conversation.

118. In Italian "tu" is further used, as *thou* is in English, in poetry, and sometimes to express anger or scorn towards the person addressed.

119. The second person plural "voi," is used by ladies and gentlemen towards their inferiors. It is also employed in commerce. Ex.

Voi parlate troppo.   You speak too much.

120. But when the Italians wish to show respect to the person they address (*whether man or woman*) instead of "voi," *you*, they use the third person singular feminine, "ella," *she*, which pronoun in that case stands for "Vostra Signoria" (*your Lordship*, or *Ladyship*). The words spoken are supposed to be addressed to the title and not to the person. Ex. "Ella ha il temperino," *instead of* "Voi avete il temperino."* *You have the penknife.*

121. In speaking to more than one person "loro," *or* "elleno" (see rule 107), *they*, which stand for "le Vostre Signorie," or "lor Signori," or "lor Signore" (*your Lordships*, or *Ladyships*), are used.*

122. In writing the exercises in this grammar, the student is strongly advised to write as many sentences as he can in the three forms; that is, in the second and third persons singular, and in the second person plural, as explained in rules 117, 119, and 120, thus:—

    Hai (tu)   tuo
    Ha ella mandato il suo quadro all' esposizione?
    Avete (voi)   vostro
    Have you sent your picture to the exhibition?

---

123 * All the words in sentences employed in connection with "Ella," "Lei" and "Loro" *should* have the feminine inflection, but many people, ignoring the pronouns ("Ella," "Lei" and "Loro") give to words the masculine or feminine inflection, according as they speak to a woman or a man, to women or men. Ex.

To a woman: "È Ella stata invitata al ballo?"
To a man: "È Ella stato invitato al ballo?"
To women: "Sono Loro state invitate al ballo?"
To men: "Sono Loro stati invitati al ballo?"
                                          Have you been invited to the ball?

§ 2. ON THE INTERROGATIVE AND NEGATIVE FORMS OF VERBS.

124. In Italian, a verb is conjugated interrogatively, simply by placing the mark of interrogation after it ;* and, in speaking, by raising the voice towards the end of the sentence.† Ex.

Avete il libro di Guglielmo?   Have you William's book?

125. A verb is conjugated negatively, by placing the negative particle "non" before it. Ex.

Carlo non ha l' oriuolo.   Charles has not the watch.

126. It is very important to notice that in Italian the Present of the Infinitive is used instead of the second person singular of the Imperative Mood, when the verb is used negatively. Ex.

Non avere il cappello.   Do not (thou) have the hat.
Non abbia il cappello. } Do not (you) have the hat.
Non abbiate il cappello. }

127. A verb is conjugated interrogatively-negatively, by placing the negative particle "non" before it, and the mark of interrogation at the end of the sentence; in speaking the voice must be raised towards the end of the sentence. Ex.

Non ha ella il libro di Carlo?   Have you not Charles' book?

VOCABULARY.

Il cappello,	the hat.	La sciarpa,	the scarf.
Il cappellino,	the bonnet.	Il giornale,	the newspaper.
L' abito,†	the coat.	Il francobollo,	the postage-stamp.
La vesta,	the dress.	Il danaro,	the money.

| Sì, | yes. | Ma, | but. | O...o, | either...or. |
| No, | no. | Quando, | when. | Non (verb) nè...nè, | neither...nor. |

EXERCISE III.

William has Henry's (92) coat. Has Elizabeth the money? Yes. We (106) have neither the newspaper nor the postage-stamp. Have you (122, a) Charles' grammar? No, I have not (125) the books. When shall we have (124) the dictionary? To-day or to-morrow. Do§ not have (126) the bonnet, but have the dress.

---

* A personal pronoun is sometimes required to avoid ambiguity. Ex. "Ha egli il libro?" *Has he the book?*

† When an interrogative sentence begins with an interrogative pronoun or an adverb, the tone of the voice in Italian is much the same as in English. Ex. "Perchè non venne ieri?" *Why did you not come yesterday?*

‡ See rule 63, in order to understand the meaning of the letters in the darker type.

128. § The auxiliaries *do, does, did*, are not translated into Italian.

VOCABULARY.

Mio padre,	my* father.	Il loro† nipote,	their nephew.
Mia madre,	my mother.	Il signore,	the gentleman.
Tuo fratello,	thy brother.	La signora,	the lady.
Tua sorella.	thy sister.	Il mio‡ scolare,	my pupil.
Suo figlio,	his *or* her son.	Il tempo,	the time.
Nostro cugino,	our cousin.	La canzone,	the song.
Vostro zio,	your uncle.	L'inchiostro.	the ink.

Gennaio,	January.	Maggio,	May.	Settembre,	September.
Febbraio,	February.	Giugno,	June.	Ottobre,	October.
Marzo,	March.	Luglio,	July.	Novembre,	November.
Aprile,	April.	Agosto,	August.	Dicembre,	December.

Eccolo, } here he is, Eccoli, m. }
        } here it is,   } here they are.   Prima di, before.
Eccola, } here she is. Eccole, f. }   Dopo, after.
                                                        Mentre, whilst.

EXERCISE IV.

My sister has the ink-stand, but she has not (125) the ink. Charles has my (131) money. My brother has Henry's song. The woman had (Imp. Ind.) my mother's dress. We had already had (Pluperf. Ind.) our (129) uncle's letter. Have you (122, 124) the postage-stamp, for the (100) newspaper? Yes, here it is. Have you William's exercises (104)? Yes, here they are. Has John my pupil's pens (100, 131)? Yes, here they are. I shall have (the) time for my lesson to-day. Their (130) nephew shall have my coat and §hat after May.‖ We shall not have my father's writing desk before to-morrow. We should have had the ink.

---

129. * *My, thy, his, her, our, your*, are translated by "mio," "tuo," "suo," "nostro," "vostro;" "mia," "tua," "sua," "nostra," "vostra," before names of kindred *in the singular*. Ex. "mio padre," *my father*.

130. † But before "loro" and when the names of kindred are *in the plural*, the article is used. Ex. "Il loro nipote," *their nephew*. "I miei fratelli, *my brothers*.

131. ‡ Before any nouns but names of kindred, *my, thy, his, her, our, your*, are translated in the singular by "il mio," "il tuo," "il suo," "il nostro," &c., and in the plural by "i miei," "i tuoi," "i suoi," "i nostri," "i vostri," "i loro." Ex. "Il mio scolare," *my pupil.*

132. § "Mio," "tuo," &c., "il mio," "il tuo," &c., must be repeated before each noun, when there are several. "Ecco qui mia madre e mia sorella," *here are my mother and sister.*

‖ See rule 74.

LESSON IV.
ON THE PARTITIVE ARTICLE.

133. The partitive articles *some* and *any*, are translated into Italian by "del," "dello," "della," to express *quantity*. Ex.

Ho comprato della carta e dell' inchiostro.	I have bought some paper and ink.

134. The partitive articles *some* and *any* are translated by "dei," "degli," "delle," to express *number*. Ex.

Gli mandai degli abiti francesi* e delle armi inglesi.	I sent him some French clothes and English arms.

135. When *some* means a limited number,† it is translated either by "qualche," which is invariable, and is followed by a noun in the singular, or by "alcuno," which agrees in gender and number with the noun to which it refers. Ex.

Vado a comprare qualche libro spagnuolo.	I am going to buy some (a few) Spanish books.
Non aveva seco che alcuni amici.	He only had with him some (a few) friends.

136. The partitive articles "del," "dello," "della," "qualche," "alcuno," "alcuni," "alcune," must be repeated before each noun, when there are several. Ex.

Ho comprato della carta e dei libri.	I have bought some paper and books.

137. When *some* and *any* are omitted, or could be omitted in English, the partitive articles are omitted, or could be omitted in Italian. Ex.

V'erano uomini, donne, e persino fanciulli.	There were men, women, and even children.
Ho veduto in Inghilterra cavalli bellissimi.	I have seen in England very fine horses.

138. When in a sentence there is the partitive article "del," "della," &c., in a subsequent sentence referring to it, in Italian, the partitive article must be represented by the pronoun "ne," *some, of it, of them*; and the verb must be repeated in full. Ex.

Ha, *or* ha ella del denaro?	Have you any money?
Sì, ne ho.	Yes, I have.
Avremo dell' acqua?	Shall we have some water?
Sì, ne avremo.	Yes, we shall.

---

* An *s* dotted thus ṣ, has the soft sound of the *s* in the word *rose*.

139. † But when the number is very limited (*few, a few*) *some* is translated by "pochi," m., or "poche," f. Ex.

Egli aveva pochi amici.	He had few friends.

VOCABULARY.

L'oro (21),	gold.	L'acciaio,	steel.	Il lottone,	brass.
L'argento,	silver.	Il ferro,	iron.	Lo stagno,	tin.
Il platino,	platina.	Il rame,	copper.	Il piombo,	lead.

EXERCISE V.

I have some (133) silver. Has your brother any iron? Yes; he has some iron, (136) copper, and brass. Mary had (Imp. Ind.) some paper, but she had not any pens. Charles has neither the grammar, nor the dictionary. My father has some money. We have not any ink. Have we any postage-stamps? Yes, we have (138). Yesterday we had (Imp. Ind.) my uncle's dictionary. Have you (124) any pencils? No, I have not any. Henry and William have money, but John has not any (138).

ON THE INDEFINITE ARTICLE.

140. The indefinite article *a* or *an* is translated into Italian by "un,"* before a masculine noun beginning either with a consonant or a vowel. Ex.

   Un giorno felice. A happy day.
   Un uomo amabile. An amiable man.

141. The indefinite article *a* or *an* is translated by "uno" before a masculine noun beginning with an *s* followed by another consonant, or with a *z*. Ex.

   Uno scolare diligente. A diligent pupil.
   Uno zio ricchissimo. A very rich uncle.

142. The indefinite article *a* or *an* is translated by "una," before a feminine noun beginning with a consonant. Ex.

   Una signora francese. A French lady.

143. The indefinite article *a* or *an* is translated by "un'," before a feminine noun beginning with a vowel. Ex.

   Un' anima sensibile. A sensitive soul.

144. When in a sentence there is an indefinite article, "un," "uno," &c., in a subsequent sentence referring to it, the indefinite article preceded by the pronoun "ne" (*of them*), must be repeated, if the answer be in the affirmative; but if the answer be negative "ne" only is expressed; "uno" and "una" being omitted. Ex.

Ha ella un dizionario? Have you a dictionary?
Sì, ne ho uno. No, non ne ho. Yes I have. No, I have not.

---

145. * But when *a* or *an* are numeral adjectives they are translated by "uno" or "una." Ex.

 Ella ha due libri, ma io non ne ho You have two books, but I have
  che uno.   but one.

VOCABULARY.

L'aria,*	air.	Il fuoco,†	fire.	Il fumo,	the smoke.
La luce,	light.	L'acqua,	water.	Il vento,‡	the wind.

Un secolo,	a century.	Lunedì, (69)	Monday.
Un anno,	a year.	Martedì,	Tuesday.
Un mese,	a month.	Mercoledì,	Wednesday.
Una settimana,	a week.	Giovedì,	Thursday.
Un giorno, dì,	a day.	Venerdì,	Friday.
Un' ora,	an hour.	Sabato,	Saturday.
Un minuto,	a minute.	Domenica,	Sunday.

Una chiesa.	a church.	Una stanza, } Una camera, }	a room.
Un palazzo,	a palace.		
Una strada,	a street.	La sedia,	the chair.

Perchè?	why	No, mai, giammai, } Non (verb) mai, }	never,	Sempre,	always.
Perchè,	because.			Subito,	at once.
Mai?	ever?	Spesso, sovente,	often.	Fra poco,	very soon.

EXERCISE VI.

Mary has a pencil. We have a writing-desk. Have you (124) ever had a lesson from my (131) master?§ Never. Charles has never had a penknife. When shall I have my dictionary? Very soon, on‖ Friday, or Saturday (74). To-morrow Elizabeth will have a dress, and Mary will have a bonnet. Henry shall not have my brother's slate. Shall we not (127) have some water? Yes, we shall (138). William, do not (126) have (thou) any (133) fire in your (thy) room to-day. He had (Imp. Ind.) his book on¶ a chair, in my cousin's garden. We shall have the book at once.

---

* See rule 63, in order to understand the meaning of the letters in the darker type.

† Notice that an *o* preceded by a *u* has always the broad sound of the *o* in the word *orphan*.

‡ An *e*, dotted thus ẹ, has the broad sound of the *a* in the word *gate*.

146. § *Master* is translated into Italian by "maestro," when it means *a teacher*, and by "padrone," when it means *a master (an owner)*.

147. ‖ *On* is not translated into Italian before Monday, Tuesday, &c., nor before any name of time. Ex. "Il primo gennaio," *On the first of January.*

148. ¶ The preposition "su," *on, upon*, takes an *r* ("sur"), before a vowel, for the sake of euphony. Ex.

L'ho trovato sur una tavola.   I found it on a table.

LESSON V.

THE VERB "ESSERE," *TO BE.*
INFINITIVE MOOD.

PRESENT.		PAST.
Essere, *to be.*		Essere stato,* *to have been.*

GERUND.	PAST PARTICIPLE.	PAST GERUND.
Essendo, *being.*	Stato-a-i-e, *been.*	Essendo stato, *having been.*

INDICATIVE MOOD.

PRESENT.	IMPERFECT.	PAST DEFINITE.
Sono,	Ero,‡	Fui,
Sei,	Eri,	Fosti,
È; (69)	Era;	Fu;
Siamo,†	Eravamo,	Fummo,
Siete,	Eravate,	Foste,
Sono.	Erano.	Furono.
I am, &c.	*I was, &c.*	*I was, &c.*

PAST INDEFINITE.	PLUPERFECT.	PAST ANTERIOR.
Sono stato, &c.	Ero stato, &c.	Fui stato, &c.
I have been, &c.	*I had been, &c.*	*I had been, &c.*

FUTURE.	CONDITIONAL.	IMPERATIVE MOOD.
Sarò,	Sarei,	*No first person.*
Sarai,	Saresti,	Sii,
Sarà;	Sarebbe;	Sia;
Saremo,	Saremmo,	Siamo,
Sarete,	Sareste,	Siate,
Saranno.	Sarebbero.	Siano.
I shall be, &c.	*I should be, &c.*	*Be (thou), &c.*

FUTURE ANTERIOR.	CONDITIONAL PAST.	
Sarò stato, &c.	Sarei stato, &c.	*The Past of the Imperative is seldom used.*
I shall have been, &c.	*I should have been, &c.*	

---

149. * Notice that the compound tenses of "essere," are formed by using the same verb as auxiliary, or that its past participle "stato," is variable. Ex. Sono stato, *or* stata (110) a Parigi.   I have been to Paris.

150. † The following forms are often used in poetry: "semo," instead of "siamo," "sete," instead of "siete," "fue," instead of "fu," "furo," instead of "furono," "fia," instead of "sarà," "fiano," or "fieno," instead of "saranno," "saria," instead of "sarei" and "sarebbe," "sariano," instead of "sarebbero," "fora," instead of "sarebbe" and "sarebbero," "sie," instead of "sia," and "sieno" instead of "siano."

‡ *Or* "era"; see rule 108.

SUBJUNCTIVE MOOD.

PRESENT.	IMPERFECT.
Che io sia,	Che *or* se (112) io fossi,
Che tu sia,	Che *or* se tu fossi,
Che [egli/ella] sia;	Che [*or se* egli / *or se* ella] fosse;
Che siamo,	Che *or* se fossimo,
Che siate,	Che *or* se foste,
Che [essi/esse] siano,	Che [*or se* essi / *or se* esse] fossero.

That I may be, &c. — *That I might be, &c.*

PAST. — PLUPERFECT.
Che io sia stato, &c. — Che *or* se io fossi stato, &c.
That I may have been, &c. — *That I might have been, &c.*

VOCABULARY.

Buono,*	good.	Uno,	1.	Primo—a,	I.
Felice,*	happy.	Due,	2.	Secondo—a,	II.
Grande,	tall, large.	Tre,	3.	Terzo—a,	III.
Piccolo,	small, little.	Quattro,	4.	Quarto—a,	IV.
Bello,	beautiful, fine.	Cinque,	5.	Quinto—a,	V.
Orgoglioso,	proud.	Sei,	6.	Sesto—a,	VI.

Dove, where. Dentro, within. Lontano, far. Cotesto,† that.
Qui, here. Fuori, without. Questo, this. Quello,‡ that.

EXERCISE VII.

John is tall, but his brother Charles is little. This church is beautiful. Where is Elizabeth? She (106, *a*) is here. These tables are small, but they are good. Where are Henry and John? They are not (125) here; they are in our uncle's garden. Where shall we be on (147) Thursday? We shall be in our (100, 129) cousin's room. Where have you been (124, 149)? I have been in my brother's room. Will you be here on Wednesday? Yes; I shall be either here, or at my sister's house. Where are my pens? They are in that (152) writing desk. Be (122) good, William, and you will be happy. Do (128, 122, 126) not be proud.

---

151. * Adjectives agree in gender and number with the nouns they qualify; those ending in *o*, change the *o* into *a* for the feminine, and form their masculine plural by changing *o* into *i*, and their feminine plural by changing *a* into *e*, as "buono," "buona," "buoni," "buone." Adjectives ending in *e* do not change for the feminine; the plural for both genders is formed by changing the *e* into an *i*; as "felice," "felici."

152. † "Cotesto," "cotesta," &c., mean *that*, near the person spoken to.

153. ‡ "Quello," "quella," &c., mean *that*, distant from the speaker, and the person addressed.

THE VERB "ESSERE," WITH "CI" AND "VI."

154. The verb "Essere" is very often employed as an impersonal verb, with the adverbs "ci" and "vi."*

INFINITIVE MOOD.	PRESENT.	Esserci, *or* esservi, *to be there* or *in it*, &c.
	PAST.	Esserci stato, *to have been there*, &c.
	GERUND.	Essendoci, *being there*, &c.
	PAST GER.	Essendoci stato, *having been there*, &c.
INDICATIVE MOOD.	PRESENT.	C'è, *or* v'è, *there is*, or *there is in it*, &c.
		Ci sono, *or* vi sono, *there are*, &c.
	IMPERFECT.	C'era, *or* v'era, *there was*, &c.
		C'erano, *or* v'erano, *there were*, &c.
	PAST INDEF.	C'è stato, *or* stata, *there has been*, &c.
		Ci sono stati, *or* state, *there have been*, &c.
	FUTURE.	Ci *or* vi sarà, Ci *or* vi saranno, } *there will be*, &c.
CONDITIONAL MOOD.		Ci *or* vi sarebbe, Ci *or* vi sarebbero, } *there would be*, &c.

INTERROGATIVELY.   NEGATIVELY.

C'è *or* v'è? *is there?* &c.   Non c'è *or* v'è, *there is not*, &c.
Ci *or* vi sono? *are there?* &c.   Non ci *or* vi sono, *there are not*, &c.

VOCABULARY.

| Il castello, | the castle. | Il salotto, | the parlour. |
| La torre, | the tower. | Il fanciullo, | the child. |

| Il medesimo, Lo stesso, } | the same. | Poco, (21) *a little.* Molto, *very, much.* | Troppo, *too much.* Troppo poco, *too little.* |

EXERCISE VIII.

Charles is the first, I, (106 *b*) am the second, and Elizabeth is the third. My brother's house is too large. Where is Mary? She is in my sister's room. Is there a man in the street? Yes; there is a man and a child. Is there a table in our parlour? No; there are three chairs, but there is no (125) table. There was a small inkstand in my uncle's room. There is too much ink in this pen. Is there a pencil in my brother's writing-desk? No, there are three pens and some paper. There will be a book for the pupil, and a writing-desk for the master (146).

---

* "Ci" means *here* and *in it*, "vi" means *there* and *in it*, but the two words are used indiscriminately; "ci" is used oftener than "vi."

LESSON VI.

ON THE VERBS.

155. Verbs are of five kinds; Active,* Passive, Neuter, Pronominal, and Impersonal; besides the two Auxiliaries, "Avere" and "Essere,"†‡ which have already been given.

156. Verbs are either Regular, Irregular, or Defective.§

157. Italian regular verbs are generally classified into three conjugations, which are distinguished by the termination of the Present of the Infinitive Mood.

The first ends in ARE, as COMPRARE, *to buy*.‖
" second " " ERE, as CREDERE, *to believe*.¶
" third " " IRE, as FINIRE, *to finish*.**

---

158. * Active Verbs are either Active Transitive, or Active Intransitive.

159. An Active Transitive Verb is a verb expressing an action which passes to the object in the sentence, without the help of a preposition. In the phrase "Giovanni ha comprato il libro," *John bought the book*, "Giovanni" is the subject, "ha comprato" is the verb, *active transitive*, and "il libro" is the object, called *direct object*.

160. An Active Intransitive Verb is a verb expressing an action which passes to the object in the sentence through a preposition. In the phrase, "Maria ha parlato a Carlo," *Mary spoke to Charles*, "Maria" is the subject, "ha parlato," the verb, *active intransitive*, and "a Carlo" is the object, in this case called *indirect object*.

161. † "Avere" is *really* an active transitive verb, and "Essere" is *really* a neuter verb, but they are generally called auxiliary verbs, because the compound tenses of all other verbs are formed with the help of either of them.

‡ See rule 63, in order to understand the meaning of the letters in the darker type.

§ Page 66 and following contain all the important irregular and defective verbs used in the Italian language, arranged alphabetically.

162. ‖ There are altogether about 7,000 verbs in Italian, of which 6,000 are of the first conjugation, and are all regular, like "comprare," *to buy*, except three :— "Andare," *to go ;* "Dare," *to give ;* and "Stare," *to stay, to be in health, to dwell,* and *to remain*.

163. ¶ The second conjugation includes 500 verbs, of which only 60 are regular: —of the 440 irregular, 60 end in "ere," long, (*Parole piane*, like "temere," *to fear*), and 380 in "ere," short ; (*Parole sdrucciole*, like "Credere," *to believe*).

164. ** There are 500 verbs of the third conjugation, in "ire ;" of these 430 are regular, conjugated either like "Finire," *to finish* (390 of them), or like "Servire," *to serve* (40 of them) ;—70 are irregular.

ON THE CONJUGATION OF ACTIVE VERBS.

MODEL OF THE FIRST CONJUGATION IN "ARE."

"COMPRARE," *TO BUY.*

INFINITIVE MOOD.

PRESENT.	PAST.
Compr are,* *to buy.*	Aver† compr ato, *to have bought.*

GERUND.	PAST PARTICIPLE.	PAST GERUND.
Compr ando,‡ *buying.*	Compr ato-a-i-e,§ *bought.*	Avendo compr ato, *having bought.*

INDICATIVE MOOD.

PRESENT.	IMPERFECT.	PAST DEFINITE.
Compr o,	Compr avo,‖	Compr ai,
Compr i,	Compr avi,	Compr asti,
Compr a;	Compr ava;	Compr ò;
Compr iamo,	Compr avamo,	Compr ammo,
Compr ate,	Compr avate,	Compr aste,
Compr ano.	Compr avano.	Compr arono.¶

I buy, &c. — *I bought, &c.* — *I bought, &c.*

PAST INDEFINITE.	PLUPERFECT.	PAST ANTERIOR.
Ho comprato, &c.	Avevo comprato, &c.	Ebbi comprato, &c.
I have bought, &c.	*I had bought, &c.*	*I had bought, &c.*

165. * A verb consists of two parts; the root which is invariable, and the termination, which varies to indicate mood, tense, person and number. In the verb "comprare," "comp" is the root, and "are" the termination.

166. † The compound tenses of *all* active verbs are formed with "avere."

‡ The Present Participle of "comprare" (see rule 105) is "comprante," seldom used. The Pres. Part. of "parlare" is "parlante," of "amare," "amante," and so of all the verbs of the first conjugation.

167. § The Past Participle of active transitive verbs remains invariable, that is to say it ends in *o*, when the *direct object* in the sentence follows it. Ex. "Ho comprato tre libri." *I have bought three books.* But when the *direct object* precedes the past participle, the latter is variable. Ex. "Ecco i libri che ho comprati." *Here are the books I have bought.*

168. The Past Participle of active intransitive verbs always remains invariable. Ex. "Ci hanno parlato." *They spoke to us.*

‖ *Or* "comprava;" see rule 108.

169. ¶ In poetry "compràro" is often used instead of "comprarono;" in the same way "parlâro," instead of "parlarono," *they spoke*, "andâro," instead of "andârono," *they went*, etc.

FUTURE.	CONDITIONAL.	IMPERATIVE MOOD.
Compr erò,	Compr erei,*	*No first person.*
Compr erai,	Compr eresti,	Compr a,
Compr erà;	Compr erebbe;	Compr i;
Compr eremo,	Compr eremmo,	Compr iamo,
Compr erete,	Compr ereste,	Compr ate,
Compr eranno.	Compr erebbero.	Compr ino.

I shall buy, &c. — *I should buy, &c.* — *Buy (thou), &c.*

FUTURE ANTERIOR.	CONDITIONAL PAST.	
Avrò comprato, &c.	Avrei comprato, &c.	The Past of the Imperative is seldom used.
I shall have bought, &c.	*I should have bought, &c.*	

SUBJUNCTIVE MOOD.

PRESENT.	IMPERFECT.
Che io compr i,	Che *or* se (112) io compr assi,
Che tu compr i,	Che *or* se tu compr assi,
Che [egli/ella] compr i;	Che [or se egli/or se ella] compr asse ;
Che compr iamo,	Che *or* se compr assimo,
Che compr iate,	Che *or* se compr aste,
Che [essi/esse] compr ino.	Che [or se essi/or se esse] compr assero.

That I may buy, &c. — *That I might buy, &c.*

PAST.	PLUPERFECT.
Che io abbia comprato, &c.	Che *or* se io avessi comprato, &c.
That I may have bought, &c.	*That I might have bought, &c.*

IMPORTANT REMARKS.

170. Verbs ending in "care," and "gare," as "peccare," *to sin*, and "pregare," *to pray*, require an *h* after the *c* and *g*, when followed by *e* or *i*, because the *c* and *g* are to be pronounced hard throughout the conjugation. Ex. "pecco," "pecchi," "pecca," "pecchiamo," &c.; "prego," "preghi," "prega," "preghiamo," &c.

171. Verbs ending in "ciare" and "giare," as "scacciare," *to drive away*, and "mangiare," *to eat*, drop the *i* before another *i*, or an *e*, as "scaccerò," &c. ; " mangerei," &c.

172. Verbs ending in "iare," as "odiare," *to hate*, retain the *i* in the root when the termination is marked by one *i* only. Ex. "odio," "odii," "odia," "odiamo," &c.

173. Verbs ending in "gnare," as "regnare," *to reign*, omit the *i* of the termination of the first person plural of the Present Indicative. Ex. "regno," "regni," "regna," "regnamo," &c.

---

174. * In poetry "compreria" is often used instead of "comprerei," and "comprerebbe," and "compreriano" instead of "comprerebbero"; in the same way "parleria," instead of "parlerei" and "parlerebbe," &c.

REGULAR VERBS OF THE FIRST CONJUGATION.

Alloggiare,	to lodge.	Licenziare,	to dismiss.
Amare,	to love, to like.	Migliorare,	to improve.
Augurare,*	to augur, to wish.	Minacciare,	to threaten.
Baciare,	to kiss.	Mirare,	to gaze, to look at.
Ballare,	to dance.	Pesare,	to weigh.
Biasimare,*	to blame.	Portare,	to carry.
Caricare,*	to load.	Predicare,*	to preach.
Cercare,	to look for.	Privare,	to deprive.
Coniugare,*	to conjugate.	Raccontare,	to relate.
Disprezzare,	to despise.	Rispettare,	to respect.
Disputare,*	to dispute.	Rubare,	to steal.
Evitare,*	to avoid.	Scappare,	to escape.
Fumare,	to smoke.	Scherzare,	to joke.
Giudicare,*	to judge.	Spaventare,	to frighten.
Guadagnare,	to earn.	Sperare,	to hope.
Guardare,	to look.	Stampare,	to print.
Guastare,	to spoil.	Stimare,	to esteem.
Imparare,	to learn.	Stracciare,	to tear.
Ingannare,	to deceive.	Tagliare,	to cut.
Mendicare,*	to beg.	Trascurare,	to neglect.
Meritare,*	to merit.	Volare,	to fly.

175. The following verbs, and about thirty more, have two past participles; a long one, which expresses an action, and an abbreviated one, which is a kind of adjective:—

Adattare,	to adapt.	adattato, *and* adatto.	*Participles.*
Adornare,	to adorn.	adornato, *and* adorno.	
Avvezzare,	to accustom.	avvezzato, *and* avvezzo.	
Caricare,	to load.	caricato, *and* carico.	
Saziare,	to satiate, satisfy.	saziato, *and* sazio.	
Svegliare,	to wake up.	svegliato, *and* sveglio.	

Ex. { Ho caricato il mio schioppo.   I have loaded my gun.
      { Il mio schioppo è carico.   My gun is loaded.

176. * The "Tonic Accent" in all the regular verbs of the first conjugation is the same as in "Comprare," but in the verbs in the list above, marked with an asterisk (*), and in about seventy more, the three persons in the singular of the Present Indicative, Imperative, and Subjunctive are "sdrùcciole," and the third persons plural of the same tenses are "bisdrùcciole." Ex.

Auguro,	auguri,	augura;
Auguriamo,	augurate,	augurano.

VOCABULARY.

L' Inghilterra,	England.	Inglese,	Englishman, English.
La Francia,	France.	Francese, (48)	Frenchman, French.
La Germania,	Germany.	Tedesco.	German.
L' Italia,	Italy.	Italiano,	Italian.
La Spagna,	Spain.	Spagnuolo,	Spaniard, Spanish.

La situazione,	the situation.	La porta, l' uscio,	the gate, door.
Questa città,	this town, city.	La lingua,	tongue, the language.

Facile,	easy.	Politico,	political.
Difficile,	difficult.	Commerciale,	commercial.

NOTE.—*In this and the following exercises the verbs are given in the Present of the Infinitive Mood; it is left to the student to put them in the proper mood, tense, number, and person.*

EXERCISE IX.

I do (128) not (125) find (a) the Italian* language difficult. William speaks (b) French,† but does not speak German. I am buying‡ some (134) books for my brother. I blame (c) my sister, because she was listening (d) at the door. Shall you (117—122) vote (e) to-morrow? Yes. John found§ this letter on (148) a chair, in my brother's room. I have sent (f) Henry's Spanish grammar to my mother. Charles always|| studies (g) in our uncle's garden. We admire (h) the situation of this town. I have left (i) William's book on my writing-desk. Elizabeth will play, (j) I (106, b) shall sing, (k) and Charles will draw (l).

(a) Trovare. (b) Parlare. (c) Biasimare. (d) Ascoltare. (e) Votare. (f) Mandare. (g) Studiare. (h) Ammirare. (i) Lasciare. (j) Suonare. (k) Cantare. (l) Disegnare.

177. * Adjectives indicating shape, colour, and nationality are put after the noun they qualify, in Italian. Ex. La lingua italiana. *The Italian language.*

178. † English, French, &c., meaning the English, the French language, &c., are also translated by "l' inglese," "il francese," &c., or "la lingua inglese," "la lingua francese," &c.

179. ‡ The English expressions "I am buying," "She was listening," "I shall be writing," &c., are translated into Italian as if they were "I buy," "she listened" (Imp. Ind.), "I shall write," &c.

180. § Translate as if it were "has found," because, in Italian, when the time at which an action occurred is not stated, the verb must be put in the Past Indefinite.

181. || "Sempre," *always,* and "mai," *ever, never,* are generally placed after the verb.

VOCABULARY.

L' Europa,	Europe.	Europeo,*	European.
L' America,	America.	Americano,	American.
La Scozia,	Scotland.	Scozzese,	Scotchman, Scotch.
L' Irlanda,	Ireland.	Irlandese,	Irishman, Irish.

La sottoveste,	the waistcoat.	Ieri sera,†	last night.
Il mondo,	the world.	Un quadro,	a picture.
Una scoperta,	a discovery.	La larghezza,	the breadth.
Una rivoluzione,	a revolution.	La lunghezza,	the length.
La riunione,	the meeting.	Una ciliegia,	a cherry.
Una regola,	a rule.	Dell' uva,	some grapes.
Il pianoforte,	the pianoforte.	Del vino,	some wine.
Questa mattina,	this morning.	Dell' acquavite,	some brandy.

EXERCISE X.

I have bought two Italian (177) books, one (145) for Henry, and one for William. You (106 b)were dining (179) (a), whilst I was studying. Mary will embroider (b) a waistcoat for my father. The discovery of (the) America caused (c) (Past Def.) a revolution in the commercial world. When I entered (d)‡ the room he was working (e). Did you speak (Past Def.) at the meeting last night? No, I did not (125) speak (Past Def.). I shall explain (f) (170) this rule this evening. I shall have built (g) my house before October (74). Measure (h) (122) the length and (115) breadth of this room, before§ buying the pianoforte. We shall preserve (i) these cherries with (in the) brandy. If (112) I had money, I would buy this picture.

(a) Pranzare. (b) Ricamare. (c) Cagionare. (d) Entrare. (e) Lavorare. (f) Spiegare. (g) Fabbricare. (h) Misurare. (i) Conservare.

---

* Notice that in the terminations "eo," "ea," "ei," and "ee" the *e* has the broad sound of *a* in the word *gate*.

182. † "Sera" means *evening*. "Ieri sera" means *yesterday evening*. Last night, meaning the night time, is translated by "Questa notte," or "La notte passata."

183. ‡ "Entrare," *to enter*, is a neuter verb, and is always followed by "in." Ex.
   Entrai nel teatro alle sei. I entered the theatre at six o'clock.

184. § All prepositions (except "dopo," *after*,) in Italian are followed by the Infinitive Present, or Past. Ex.
   Prima di andare a Parigi. Before going to Paris.
   Prima di aver parlato. Before having spoken.

185. § The preposition "dopo," *after*, is always followed by the Past of the Infinitive. Ex.
   Partirò dopo aver parlato. I shall start after having spoken.

LESSON VII.

ON THE PERSONAL PRONOUNS.

PERSONAL PRONOUNS USED AS SUBJECTS* OF VERBS.

186. The personal pronouns are translated into Italian as follows:—

Io,	*I.*	Noi,	*We.*
Tu,	*Thou.*	Voi,	*You.*
Egli, Ei, *or* Esso,	*He, it.*†	m. Essi *or* Eglino,	*They, you* (121).
Ella *or* Essa,	*She, it, you* (120).	f. Esse *or* Elleno,	

187. The pronouns "egli," "ella," "eglino," and "elleno," are used only in speaking of persons, whilst "esso," "essa," "essi," and "esse," are often employed with reference to persons, animals, and things, and are used both as the subjects and objects of verbs. "Eglino" and "elleno" are becoming obsolete; "essi" and "esse" being used instead of them. Ex.

Egli parla francese.	He speaks French.
Ei non sapeva che fare del pane che gli gettavo. (Pellico.)	He did not know what to do with the bread I threw him.
Essi andarono a Parigi.	They went to Paris.

188. As the termination of the verb, in Italian, is sufficient to indicate the person and number of the subject in the sentence, the personal pronouns, "Io," "Tu," "Egli," &c., are not expressed, except (*a*)—when two or more nouns or pronouns are used as subjects in the same sentence; (*b*)—in the present and imperfect tenses of the Subjunctive Mood, to avoid ambiguity; (*c*)—when a particular stress is laid on the pronoun. Ex.

Mentre io scrivo questa lettera, voi preparerete i miei bauli.	Whilst I write this letter, you will prepare my trunks.
Se io parlassi, sarei ruinato.	If I spoke, I should be ruined.
Io parlo quando bisogna.	I do speak when it is needful.

189. The personal pronouns "io," "tu," "egli," &c., are sometimes accompanied by "stesso," "stessa," or "medesimo," "medesima," &c., *self*, to express emphasis. Ex.

L' ho scritto io stesso (*or* medesimo),   I wrote it myself.

---

190. * A noun, or pronoun is called the *subject* of a verb when it represents the person or thing which does, or receives the action expressed by the verb. Ex.
    Pietro agisce bene; egli è stimato.   Peter acts well; he is esteemed.
In which sentence "Pietro" is the subject of "agisce," and "egli" of "è stimato."

191. † There is no neuter gender in Italian; therefore the pronoun *it* must be translated into Italian by a masculine or feminine pronoun.

PERSONAL PRONOUNS USED AS OBJECTS OF VERBS.
The Conjunctive Personal Pronouns.

192. When there is only one pronoun used as a direct,* or as an indirect† object, in the same sentence, the English pronouns *me, thee, him,* etc., and *to me, to thee, to him,* etc., are translated as follows:—

Direct Objects.		Indirect Objects.	
Mi,	*me.*	Mi,	*to me.*
Ti,	*thee.*	Ti,	*to thee.*
Lo *or* esso,	*him* or *it* (191).	Gli,	*to him.*
La *or* essa,	*her, you* (120) or *it.*	Le,	*to her, you* or *it.*
Si,	{ *himself, herself, itself* or *themselves.*	Si,	{ *to himself, to herself, to itself* or *to themselves.*
Ci *or* ne,‡	*us.*	Ci *or* ne,‡	*to us.*
Vi,	*you.*	Vi,	*to you.*
Li *or* essi,	*them,* mas.	(A) Loro *or* gli,§	*to them,* mas.
Le *or* esse,	*them,* fem.	(A) Loro *or* le,	*to them,* fem.

The Conjunctive Personal Pronouns placed before the Verb.

193. The pronouns given above ARE, AS A RULE, PLACED BEFORE THE VERB. Ex.

Egli mi parlò con rispetto.	He spoke to me with respect.
Non ci hanno mai invitati.	They never invited us.
Gli parlerò domani.‖	I shall speak to him to-morrow.

194. * A noun, or pronoun is called the *direct object* of a verb when it represents the person, or thing which receives the action of the verb directly, that is, without passing through a preposition. Ex.
    Egli chiamò Carlo e me.   He called Charles and me.
In the sentence above "Carlo" and "me" are the *direct objects* of "chiamò."

† A noun, or pronoun is called the *indirect object* of a verb when it represents the person, or thing which receives the action of the verb indirectly, that is, through a preposition. Ex. "Egli mi parlò," *he spoke to me.*
In the sentence above "mi" (a me) is the indirect complement of "parlò."

195. ‡ "Ne" is sometimes used instead of "ci," *us,* and *to us.* Ex.
    L' amicizia tua ne piace. (Tasso.) Your friendship pleases (to) us.

196. § Notice that instead of "a loro," *or* "loro," in modern Italian, "gli" (mas.), and "le" (fem.), are often used. Ex.
    Non gli (*or* le) presterei del denaro.   I would not lend them money.

197. ‖ In many cases in which, according to rule 193, the conjunctive personal pronoun ought to precede the verb, it is placed after it, and joined to it, to give force to the language. If the verb ends with an accented vowel, as "mandò," *he* or *she sent,* the consonant of the pronoun, except the *g* of "gli," is doubled, and the accent suppressed. Ex.
    Essa guardavami sovente.   She often looked at me.
    Egli mandommi a Milano.   He sent me to Milan.

N.B.—It is much better for the *beginner* to follow rule 193.

The Conjunctive Personal Pronouns Placed After the Verb.

198. The conjunctive pronouns "mi," "ti," "gli," &c., ARE PLACED AFTER THE VERB, AND JOINED TO IT (that is why they are called Conjunctive Pronouns), when they are used with verbs in the Infinitive, used Affirmatively*; in which case the final "e" of the Infinitive is dropped. Ex.

Mio padre desidera di mandarmi a Venezia. — My father desires to send me to Venice.

199. The conjunctive pronouns "mi," "ti," "gli," &c., are placed after the Gerund, used Affirmatively,* and joined to it. Ex.

Essa lo calmò parlandogli con molta bontà. — She calmed him by speaking to him very kindly.

200. The conjunctive pronouns "mi," "ti," "gli," &c., are placed after the Past Gerund, and joined to it; in which case the auxiliary, "avendo" or "essendo," is omitted, and the Past Participle alone is expressed, and is variable.† Ex.

Pagatimi (used instead of avendomi pagato) i libri, andò via. — Having paid me for the book, he went away.

Adagiatasi (essendosi‡ adagiata) sulla sedia, essa narrò le sue avventure. — Having seated herself on the chair, she narrated her adventures.

201. The conjunctive pronouns "mi," "ti," "gli," &c., are placed after the second person singular, and the first and second persons plural of the Imperative, used affirmatively,§ and are joined to them. Ex.

Parlami ora caro fratello. — Speak to me now, dear brother.
Mandateci∥ un mazzo di fiori. — Send us a bunch of flowers.

---

202. * When the Infinitive (see rule 126) and the Gerund are preceded by a negative, the pronouns are *sometimes* put before the verb. Ex.
  Non ti scordar di me. — Do not forget me.
  Non gli piacendo la stanza. — As he did not like the room.

203. † Notice that this rule of leaving out "avendo" or "essendo" in the Past Gerund holds good whether there is a pronoun or not. Ex.
  Comprato (avendo comprato) il cavallo, andò via. — Having bought the horse, he went away.

204. ‡ Notice that in the compound tenses of reflexive verbs (see page 59) "essere" is used.

205. § When the Imperative is used negatively, the Conjunctive Pronouns precede the verbs, according to rule 193. Ex.
  Non mi parlare ora, caro fratello. — Do not speak to me now, dear brother.

206. ∥ Here the student is reminded that, instead of "voi," *you*, the Italians very often use "Ella," *your Lordship* or *Ladyship* (see rule 120); in which case the pronouns precede the verbs, according to rule 193. Ex.
  Ci mandi un mazzo di fiori. — Send us a bunch of flowers.

VOCABULARY.

Londra,	London.	Firenze,	Florence.	Glasgovia,	Glasgow.
Parigi,	Paris.	Dublino,	Dublin.	Napoli,	Naples.
Roma,	Rome.	Venezia,	Venice.	Genova,	Genoa.

Federico,	Frederick.	Giacomo,	James.	Margherita,	Margaret.
Giorgio,	George.	Filippo,	Philip.	Luigia,	Louisa.
Odoardo,	Edward.	Giuseppe,	Joseph.	Francesca,	Frances.

Il caffè,	coffee.	La crema,	cream.	Il butirro,	butter.
Il tè,	tea.	L'olio,	oil.	Lo zucchero,	sugar.
Il latte,	milk.	L'aceto,	vinegar.	La cioccolata,	chocolate.

EXERCISE XI.

Where did you (120, 122) buy (have you bought) this coffee? I bought it (192, 193) in* London. Does (128) Edward speak Italian? Yes, he does.† Where did you study (have you studied) the French language? I studied (have studied) it in France. Has Louisa sent to-day's newspaper to my father? Yes; she sent (has sent) it this morning. Charles always speaks to me (193) when he meets (a) me. My father taught (b) us yesterday, and will teach us to-day. My mother never (non. . . mai, 181) sends us (193) here. I shall not speak to him (193) to-day. Have you bought any sugar? Yes, I have (138, 208). George has made me (193) a present of (c) some Italian books. If (112) they had any (133) money, they would send (to) him some tea and (136), bread.

(a) Incontrare.   (b) Insegnare.   (c) Regalare (to make a present of).

207. * The prepositions *in* and *to* are translated into Italian by "a," before the name of a town, and by "*in*" before the name of a continent, an empire, a kingdom, a duchy, or a province. Ex.
  Andò a Parigi, in Francia.   He went to Paris, in France.

208. † In answering a question, the verb contained in the question, and not merely the translation of "I do," "he does," "it does," "I have," "he did," "I will," &c., must be expressed in the answer, in Italian, and the verb must be in the same tense as in the question; and if there is a noun in the question, that noun also must be represented in the answer by a pronoun, agreeing in gender and number with the noun it represents. Ex.
  Giovanni, parla il tedesco? Sì, lo parla.   Does John speak German? Yes, he does.

209. The above rule holds good also when "I do," "I did," "I have," &c., have reference to a previous verb in the sentence. Ex.
  Avevo promesso di portare il mio oriuolo,   I had promised to bring my watch,
    e l'ho portato,   and I have brought it.

THE DISJUNCTIVE PERSONAL PRONOUNS.

210. When in the same sentence there are more than one direct (195) or more than one indirect (196) objects, relating to different persons or things, or when they desire to lay a particular stress on the object in the sentence, the Italians place the following personal pronouns after the verb, but not joined to it—that is why they are called Disjunctive Personal Pronouns.

DIRECT OBJECTS (195).		INDIRECT OBJECTS (196).	
Me,	me.	A me,	to me.
Te,	thee.	A te,	to thee.
Lui or esso,	him or it (191).	A lui or a esso,	to him or it.
Lei or essa,	her, you or it.	A lei or a essa,	to her, you or it.
Sè,	{ himself, herself, itself or themselves.	A sè,	{ to himself, herself. to itself or themselves.
Noi,	us.	A noi,	to us.
Voi,	you.	A voi,	to you.
Loro or essi,	them, mas.	(A) loro or a essi,	to them, mas.
Loro or esse,	them, fem.	(A) loro or a esse,	to them, fem.

EXAMPLES.

Il generale parlò a me, ma non parlò a mio nipote. — The general spoke to me, but he did not speak to my nephew.

Parlo a Lei, Signore; perchè non mi risponde? — I speak to you, Sir; why do you not answer me?

211. Notice that in the case explained in rule 210, "gli" and "le" (see rule 196) could not be used instead of "a loro." Ex.

Manderò un libro a lui, e a loro manderò del denaro. — I shall send him a book, and some money to them.

212. Notice that not only "a" *to*, but all the other prepositions "di," *of*, "do," *from*, "con," *with*, "per," *for, through*, &c., are used to form the indirect objects of verbs, but, as they always follow the verb, they offer no difficulty to the student. Ex.

Carlo parlerà per me.* — Charles will speak for me.
Vuol ella venir con me?† — Will you come with me?
Partì con loro.‡ — He went away with them.

---

213. * Instead of "per me," "per te," "per lui," and "per lei," &c., the conjunctive forms "mi," "ti," "gli," and "le," &c., are used with such verbs as "fare," *to do, to make*, "fabbricare," *to build*, "dipingere," *to paint*, &c., when the sentence contains also a direct object. Ex.
Gli (per lui) fabbricarono una casa. They built him (for him) a house.

214. † "Meco," "teco," "seco," are sometimes used instead of "con me," "con te," "con sè." Ex. Vuol ella venir meco? *Will you come with me?*

215. ‡ Formerly the pronoun "esso," (invariable) was sometimes used pleonastically before "lui," "lei," "loro." Ex.
Andai con essoloro (D'Azeglio). I went along with them.

VOCABULARY.

| Il marmo, | marble. | Il mattone, | brick. | Il cristallo, | crystal. |
| La pietra, | stone. | Il legno, | wood. | Il vetro, | glass. |

| Paolo, | Paul. | Stefano, | Stephen. | Carlotta, | Charlotte. |
| Andrea, | Andrew. | Antonio, | Anthony. | Maddalena, | Madeline. |

La statua,	the statue.	Il fazzoletto,	the handkerchief.
La testa,	the head.	Uno (141) specchio,	a looking-glass.
Gli occhi,	the eyes.	Un leggìo,	a reading-desk.
I capelli,	the hair.	Carta sugante,	blotting-paper.
Il braccio,	the arm.	Ceralacca,	sealing-wax.
La mano,	the hand.	Un acquarello,	a water-colour.
Il dito,	the finger.	Mio suocero,	my father-in-law.
Il piede,*	the foot.	Mia cognata,	my sister-in-law.
L'anello,	the ring.	Vostro genero,	your son-in-law.

EXERCISE XII.

I condemned (a) (Past Def.) him, and I pardoned (b) my (129) brother. Paul always (181) speaks of himself (212). Charlotte (113) spoke to me (210), but she did not speak to my (130) sisters. I speak to you (210); why do (128) you not answer? You never pay attention (c) to me. He always speaks of me, but I never speak of him. They sent (Past Def.) a reading-desk to me (210), and a marble statue to my (146) master. Stephen will speak for me. They built him (213) a marble palace. Madeline has sent a gold ring to William, and a small water-colour to my sister-in-law. She sent (180) also a beautiful looking-glass to my sister. I shall place (d) the picture before her.‡

(a) Condannare. (b) Perdonare a. (c) Badare a.† (d) Posare

---

* Notice that the *e* in the diphthong *ie* (except in the suffixes "etto," &c.), has the broad sound of *a* in the word *gate*.

216. † "Badare" is always followed by a disjunctive personal pronoun. Ex.
    Badate a me.   Pay attention to me.
You could not say "Badatemi."

217. ‡ When the prepositions "davanti," "dinanzi," "innanzi," *before*, "didietro," "dietro," *behind*, "incontro," *against*, "sopra," "disopra," *on, upon, above*, "sotto," "disotto," *under, below*, are used with a conjunctive personal pronoun, they are placed at the end of the phrase. Ex.
    Gli andò incontro.   He went against him.

LESSON VIII.
ON DOUBLE CONJUNCTIVE PRONOUNS.

218. When two conjunctive pronouns are governed by the same verb, and one is a "direct" and the other an "indirect object," the "indirect" precedes the "direct object," and the *i* of "mi," "ti," "ci," "vi," is changed into *e*. When these pronouns come before the verb, they are written separately, but when they are placed after the verb, they are written together, and joined to it. Ex.

Me lo prestò Guglielmo.	William lent it to me.
Me li ha comprati mio zio.	My uncle bought them for me.
Egli vuol venderceloggi.	He will sell it to us to-day.
Me lo, *or* mel* disse ieri sera.	He told it to me last night.

See rule 201. { Dammelo, Me lo dia, Datemelo, } Give it to me.

219. When the pronoun "gli," *to him*, is followed by the pronouns "lo," "la," "li," "le," and "ne," instead of changing the final *i* into *e*, like the other conjunctive pronouns (see rule 218), it takes an *e* after the final *i*, and forms one word with the relative pronoun. Ex.

Glielo presterò, ma non posso darglielo.†	I will lend it to him, but I cannot give it to him.
Mi ha promesso di mandarglieli questa sera.†	He promised that he would send them to him this evening.

See rule 201. { Mandaglielo,† Glielo mandi,† Mandateglielo,† } Send it to him.

220. Notice that, for the sake of euphony, "glie" is also used for the feminine instead of "le," when followed by "lo," "la," "li," "le," and "ne." Ex.

Maria desiderava i fiori, ed io glieli ho mandati.†	Mary wished for the flowers, and I sent them to her.

221. In Italian an answer must contain the noun expressed in the question, or a pronoun in its stead, and the verb must be repeated in the answer. Ex.

Ha ella preso la mia ombrella ?	Have you taken my umbrella ?
No, non l' ho presa.	No, I have not.

---

222. * "Mel," "tel," "cel," "vel," are often used instead of "me lo," "te lo," "ce lo," "ve lo."

223. † It is important to notice that "gli" in this sentence might mean either *to him*, or *to her* (and consequently *to you*, see rule 120), or *to them* (see rule 211); but the sense of the sentence, in the context, always helps to clear up the ambiguity.

ON THE PERSONAL PRONOUNS.

VOCABULARY.

Dio, Iddio,	God.	Il sole,	the sun.
Il cielo,	Heaven, the sky,	La luna,	the moon.
La terra,	the earth.	Le stelle,	the stars.

Mio caro amico,	my dear friend.	Un regalo,	a present.
Il giorno di nascita,	the birthday.	Un album,	an album.
Questo pericolo,	this danger.	Il popolo,	the people.

Ora, adesso,   now.   Volontieri,   willingly.

EXERCISE XIII.

Speak to me (201) now, because I shall not have time tomorrow. He was speaking (179) to his master (146) when you called (a) (Past Def.) him. When will you send her (192, 193) the pictures? I will send them to her (219, 220) this evening. Do not forget (b) (125, 126). Will* you help (c) me, (192) my dear friend? Yes, willingly, I will not abandon (d) you in this danger. Will (224) you lend (e) me your penknife? Yes, I will (208). Shall you send him a present for his birthday? Yes, I shall send him an album. I have brought (f) Henry's books to† show (g) them to you (122, 218). They ordered (h) him to (226) speak to the people.

(a) Chiamare. (b) Dimenticare. (c) Aiutare. (d) Abbandonare. (e) Prestare. (f) Portare. (g) Mostrare. (h) Comandare.

224. * When *will, would, shall* and *should* are distinct verbs of themselves (not mere auxiliaries) they are translated into Italian by "Volere" or "Dovere." Ex.

Vuol' ella darmi una rosa?   Will you give me a rose?

N.B.—The Present Indicative of "volere," *to be willing*, should be studied at once; it is given on page 91.

225. † When the preposition *to* means *in order to*, it is translated into Italian by "per" or "onde." Ex.

Sono venuto per (*or* onde) parlarle.   I have come to speak to you.

226. The verbal prefix *to* is translated into Italian by "di," when it is preceded by an adjective, or a past participle (except "pronto," *ready*, "disposto," *disposed*, "prono," *inclined*, "preparato," *prepared*), and a verb expressing an idea of rest or state. Ex.

Sono decisi di andare a Venezia.   They have decided to go to Venice.

227. The verbal prefix *to* is translated into Italian by "a," when it is preceded by a verb expressing motion, or "pronto," "disposto," "prono," and "preparato." Ex.

Venga a trovarmi fra due mesi.   Come to see me in two months' time.

FURTHER REMARKS ON THE PERSONAL PRONOUNS.

228. "E'" is sometimes used instead of "egli," "esso," and "essi." Ex.

Picchia anche lì e aspetta, e' poteva aspettare. (Manz.) — He also knocks there and waits, and he might wait.

Cortesemente domandò chi, e' fossero. (Boccaccio.) — Courteously he asked who they were.

229. "Desso," "dessa," "dessi," "desse," are elegantly used instead of "esso," "essa," &c., with the verbs "essere," and "parere." Ex.

Quegli è desso; lo conosco. — It is he; I know him.

230. "Egli," or simply "gli," and "e'" are sometimes used as "ripieni," that is pleonastically; they correspond to the English neuter pronoun *it*. Ex.

E s'egli è ver che tua potenza sia nel cielo. (Petrarca.) — And if it be true that thy power is in heaven.

E' risica d' essere una giornata peggio di ieri. (Manz.) — It risks to be a day worse than yesterday.

231. Instead of the subjective pronouns "io," "tu," "egli," "ella," "essi," and "esse," the objective pronouns "me," "te," "lui," "lei," and "loro" are used after the words "ma," *but*, "anche," *also*, "come," "siccome," *as*, "quanto," *as much as*, "nemmeno," *not even*, &c., for the sake of euphony, and in other cases solely for the purpose of giving more prominence to the pronoun. Ex.

Ma Lei non mi scrive mai. — But you never write to me.
Si levò anche lui il cappello. — He also took off his hat.
Lei è ricca, ma io son povero. — You are rich, but I am poor.
Le parole che dicon loro vanno via e spariscono. (Manz.) — The words which they say fly away and disappear.

232. Sometimes, in the colloquial style, "la," and "le," are used instead of "ella" and "esse." Ex.

La c'è; l' ho trovata! (Manz.) — She is there; I found her!
Le son tutte qui. (Manz.) — They are all here.

233. When several verbs govern the same pronouns, the latter are generally repeated with each verb. Ex.

Gli* amiamo e gli* stimiamo. — We love and esteem them.

234. "Non lo" is often contracted into "nol." Ex.

Egli nol disse a nessuno. — He did not tell it to anybody.

235. "Il" in poetry, is sometimes used instead of "lo." Ex.

Oimè! bene il conosco. (Tas.) — Alas! I know him well.

236. Notice that before a verb beginning with a vowel, or an *s* followed by another consonant, "gli" is used instead of "li."

LESSON IX.

ON THE WORDS "CI," "VI," AND "NE."

237. Besides being used as conjunctive personal pronouns (see rules 192, 197), "ci," "vi," and "ne," are used as relative pronouns, and as adverbs.

238. "Ci" and "vi," used as relative pronouns, signify *of it, of them; about it, about them; to it, to them; for it, for them; in it, in them.* Ex.

Non indovinerei, se ci pensassi un anno.	I could not guess it, if I thought a year about it.
Questo quadro mi va a genio; ci ho fatto fare una bella cornice.	I like this picture very much; I have had a fine frame made for it.
Ci ho dato una mano di vernice.	I have given it a coat of varnish.

239. When "ci" and "vi" are used as adverbs, they always refer to an antecedent; "ci" means *here*, and "vi" means *there*.* Ex.

Francesco viene qui tutte le mattine, e ci sta fino alle otto della sera.	Francis comes here every morning, and stays till eight o'clock in the evening.
Non sono mai stato in Italia, ma faccio i conti d'andarvi questa primavera.	I have never been to Italy, but I intend to go there this Spring.

240. "Ne," used as a relative pronoun, means *some, any, of it, of them; concerning* (or *about*) *him, her, it; for it, for them, from it, from them.* As stated already (rule 138) in an answer, "ne" must always be expressed in Italian (although *some, any, of it, of them,* &c., are seldom expressed in English), and the verb, in the answer, must also be expressed in full. Ex.

Ha ella per caso qualche libro italiano da prestarmi?	Have you perchance any Italian books to lend me?
Sì, ne ho due o tre, e glieli presterò volontieri.	Yes, I have two or three, which I shall be very glad to lend you.
Sono certo che le piace la musica, perchè ne parla sempre.	I am certain that you are fond of music, for you are always speaking about it.
Vado ai bagni di mare ogni anno, e ne derivo sempre molto bene.	I go to the sea-side to bathe every year, and I always derive great benefit from it.

241. * For the sake of euphony "ci" is sometimes used instead of "vi." Ex. Andateci, e vi troverete Carlo.   Go there, and you will find Charles.

242. When "ne" is used as an adverb, it means *thence*. Ex.

| Sono stato a Parigi; ne vengo appunto. | I have been to Paris; I have just returned from there. |

243. When "ci," "vi," and "ne," are used as relative pronouns, and as adverbs, they occupy the same position with regard to the verb as when they are conjunctive personal pronouns (see rules 192-201) and the *i* of "ci," "vi," is changed into *e* (218) when "lo," "la," "li," "le," and "ne," follow them. Ex.

Egli va sovente al teatro, e vi mena seco sua sorella.	He often goes to the theatre and takes his sister with him.
Mia zia aveva dei biglietti, e me ne diede tre.	My aunt had some tickets, and she gave me three.
Non l'ho mai condotto a casa nostra; ma ho promesso di condurcelo.	I had never taken him to our house, but I have promised to do so.

On the Personal Pronouns used Reflectively.

244. We have seen (rule 189) that when *myself, thyself,* &c., are used merely to express emphasis, or to indicate discrimination, they are translated by "stesso," "stessa," &c., or "medesimo," "medesima," &c.; but when these pronouns are used as Reflective Pronouns, they are expressed by "mi," "ti," "si;" "ci," "vi," "si," and are subject to all the rules given above, concerning the personal pronouns. Ex.

Non mi vesto mai prima delle dieci.	I never dress before ten o'clock.
Preparati, *or* preparatevi, *or* si prepari subito.	Get ready without losing a minute.
Raccolse i panni di suo fratello, e se ne vestì.	He took up his brother's clothes, and dressed himself in them.

"Ecco," *behold*, used with Personal and Relative Pronouns.

245. When a conjunctive pronoun, personal or relative, is used with the word "ecco," *behold*,* *here is, there is, this is, these are, here are, there are*, it must be placed after it, and joined to it; as "eccomi," "eccoti," "eccoci," "eccoli," "eccole," "eccone."† Ex.

| Eccomi. Eccoci pronti. | Here I am. Here we are ready. |
| Se ama le incisioni, eccone qui delle bellissime. | If you are fond of engravings, here are some beautiful ones. |

246. * Sometimes "ecco" is followed by two pronouns. Ex.
Eccoteli umiliati. Here they are humbled.

247. † Sometimes "ecco" is rendered more graphic by adding to it the adverbs "qui," *here,* and "là," *there.* Ex. "Eccolo là." There he is.

VOCABULARY.

Un orologio, (21)	a clock.	Questo paese,	this country.
Il mio oriuolo,	my watch.	Alla campagna,	into the country.
Una rosa,*	a rose.	Casa di campagna,	country house.
Il frutto,	the fruit.	Questo canestro,	this basket.
Un ombrello,	an umbrella.	Un errore,	a fault.
Un ombrellino,	a parasol.	Uno sbaglio,	a mistake.
Un porta-lapis,	a pencil-case.	Alla posta,	to the post.

Rosso,	red.	Verde,	green.	Bianco,	white.
Turchino,	blue.	Giallo,	yellow.	Nero,	black.

EXERCISE XIV.

I have brought my exercise to (225) show it to you (122, 218); you will find few (139) faults in it (238). Henry has brought (167) us (192, 193) a basket of roses. I should not have spoken to her, if I had thought (a) of † it (238). Before speaking to us, (210) speak to my father. He was speaking to us, (179, 192, 193) when they called (Past Def.) him into the garden. Have you an English watch? Yes, I have (144). If I had thought of it, I should never have lent him my pencil-case. When will you take (b) these letters (89) to the post? I will take them (there) (239, 243) at once, if you will (224) lend me your umbrella. Have you spoken to William? No, I have not, (208) but I will speak to him when‡ I have time. Why did (128) you burn (c) (Past Indef.) that (152) letter? I burnt it (167) by§ mistake. Have you paid (d) for‖ your parasol? No, but I will pay for it when Henry returns (e).

(a) Pensare. (b) Portare. (c) Abbruciare. (d) Pagare. (e) Ritornare.

---

* An *s* dotted thus ṣ, has the soft sound of the *s* in the word *rose*.

248. † *To think of* is translated by "pensare a." "Pensare di," means *to have an opinion about*. Ex.
Che pensa di questo poema?   What do you think of this poem?

249. ‡ A verb preceded by the adverbs *when, as soon as*, &c., indicates a future time; therefore the future, and *not* the present tense, must be used in Italian. Ex.
Scriverò quando avrò il tempo.   I shall write when I have time.

250. § When a *common* noun begins with an *s*, followed by another consonant, and is preceded by "per," *by, through*, "in," *in, into*, "con," *with*, and "non," *no, not*, an *i* is put before the *s* for the sake of euphony; as "Per isbaglio," *by mistake*.

251. ‖ *For* is not translated into Italian, after the active verbs *to pay, to buy, to sell, to ask, to look, to wait, to wish*.

LESSON X.

MODEL OF THE SECOND CONJUGATION IN "ERE."
"CREDERE," *TO BELIEVE.*

INFINITIVE MOOD.

Present.	Past.
Cred ere, *to believe.*	Aver cred uto, *to have believed.*

Gerund.	Past Participle.	Past Gerund.
Cred endo,* *believing.*	Cred uto-a-i-e, *believed.*	Avendo cred uto, *having believed.*

INDICATIVE MOOD.

Present.	Imperfect.	Past Definite.
Cred o,	Cred evo,	Cred ei, *or* etti,
Cred i,	Cred evi,	Cred esti,
Cred e;	Cred eva;	Cred è, ette;
Cred iamo,	Cred evamo,	Cred emmo,
Cred ete,	Cred evate,	Cred este,
Cred ono.	Cred evano.	Cred erono, *or* ettero.

I believe, &c.   *I believed, &c.*   *I believed, &c.*

Past Indefinite.	Pluperfect.	Past Anterior.
Ho creduto, &c.	Avevo creduto, &c.	Ebbi creduto, &c.
I have believed, &c.	*I had believed, &c.*	*I had believed, &c.*

Future.	Conditional.	IMPERATIVE MOOD.
Cred erò,	Cred erei,	*No first person.*
Cred erai,	Cred eresti,	Cred i,
Cred erà;	Cred erebbe;	Cred a;
Cred eremo,	Cred eremmo,	Cred iamo,
Cred erete,	Cred ereste,	Cred ete,
Cred eranno.	Cred erebbero.	Cred ano.

I shall believe, &c.   *I should believe, &c.*   *Believe (thou), &c.*

Future Anterior.	Conditional Past.	
Avrò creduto, &c.	Avrei creduto, &c.	The Past of the Imperative is seldom used.
I shall have believed, &c.	*I should have believed, &c.*	

---

* Notice that the *e* in the gerundial termination *endo*, has always the broad sound of the *a* in the word *gate*.

SUBJUNCTIVE MOOD.

PRESENT.		IMPERFECT.	
Che io cred a,	*That I may believe, &c.*	Che or se (112) io cred essi,	*That or if I might believe, &c.*
Che tu cred a,		Che or se tu cred essi,	
Che [egli/ella] cred a ;		Che or se [egli/ella] cred esse ;	
Che cred iamo,		Che or se cred essimo,	
Che cred iate,		Che or se cred este,	
Che [essi/esse] cred ano.		Che or se [essi/esse] cred essero.	

PAST.	PLUPERFECT.
Che io abbia creduto, &c.	Che or se io avessi creduto, &c.
That I may have believed, &c.	*That or if I might have believed, &c.*

POETICAL FORMS.

252. In poetry "crederìa" is often used instead of "crederei," and "crederebbe" and "crederìano" instead of "crederebbero"; in the same way "temerìa," instead of "temerei" and "temerebbe," &c.

253. In poetry "credêro" is often used instead of "crederono"; in the same way "temêro" instead of "temerono," &c.

REGULAR VERBS OF THE SECOND CONJUGATION.

Assistere, (a)	to assist.	Precedere,*	to precede.
Cedere,*	to yield.	Premere,*	to press.
Dipendere,	to depend.	Procedere,	to proceed.
Eccedere,*	to exceed.	Resistere, (e)	to resist.
Fendere, (b)	to split.	Ricevere,*	to receive.
Fremere,*	to rage.	Risolvere, (f)	to resolve.
Gemere,	to groan.	Spandere,*	to shed.
Godere,	to enjoy.	Splendere,	to shine.
Mescere, (c)	to pour out.	Temere,	to fear.
Pascere, (d)	to feed.	Vendere,	to sell.

254. * Those verbs in the above list, marked thus,* form their Past Definite either in *ei*, or in *etti*; as "cedei," or "cedetti," "cedesti," "cedè," or "cedette"; "cedemmo," "cedeste," "cederono," or "cedettero." But all the others have only the termination *ei*.

(a) The Past Participle of "Assistere" is "assistito."
(b) ... ... "Fendere" is "fesso."
(c) ... ... "Mescere" is "mesciuto."
(d) ... ... "Pascere" is "pasciuto."
(e) ... ... "Resistere" is "resistito."
(f) ... ... "Risolvere" is "risoluto."

VOCABULARY.

Il generale,	the general.	La vista,	the sight.
Il colonello,	the colonel.	Il Natale,	Christmas.
Un soldato,	a soldier.	La Pasqua,	Easter.
Un ordine,	an order.	Il medico,	the doctor.
Una fortezza,	a fortress.	Questo dono,	this gift.
Il presidio,	the garrison.	La sua salute,	his health.
Un cannone,	a cannon.	La confidenza,	confidence.
Un fucile,	a gun.	Qual pegno di,	as a mark of.
Il campanello,	the bell.	Una volta,	once.
La folla, calca,	the crowd.	Due volte,	twice.

Signore, { Mr. / Sir. } Signora, { Mrs. / Madam. } Signorina, { Miss. / Madam. }

EXERCISE XV.

I receive (a) letters from Mr.* James. The soldiers have received the general's order. My sister enjoys (b) good health in this country. He groans (c) at the sight of the doctor. Receive (122) this gift as a mark of my confidence. Believe me, (201, 122) general,† we shall beat (d) them (236). Who (chi) is knocking at (e) (179) the door? Charles; he has already knocked twice, and rang (f) the bell. The cannon beat down (g) (180) the fortress. I have received a letter from my father; he thinks (h) (che) that he will be in London before Christmas. I have sold (i) my (131) country-house to Mr. John. Yesterday he lost (j) his umbrella in the crowd. We have resolved (k) to yield (l) to him (198).

(a) Ricevere. (b) Godere. (c) Gemere. (d) Sconfiggere. (e) Battere, or Bussare a. (f) Suonare. (g) Buttar giù. (h) Credere. (i) Vendere. (j) Perdere. (k) Risolvere di. (l) Cedere a.

255. * In speaking or writing to people, the words Mr., Sir, are translated by "Signore" (plural "Signori"), Mrs., Madam, by "Signora" (plural "Signore"), Miss, by "Signorina" (plural "Signorine.") But in speaking or writing about persons, Mr., Sir, &c., are translated by "il Signore," "i Signori," "la Signora," "la Signorina," "le Signorine," "le Signore." When "Signore" is followed by the name of the person referred to, the e is omitted. Ex.

Il Signor John ha ricevuto una lettera dalla Signora James. Mr. John has received a letter from Mrs. James.
I Signori John sono amici delle Signorine James. Messrs. John are friends of the Misses James.

256. † The Italians, out of politeness, use the words Signor and Signora before titles, dignities, and names of rank, when they address a person equal or superior to themselves. Ex. "Caro Signor Marchese," *Dear Marquis.*

VOCABULARY.

Il fiore,*	the flower.	Questa capra,	this goat.
Una fragola,	a strawberry.	La montagna,	the mountain.
Questo bicchiere,	this glass.	La notizia,	the news.
La mia volontà,	my will.	La bellezza,	the beauty.
Fortificazioni, f.	entrenchments.	La freschezza,	the freshness.
Il tumulto,	the turmoil.	Il suo successo,	his success.
Il mio pensiero,	my thought.	Un' impresa,	an undertaking.
Contento,	glad.	Insieme,	together.
Valorosamente,	bravely.	Tutto,	everything.
Quietamente,	quietly.	Ad onta di,	in spite of.
Che cosa?	what?	Per piacere,	if you please.

EXERCISE XVI.

What does (128) this woman sell? She sells (134-137), fruit (fruits) and flowers; yesterday she sold me some beautiful roses, and some good strawberries. Who will succeed† him (192, 193) in the business?‡ I think (I believe)§ his brother Edward will succeed him. He and his sister have left London, and are enjoying the beauty of the country, and the freshness of the air. She shudders (a) at the thought of meeting (b) (184, 198) him. Do you believe the news (260) he told us? (c) No, I do not believe it (193). It does not depend upon (d) my sister. The French fought (e) bravely, within the (102) entrenchments. The goats browse (f) quietly on the mountains in spite of the turmoil of (the) men (uomini). I shall never forget (g) the happy days (260) we have enjoyed (167) together. Everything will depend upon the success of the undertaking. Shall I pour you out (to pour out) (h) a glass of wine, Mr. John? Yes, if you please.

(a) Fremere. (b) Incontrare. (c) Raccontare. (d) Dipendere da. (e) Combattere. (f) Pascere. (g) Dimenticare. (h) Mescere a.

---

257. * Nouns ending in *e*, in the singular, form their plural by changing the *e* into *i*; as "il fiore," plural "i fiori."
258. † When *to succeed* means *to take the place of*, it is translated by "Succedere a;" but when it means *to be successful*, it is translated by "Riuscire."
259. ‡ *Business* is translated by "Affare," or "Affari," when it means *concern, affairs*; but when it is translated by "Negozio," when it means *shop, trade*.
260. § In Italian the conjunction "che," *that*, and the relative pronoun "che," *or* "il quale," &c., *that*, or *which* cannot be omitted before the personal pronoun. Ex.

Credo ch' egli sia a Vienna. I believe (that) he is in Vienna.
Le notizie che ci ha recate. The news (that) he brought us.

LESSON XI.

MODEL OF THE THIRD CONJUGATION IN "IRE".
"FINIRE," *TO FINISH.*

INFINITIVE MOOD.

Present.	Past.
Fin ire, *to finish.*	Aver fin ito, *to have finished.*

Gerund.	Past Participle.	Past Gerund.
Fin endo, *finishing.*	Fin ito-a-i-e, *finished.*	Avendo fin ito, *having finished.*

INDICATIVE MOOD.

Present.	Imperfect.	Past Definite.
Fin isco,	Fin ivo, (108)	Fin ii,
Fin isci,	Fin ivi,	Fin isti,
Fin isce ;	Fin iva ;	Fin ì ;*
Fin iamo,	Fin ivamo,	Fin immo,
Fin ite,	Fin ivate,	Fin iste,
Fin iscono.	Fin ivano.	Fin irono.*
I finish, &c.	*I finished, &c.*	*I finished, &c.*

Past Indefinite.	Pluperfect.	Past Anterior.
Ho finito, &c.,	Avevo finito, &c.,	Ebbi finito, &c.,
I have finished, &c.	*I had finished, &c.*	*I had finished, &c.*

Future.	Conditional.	IMPERATIVE MOOD.
Fin irò,	Fin irei,*	No first person.
Fin irai,	Fin iresti,	Fin isci,
Fin irà ;	Fin irebbe ;*	Fin isca ;
Fin iremo,	Fin iremmo,	Fin iamo,
Fin irete,	Fin ireste,	Fin ite,
Fin iranno.	Fin irebbero.*	Fin iscano.
I shall finish, &c.	*I should finish, &c.*	*Finish (thou), &c.*

Future Anterior.	Conditional Past.	
Avrò finito, &c.	Avrei finito, &c.	The Past of the Imperative is seldom used.
I shall have finished, &c.	*I should have finished, &c.*	

261. * In poetry "finìo" is sometimes used instead of "finì," "finìro" instead of "finirono," "finirìa," instead of "finirei" and "finirebbe" and "finirìano," instead of "finirebbero."

SUBJUNCTIVE MOOD.

PRESENT.

Che io* fin isca,
Che tu fin isca,
Che [egli/ella] fin isca;
Che fin iamo,
Che fin iate,
Che [eglino/esse] fin iscano.

That I may finish, &c.

IMPERFECT.

Che or se (112) io fin issi,
Che or se tu fin issi,
Che or se [egli/ella] fin isse;
Che or se fin issimo,
Che or se fin iste,
Che or se [eglino/esse] fin issero.

That or if I might finish, &c.

PAST.
Che io abbia finito, &c.
That I may have finished, &c.

PLUPERFECT.
Che or se io avessi finito, &c.
That or if I might have finished, &c.

LIST OF VERBS CONJUGATED LIKE "FINIRE."

Abbellire,	to embellish.	Indebolire,	to weaken.
Abolire,	to abolish.	Inferocire,	to become ferocious.
Aderire,	to adhere.	Inghiottire,	to swallow.
Agire,	to act.	Inorgoglire,	to become proud.
Apparire,	to appear.	Intenerire,	to touch, move.
Ardire,	to dare.	Invaghire,	to enchant, charm.
Arrossire,	to blush.	Marcire,	to rot.
Colpire,	to strike.	Munire,	to furnish.
Condire,	to season.	Patire,	to suffer.
Conferire,	to confer.	Profferire,	to proffer.
Differire,	to differ, delay.	Progredire,	to progress.
Digerire,	to digest.	Proibire,	to prohibit.
Eseguire,	to execute.	Pulire,	to clean.
Esibire,	to offer.	Riverire,	to reverence.
Garantire,	to guarantee.	Sbigottire,	to disconcert.
Guarire,	to cure.	Schernire,	to despise.
Impallidire,	to turn pale.	Sparire,	to disappear.
Impaurire,	to frighten.	Starnutire,	to sneeze.
Impazzire,	to become mad.	Stupire,	to astonish.
Impedire,	to hinder.	Suggerire,	to suggest.
Incivilire,	to civilize, polish.	Svanire,	to vanish.

* An *o*, dotted thus ǫ, has the broad sound of the *o* in the word *orphan*.

ON VERBS CONJUGATED LIKE "SERVIRE," *TO SERVE.*

262. As already stated in rule 164, most verbs in "ire" (390 out of 500) are conjugated regularly like "Finire." But there are a few (about 40) which are conjugated like "Servire," *to serve.* These differ from "Finire" in the Present Indicative, Imperative, and in the Present Subjunctive, as is shown in the appended paradigm:—

INDICATIVE MOOD.		IMPERATIVE MOOD.		SUBJUNCTIVE MOOD.	
PRESENT.				PRESENT.	
Serv o,	⎫	No 1st per.	⎫	Che io serv a,	⎫
Serv i,	⎪ *I serve, &c.*	Serv i,	⎪ *Serve (thou), &c.*	Che tu serv a,	⎪ *That I may serve, &c.*
Serv e;	⎬	Serv a;	⎬	Che [egli/ella] serv a;	⎬
Serv iamo,	⎪	Serv iamo,	⎪	Che serv iamo,	⎪
Serv ite,	⎪	Serv ite,	⎪	Che serv iate,	⎪
Serv ono.	⎭	Serv ano.	⎭	Che [essi/esse] serv ano.	⎭

THE FOLLOWING VERBS ARE CONJUGATED LIKE "SERVIRE."

Consentire,	to consent.	Sentire,	to hear, to feel.
Divertire,	to amuse.	Soffrire,	to suffer.
Investire,	to invest.	Sovvertire,	to subvert.
Partire,*	to depart.	Tossire,	to cough.
Seguire,	to follow.	Vestire,	to dress.

REMARKS ON SOME PREFIXES USED IN ITALIAN.

263. The prefix "dis," or simply "s," *often* means *the undoing* the action expressed by the verb to which it is joined, or *the nullifying* the quality expressed by the noun or adjective before which it is placed; as "disarmare," *to disarm,* "disfare," or "sfare," *to undo,* "disordine," *disorder,* "svantaggio," *disadvantage,* "disutile," *useless.*

264. The prefix "ri" *often* means *a repetition* of the action expressed by the verb to which it is joined; as "ribolire," *to boil again,* "ridire," *to say again.*

265. The prefix "stra" means *the overdoing* the action expressed by the verb to which it is joined, or *the exaggerating* the quality expressed by the noun or adjective before which it is placed; as "strafare," *to overdo,* "stracuocere," *to overcook,* "straccarico," *overloaded.*

---

* "Partire," meaning *to divide*, is conjugated like "finire."

VOCABULARY.

Questa fanciulla,	this girl.	Un bosco,	a wood.
Una scienza	a science.	Una sorgente,	a spring.
La scuola,	the school.	Un fiume,	a river (large).
Il mio dovere,	my duty.	La finestra,	the window.
Questa famiglia,	this family.	Il piacere,	the pleasure.
La mia condotta,	my conduct.	L'animo,	the mind.
La mattina,	the morning.	L'anima,	the soul.
La sera,	the evening, night.	Una legge,	a law.
La notte,	the night.	La fragranza,	the fragrance.

Nuovo,	new.	Dolce,	sweet.	Caldo,	warm.
Vecchio,	old.	Amaro,	bitter.	Freddo,	cold.

Severamente,   severely.   Probabilmente,   probably.

EXERCISE XVII.

They punish (a) him (192, 193) too severely. He has enriched (b) (the) science with* new discoveries. Does this boy understand (c) Italian? Yes he understands it (192, 193) but he does not speak it. Will you have finished before to-morrow? Probably I shall (208). I shall finish this exercise before (184) going to school. He always (181) fulfils (d) his duty. They will never betray (e) us. He will inform (f) my family of my conduct. Yesterday my sister was sewing (g) (Past Def.) from (the) morning to (the) night. The singing† of the birds, the murmuring (h) of the springs, the fragrance of the flowers contribute (i) to the pleasures of the mind. He will obey (j) the laws of this country. We shall start (k) for the country on (147, 74) Thursday.

(a) Punire.‡   (b) Arricchire.‡   (c) Capire.‡   (d) Adempire.
(e) Tradire.‡   (f) Istruire.‡   (g) Cucire.   (h) Mormorare.   (i) Contribuire.‡   (j) Obbedire a.‡   (k) Partire.

---

266. * "*With*," preceded by a past particle, is translated by "di," *of*, except when it means *in company with*, or *by means of;* then it is translated by "con." Ex. "Uno scettro adorno di gioie."   A sceptre adorned with jewels.

267. † To translate into Italian the English expressions "the singing of the birds," "the murmuring of the springs," &c., the verb must be employed in the present of the Infinitive Mood; or the participle, "singing," &c., must be changed into a noun. Ex.

Il cantare, *or* il canto degli uccelli   The singing of birds delights me
  mi diletta oltremodo.   immensely.

‡ This verb is conjugated like "Finire;" see page 50.

LESSON XII.
ON VERBS USED PASSIVELY.

268. A verb used passively expresses an action received by the subject in the sentence. The passive voice, in Italian, is formed by using the auxiliary "essere," followed by the past participle of the verb to be expressed passively. The past participle always agrees with the subject in the sentence. Ex.

I suoi fratelli sono stimati.   His brothers are esteemed.

"STIMARE," *TO ESTEEM.*—CONJUGATED PASSIVELY.

INFINITIVE MOOD.

Present.	Past.
Essere stimato-a, *to be esteemed.*	Essere stato stimato, *to have been esteemed.*

Gerund.	Past Participle.	Past Gerund.
Essendo* stimato-a-i-e, *being esteemed.*	Stimato-a-i-e, *esteemed.*	Essendo stato stimato, *having been esteemed.*

INDICATIVE MOOD.

Present.		Imperfect.		Past Definite.	
Sono stimato-a,	⎫	Ero stimato-a,	⎫	Fui stimato-a,	⎫
Sei stimato-a,	⎬ *I am esteemed, &c.*	Eri stimato-a,	⎬ *I was esteemed, &c.*	Fosti stimato-a,	⎬ *I was esteemed, &c.*
È stimato-a ;		Era stimato-a ;		Fu stimato-a ;	
Siamo stimati-e,		Eravamo stimati-e,		Fummo stimati-e,	
Siete stimato-a-i-e,		Eravate stimato-a-i-e,		Foste stimato-a-i-e,	
Sono stimati-e.	⎭	Erano stimati-e.	⎭	Furono stimati-e.	⎭

Past Indefinite.	Pluperfect.	Past Anterior.
Sono stato stimato, &c.	Ero stato stimato, &c.	Fui stato stimato, &c.
I have been esteemed, &c.	*I had been esteemed, &c.*	*I had been esteemed, &c.*

Future.		Conditional.	
Sarò stimato-a,	⎫	Sarei stimato-a,	⎫
Sarai stimato-a,	⎬ *I shall be esteemed, &c.*	Saresti stimato-a,	⎬ *I should be esteemed, &c.*
Sarà stimato-a ;		Sarebbe stimata-o ;	
Saremo stimati-e,		Saremmo stimati-e,	
Sarete stimato-a-i-e,		Sareste stimato-a-i-e,	
Saranno stimati-e.	⎭	Sarebbero stimati-e.	⎭

Future Anterior.	Conditional Past.
Sarò stato stimato, &c.	Sarei stato stimato, &c.
I shall have been esteemed, &c.	*I should have been esteemed, &c.*

---

* An *e*, dotted thus ẹ, has the broad sound of the *a* in the word *gate*.

IMPERATIVE MOOD.

SINGULAR.	PLURAL.
Sii stimato-a, *be (thou) esteemed*, &c.	Siamo stimati-e,
Sia stimato-a;	Siate stimato-a-i-e,
	Siano stimati-e.

SUBJUNCTIVE MOOD.

PRESENT.
Che io sia stimato-a,
Che tu sia stimato-a,
Che [egli/ella] sia stimato-a;
Che siamo stimati-e,
Che siate stimato-a-i-e,
Che [essi/esse] siano stimati-e.

} *That I may be esteemed, &c.*

IMPERFECT.
Che *or* se (112) io fossi stimato-a,
Che *or* se tu fossi stimato-a,
Che *or* se [egli/ella] fosse stimato-a;
Che *or* se fossimo stimati-e,
Che *or* se foste stimato-a-i-e,
Che *or* se [essi/esse] fossero stimati-e.

} *That I might be, or if I were esteemed, &c.*

PAST.
Che io sia stato stimato, &c.
That I may have been esteemed, &c.

PLUPERFECT.
Che *or* se io fossi stato stimato, &c.
That or if I might have been esteemed, &c.

VOCABULARY

Il re,	the king.	Una battaglia,	a battle.
La regina,	the queen.	Un ballo,	a ball (party).
Un principe,	a prince.	Un invito,	an invitation.
Tutti, tutte,	all, everybody.	Parecchi-e,	several, many.

EXERCISE XVIII.

She is loved (a)* and esteemed (b) by† everybody. The city of Rome has been sacked (c) several times. Have you (122) been invited (d) to the ball? No, but I expect (e) an invitation. His son and his brother were wounded (f) (Past Definite, passive form) in the battle. Margaret would have been blamed by my mother, if (112) she had spoken. Will these ladies be presented (g) (269) to the Queen by the Prince? I believe they will.‡ We should be despised (h) if we abandoned him (192, 193) in this danger.

(a) Amare. (b) Stimare. (c) Saccheggiare. (d) Invitare. (e) Aspettare. (f) Ferire. (g) Presentare. (h) Disprezzare.

269. * The past participle of verbs used passively is variable. Ex. "Ella è amata." *She is loved.*

270. † The preposition *by*, preceded by a past participle, is translated into "da," in Italian. Ex. "Egli è ammirato da tutti." He is admired by everybody.

271. ‡ The English expressions *I believe he is, I believe they are, I think so,* are elegantly translated into Italian by "Credo di sì." And *I believe they are not, I do not think so,* are translated by "Credo di no."

LESSON XIII.
ON NEUTER VERBS.

272. A neuter verb, properly speaking, is a verb which is neither active nor passive; in that case "essere," *to be*, is the only *real* neuter verb; but any active verb which can be used without any object (direct or indirect) is, in Italian, called a neuter verb. Ex. Abbiamo riso.* *We laughed.*

THE NEUTER VERB "NUOTARE," *TO SWIM*.
INFINITIVE MOOD.

Present.	Past.
Nuotare, *to swim*.	Aver nuotato, *to have swam*.

Gerund.	Past Participle.	Past Gerund.
Nuotando,† *swimming*.	Nuotato, *swam*.	Avendo nuotato, *having swam*.

INDICATIVE MOOD.

Present.	Imperfect.	Past Definite.
Nuoto,	Nuotavo,‡	Nuotai,
Nuoti,	Nuotavi,	Nuotasti,
Nuota;	Nuotava;	Nuotò;
Nuotiamo,	Nuotavamo,	Nuotammo,
Nuotate,	Nuotavate,	Nuotaste,
Nuotano.	Nuotavano.	Nuotarono.

I swam, &c. (for all three)

Past Indefinite.	Pluperfect.	Past Anterior.
Ho nuotato, &c.	Avevo nuotato, &c.	Ebbi nuotato, &c.
I have swam, &c.	*I had swam, &c.*	*I had swam, &c.*

Future.	Conditional.
Nuoterò, &c.	Nuoterei, &c.
I shall swim, &c.	*I should swim, &c.*

Future Anterior.	Conditional Past.
Avrò nuotato, &c.	Avrei nuotato, &c.
I shall have swam, &c.	*I should have swam, &c.*

---

273. * Notice that the past participle of neuter verbs, conjugated with "avere," always remains *invariable*.

† The Present Participle is "nuotante."

‡ Or "nuotava;" see rule 108.

ON NEUTER VERBS.

IMPERATIVE MOOD.	SUBJUNCTIVE MOOD.	
	PRESENT.	IMPERFECT.
No first person.	Che io nuoti,	Che *or* se io nuotassi,
Nuota,	Che tu nuoti,	Che *or* se tu nuotassi,
Nuoti ;	Che [egli/ella] nuoti ;	Che *or* se [egli/ella] nuotasse ;
Nuotiamo,	Che nuotiamo,	Che *or* se nuotassimo,
Nuotate,	Che nuotiate,	Che *or* se nuotaste,
Nuotino.	Che [essi/esse] nuotino.	Che *or* se [essi/esse] nuotassero.

(Imperative: *Swim (thou), &c.*; Present Subj.: *That I may swim, &c.*; Imperfect Subj.: *That or if I might swim, &c.*)

PAST.
Che io abbia nuotato, &c.
That I may have swam, &c.

PLUPERFECT.
Che *or* se io avessi nuotato, &c.
That or *if I might have swam, &c.*

274. There are about 600 neuter verbs in the Italian language, upwards of 550 of which require " Avere " for auxiliary. Ex.

Abbiamo dormito fino alle nove. We slept till nine o'clock.

For the auxiliaries used with the other 50 see rules 275, and 276.

LIST OF THE PRINCIPAL NEUTER VERBS WHICH ARE CONJUGATED WITH " AVERE."

Camminare,	to walk.	Regnare,	to reign.
Dormire,	to sleep.	Ridere,	to laugh.
Gridare,	to cry.	Sbadigliare,	to yawn.
Passeggiare,	to take a walk.	Tacere,	to be silent.
Piangere,	to weep.	Tossire,	to cough.
Pranzare,	to dine.	Viaggiare,	to travel.

275. The following eighteen neuter verbs require " **essere** " for auxiliary, because they indicate *a state*, rather than *an action*.

Andare,	to go.	Giungere,	to arrive.	Restare,	} to remain.
Apparire,	to appear.	Morire,	to die.	Rimanere,	
Arrivare,	to arrive.	Nascere,	to be born.	Sorgere,	to rise.
Cadere,	to fall.	Partire,	to depart.	Sortire,	} to go out.
Divenire,	to become.	Perire,	to perish.	Uscire,	
Entrare,	to enter.	Pervenire,	to arrive at.	Venire,	to come.

EXAMPLES.

Sono andati alla campagna.   They have gone into the country.
Sono divenute ricchissime.   They have become very rich.

---

* Notice that *o* preceded by *u* has always the broad sound of the *o* in the word *orphan*.

ON NEUTER VERBS.

276. There are 32 neuter verbs, like "Salire," *to ascend*, "Scendere," *to descend*, "Fuggire," *to escape*, "Passare," *to pass*, which require either "avere," or "essere" as auxiliary; "avere" when *an action* is expressed, "essere," when *a state* is denoted. Ex.

Abbiamo salito il monte.	We ascended the mountain.
Andrea è salito sulla torre.	Andrew is on the tower.
La cattiva stagione è passata.	The bad season is passed.

VOCABULARY.

Questa instituzione,	this institution.	Il tempo,	the weather.
La sua bontà, (69)	his kindness.	La stagione,	the season.
Una prigione,	a prison.	La primavera,	Spring.
Questo ponte,	this bridge.	L'estate, (f.),	Summer.
Questo parco,	this park.	L'autunno,	Autumn.
Una pecora,	a sheep.	L'inverno,	Winter.

Su, sopra, upon, over.   Molti, } many.   Qualcosa, something.
Molto, much, very.   Molte, }   Abbastanza, enough.

EXERCISE XIX.

We have travelled (a) (274, 273) much. I have passed (276) over the bridge with my brother. It was a beautiful sight in the park, the sheep were browsing, (b) (179) the goats were skipping about, (c) the birds were warbling, (d) and the children were playing (e). This institution has been established (f)* these five years. Has your sister arrived? (275). Yes, she has (208). He escaped (180, 276) from his prison by† jumping (g) from a window. He slept (274) whilst we were working (Past Indef.). We lived (h) (180) three years in America, and received much kindness from the Americans. Do not (126, 122) travel this winter.

(a) Viaggiare. (b) Pascere. (c) Saltellare. (d) Cantare. (e) Giuocare. (f) Stabilire. (g) Saltare. (h) Dimorare.

277. * When the verb expresses an action (or a state) which has lasted for some time past, and is still lasting, it must be put in the *Present Indicative* in one of the two following ways:—

Dimoro in questa casa da cinque anni, *or* } I have been living in this
Sono cinque anni che dimoro in questa casa. } house these five years.

278. † The Italian Gerund is never preceded by any preposition; instead of the Gerund the present of the Infinitive, with a preposition, may be used. Ex.

Saltando, *or* col saltare da una finestra.   By jumping from a window.

LESSON XIV.

ON THE REFLECTIVE AND RECIPROCAL VERBS.

279. A reflective verb is a verb the action of which reacts upon its subject, and a reciprocal verb is a verb the action of which is reciprocated between two, or several persons, or things.

280. The compound tenses of reflective and reciprocal verbs are formed with the auxiliary "Essere." Ex.

    Francesco si è vestito.   Francis has dressed himself.

THE VERB "LODARSI," *TO PRAISE ONE'S-SELF.*

INFINITIVE MOOD.

PRESENT.		PAST.
Lodarsi, *to praise one's-self.*		Essersi lodato, *to have praised one's-self.*
GERUND.	PAST PARTICIPLE.	PAST GERUND.
Lodandosi, *praising one's-self.*	Lodatosi, (200) *having praised himself.*	Essendosi lodato, *having praised one's-self.*

INDICATIVE MOOD.

PRESENT.		IMPERFECT.		PAST DEFINITE.	
Mi lodo,		Mi lodavo,*		Mi lodai,	
Ti lodi,		Ti lodavi,		Ti lodasti,	
Si loda;	*I praise myself, &c.*	Si lodava;	*I praised myself, &c.*	Si lodò;	*I praised myself, &c.*
Ci lodiamo,		Ci lodavamo,		Ci lodammo,	
Vi lodate,		Vi lodavate,		Vi lodaste,	
Si lodano.		Si lodavano.		Si lodarono.	

PAST INDEFINITE.	PLUPERFECT.	PAST ANTERIOR.
Mi sono lodato, &c.	Mi ero lodato, &c.	Mi fui lodato, &c.
I have praised myself, &c.	*I had praised myself, &c.*	*I had praised myself, &c.*

IMPERATIVE MOOD.

FUTURE.	CONDITIONAL.	*No first person.*	
Mi loderò, &c.	Mi loderei, &c.	Lodati,	
I shall praise myself, &c.	*I should praise myself, &c.*	Si lodi;	*Praise thyself, &c.*
FUTURE ANTERIOR.	CONDITIONAL PAST.	Lodiamoci,	
Mi sarò lodato, &c.	Mi sarei lodato, &c.	Lodatevi,	
I shall have praised myself, &c.	*I should have praised myself, &c.*	Si lodino.	

---

* *Or* "lodava;" see rule 108.

SUBJUNCTIVE MOOD.

PRESENT.		IMPERFECT.	
Che io mi lodi,	*That I may praise myself, &c.*	Che or se (112) io mi lodassi,	*That or if I might praise myself, &c.*
Che tu ti lodi,		Che or se tu ti lodassi,	
Che [egli/ella] si lodi;		Che or se [egli/ella] si lodasse;	
Che ci lodiamo,		Che or se ci lodassimo,	
Che vi lodiate,		Che or se vi lodaste,	
Che [eglino/esse] si lodino.		Che or se [eglino/esse] si lodassero.	

PAST.   PLUPERFECT.
Che io mi sia lodato, &c.   Che or se io mi fossi lodato, &c.
That I may have praised myself, &c. That or if I might have praised myself, &c.

281. Notice that "lodarsi" might mean *to praise one's-self*, or *to praise one another*; hence many verbs may be used, in the plural, either reflectively or reciprocally.

VOCABULARY.

L'assemblea,	the assembly.	L'imprudenza,	imprudence.
A mia spesa,	at my expense.	Un bastimento, vascello, una nave.	a ship.
Il preparativo,	the preparation.		
L'elezione,	the election.	Una barca,	a bark.
Lo spirito,	wit, the mind.	Questa canzone,	this song.
Il sapere,	learning.	La chitarra,	the guitar.

Ogni, every, each. Alle sei, at six o'clock. A mezzogiorno, at noon.

EXERCISE XX.

I presented myself (a) to the (103) assembly. He was arming himself (b) for the battle. Elizabeth praises herself too much. These two men always praise one another (281). The king surrounded himself (c) (Past Def.) with (266) soldiers. She sang two Spanish (177, 74) songs, accompanying herself (d) with the guitar. Are the children dressing themselves? (e) (244). No, they are not (208). When I entered (183) the room, they were busying themselves (f) with the preparations for the election. He has (280) enriched himself (g) at my expense. They praise themselves too much.

(a) Presentarsi. (b) Armarsi. (c) Circondarsi. (d) Accompagnarsi. (e) Vestirsi.* (f) Affaccendarsi. (g) Arricchirsi.†

* This verb is conjugated like "Servire;" see page 52.
† This verb is conjugated like "Finire;" see page 50.

282. The Following Verbs, and a few more, are reflective in Italian and not reflective in English.

Italian	English	Italian	English
Accorgersi di, or che,*	} to perceive.	Dimenticarsi di, Scordarsi di,	} to forget.
Avvedersi di, or che,*		Dolersi di,*	to grieve at.
		Fidarsi di,	to trust.
Addormentarsi,	to fall asleep.	Imbarcarsi,	to embark.
Affrettarsi di,	} to hasten. to make haste.	Impadronirsi di,†	to seize.
Sbrigarsi,		Infastidirsi di,†	to get weary.
Spicciarsi,		Ingegnarsi,	to endeavour.
Alzarsi,	} to rise.	Ingerirsi di,	to meddle with.
Levarsi,		Innamorarsi di,	to fall in love with.
Ammogliarsi,	a man to marry (a woman).	Lagnarsi di,	to complain of.
Maritarsi,	a woman to marry (a man).	Lamentarsi di,	to complain of.
Annoiarsi,	to get tired.	Maravigliarsi di,	to wonder at.
Appoggiarsi a,	to lean against.	Offendersi di,	to take offence at.
Approssimarsi a,	} to approach.	Opporsi a,*	to oppose.
Accostarsi a,		Pascersi di,	to feed upon.
Avvicinarsi a,		Pentirsi di,‡	to repent.
Arrendersi,	to surrender.	Querelarsi,	{ to complain. to dispute.
Astenersi,*	to abstain.		
Attristarsi di,	to get sad at.	Rallegrarsi di,	to rejoice at.
Avanzarsi,	to advance.	Rammentarsi di,	to recollect.
Avvezzarsi a,	to get accustomed.	Ricordarsi di,	to remember.
Avviarsi,	to set out.	Riposarsi a,	to rest.
Bagnarsi,	to bathe, to get wet.	Rompersi,*	to get broken.
Compiacersi di,*	to take pleasure in.	Sbagliarsi,	to mistake.
Congratularsi di,	to congratulate upon.	Sentirsi bene,‡	to feel well.
Contentarsi di,	to be satisfied with.	Sentirsi male,‡	to feel unwell.
Crucciarsi di,	} to get angry with.	Svegliarsi,	to awake.
Adirarsi di,		Vantarsi di,	to boast of.
Arrabbiarsi di,		Vestirsi,‡	to dress.
Dilettarsi di,	to delight in, with.	Vergognarsi di,	to be ashamed of.

EXERCISE XXI.

I rise every morning at six o'clock. Do you remember Charles' birthday? Yes, I do (208). They embarked (Past Def.) in an English ship. I shall remember to bring my mother's umbrella. He has not repented of his imprudence. Children, make haste, we shall start (partire) at noon. She does not feel well to-day.

---

* This is an irregular verb; its irregular forms will be given farther on.
† This verb is conjugated like "Finire;" see page 50.
‡ This verb is conjugated like "Servire;" see page 52.

LESSON XV.
IMPERSONAL VERBS.

283. In Italian, Impersonal Verbs, like "Bastare," *to suffice*, are used in the third person, both in the singular and plural, and their compound tenses are formed with "Essere." Ex.

Questo denaro basta.   This money suffices.
Questi libri basteranno.   These books will suffice.

THE IMPERSONAL VERB "BASTARE," *TO SUFFICE.*
INFINITIVE MOOD.

PRESENT.   PAST.
Bastare, *to suffice*.   Essere bastato, *to have sufficed.*

GERUND.   PAST PARTICIPLE.   PAST GERUND.
Bastando,* *sufficing*.   Bastato, *sufficed*.   Essendo bastato, *having sufficed.*

INDICATIVE MOOD.

PRESENT.   IMPERFECT.   PAST DEFINITE.
Basta, it† *suffices ;*   Bastava, *it sufficed ;*   Bastò, *it sufficed ;*
Bastano, *they suffice.*   Bastavano, *they sufficed.*   Bastarono, *they sufficed.*

PAST INDEFINITE.   PLUPERFECT.
È bastato,   Sono bastati,   Era bastato,   Erano bastati,
It has sufficed.   *They have sufficed.*   *It had sufficed.*   *They had sufficed.*

FUTURE.   CONDITIONAL PRESENT.
Basterà, *it will suffice ;*   Basterebbe, *it would suffice ;*
Basteranno, *they will suffice.*   Basterebbero, *they would suffice.*

FUTURE ANTERIOR.   CONDITIONAL PAST.
Sarà bastato,   Sarebbe bastato,
It will have sufficed.   *It would have sufficed.*
Saranno bastati,   Sarebbero bastati,
They will have sufficed.   *They would have sufficed.*

SUBJUNCTIVE MOOD.

PRESENT.   IMPERFECT.
Che basti,   Che bastasse, *that it might suffice ;*
That it may suffice.   Che bastassero, *that they might suffice ;*
Che bastino,   Se bastasse, *if it sufficed ;*
That they may suffice.   Se bastassero, *if they sufficed.*

PAST.   PLUPERFECT.
Che sia bastato,   Che fosse bastato, *that it might have sufficed ;*
That it may have sufficed.   Che fossero bastati, *that they might have sufficed;*
Che siano bastati,   Se fosse bastato, *if it had sufficed ;*
That they may have sufficed.   Se fossero bastati, *if they had sufficed.*

---

* The Present Participle of "bastare" is "bastante," plural "bastanti."
284. † The pronoun *it* is not translated into Italian.

ON IMPERSONAL VERBS.

285. The following Impersonal Verbs are of the first regular conjugation, like "bastare."

Arrivare,	*to happen.*	Capitare,	*to happen.*
Bisognare,	*to be necessary.*	Sembrare,	*to seem.*

286. The following Impersonal Verbs are of the second and third conjugation, and irregular:—

Accadere,* }		Occorrere,§ {	*to happen, to want,*
Avvenire,† }	*to happen.*		*to be needful.*
Convenire,‡	*to be useful.*	Parere,¶	*to appear.*

EXAMPLES.

Ciò accade sovente.	That often happens.
Accadono strane cose.	Strange things happen.

287. The Impersonal Verbs given above (used in the third person singular) govern a verb in the Present of the Infinitive to express an action which does not refer to any person in particular; but they govern a verb in the Subjunctive Mood (Present or Imperfect) preceded by the conjunction "che," *that,* when the action expressed by the verb has reference to some person or persons. Ex.

Bisogna parlare.	It is necessary to speak.
Bisogna che io parli.	It is necessary that I should speak.

288. The Impersonal Verbs given in the above rules, 285 and 286, are very often used with the conjunctive personal pronouns "mi," *to me,* "ti," *to thee,* "gli," *to him,* &c., as shown in the paradigm appended to this rule, and are followed either by a noun, or a verb in the Present of the Infinitive.

INDICATIVE MOOD. PRESENT.

Mi accade,	it happens to me.			
Ti accade,	„	„	„ thee.	
Gli accade,	„	„	„ him.	
Le accade,	„	„	„ her, to it, *or* to you (sing.)	
Ci accade,	„	„	„ us.	
Vi accade,	„	„	„ you.	
Accade (a) loro	„	„	„ them, *or* to you (plur.)	

EXAMPLES.

Mi accade sovente d'incontrarlo.	It often happens that I meet him.
Che cosa le occorre, Signora?	What do you want, Madam?
Mi occorrono dei guanti.	I want some gloves.

---

* The Past Def. is "accadde." Fut. "accadrà." Cond. "accadrebbe."
† The Past Part. is "avvenuto." Pres. Ind. "avviene." Past Def. "avvenne." Fut. "avverrà." Cond. "avverrebbe." Pres. Subj. "che avvenga."
‡ Past Part. is "convenuto." Pres. Ind. "conviene." Past Def. "convenne." Fut. "converrà." Cond. "converrebbe." Pres. Subj. "che convenga."
§ The Past Part. is "occorso." Past Def. "occorse."
¶ The Past Part. is "parso." Past Def. "parse" or "parve." Fut. "parrà." Cond. "parrebbe." Pres. Subj. "che paia."

ON IMPERSONAL VERBS.

289. The following Impersonal Verbs of the three conjugations, mostly irregular, are also very often used with the conjunctive personal pronouns "mi," *to me*, "ti," *to thee*, "gli," *to him*, &c., and are followed either by a noun or by a verb in the Present of the Infinitive:—

Abbisognare,	*to be in want of.*	Piacere,‡	*to please, to like.*
Tardare,	*to long for.*	Dispiacere,§	*to displease.*
Calere,*	*to care about.*	Premere,	*to have at heart.*
Dolere,†	*to ache.*	Rincrescere,¶	*to be sorry for.*

EXAMPLES.

Mi abbisognano dei libri.	I am in want of books.
Gli tarda di veder l' Italia.	He longs to see Italy.
Mi preme la sua salute.	I am anxious about your health.
Le rincresce di partire.	She is sorry to go away.

VOCABULARY.

Una tragedia,	a tragedy.	Un romanzo,	a novel.
Una commedia,	a comedy.	Il suo motivo,	his motive.
Sapiente,	wise.	Quanto? quanta?	how much?
Correttamente,	correctly.	Quanti? quante?	how many?
Prudentemente,	prudently.	Non ancora,	not yet.

EXERCISE XXII.

I must (a) (287) sell (b) my horse before Saturday. What (che cosa, *mas.*) do you (122, 193) want (c)? I want some Italian books. How many do you want (of them)? (240). I want three (of them); Alfieri's tragedies, Goldoni's comedies, and a good Italian novel. It is not necessary (c) to be very wise to (225) guess (d) his motive. How do you like (e) (289) this palace? I do not like it much. It is not enough (f) to speak correctly, it is also necessary (a) to speak prudently. It appears (g) that you have not attended (h) to the business (259). No, not yet. I have at heart (i) your success.

(a) Bisognare. (b) Vendere. (c) Occorrere. (d) Indovinare. (e) Piacere. (f) Bastare. (g) Parere. (h) Accudire a. (i) Premere.

---

* The Past Def. is "mi calse. Pres. Subj. "che mi caglia."

† The Pres. Ind. is "mi duole." Past Def. "mi dolse." Fut. "mi dorrà." Cond. "mi dorrebbe." Pres. Subj. "che mi doglia."

‡ The Past Part. is "piaciuto." Past Def. "piacque." Pres. Subj. "che piaccia."

§ The Past Part. is "dispiaciuto." Past Def. "dispiacque." Pres. Subj. "che dispiaccia."

¶ The Past Part. is "rincresciuto." Past Def. "rincrebbe." Pres. Subj. "che mi rincresca."

LESSON XVI.
IMPERSONAL VERBS EXPRESSIVE OF THE STATE OF THE WEATHER

290. The following Impersonal Verbs expressive of the state of the weather are used only in the third person singular, and their compound tenses are formed either with "Essere" or "Avere."

Piovigginare,	to drizzle.	Tuonare,	to thunder.
Nevicare,	to snow.	Balenare,	} to lighten.
Grandinare,	to hail.	Lampeggiare,	
Gelare,	to freeze.	Albeggiare,	to dawn.
Digelare,	to thaw.	Annottare,	to grow dark.

291. The only verb of this class of the second conjugation is "Piovere," *to rain*, and it is irregular only in the Past Definite, which is "piovve," *it rained*.

EXAMPLES.

Pioviggina,	it drizzles.	È tuonato,	it has thundered.
Nevicava,	it snowed.	Digelerà,	it will thaw.
Grandina,	it hails.	Se piovesse,	if it rained.

VOCABULARY.

La pioggia,	the rain.	Il lampo,	} the lightning.
La neve,	the snow.	Il baleno,	
Il ghiaccio,	the ice.	Il pattino,	the skate.
La grandine,	the hail.	Il lago,	the lake.
La nebbia,	the fog.	Il contadino,	the peasant.

Straordinario,	extraordinary.	Niente,	nothing.
Terribilmente,	awfully.	Ecco tutto,	that is all.
Durante,	during.	Non è vero?	is it not so?

EXERCISE XXIII.

Does it (284) rain now? No, it does not (208). It has been raining during the night. The wind blows (a). In my country it never (181) snows. The thunder re-echoed (b) awfully. The lake is frozen. The peasants will sell the ice in the town. If (112) I had skates I would skate (c). It is getting dark, we must (285, 288) return to the castle. What (che cosa, *mas.*) has happened (d)? Nothing (of) extraordinary; it snows, that is all. Has anything (qualche cosa, *mas.*) happened (d) to George? Nothing; he is in the garden playing† with William.

(a) Soffiare. (b) Rimbombare. (c) Pattinare. (d) Accadere.

292. † When the present participles *speaking, playing*, &c., are used separately from their auxiliary, *I am, He is, He was, I shall be*, &c., they are translated by the simple tenses ("parlo," "giuocava," &c.) preceded by the conjunction "che." Ex.
   Luigi è nel suo studio che lavora.   Louis is in his studio working.

LESSON XVII.
ON THE IRREGULAR VERBS.

ALPHABETICAL LIST OF ALL THE IMPORTANT IRREGULAR, AND DEFECTIVE VERBS USED IN THE ITALIAN LANGUAGE.

293. The student is strongly advised to learn by heart, first of all, the verbs which in the following list are preceded by two asterisks (**); this will enable him to write easily the exercises on the irregular verbs. Afterwards he should learn those preceded by one asterisk (*); leaving those not marked to the last.

294. Only the irregular forms of the verbs are given. The rest of the verbs is conjugated according to the regular paradigms; those ending in "are" are conjugated like "Comprare" (see page 29); those ending in "ere" are conjugated like "Credere"* (see page 46); and those ending in "ire" are conjugated either like "Finire" (see page 50) or like "Servire" (see page 52), as will be stated in the foot-notes.

A

Accẹndere, *to light.* Past Part. acceso.

PAST DEFINITE.†

Accesi,	Accẹnd emmo,
Accẹnd esti,‡	Accẹnd este,
Accese;§	Accesero.

Accadere, *to happen* (Imper. 286). Past Def. accàdde, &c. Fut. accadrà, &c.‖

Accingersi, *to prepare one's-self.* Past Part. accinto si (200). Past Def. mi accinsi, &c.‖

Accludere, *to enclose.* Past Part. accluso. Past Def. acclusi, &c.

---

* See rule 63, in order to understand the meaning of the letters in the darker type.

VERY IMPORTANT NOTE.

295. † It is most important to notice that most of the Italian irregular verbs are, like "accẹndere," irregular only in the Past Participle, and in the Past Definite, and that of the six persons in a Past Definite, only three can be irregular:—the first person singular, which always ends in *i*, the third person singular, which always ends in *e*, and the third person plural, which always ends in *ero*;—so that, one of the three persons being known, the others are known, as a matter of course.

‡ An *e*, dotted thus ẹ, has the broad sound of the *a* in the word *gate.*

296. § Notice that the third person singular of an irregular Past Definite is never accented.

‖ The compound tenses of this verb are formed with "Ẹssere."

Accogliere (bene), *to receive (kindly).* Past Part. accolto. Pres. Ind. accolgo, accogli, accoglie; accogliamo, accogliete, accolgono. Past Def. accolsi, accogliesti, accolse; accogliemmo, accoglieste, accolsero. Imperative, accogli, accolga; accogliamo, accogliete, accolgano. Pres. Subj. che io accolga, &c.

Accorgersi, *to perceive.* Past Part. accortosi. Past Def. mi accorsi, &c.†

Accorrere, *to run to.* Past Part. accorso. Past Def. accorsi, &c.†

Accrescere, *to augment.* Past Part. accresciuto. Past Def. accrebbi, &c.

Addurre, *to bring forth, to allege,* is contracted from "Adducere," and is, therefore, conjugated thus: Ger. adducendo. Pres. Ind. adduco, adduci, adduce; adduciamo, adducete, adducono. Imp. Ind. adducevo, &c.

Its irregular forms are: Past Part. addotto. Past Def. addussi, adducesti,‡ addusse, &c. Fut. addurrò (69), addurrai, addurrà; addurremo, addurrete, addurranno. Cond. addurrei, addurresti, addurrebbe; addurremmo, addurreste, addurrebbero.§

Adempire (*or* adempiere), *to perform, to fulfil.* Pres. Ind. adempio, adempi, adempie, &c. Imperative, adempi, adempia, &c. Pres. Subj. che io adempia, &c.

VOCABULARY.

La serva,	the woman-servant.	Una ragione,	a reason.
La lampada,	the lamp.	Una scusa,	an excuse.

Raramente, seldom. Però, but still, however.

EXERCISE XXIV.

Where is the servant? She is in the parlour lighting (292) the fire. Yesterday morning I lit my (131) lamp at six o'clock. Your uncle received me well (Past Def.). What (che) reason did he allege? (has he alleged?) He did not allege any reason. He seldom fulfils his duty. But still he will adduce good excuses.

---

† The compound tenses of this verb are formed with "Essere."
‡ Notice that the regular forms of the Past Definite (295), namely, the second person singular, and the first and second persons plural, are derived from the root (165) of the Present Infinitive in its full form, "Adduc ere."
§ Notice that the Conditional always follows the Future in its irregularities.

*Affliggere, *to afflict.* Past Part. afflitto. Past Def. afflissi, &c.
*Aggiungere, *to add.* Past Part. aggiunto. Past Def. aggiunsi, &c.
*Alludere, *to allude.* Past Part. alluṣo.† Past Def. alluṣi, &c.
Ammettere, *to admit.* Past Part. ammesso. Past Def. ammiṣi, &c.
**Andare, *to go.* Ger. andando. Pres. Ind. vado, *or* vo, vai, va; andiamo, andate, vanno. Fut. anderò (*or* andrò), &c. Imperative, va, vada; andiamo, andate, vadano. Pres. Subj. che io vada, &c.‡

Anteporre, *to prefer,* is contracted from "Anteponere." See "Porre."

Apparire,§ *to appear.* Past Part. apparso. Past Def. apparvi (*or* apparii), &c.‡

**Appartenere, *to belong.* Pres. Ind. appartengo, appartieni, appartiene; apparteniamo, appartenete, appartengono. Past Def. appartenni, &c. Fut. apparterrò, &c. Cond. apparterrei, &c.¶ Imperative, appartieni, appartenga, &c. Pres. Subj. che io appartenga, &c.

Appendere, *to hang up.* Past Part. appeso. Past Def. appesi, &c.
Apprendere,‖ *to learn.* Past. Part. appreso. Past Def. appresi, &c.
**Aprire,†† *to open.* Past. Part. aperto.
Ardere, *to burn.* Past. Part. arso. Past Def. arsi, &c.
Arrendersi, *to surrender.* Past. Part. arreso. Past. Def. mi arresi, &c.‡
Arridere, *to smile.* Past. Part. arriso. Past. Def. arrisi, &c.
*Ascendere, *to ascend.* Past. Part. asceso. Past. Def. ascesi, &c.
Ascondere, *to hide.* Past Part. ascoso. Past Def. ascosi, &c.
Ascrivere, *to ascribe.* Past Part. ascritto. Past Def. ascrissi, &c.
*Assalire, *to assail, to assault.* Pres. Ind. assalgo, assali, assale; assagliamo, assalite, assalgono. Past. Def. assalsi (*or* assalii), &c. Imperative, assali, assalga, assagliamo, &c. Pres. Subj. che io assalga, &c.
*Assistere, *to assist.* Past Part. assistito.
Assolvere, *to absolve.* Past Part. assolto (*or* assoluto).
Assorbere (*or* assorbire), *to absorb.* Past Part. assorto.

---

† An *s*, dotted thus ṣ, has the soft sound of the *s* in the word *rose.*
‡ The compound tenses of this verb are formed with "Ęssere."
§ In the regular forms it is conjugated like "Finire."
¶ Notice that the Conditional always follows the Future in its irregularities.
297. ‖ Apprendere means *to learn* (a fact); *to learn* (a lesson, a language) is translated by "Imparare."
†† In the regular forms it is conjugated like "Ṣervire."

Assumere, *to assume.* Past Part. assunto. Past Def, assunsi, &c.
Astenersi, *to abstain.* See " Tenere."
Attorcere, *to twist.* Past Part. attorto. Past Def. attorsi, &c.
*Attrarre, *to attract*, is contracted from "Attraere." Ger. attraendo.
  Past Part. attratto. Pres. Ind. attraggo, attrai, attrae; attraiamo (*or* attraggiamo), attraete, attraggono. Imp. Ind. attraevo, &c. Past Def. attrassi, attraesti, &c. Fut. attrarrò, &c. Cond. attrarrei, &c. Imperative, attrai, attragga; attraiamo, attraete, attraggano. Imp. Subj. che io attraessi, &c.
Avvedersi, *to perceive.* Past Part. avvedutosi. Past Def. mi avvidi, &c.
Avvenire, *to happen* (Imper. 286). Past Def. mi avvenne, &c.
Avvincere, *to bind.* Past Part. avvinto. Past Def. avvinsi, &c.
Avvolgere, *to wrap round.* Past Part. avvolto. Past Def. avvolsi, &c.

B

Benedire, *to bless*, is contracted from "Benedicere," and is, therefore, conjugated thus: Ger. benedicendo. Pres. Ind. benedico, benedici, &c.

Its irregular forms are: Past Part. benedetto. Past Def. benedissi, &c.

VOCABULARY.

Un cavallo,	a horse.	Questo gatto,	this cat.
Il mio cane,	my dog.	L'anno passato,	last year.

Fino,	until.	Fino a, as far as.	Verso, towards.

EXERCISE XXV.

Where are you (122) going (179)? I am going to Paris. Do not (126, 122) go now; wait until the autumn and we will go (there) (239) together. We went there last year. If (112) you went there (239) now you would meet my father-in-law. This dog belongs to my brother-in-law. The door is open (269). They pride themselves on† their wit, and (on their) learning.

---

298. † The preposition *on* ("su," "sopra,") is never translated literally in Italian except when it is taken in a literal sense; as, "Sulla tavola." *On the table.* As explained in rule 147, before a name of time *on* is not translated at all. Sometimes, however, *on* is translated into Italian by another preposition. Ex.

S'inorgogliscono del loro spirito.	They pride themselves on their wit.
Parlai in quell' occasione.	I spoke on that occasion.
A condizione ch' ella canti.	On condition that you sing.
Parlò di un affare d' importanza.	He spoke on a matter of importance.

ON THE IRREGULAR VERBS.

**Bere, *to drink,* is contracted from "Bevere," and is, therefore, conjugated thus: Ger. bevendo. Pres. Ind. bevo, &c.
Its irregular forms are: Past Def. bevvi, &c. Fut. berrò, &c.

C

**Cadere, *to fall.* Past Def. caddi, &c. Fut cadrò, &c.†

Calere, *to care for* (Imper. 289) is only used in the following tenses: Pres. Ind. mi cale, &c. Imp. Ind. mi caleva, &c. Past Def. mi calse, &c. Pres. Subj. che mi caglia, &c. Imp. Subj. che mi calesse, &c.

**Chiedere, *to ask.* Past Part. chiesto. Pres. Ind. chiedo (*or* chieggo), chiedi, &c. Past Def. chiesi, &c. Imperative, chiedi, chieda (*or* chiegga), &c. Pres. Subj. che io chieda (*or* chiegga), &c.

**Chiudere, *to shut, to shut up.* Past Part. chiuso. Past Def. chiusi, &c.

Cingere, *to gird.* Past Part. cinto. Past Def. cinsi, &c.

Cingersi, *to prepare one's-self.* Conjugated like "Cingere."

**Cogliere (contracted into "Corre"), *to gather.* Past Part. colto. Pres. Ind. colgo, cogli, coglie; cogliamo, cogliete, colgono. Past Def. colsi, &c. Fut. coglierò (*or* corrò), &c. Imperative, cogli, colga; cogliamo, &c. Pres. Subj. che io colga, &c.

*Commettere, *to commit.* Past Part. commesso. Past Def. commisi, &c.

Commuovere,‡ *to affect, to move.* Past Part. commosso. Pret. Ind. commossi, &c.

Comparire§, *to appear suddenly.* Past Part. comparso. Past Def. comparvi, &c.†

Compiacere, *to comply with, to please.* Past Part. compiaciuto. Pres. Ind. compiaccio, compiaci, compiace; compiacciamo, compiacete, compiacciono. Past Def. compiacqui, &c. Imperative, compiaci, compiaccia; compiacciamo, compiacete, compiacciano.

Compiacersi di, *to take delight in,* is conjugated like "Compiacere."

---

† The compound tenses of this verb are formed with "Essere."
‡ When in the verb "Commuovere," the tonic accent does not fall on the second *o*, the letter *u* may be omitted; "commovendo," "commoviamo," "commoverò" instead of "commuovendo," &c.
§ In the regular forms it is conjugated like "Finire."

*Compiangere, *to pity, to lament*. Past Part. compianto. Past Def. compiansi, &c. Pres. Subj. che io compianga, &c.

Compire (*or* compiere), *to fulfil, to complete*. Pres. Ind. compio, compi, compie, &c. Imperative, compi, compia, &c. Pres. Subj. che io compia, &c.

**Comporre, *to compose*, is contracted from "Componere," and is, therefore, conjugated thus: Ger. componendo. Imp. Ind. componevo, &c.

    Its irregular forms are: Past Part. composto. Pres. Ind. compongo, componi, compone; componiamo, componete, compongono. Past Def. composi, &c. Fut. comporrò, &c. Imperative, componi, componga, &c. Pres. Subj. che io componga, &c.

*Comprendere, *to comprehend, to contain, to impress*. Past Part. compreso. Past Def. compresi, &c.

Comprimere, *to compress*. Past Part. compresso. Past Def. compressi, &c.

*Compromettere, *to compromise*. Past Part. compromesso. Past Def. compromisi (*or* compromessi), &c.

Compungere, *to grieve*. Past Part. Compunto. Past Def. compunsi, &c.

*Conchiudere, *to conclude*. Past Part. conchiuso. Past Def. conchiusi, &c.

Concludere, *to conclude*. Past Part. concluso. Past Def. conclusi, &c.

*Concorrere, *to concur, to compete*. Past Part. concorso. Past Def. concorsi, &c.

EXERCISE XXVI.

I always drink coffee in the morning and tea in the evening. What do the Italians drink? They drink wine. If (112) I had money I should always drink good wine. Henry has fallen from the chair. Who (chi) has shut the door? I; I shut it (180, 193) because all the windows are open (269). Where is Charles? He is in the garden gathering (292) flowers for his sister. When I entered (183) the room they were composing a letter. I have just† composed an Italian song. Gather (122) some flowers for me (213).

---

299. † *I have just* is translated into Italian by "ho appunto."

Condiscendere, *to condescend*. Past Part. condisceso. Past Def. condiscesi, &c.

**Condurre, *to lead*, is contracted from "Conducere," and is therefore conjugated thus: Ger. conducendo. Pres. Ind. conduco, &c.

Its irregular forms are: Past Part. condotto. Past Def. condussi, &c. Fut. condurrò, &c.

**Confondere, *to confound, to confuse*. Past Part. confuso. Past Def. confusi, &c.

Congiungere, *to join*. Past Part. congiunto. Past Def. congiunsi, &c.

Connettere, *to connect*. Past Part. connesso. Past Def. connessi, &c.

**Conoscere, *to know, to be acquainted with* (through the senses). Past Part. conosciuto. Past Def. conobbi, &c.

*Consistere, *to consist* (Imper. 284). Past Part. consistito.†

Costruire,‡ *to construct*. Past Part. costrutto (*or* costruito). Past Def. costrussi, &c.

Contendere, *to quarrel*. Past Part. conteso. Past Def. contesi, &c.

**Contenere, *to contain*. Pres. Ind. contengo, contieni, contiene; conteniamo, contenete, contengono. Past Def. contenni, &c. Fut. conterrò, &c. Imperative, contieni, contenga; conteniamo, &c. Pres. Subj. che io contenga, &c.

*Contradire, *to contradict*, is abbreviated from "Contradicere," and is, therefore, conjugated thus: Ger. contradicendo. Pres. Ind. contradico, contradici, &c.

Its irregular forms are: Past Part. contradetto. Past Def. contradissi, &c.

Contrapporre, *to oppose*, is contracted from "Contrapponere." See "Porre."

*Contrarre, *to contract*, is contracted from "Contraere." See "Trarre."

**Convenire, *to suit*, (286) *to agree upon, to meet by appointment*. Past. Part. convenuto. Pres. Ind. convengo, convieni, conviene; conveniamo, convenite, convengono. Past. Def. convenni, &c. Fut. converrò, &c. Imperative, convieni, convenga, conveniamo, &c. Pres. Subj. che io convenga, &c.†

---

† The compound tenses of this verb are formed with "Essere."
‡ In the regular forms it is conjugated like "Finire."

*Convincere, *to convince.* Past Part. convinto. Past Def. convinsi, &c.
**Coprire,† *to cover.* Past Part. coperto.
**Correggere, *to correct.* Past Part. corretto. Past Def. corressi, &c.
**Correre, *to run.* Past Part. corso. Past Def. corsi, &c.‡
*Corrispondere, *to correspond.* Past Part. corrisposto. Past Def. corrisposi, &c.
Corrodere, *to corrode.* Past Part. corroso. Past Def. corrosi, &c.
*Corrompere, *to corrupt.* Past Part. corrotto. Past Def. corruppi, &c.
Costringere, *to constrain.* Past Part. costretto. Past Def. costrinsi, &c.
*Crescere, *to grow.* Past Part. cresciuto. Past Def. crebbi, &c.‡
*Cucire, *to sew.* Pres. Ind. cucio, cuci, cuce, &c. Imperative, cuci, cucia, &c. Pres. Subj. che io cucia, &c.
**Cuocere, *to cook.* Past Part. cotto. Pres. Ind. cuocio, &c. Past Def. cossi, &c.

D

**Dare, *to give.* Ger. dando. Past Part. dato. Pres. Ind. do, dai, dà; diamo, date, danno. Past Def. diedi (*or* detti), desti, diede (diè *or* dette); demmo, deste, diedero (*or* dettero). Fut. darò, &c. Imperative, dà, dia; diamo, date, diano. Pres. Subj. che io dia, &c. Imperf. Subj. che io dessi, &c.
Decadere, *to decay.* See "Cadere."

EXERCISE XXVII.

I conducted (Past Def.) them (*mas.* 193) into the (102) house. I do not know my uncle's friend. If (112) I knew that lady, I would speak to her (193). The castle contains many good pictures. I always cover the bird's cage (in) the evening. I corrected (Past Def.) his exercises yesterday, and I shall correct George's exercises to-morrow morning. When I met (Past Def.) him he was running (179) towards the church. Why did you give him (why have you given him) (193, 122) your dictionary? I gave (Past Def.) it (to) him (219) because he asked (domandare a) me for it (218, 251). Give him (201) a watch. I desire to take (condurre) him§ to school.

---

† In the regular forms it is conjugated like "Servire."
‡ The compound tenses of this verb are formed with "Essere."
§ When personal pronouns are joined to verbs in the infinitive (198) ending in *rre*, the *re* is omitted.

Decidere, *to decide.* Past Part. deciso. Past Def. decisi, &c.

*Dedurre, *to deduce, to deduct,* is contracted from "Deducere," and is, therefore, conjugated thus: Ger. deducendo. Pres. Ind. deduco, &c.

    Its irregular forms are: Past Part. dedotto. Past Def. dedussi, &c. Fut. dedurrò, &c.

*Deludere, *to delude.* Past Part. deluso. Past Def. delusi, &c.

*Deporre, *to depose,* is contracted from "Deponere." See "Porre."

Deprimere, *to depress.* Past Part. depresso. Past Def. depressi, &c.

*Deridere, *to deride.* Past Part. deriso. Past Def. derisi, &c.

**Descrivere, *to describe.* Past Part. descritto. Past Def. descrissi, &c.

Detrarre, *to detract,* is contracted from "Detraere." See "Trarre."

**Difendere, *to defend.* Past Part. difeso. Past Def. difesi, &c.

Diffondere, *to squander, to spread out.* Past Part. diffuso. Past Def. diffusi, &c.

**Dipingere, *to paint.* Past Part. dipinto. Past Def. dipinsi, &c.

**Dire, *to tell, to say,* is contracted from "Dicere," and is, therefore, conjugated thus: Ger. dicendo. Pres. Ind. dico, dici, dice; diciamo, dite, dicono.

    Its irregular forms are: Past Part. detto. Past Def. dissi, dicesti, disse; dicemmo, diceste, dissero. Fut. dirò, &c. Imperative, di', dica; diciamo, dite, dicano. Pres. Subj. che io dica, &c.

*Dirigere, *to direct.* Past Part. diretto. Past Def. diressi, &c.

*Discendere, *to descend.* Past Part. disceso. Past Def. discesi, &c.

*Discorrere, *to speak, to discourse.* Past Part. discorso. Past Def. discorsi, &c.

*Discutere, *to discuss.* Past Part. discusso. Past Def. discussi, &c.

Disdire, (263) *to deny, to be unbecoming.* ⎱ Conjugated like "Dire."
Disdirsi,† (263) *to unsay.* ⎰

Dispergere, *to disperse.* Past Part. disperso. Pret. Ind. dispersi, &c.

**Dispiacere a, (263, 289) *to displease.* Past Part. dispiaciuto. Pres. Ind. dispiaccio, dispiaci, dispiace; dispiacciamo, dispiacete, dispiacciono. Past Def. dispiacqui, &c. Imperative, dispiaci, dispiaccia; dispiacciamo, dispiacete, dispiacciano. Pres. Subj. che io dispiaccia, &c.

---

† The compound tenses of this verb are formed with "Essere."

ON THE IRREGULAR VERBS.

**Disporre, *to dispose*, is contracted from "Disponere," and is, therefore, conjugated thus: Ger. disponendo. Imp. Ind. disponevo, &c.

Its irregular forms are: Past Part. disposto. Pres. Ind. dispongo, disponi, dispone; disponiamo, disponete, dispongono. Fut. disporrò, &c. Past Def. disposi, &c. Imperative, disponi, disponga, &c. Pres. Subj. che io disponga, &c.

Dissolvere, *to dissolve*. Past Part. dissolto (*or* dissoluto).
Dissuadere, *to dissuade*. Past Part. dissuaso. Past Def. dissuasi, &c.
Distendere, *to extend, to stretch out*. Past Part. disteso. Past Def. distesi, &c.
*Distinguere, *to distinguish*. Past Part. distinto. Past Def. distinsi, &c.
Distogliere (contracted into "Distorre") *to divert from*. See "Togliere."
Distrarre, *to distract*. See "Trarre."
*Distruggere, *to destroy*. Past Part. distrutto. Past Def. distrussi, &c.
**Divenire, *to become*. Past Part. divenuto. Pres. Ind. divengo, divieni, diviene; diveniamo, divenite, divengono. Past Def. divenni, &c. Fut. diverrò, &c. Imperative, divieni, divenga; diveniamo, &c. Pres. Subj. che io divenga, &c.†
**Dividere, *to divide*. Past Part. diviso. Past Def. divisi, &c.

EXERCISE XXVIII.

I have decided to travel during the winter. They defended (Past Def.) me bravely. He described (Past Def.) the town correctly. He desired‡ (Past Def.) me to paint (for) him (213) a picture. She always tells the truth, and yet nobody believes (to) her (193). I will tell it to him (219) again this evening. If I told her what you have said, she would get cross (adirarsi). He disposes of his money wisely. Frederick became (Past Def.) rich in three years. Divide these strawberries between you and Elizabeth.

---

† The compound tenses of this verb are formed with Essere."
300. ‡ When *to desire* means *to wish*, it is translated by "Desiderare." Ex. Desidera di andare alla campagna. He wishes to go into the country.
301. When *to desire* means *to ask, to beg*, it is translated by "Pregare" or "Dire." Ex. Mi pregò d' assistere alla ceremonia. He desired me to be present at the ceremony.
302. When *to desire* means *to command*, it is translated by "Comandare." Ex. Mi comandò di partir subito. He desired me to leave at once.

*Dolere, *to ache.* Past Part. doluto. Pres. Ind. dolgo, duoli, duole; dogliamo, dolete, dolgono. Past Def. dolsi, &c. Fut. doglierò (*or* dorrò), &c. Pres. Subj. che io dolga, &c.

**Dolersi, *to complain,* is conjugated like "Dolere," but it is used also in the Imperative: duoliti, si dolga; dogliamoci, doletevi, si dolgano.†

**Dovere, *to owe, to be obliged.* Past Part. dovuto. Pres. Ind. devo‡ (debbo, *or* deggio), devi, deve (*or* dee); dobbiamo, dovete, devono (*or* debbono). Fut. dovrò, &c. Pres. Subj. che io debba (*or* deggia), che tu debba, ch' egli debba; che dobbiamo, che dobbiate, che debbano (*or* deggiano).

E

*Eleggere, *to elect.* Past Part. eletto. Pres. Ind. elessi, &c.

Emergere, *to emerge.* Past Part emerso. Past Def. emersi, &c.

Erigere, *to erect.* Past Part. eretto. Past Def. eressi, &c.

*Escludere, *to exclude.* Past Part. escluso. Past Def. esclusi, &c.

Esigere, *to exact.* Past Part. esatto.

Espellere, *to expel.* Past Part. espulso. Past Def. espulsi, &c.

**Esporre, *to expose,* is contracted from "Esponere."

Its irregular forms are: Past Part. esposto. Pres. Ind. espongo, esponi, espone; esponiamo, esponete, espongono. Past Def. esposi, &c. Fut. esporrò, &c. Imperative, esponi, esponga, &c. Pres. Subj. che io esponga, &c.

*Esprimere, *to express.* Past Part. espresso. Past Def. espressi, &c.

*Estendere, *to extend.* Past Part. esteso. Past Def. estesi, &c.

*Estinguere, *to extinguish.* Past Part. estinto. Past Def. estinsi, &c.

*Estrarre, *to extract,* is contracted from "Estraere." See "Trarre."

F

**Fare, *to do, to make,* is contracted from "Facere," and is therefore conjugated thus: Ger. facendo. Imp. Ind. facevo, &c.

Its irregular forms are: Past Part. fatto. Pres. Ind. faccio *or* fo, fai, fa; facciamo, fate, fanno. Past Def. feci, facesti, fece; facemmo, faceste, fecero. Fut. farò, &c. Imperative, fa, faccia; facciamo, fate, facciano. Pres. Subj. che io faccia, &c. Imp. Subj. che io facessi, &c.

---

† The compound tenses of this verb are formed with "Essere."
‡ "Devo," "devi," "deve," &c., mean also *I must, you must, he must,* &c.

Fendere, *to split*. Past Part. fesso.
*Fingere, *to feign*. Past Part. finto. Past Def. finsi, &c.
*Fondere, *to melt*. Past Part. fuso. Past Def. fusi, &c.
Frammettere, *to interpose*. Past Part. frammesso. Past Def. frammisi, &c.
Frangere, *to break*. Past Part. franto. Past Def. fransi, &c.
Friggere, *to fry*. Past Part. fritto. Past Def. frissi, &c.

G

Giacere, *to lie down*. Past Part. giaciuto. Past Def. giacqui, &c.
**Giungere, *to arrive*. Past Part. giunto. Past Def. giunsi, &c.†

I

Illudere, *to delude*. Past Part. illuso. Past Def. illusi, &c.
Immergere, *to immerge*. Past Part. immerso. Past Def. immersi, &c.
*Imporre, *to impose*, is contracted from "Imponere." See "Porre."
†Imprimere, *to impress*. Past Part. impresso. Past Def. impressi, &c.
*Incidere, *to engrave*. Past Part. inciso. Past Def. incisi, &c.
*Includere, *to include*. Past Part. incluso. Past Def. inclusi, &c.
*Incorrere, *to incur*. Past Part. incorso. Past Def. incorsi, &c.
Increscere, *to be sorry, to be weary* (Impersonal), Past Part. incresciuto. Past Def. increbbe, &c.
**Indurre, *to induce*, is contracted from "Inducere," and is, therefore, conjugated thus: Ger. inducendo. Pres. Ind. induco, &c.

   Its irregular forms are: Past Part, indotto. Past Def. indussi, &c. Fut, indurrò, &c.
Infondere, *to infuse*. Past Part. infuso. Past Def. infusi, &c.
Inscrivere, *to inscribe*. Past Part. inscritto. Past Def. inscrissi, &c.
Insistere, *to insist*. Past Part. insistito.

EXERCISE XXIX.

James complains of your conduct. I am obliged to go to Paris to buy some presents for my cousin Margaret. We owe (to) him some money for the house he built for us (213). If (112) I were obliged to (226) speak before this crowd of people, it would displease me very much. What (che cosa) are you doing (179) now, Louisa? I am making a bonnet for Charlotte. Yesterday I made a waistcoat for Frederick. I shall induce Charles to go to Scotland.

---

† The compound forms of this verb are formed with "Essere."

*Intẹndere, *to understand.* Past Part. inteso. Past Def. intesi, &c.
Interporre, *to interpose,* is contracted from "Interponere. See "Porre."
*Interrompere, *to interrupt.* Past Part. interrotto. Past Def. interruppi, &c.
*Intraprendere, *to undertake.* Past Part. intrapreso. Past Def. intrapresi, &c.
**Introdurre, *to introduce,* is contracted from "Introducere," and is therefore conjugated thus: Ger. introducẹndo. Pres. Ind. introduco, &c.
    Its irregular forms are: Past Part. introdotto. Past Def. introdussi, &c. Fut. introdurrò, &c.
*Intrudere, *to intrude.* Past Part. intruṣo. Past Def. intruṣi, &c.
*Invadere, *to invade.* Past Part. invaṣo. Past Def. invaṣi, &c.
*Invọlgere, *to involve, to wrap in.* Past Part. invọlto. Past Def. invọlsi, &c.
Istruire,† *to instruct.* Past Def. istrussi, &c.

L

Ledere, *to offend.* Past Part. leṣo. Past Def. leṣi, &c.
**Leggere, *to read.* Past Part. letto. Past Def. lessi, &c.

M

Maledire, *to curse,* is contracted from "Maledicere." See "Dire."
**Mantenere, *to maintain.* Pres. Ind. mantengo, mantiẹni, mantiene; manteniamo, mantenete, mantengono. Past Def. mantenni, &c. Fut. manterrò, &c. Imperative, mantiẹni, mantenga; manteniamo, &c. Pres. Subj. che iọ mantenga, &c.
**Mettere, *to put.* Past Part. messo. Past Def. miṣi (*or* messi), &c.
*Mọrdere, *to bite.* Past Part. mọrso. Past Def. mọrsi, &c.
*Mọrire, *to die.* Past Part. mọrto. Pres. Ind. muọio, muọri, muọre; moriamo, morite, muọiono (*or* muọrono). Fut. morirò (*or* morrò), &c. Imperative, muọri, muọia; moriamo, morite, muọiano. Pres. Subj. che iọ muọia, &c.†
Mungere, *to milk.* Past Part. munto. Past Def. munsi, &c.
Muọvere,‡ *to move.* Past Part. mọsso. Past Def. mọssi, movesti, &c.

---

  † The compound tenses of this verb are formed with "Essere."
  ‡ When in the verb "Muọvere" the tonic accent does not fall on the *o*, the letter *u* may be omitted; as "movẹndo," "moviamo," "moverò," instead of 'muovẹndo," &c.

N

**Nascere, *to be born.* Past Part. nato. Past Def. nacqui,† &c.
**Nascondere, *to hide.* Past Part. nascosto (*or* nascoso). Past Def. nascosi, &c.
*Negligere, *to neglect.* Past Part. negletto. Past Def. neglessi, &c.
Nuocere,‡ *to hurt.* Past Part. nociuto. Past Def. nocqui, &c.

O

Occorrere, *to be in need of, to happen* (Imper. 286). Past Part. occorso. Past Def. occorse.†
**Offendere, *to offend.* Past Part. offeso. Past Def. offesi, &c.
**Offrire,§ *to offer.* Past Part. offerto. Past Def. offersi (*or* offrii), &c.
*Ommettere, *to omit.* Past Part. ommesso. Past Def. ommisi, &c.
**Opporre, *to oppose,* is contracted from " Opponere," and is, therefore, conjugated thus: Ger. opponendo. Imp. Ind. opponevo, &c.

Its irregular forms are: Past Part. opposto. Pres. Ind. oppongo, opponi, oppone; opponiamo, opponete, oppongono. Past Def. opposi, &c. Fut. opporrò, &c. Imperative, opponi, opponga; &c. Pres. Subj. che io opponga, &c.

VOCABULARY.

| Una satira, | a satire. | Questa elezione, | this election. |
| Una cornice, | a frame. | La mia patria, | my native land. |

EXERCISE XXX.

Has your brother read " La Gerusalemme Liberata ? " Yes, he has (208); and he is now reading (179) " L' Orlando Furioso." Do not read satires, you will learn little from (in) them (238). Louisa always (181) puts her books on my table. Here is the picture; put a frame to it (238). Charles was born in England. Dante was born¶ in Florence in the (103) year 1265. Do not offend Henry; he will not pardon you. I oppose his election because he does not love his native land.

---

† The compound tenses of this verb are formed with " Essere."
‡ When in the verb " Nuocere " the tonic accent does not fall on the *o*, the lettre *u* may be omitted; as " nocendo," " nociamo," " nocerò," instead of " nuocendo," &c.
§ In the regular forms it is conjugated like " Servire."
303. ¶ *I was born, thou wast born,* &c., must be translated by " sono nato," " sei nato," &c., when we speak of persons still living; but by " nacque," " nacquero," when speaking of persons dead.

Opporsi, *to oppose*, is conjugated like "Opporre."†
*Opprimere, *to oppress*. Past Part. oppresso. Past Def. oppressi, &c.
**Ottenere, *to obtain*. Pres. Ind. ottengo, ottieni, ottiene; otteniamo, ottenete, ottengono. Past Def. ottenni, &c. Fut. otterrò, &c. Imperative, ottieni, ottenga; otteniamo, &c. Pres. Subj. che io ottenga, &c.

P

**Parere, *to appear*. Past Part. parso. Pres. Ind. paio, pari, pare; paiamo, parete, paiono. Past Def. parsi (*or* parvi), &c. Fut. parrò, &c. Imperative, pari, paia; paiamo, parete, paiano. Pres. Subj. che io paia, &c.†
Pendere, *to hang up, to incline*. Past Part. peso. Past Def. pesi, &c.
Percorrere, *to go over*. Past Part. percorso. Past Def. percorsi, &c.
*Percuotere,‡ *to strike*. Past Part. percosso. Past Def. percossi, &c.
**Permettere, *to permit*. Past Part. permesso. Past Def. permisi, &c.
Persistere, *to persist*. Past Part. persistito.
*Persuadere, *to persuade*. Past Part. persuaso. Past Def. persuasi, &c.
**Piacere a, *to please*. Past Part. piaciuto. Pres. Ind. piaccio, piaci, piace; piacciamo, piacete, piacciono. Past Def. piacqui, &c. Imperative, piaci, piaccia; piacciamo, &c. Pres. Subj. che io piaccia, &c.
**Piangere,§ *to weep*. Past Part. pianto. Past Def. piansi, &c.
Pingere,§ *to paint*. Past Part. pinto. Past Def. pinsi, &c.
*Piovere, *to rain* (Imper. 291). Past Part. piovuto. Past Def. piovve.
*Porgere, *to present, to hand*. Past Part. porto. Past Def. porsi, &c.
**Porre, *to put*, is contracted from "Ponere," and is therefore conjugated thus: Ger. ponendo. Imp. Ind. ponevo, &c.
  Its irregular forms are: Past Part. posto. Pres. Ind. pongo, poni, pone; poniamo, ponete, pongono. Past Def. posi, &c. Fut. porrò, &c. Imperative, poni, ponga, &c. Pres. Subj. che io ponga, &c.
Posporre, *to postpone*, is contracted from "Posponere. See "Porre."

---

† The compound tenses of this verb are formed with "Essere."
‡ When in the verb "Percuotere" the tonic accent does not fall on the *o*, the letter *u* may be omitted; as "percotendo," "percotiamo," "percoterò," instead of "percuotendo," &c.
§ In verbs ending in "angere," "engere," "ingere," and "ungere," the *n* is sometimes placed after the *g*. Ex. "Egli piagne," *he weeps*, instead of "Egli piange."

*Possedere, *to possess.* Past Part. posseduto. Pres. Ind. possiedo (*or* posseggo), possiedi, possiede; possediamo, possedete, possiedono (*or* posseggono). Imperative, possiedi, possegga, &c. Pres. Subj. che io possegga, &c.

**Potere, *to be able.* Pres. Ind. posso, puoi, può; possiamo, potete, possono. Fut. potrò, &c. Pres. Subj. che io possa, &c.

Precorrete, *to forerun.* Past Part. precorso. Past Def. precorsi, &c.

*Predire, *to predict,* is contracted from " Predicere." See " Dire."

Prefiggere, *to prefix.* Past Part. prefisso. Past Def. prefissi, &c.

Premettere, *to place before.* See " Mettere."

**Prendere, *to take.* Past Part. preso. Past Def. presi, &c.

Preporre, *to prefer,* is contracted from " Preponere." See " Porre."

*Prescrivere, *to prescribe.* Past Part. prescritto. Past Def. prescrissi, &c.

Presumere, *to presume.* Past Part. presunto. Past Def. presunsi, &c.

*Pretendere, *to claim.* Past Part. preteso. Past Def. pretesi, &c.

*Prevalere, *to prevail.* See " Valere."

Prevedere, *to foresee.* See " Vedere."

**Produrre, *to produce,* is contracted from " Producere," and is therefore conjugated thus: Ger. producendo. Pres. Ind. produco, &c.

Its irregular forms are: Past Part. prodotto. Past Def. produssi, &c. Fut. produrrò, &c. Imperative, produci, produca, &c. Pres. Subj. che io produca, &c.

EXERCISE XXXI.

My brother always obtains what (ciò che) he desires (300). They appear rich, but they are very poor. The king permitted (Past Def.) (to) us to enter (183) the city. When they heard (Past Def.) the news, they wept. I put (Past Def.) the ring on your table. If (112) I could† induce William to go‡ with us, I should be happy. He could (potere) (Past Def.) not answer my question.§

---

304. † When *I could* means *I might* it is translated by " Potere."

305. ‡ When *to go* is used in the sense of *to accompany,* it is translated *not* by " Andare," but by " Accompagnare " *to accompany,* or " Venire," *to come.* Ex. Vuol' ella venire in Italia con me? Will you go to Italy with me?

306. § When *question* means *argument,* it is translated into Italian by " Questione;" when it means *dispute,* it is translated by " Lite "; but when it means *inquiry,* it is translated by " Domanda," " Interrogazione," " Quesito."

Profondere, *to dissipate.* Past Part. profuso. Past Def. profusi, &c.
**Promettere, *to promise.* Past Part. promesso. Past Def. promisi, &c.
Promuovere,† *to promote.* Past Part. promosso. Past Def. promossi, &c.
**Proporre, *to propose,* is contracted from " Proponere." See " Porre."
Prorompere, *to break forth.* Past Part. prorotto. Past Def. proruppi, &c.
Proscrivere, *to proscribe.* Past Part. proscritto. Past Def. proscrissi, &c.
**Proteggere, *to protect.* Past Part. protetto. Past Def. protessi, &c.
*Provvedere, *to provide.* See " Vedere."
Protrarre, *to protract,* is contracted from " Protraere." See " Trarre."
Pungere, *to prick.* Past Part. punto. Past Def. punsi, &c.

R

**Raccogliere, *to pick up, to collect.* Past Part. raccolto. Pres. Ind. raccolgo, raccogli, raccoglie; raccogliamo, raccogliete, raccolgono. Past Def. raccolsi, &c. Fut. raccoglierò, (*or* raccorrò), &c. Imperative, raccogli, raccolga, &c. Pres. Subj. che io raccolga, &c.
Radere, *to shave.* Past Part. raso. Past Def. rasi, &c.
Raggiungere, *to overtake.* Past Part. raggiunto. Past Def. raggiunsi, &c.
Redimere, *to redeem.* Past Part. redento. Past Def. redensi, &c.
Reggere, *to rule, to support.* Past Part. retto. Past Def. ressi, &c.
**Rendere, *to render, to restore.* Past Part. reso. Past Def. resi, &c.
Reprimere, *to repress.* Past Part. represso. Past Def. repressi, &c.
Ricomporre, *to compose again,* is contracted from " Ricomponere." See " Porre."
**Riconoscere, *to recognise.* See " Conoscere."
Ricorrere, *to have recourse.* Past Part. ricorso. Past Def. ricorsi, &c.
**Ridere, *to laugh.* Past Part. riso. Past Def. risi, &c.
Ridire, (264) *to repeat,* is contracted from " Ridicere." See " Dire."

---

† When in the verb " Promuovere " the tonic accent does not fall on the *o*, the letter *u* may be omitted ; as " promovendo," " promoviamo," " promoverò," instead of " promuovendo," &c.

**Ridurre, *to reduce*, is contracted from "Riducere," and is, therefore, conjugated thus: Ger. riducendo. Pres. Ind. riduco, &c. Its irregular forms are: Past Part. ridotto. Past Def. ridussi, &c. Fut. ridurrò, &c.

**Rimanere, *to remain*. Past Part. rimasto (*or* rimaso). Pres. Ind. rimango, rimani, rimane; rimaniamo, rimanete, rimangono. Past Def. rimasi, &c. Fut. rimarrò, &c. Imperative, rimani, rimanga, &c. Pres. Subj. che io rimanga, &c.†

Rinchiudere, *to shut up*. Past Part. rinchiuso. Past Def. rinchiusi, &c.

*Rincrescere, *to weary, to vex* (as an impersonal verb, *to be sorry for*; see rule 289). Past Part. rincresciuto. Past Def. rincrebbi, &c.

Riprendere, *to take back, to correct*. Past Part. ripreso. Past Def. ripresi, &c.

*Riscuotere,‡ *to receive in payment, to exact*. Past Part. riscosso. Past Def. riscossi, &c.

Risorgere, *to rise again*. Past Part. risorto. Past Def. risorsi, &c.

**Rispondere, *to answer*. Past Part. risposto. Past Def. risposi, &c.

Ritorcere, *to twist, to wring*. Past Part. ritorto. Past Def. ritorsi, &c.

VOCABULARY.

La stravaganza,	the extravagance.	Il nemico,	the enemy.
Il travestimento,	the disguise.	La povertà,	poverty.

Ebbene! Well!   Contro, incontro, against.   Indietro, behind.

EXERCISE XXXII.

Do you not remember that you promised (180) to give me (198) your (131) dog? Yes, and I will give it to you (218-220) on (147) Saturday. Man proposes, God disposes. We shall protect him (193) against all his enemies. I shall restore to him the paintbrushes (260) he lent (Past Def.) (to) me last week. In spite of his disguise she recognised (Past Def.) him at once. His extravagance will soon reduce him to (the) poverty. Why did you remain (Past Def.) behind yesterday? I remained behind to (225) see if I could induce Frederick to go (305) with us. He answered (Past Def.) very prudently.

† The compound tenses of this verb are formed with "Essere."
‡ When in the verb "Riscuotere" the tonic accent does not fall on the *o*, the letter *u* may be omitted; as "riscotendo," "riscotiamo," "riscoterò," instead of "riscuotendo," &c.

Ritrarre, *to draw out, to portray.* See " Trarre."
**Riuscire (*or* Riescire) *to succeed.* Past Part. riuscito. Pres. Ind. riesco, riesci, riesce ; riusciamo (*or* riesciamo), riuscite, riescono. Imperative, riesci, riesca ; riusciamo, riuscite, riescano. Pres. Subj. che io riesca, &c.†
Rivolgere, *to turn over, to revolve.* Past Part. rivolto. Past Def. rivolsi, &c.
Rivolgersi, *to direct one's-self to*, is conjugated like " Rivolgere."
Rodere, *to gnaw.* Past Part. roso. Past Def. rosi, &c.
**Rompere, *to break.* Past Part. rotto. Past Def. ruppi, &c.
Rompersi, *to get broken*, is conjugated like " Rompere."†

S

**Salire, *to ascend.* Pres. Ind. salgo, sali, sale ; sagliamo, salite, salgono. Past Def. salsi (*or* salii), &c. Imperative, sali, salga ; sagliamo, &c. Pres. Subj. che io salga, &c.
**Sapere, *to know* (through the mind). Past Part. saputo. Pres. Ind. so, sai, sa ; sappiamo, sapete, sanno. Past Def. seppi, &c. Fut. saprò, &c. Imperative, sappi, sappia ; sappiamo, sappiate,‡ sappiano. Pres. Subj. che io sappia, &c.
Scadere, *to decline* (in value, health), *to come due.* Past Part. scaduto. Past Def. scaddi, &c. Fut. scadrò, &c.†
**Scegliere (*or* Scerre), *to choose.* Past Part. scelto. Pres. Ind. scelgo, scegli, sceglie ; scegliamo, scegliete, scelgono. Past Def. scelsi, &c. Fut. sceglierò (*or* scerrò), &c. Imperative, scegli, scelga ; scegliamo, &c. Pres. Subj. che io scelga, &c.
*Scendere, *to descend.* Past Part. sceso. Past Def. scesi, &c.
Sciogliere (*or* sciorre), *to untie, to unravel.* Past Part. sciolto. Pres. Ind. sciolgo, sciogli, scioglie ; sciogliamo, sciogliete, sciolgono. Past Def. sciolsi, &c. Fut. scioglierò (*or* sciorrò), &c. Imperative, sciogli, sciolga ; sciogliamo, &c. Pres. Subj. che io sciolga, &c.
*Scommettere, *to bet.* Past Part. scommesso. Past Def. scommisi (*or* scommessi), &c.
Scomporre, *to discompose*, is contracted from " Scomponere." See " Porre."
Sconfiggere, *to defeat.* Past Part. sconfitto. Past Def. sconfissi, &c.

---

† The compound tenses of this verb are formed with " Essere."
‡ Notice the irregularity of " Sapere " in the Imperative Mood.

Sconvolgere, *to overturn.* Past Part. sconvolto. Past Def. sconvolsi, &c.
*Scoprire (263), *to discover.*† Past Part. scoperto.
*Scorgere, *to perceive, to discern, to guide.* Past Part. scorto. Past Def. scorsi, &c.
Scorrere, *to flow, to glide, to run quickly.* Past Part. scorso. Past Def. scorsi, &c.
**Scrivere, *to write.* Past Part. scritto. Past Def. scrissi, &c.
Scuotere,‡ *to shake.* Past Part. scosso. Past Def. scossi, &c.
**Sedere, *to sit down.* Past Part. seduto. Pres. Ind. seggo, siedi, siede; sediamo, sedete, seggono. Imperative, siedi, segga; sediamo, sedete, seggano. Pres. Subj. che io segga, &c.
Sedersi, *to sit down,* conjugated like "Sedere."§

VOCABULARY.

Una pianura,	a plain.	L' indirizzo,	the address.
Una collina,	a hill.	Questo colore,	this colour.
Alla moda,	in the fashion.	Benissimo,	very well.

EXERCISE XXXIII.

Well, have you succeeded (258) in your undertaking? No; I shall never succeed. I ascend the hill every morning. It is necessary (bisognare)‖ to start at once. If I knew Mr. John's address, I would write (to) him a letter. Can¶ he read? Yes, he can read and write very well. Why have you chosen this colour? I chose (180) it because it is in fashion. I would write to him every day, if (112) I had time. Have you written to the girl's uncle? Yes, I wrote (Past Def.) to him yesterday.

---

† In the regular forms it is conjugated like "Servire."
‡ When in the verb "Scuotere" the tonic accent does not fall on the *o*, the letter *u* may be omitted; as "scotendo," "scotiamo," "scotete," instead of "scuotendo," &c.
§ The compound tenses of this verb are formed with "Essere."
307. ‖ The verbs "Bisognare," *to be necessary,* "Fare," *to make,* "Lasciare," *to allow,* "Dovere," *to be obliged,* "Intendere," *to hear,* "Potere," *to be able,* "Sapere," *to know how,* "Solere," *to be accustomed,* "Volere," *to be willing,* "Sentire," *to feel,* or *to hear,* and "Udire," *to hear,* do *not* require any preposition after them, when they are followed by a verb in the Infinitive. Ex.
Bisogna esser forte per lottare con lui. One must be strong to wrestle with him.
Dovreste comprargli un paio di stivali. You ought to buy him a pair of boots.
Voglio sapere se il Conte è arrivato. I want to know if the Count has arrived.
308. ¶ When *can* and *could* are used in the sense of *to know how,* they are translated into Italian by "Sapere."

Sedurre, *to seduce*, is contracted from "Seducere," and is, therefore, conjugated thus: Ger. seducendo. Pres. Ind. seduco, &c.
    Its irregular forms are: Past Part. sedotto. Past Def. sedussi, &c. Fut. sedurrò, &c.

Seppellire, *to bury.* Past Part. sepolto *or* seppellito.

Smettere, (263) *to leave off.* Past Part. smesso. Past Def. smisi (*or* smessi), &c.

Socchiudere, *to half shut.* Past Part. socchiuso. Past Def. socchiusi, &c.

*Soccorrere, *to succour.* Past Part. soccorso. Past Def. soccorsi, &c.

Sodisfare, *to satisfy*, is contracted from "Sodisfacere," and is, therefore, conjugated thus: Ger. sodisfacendo. Imp. Ind. sodisfacevo, &c.
    Its irregular forms are: Past Part. sodisfatto. Pres. Ind. sodisfaccio (*or* sodisfo), sodisfi, sodisfa; sodisfacciamo, sodisfate, sodisfano. Past Def. sodisfeci, sodisfacesti, sodisfece, &c. Fut. sodisfarò, &c. Imperative, sodisfa, sodisfaccia; sodisfacciamo, sodisfate, sodisfano. Pres. Subj. che io sodisfaccia, &c.

*Soffrire, *to suffer.* Past Part. sofferto. Past Def. soffersi (*or* soffrii), &c.

*Soggiungere, *to add.* Past Part. soggiunto. Past Def. soggiunsi, &c.

Sommergere, *to submerge.* Past Part. sommerso. Past Def. sommersi, &c.

**Solere (*or* Esser solito), *to be accustomed.* Past Part. solito. Pres. Ind. soglio, suoli, suole; sogliamo, solete, sogliono; *or* sono solito, sei solito, &c. Imp. Ind. solevo, &c., *or* ero solito, &c. Pres. Subj. che io soglia, &c., *or* che io sia solito, &c. Imp. Subj. che io solessi, &c., *or* che io fossi solito, &c.

Sommettere, *to submit.* See "Mettere."

Sopraggiungere, *to come unexpectedly.* See "Giungere."

Soprastare, *to be above, to domineer.* See "Stare."†

Sopravvivere, *to survive.* See "Vivere."

Sopprimere, *to suppress.* Past Part. soppresso. Past Def. soppressi, &c.

---

† The compound tenses of this verb are formed with "Essere."

ON THE IRREGULAR VERBS.

*Sorgere, *to rise.* Past Part. sorto, &c. Past Def. sorsi, &c.
*Sorprendere, *to surprise.* Past Part. sorpreso. Past Def. sorpresi, &c.
Sorreggere, *to support.* Past Part. sorretto. Past Def. sorressi, &c.
Sorridere, *to smile.* Past Part. sorriso. Past Def. sorrisi, &c.
Sospendere, *to suspend.* Past Part. sospeso. Past Def. sospesi, &c.
Sospingere, *to push.* Past Part. sospinto. Past Def. sospinsi, &c.
**Sostenere, *to sustain.* Pres. Ind. sostengo, sostieni, sostiene; sosteniamo, sostenete, sostengono. Past Def. sostenni, &c. Fut. sosterrò, &c. Imperative, sostieni, sostenga; sosteniamo, &c. Pres. Subj. che io sostenga, &c.
Sottintendere, *to be understood.* Past Part. sottinteso. Past Def. sottintesi, &c.
*Sottomettere, *to submit.* See "Mettere."
Sottomettersi, *to submit*, is conjugated like "Sottomettere."†
Sottoporre, *to subdue.* Past Part. sottoposto. Past Def. sottoposi, &c.
*Sottoscrivere, *to subscribe.* See "Scritto."
Sottrarre, *to draw away*, is contracted from "Sottraere." See "Trarre."

EXERCISE XXXIV.

My father is accustomed (307) to get up (alzarsi) every morning at six o'clock. My uncle spent (Past Def.) too much money in (278) building his house. What is the name of‡ that lady? I do not know; but I believe she is called Mrs. James. You would have succeeded (258) in your undertaking, but you have to deal with§ a rascal, who cheats (ingannare) everybody.

---

† The compound tenses of this verb are formed with "Essere."

309. ‡ The expressions *What is the name of? What is called? What do you call?* are expressed in Italian by the verb "Chiamarsi." Ex.

Come si chiama?	What is his name?
Si chiama il colonnello Silvestri.	He is called Colonel Silvestri.

310. § *To deal with* is translated by "Aver da fare con." When the preposition *to* precedes a verb in the Infinitive Mood, which depends on the verbs *to have* or *to be*, it is expressed by "da," or by "a";—by "da" when an idea of right or duty is to be indicated, and by "a" when *no* idea of right or duty is to be expressed. Ex.

Avete da fare con un birbante.	You have to deal with a rascal.
È da considerarsi (*or* considerare) che...	It is to be considered that....
Ho da scrivere tre lettere.	I have three letters to write.
Non è da negarsi che....	It is not to be denied that....
È facile a capirsi.	It is easily understood.
Questi fiori sono belli a vedersi.	These flowers are beautiful to look at.

Sovvenire, *to help*, is conjugated like "Venire."
Sovvenirsi, *to remember*, is conjugated like "Venire."†
Spandere, *to spread*. Past Part. spanto. Past Def. spansi, &c.
*Spargere, *to scatter*. Past Part. sparso. Past Def. sparsi, &c.
**Spendere, *to spend*. Past Part. speso. Past Def. spesi, &c.
Spengere (*or* spegnere), *to extinguish*. Past Part. spento. Pres. Ind. spengo, spegni, spegne; spegnamo, spegnete, spengono. Past Def. spensi, &c. Imperative, spegni, spenga; spegnamo, spegnete, spengano. Pres. Subj. che io spenga, &c.
Spingere, *to push*. Past Part. spinto. Past Def. spinsi, &c.
Sporgere, *to project*. Past Part. sporto. Past Def. sporsi, &c.
**Stare, *to be in health (to do), to dwell, to stay*. Ger. stando. Pres. Ind. sto, stai, sta; stiamo, state, stanno. Past Def. stetti, stesti, stette; stemmo, steste, stettero. Fut. starò, &c. Imperative, sta, stia; stiamo, state, stiano (*or* stieno). Pres. Subj. che io stia, &c. Imp. Subj. che io stessi, che tu stessi, &c.†
*Stendere, *to extend*. Past Part. steso. Past Def. stesi, &c.
Storcere, *to twist*. Past Part. storto. Past Def. storsi, &c.
Stravolgere, (265) *to twist, to distort*. Past Part. stravolto. Past Def. stravolsi, &c.
*Stringere, *to grasp, to tighten*. Past Part. stretto. Past Def. strinsi, &c.
Struggere, *to melt, to dissolve*. Past Part. strutto. Past Def. strussi, &c.
Suddividere, *to subdivide*. Past Part. suddiviso. Past Def. suddivisi, &c.
Svellere, *to pluck up*. Past Part. svelto. Past Def. svelsi, &c.
Svenire *and* Svenirsi, *to faint away*.† See "Venire."
Svolgere, *to unfold, to develop, to dissuade*. Past Part. svolto. Past Def. svolsi, &c.
*Supporre, *to suppose, to guess*, is contracted from "Supponere." See "Porre."

T

**Tacere, *to be silent*. Past Part. taciuto. Pres. Ind. taccio, taci, tace; tacciamo, tacete, tacciono. Past Def. tacqui, &c. Imperative, taci, taccia; tacciamo, &c.

---

† The compound tenses of this verb are formed with "Essere."

Tẹndere, *to tend, to incline to, to stretch.* Past Part. teso. Past Def. tesi, &c.

**Tenere, *to keep, to hold.* Pres. Ind. tẹngo, tiẹni, tiẹne; teniamo, tenete, tẹngono. Past Def. tenni, &c. Fut. terrò, &c. Imperative, tiẹni, tẹnga; teniamo, &c. Pres. Subj. che io tẹnga, &c.

Tẹrgere, *to clean, to dry up.* Past Part. terso. Past Def. tersi, &c.

Tingere, *to dye.* Past Part. tinto. Pret. Ind. tinsi, &c.

**Tọgliere (*or* Tọrre), *to take away.* Past Part. tọlto. Pres. Ind. tọlgo, tọgli, tọglie; togliamo, togliete, tọlgono. Past Def. tọlsi, &c. Fut. toglierò (*or* tọrrò), &c. Imperative, tọgli, tọlga; togliamo, &c. Pres. Subj. che io tọlga, &c.

Tọrcere, *to twist.* Past Part. tọrto. Past Def. tọrsi, &c.

**Tradurre, *to translate,* is contracted from "Traducere," and is, therefore, conjugated thus: Ger. traducẹndo. Pres. Ind. traduco, &c.

Its irregular forms are: Past Part. tradotto. Past Def. tradussi, &c. Fut. tradurrò, &c. Cond. tradurrẹi, tradurresti, tradurrẹbbe; tradurremmo, tradurreste, tradurẹbbero.‡

VOCABULARY.

Buọn giorno,	good morning.	Come sta?	how do you do?
Un villaggio,	a village.	Versi sciọlti,	blank verse.
Un canto,	a canto.	Il vicinato,	the neighbourhood.

EXERCISE XXXV.

Good morning, sir, how do you do (120)? I am very well to-day, thank (ringraziare) you (122, 193). Where do you live (stare) now? I live in the country; in a small village near Brighton. Have you been (149) to Paris? No, I have not been there (239). My brother is translating "La Divina Commedia," in blank verse. Yesterday he translated (Past Def.) two cantos (of it) (240). If I had friends in this neighbourhood, I would remain here (239) for§ a week.

---

† See last note (§) on page 80.

‡ Notice that the initial *e* of the termination of the 1st and 3rd pers. sing. and the 3rd pers. plur. of the Conditional has always the broad sound of the *a* in the word *gate*.

311. § When *for* precedes a noun indicating time, it is either not translated into Italian, or it is translated by "Durante." Ex.

Parlò tre ore di sẹguito.   He spoke for three hours consecutively.
Sono stato a Parigi sẹi giorni.   I have been to Paris for six days.

ON THE IRREGULAR VERBS.

Trarre, *to draw, to lead, to live,* is contracted from "Traere." Ger. traendo. Past Part. tratto. Pres. Ind. traggo, trai, trae; traiamo (*or* traggiamo), traete, traggono. Imp. Ind. traevo, &c. Past Def. trassi, traesti, &c. Fut. trarrò, &c. Imperative, trai, tragga; traiamo, traete, traggano. Imp. Subj. che io traessi, &c.

Trarsi, *to betake one's-self.* Conjugated like "Trarre."†

Trascendere, *to go beyond.* Past Part. trasceso. Past Def. trascesi, &c.

Trascorrere, *to elapse, to pass over quickly.* Past Part. trascorso. Past Def. trascorsi, &c.

Trasmettere, *to transmit.* Past Part. trasmesso. Past Def. trasmisi (*or* trasmessi), &c.

Trattenere, *to stop, to entertain.* See "Tenere."

U

*Uccidere, *to kill.* Past Part. ucciso. Past Def. uccisi, &c.

**Udire, *to hear.* Pres. Ind. odo, odi, ode; udiamo, udite, odono. Fut. udrò (*or* udirò), &c. Imperative, odi, oda; udiamo, udite, odano. Pres. Subj. che io oda, &c.

Ungere, *to anoint.* Past Part. unto. Past Def. unsi, &c.‡

**Uscire (*or* Escire), *to go out.* Past Part. uscito. Pres. Ind. esco, esci, esce; usciamo, uscite, escono. Imperative, esci, esca; usciamo, uscite, escano. Pres. Subj. che io esca, &c.†

**Valere, *to be worth.* Pres. Ind. valgo, vali, vale; valghiamo (*or* vagliamo), valete, valgono. Past Def. valsi, &c. Fut. varrò, &c. Imperative, vali, valga; valghiamo (*or* vagliamo), &c. Pres. Subj. che io valga, &c.

**Vedere, *to see.* Past Part. visto (*or* veduto). Pres. Ind. vedo (veggo, *or* veggio), vedi, vede; vediamo, vedete, vedono (*or* veggono). Past Def. vidi, &c. Fut. vedrò, &c. Imperative, vedi (*or* ve'), veda (*or* vegga); vediamo, &c. Pres. Subj. che io vegga, &c.

**Venire, *to come.* Past Part. venuto. Pres. Ind. vengo, vieni, viene; veniamo, venite, vengono. Past Def. venni, &c. Fut. verrò, &c. Imperative, vieni, venga; veniamo, &c. Pres. Subj. che io venga, &c.

---

† The compound tenses of this verb are formed with "Essere."
‡ See last note (§) on page 80.

Vilipendere, *to vilify.* Past Part. vilipeso.† Past Def. vilipesi, &c.†
**Vincere, *to win, to vanquish.* Past Part. vinto. Past Def. vinsi, &c.
**Vivere, *to live.* Past Part. vissuto (*or* vivuto). Past Def. vissi, &c.
**Volere, *to be willing.* Pres. Ind. voglio (*or* vo'), vuoi, vuole; vogliamo, volete, vogliono. Past Def. volli, &c. Fut. vorrò, &c. Imperative, vogli, voglia;‡ vogliate, vogliano. Pres. Subj. che io voglia, &c.
*Volgere, *to turn.* Past Part. volto. Past Def. volsi, &c.

VOCABULARY.

La voce,	the voice.	Un miglio,	a mile.
La colazione,	the breakfast.	Una rivista,	a review.
Il pranzo,	the dinner.	Il mio consiglio,	my advice.

Solamente, only. Di vista, by sight. A mente, by heart.

EXERCISE XXXVI.

I hear William's voice; do you? (do you hear it?) My brother is gone out; I do not know when he will return. William will go out with me on (147) Saturday morning. I go out every morning before (to make) breakfast. Do not go out, (122, 126) Henry; your father-in-law wishes (300) to speak to you. Frederick has got the book, but he will (volere) not give it to me.§ Do you know Mrs. James? I know her only by sight; her house is‖ a mile from this village. I heard him¶ singing Italian songs. He knows many of them (240) by heart. How much is this ring worth? I could** not tell you. One must have†† much money, to (225) buy good rings. Your brother always comes to see me when he is in London. If you had gone out then, you would have seen the review. He would (224) not give me his advice. I like to hear him translating.¶

---

† Notice that the *s* in Past Participles in "eso" and Past Definites in "esi" has no dot under it, and is therefore pronounced like the *s* in the English word *spirit.*

‡ Notice that "Volere" has no first person plural in the Imperative.

312. § When the verbs "dovere," "potere," "sapere" and "volere," followed by another verb in the Infinitive Mood, are used with any of the Conjunctive Personal Pronouns ("me lo," "glie la," &c.), these may be placed either before or after "dovere," "potere," "sapere" and "volere," thus: "Non me lo vuol dare," or "Non vuol darmelo."

313. ‖ The Italians say, "My house is *at* a mile from this village."

314. ¶ When two or three verbs follow one another, the second and third must be in the Infinitive Mood.

315. ** When *can* and *could* are used in the sense of *to be able* they are translated by "Potere."

316. †† The expression *One must have* is translated into Italian by "Ci vuole."

POETICAL AND DEFECTIVE FORMS OF VERBS.*

317. Having given on page 17 (rule 111), the poetical forms of "Avere," on page 25 (rule 150), the poetical forms of "Essere," on page 29 (rule 169), and on page 30 (rule 174), some hints concerning the poetical forms of Regular Verbs of the First Conjugation, on page 47 (rules 252 and 253), some hints concerning the poetical forms of Regular Verbs of the Second Conjugation, on page 50 (rule 261), some hints concerning the poetical forms of Regular Verbs of the Third Conjugation, I shall now give the most important forms of the Defective Verbs arranged in alphabetical order.

318. **Algere**, *to freeze*, is only used in the 2nd and 3rd pers. sing. and the 3rd pers. plur. of the Past Def. "alsi," "alse;" "alsero."

319. **Angere**, *to torment*, is only used in the 3rd pers. sing. of the Pres. Ind. "ange."

320. **Colere**, *to honour, to worship*, is only used in the 3rd pers. sing. of the Pres. Ind. "cole."

321. **Fiedere** (*or* Fedire), *to wound*, is only used in the three pers. sing. and the 3rd pers. plur. of the Pres. Ind.: "fiedo," "fiedi," "fiede;" "fiedono."

322. **Gire**, *to go*, is used in the Past Part. "gito," in the Imperf. Ind. "givo," "givi," &c., in the Past Def. "gìi," "gisti," "gì," &c., in the Fut. "girò," &c., in the Cond. "girei," and the Imperf. Subj. "che *or* se io gissi," &c.

323. **Ire**, *to go*, is only used in the Past Part. "ito," in the Imperf. Ind. "ivo," "ivi," &c., in the 2nd pers. sing. and 3rd. pers. plur. of the Past Def. "isti," "irono."

324. **Licere**, *to be lawful*, is only used in the 3rd pers. sing. of the Pres. Ind. "lece" (*or* "lice").

325. **Molcere**, *to soothe*, is only used in the Gerund "molcendo," in the 2nd and 3rd pers. sing. of the Pres. Ind. "molci," "molce;" in the Imperf. Ind. "molcevo," &c., and in the 3rd pers. sing. of the Imperf. Subj. "che *or* se molcesse."

326. **Olire**, *to be fragrant*, is only used in the 2nd and 3rd pers. sing. of the Pres. Ind. "olisci," "olisce," and in the Imperf. Ind. "olivo," &c.

327. **Riedere** (*or* Redire), *to return*, is only used in the Pres. Ind. "riedo," "riedi," &c., in the Imperf. Ind. "riedevo," &c., and in the Past Def. "redii," "redisti," &c.

---

* The student will find the idiomatical forms of "Andare," "Dare," "Fare," "Stare," "Sapere," "Tenere," and "Venire," further on.

LESSON XVIII.

ON THE USE OF THE DEFINITE AND PARTITIVE ARTICLES.

328. In Italian the Definite Article ("il," "lo," or "la;" "i," "gli," or "le") is used before any noun (concrete or abstract) employed in a definite sense; that is to say, employed to express—(a) the whole of its genus—(b) a whole class—(c) an individual. Ex.

Gli animali sono utili all' uomo. — Animals are useful to men.
Gli uomini irosi commettono gravi errori. — Hot-tempered men commit grave errors.
L'oro è più caro che l'argento. — Gold is dearer than silver.
Persino i cattivi ammirano la virtù. — Virtue is admired even by the wicked.
L'amore della verità (69). — The love of truth.

329. In Italian the definite article is also used before titles of persons. Ex.

Il dottor Sangrado. — Doctor Sangrado.

330. In Italian the definite article is also used before the names of countries and provinces. Ex.

L'Asia è molto grande. — Asia is very large.
La Borgogna è molto fertile. — Burgundy is very fertile.

331. Notice, however, that if the name of a country or province be preceded by the preposition "in," no article is used. Ex.

Egli è andato in Italia. — He is gone to Italy.

332. In Italian the definite article is also used before the names of *a few* towns, the most important of which are: Il Cairo, l'Aia (*the Hague*), la Rochelle, la Mecca, la Mirandola.

333. In Italian the definite article is also placed before the family names of very distinguished persons, who lived since the year 1200. Ex. Il Petrarca,† il Milton, il Molière, il Tiziano, il Biron, il Manzoni, il Darwin. Ex.

L'Ariosto è il pittore della natura. — Ariosto is the painter of nature.

334. Notice, that no article is used before the names of distinguished persons, when only their Christian name, or if more than one word is used to designate them. Ex.

Dante morì a Ravenna. — Dante died in Ravenna.
Carlo Darwin era modesto. — Charles Darwin was modest.

---

* See rule 63, to understand the meaning of the letters in the darker type.

335. † "Il Petrarca," "Il Tiziano," mean "Il poeta Petrarca," "Il pittore Tiziano." The Italians also say "la Saffo," *the poetess Sappho*.

336. In Italian the definite article is also placed before Adjectives, Adverbs, Prepositions, Conjunctions, Interjections and Verbs in the Infinitive Mood, when they are used as nouns. Ex.

Carlo ama l'utile. Charles is fond of what is useful.
Il saper ascoltare è utile quanto il saper parlare. To know how to listen is as useful as to know how to speak.

337. When several nouns follow one another in the same sentence (whether used as subjects or objects), the definite article must be repeated in Italian before each of them, when it is already expressed before the first. Ex.

Il ferro, l' oro e l' argento sono metalli utilissimi. Iron, gold and silver are very useful metals.

338. When two adjectives are united by the conjunction "e," and one of them is intended to qualify a substantive expressed and the other a substantive understood, the article must be repeated, in Italian, before each adjective. Ex.

Conosce la storia antica e la moderna. He knows ancient and modern history.

339. But when the adjectives, united by "e," *and*, qualify only one substantive, the article is not repeated. Ex.

Anna d'Austria, la bella e altiera regina di Francia. Anne of Austria, the proud and beautiful Queen of France.

THE WORDS REQUIRED TO COMPOSE THIS AND THE FOLLOWING EXERCISES ARE GIVEN IN THE VOCABULARY AT THE END OF THE GRAMMAR.

EXERCISE XXXVII.

Necessity (328) is the mother of invention. Flowers (328) are very dear (in) this season of the year. The Alps separate France (330) from Italy. Drawing (328) owes its origin to chance, sculpture to religion, and painting to the progress of the other arts. Fear and ignorance are the sources of superstition. The love of (328) music and poetry is universal in Italy. Captain (329) Bravo wishes to speak to your father. Go and* tell (to) him (198) that my father is in (331) France. Good (328) laws make good men.

---

340. * The preposition " a " is used in Italian instead of the English conjunction *and*, after a verb expressing motion. Ex.

Andate a prendere la mia mantellina. Go and fetch my mantle.

ON THE OMISSION OF THE DEFINITE ARTICLE.

341. The definite article is *not* required in Italian before any noun used adverbially, or preceded by "senza," *without*, "nè," *neither*, *nor*, or "sia," *whether it be*. Ex.

Luigi lavora con perseveranza.	Louis works with perseverance.
Il suo socio* è un uomo senza merito.	His partner is a man without merit.
Essa non ha nè bellezza,† nè talento.	She has neither beauty nor talent.
Sia superbia, sia timidità, essa non volle parlare.	Whether through pride or timidity, she would not speak.

342. The definite article is *not* required in Italian before nouns used in apposition with preceding words. Ex.

Dublino, capitale dell' Irlanda.	Dublin, the capital of Ireland.
Sposò Margherita, figlia di Enrico II.	He married Margaret, the daughter of Henry II.

343. The definite article is *not* required in Italian before nouns used emphatically. Ex.

Uomini, donne, fanciulli, tutto perì!	Men, women, children, everything perished!

344. The definite article is *not* required in Italian before the ordinal numbers "primo," *first*, "secondo," *second*, &c., when they come after the name of a sovereign, or after the words "libro," *book*, "capo," or "capitolo," *chapter*, "atto," *act*, "scena," *scene*. Ex.

Enrico quarto, re di Francia.	Henry IV., King of France.
Atto primo, scena quarta.	Act the first, scene the fourth.

ON THE USE OF THE PARTITIVE ARTICLE.

345. To the rules relating to the Partitive Article "del," "dello," "della," "dei," "degli," "delle," which have been given on page 22, and which the student should now read over, the following must be added.

346. The preposition "di," only (not "del," "dello," &c.) is required before a noun or name used adjectively. Ex.

Guarda, sorella mia, che bell' anello d' oro.	Look, sister, what a beautiful gold ring.
Il regno d' Italia è grande.	The kingdom of Italy is large.

347. The preposition "di," only (not "del," "dello," &c.) is required before a noun used as a complement to another noun. Ex.

Caro fratello dammi* un quinterno di carta da scrivere.	Dear brother, give me a quire of note paper.

---

* Observe that the initial letters of "mi," "ti," "lo," "la," "ci," and "vi" is doubled when these words are joined after "va," *go* (from "andare"), "dà," *give* (from "dare," and in this case the accent is not written), "fa," *do, make* (from "fare"), and "sta," *stay* (from "stare").

348. The preposition "di" only (not "del," "dello," &c.) is required before an adjective or a past participle expressed or understood. Ex.

La via era adorna di alberi. The road was lined with trees.
Il baule era coperto di polvere. The trunk was covered with dust.
Un canestro (pieno) di fiori. A basket of flowers.

349. The preposition "di," only (not "del," "dello," &c.), is required after the words "qualità," "sorte," "genere," "specie," "corso." Ex.

Egli vende tre qualità di tè. He sells three kinds of tea.

350. Notice, however, that a noun must be preceded by the partitive article "del," "dello," &c. (and not merely by the preposition "di") when it is taken in a specified sense. Ex.

Un quinterno *della* carta che comprai ieri. A quire of the paper I bought yesterday.
La via era adorna *degli* alberi che ho piantati io stesso. The road was lined with the trees I have planted myself.
Egli vende tre qualità *del* tè che viene da Ceylon. He sells three kinds of the tea which comes from Ceylon.

EXERCISE XXXVIII.

Glory (328) follows virtue like a shadow. If your brother studied with (341) perseverance, he would succeed (258). Eating, (267, 336) drinking, and sleeping are necessary to man. Last year we visited (Past Def.) Cairo, (342) the capital of Egypt. His cousin Margaret married William, (342) the son of Colonel Barducci. This bronze statue was (Imp. Ind.) formerly in the Municipal Palace of Modena. I wish to attend (assistere a) a course of lectures which (che) he will begin to-morrow evening. What shall I buy you (for you)? (213, 251) Buy me a box of steel pens (347), a dozen of quills, a quire of (347) foreign paper, and three sheets of blotting-paper. His apartments were adorned (175) with (266) the pictures which (che) he had himself (189) bought at Padova. The question is* to decide whether we shall meet again (radunarsi) to-morrow or on (147, 74) Wednesday next. The theatre was (Imperf. Ind.) full of strangers† and foreigners. The hall is full (350) of the men who have taken part in the strike. It is necessary (bisognare) (307) to start at once.

---

351. * The expressions *the question is*, or *was, the matter is*, or *was* are translated into Italian by "Sì tratta di," "Si trattava di."

352. † *Stranger* is translated by "forestiere," and *foreigner*, by "straniero."

LESSON XIX.
ON THE USE OF THE INDEFINITE ARTICLE.

353. The indefinite article is *not* required in Italian before nouns used in apposition with preceding words. Ex.

I Rivali, bellissima commedia di Sheridan.	The Rivals, a very fine comedy by Sheridan.

354. The indefinite article is *not* used in Italian before nouns expressing nationality, title, profession and condition, used adjectively. Ex.

Sono Scozzese di nascita.	I am a Scotchman by birth.
Suo nipote è libraio.	His nephew is a bookseller.
Mio nonno era generale.	My grandfather was a general.
Egli è stato prigioniero.*	He has been a prisoner.

355. Notice that when nouns expressing nationality, &c., are qualified, the indefinite article is required before them. Ex.

Maria Stuarda era una principessa di sventurata razza.	Mary Stuart was a princess of an unfortunate race.

356. The indefinite article is *not* used in Italian before "cento," *a (one) hundred*, and "mille," *a (one) thousand.* Ex.

Hanno comprato cento quadri per mille lire sterline.	They bought a hundred pictures for a thousand pounds.

357. The indefinite article is *not* used in Italian before the title of a book, or the heading of a chapter. Ex.

Vita di Lord Macaulay.	A Life of Lord Macaulay.

358. The indefinite article is *not* used in Italian after "che," "quale," *what a*, used exclamatively. Ex.

Guardi, che bel castello!	Look, what a beautiful castle!

359. In Italian the indefinite article is placed before, and not after the adjective "tale," *such*, and the adverb "così," or "sì," *so*. Ex.

Un tal nomo è odioso.	Such a man is odious.
Una così bella opera!	So beautiful a work

360. The indefinite article is *not* used in Italian in the expressions "Far regalo di,"† *to make a present of;* "Far segno," *to make a sign;* "Far fortuna," *to make a fortune;* "Metter fine," *to put an end to.*

---

* Notice that an *e* preceded by an *i* has always the broad sound of the *a* in the word *gate*.

361. † When the words "regalo," "segno" and "fortuna" are qualified, the article is required. Ex. "Fece una gran fortuna," *he made a large fortune.*

ON THE DIFFERENT USE OF THE ARTICLE.

362. Before the names of measure, weight, number and time, the Italians use the definite article instead of the indefinite article which is employed by the English. Ex.

Ho pagato questo panno cinque scellini il braccio.	I have paid five shillings a yard for this cloth.
Queste pere costano due soldi la libbra.	These pears cost a penny a pound.
Questi aranci si vendono un franco la dozzina.	These oranges are sold a franc a dozen.
Abbiamo lezione di canto tre volte la settimana.	We have singing lessons three times a week.
Egli guadagna due scellini l'ora.	He earns two shillings an hour.

EXERCISE XXXIX.

Michelangelo was (355) a sculptor, a painter, an architect, and a poet of great celebrity. When I made his acquaintance he was a banker (354); now he is a poor workman (355). What are you reading, Henry? "I Lombardi alla prima Crociata," a (353) splendid poem, by (of) Tommaso Grossi. My father is a captain (354) in the French army. We bought (180) a hundred (356) Turkish carpets for a thousand (356) guineas. This cloth costs six shillings a (362) yard. The best coffee comes from Mocha, a (353) town in (of) Arabia. I give four shillings a day to my gardener. What is the title of Charles' new book? "A (357) life of Lord Palmerston." What a (358) beautiful morning! shall we go out for a walk? Yes, as soon as (249) I have written my letters. What a beautiful horse! where did you buy it? (193) I bought it from Colonel James. This man works by the hour;* he earns three shillings an (362) hour. Her father knows† a great deal; he earns six hundred guineas a year. Captain Cook was a navigator of great celebrity (355).

---

363. * The expressions *to work by the hour, by the day, by the week*, &c. are translated into Italian by "lavorare all'ora," "al giorno," "alla settimana," &c.

364. † When *to know*, means *to know through the mind*, and *to know how*, it is translated by "Sapere." Ex.

Mio cugino sa il tedesco.	My cousin knows German.
Voi non sapete la vostra lezione.	You do not know your lessons.
Suo figlio non sa comportarsi.	Your son does not know how to behave.

365. But when *to know* means *to be acquainted with* (through the senses), it is translated by "Conoscere." Ex.

Conosco il Presidente.	I know the President (Chairman).

LESSON XX.
ON THE GENDER AND NUMBER OF NOUNS.

366. In Italian, nouns are either of the masculine or of the feminine gender—there is no neuter—and the gender of Italian nouns is determined either by their meaning, or by their termination.

DETERMINATION OF THE GENDER OF NOUNS BY THEIR MEANING.

367. Appellations of men, and the names of male animals are masculine, whilst appellations of women, and the names of female animals are feminine.*

ON THIS POINT THE FOLLOWING OBSERVATIONS ARE NECESSARY:—

368. The words " Maestà," *majesty*, " Santità," *holiness*, " Eminenza," *Eminence*, " Eccellenza," *Excellency*, and " Signoria," *Lordship* or *Ladyship*, are feminine, and, therefore, the Italians call a king " Sua Maestà," and the pope, " Sua Santità."

369. The Italians apply the words "una sentinella," *a sentry*, "una recruta," *a recruit*, "una guardia," *a guard, a keeper*, "una guida," *a guide*, "una spia," *a spy*, "una vittima," *a victim*, to a man as well as to a woman.

370. The appellations " compatriota," *compatriot*, " artista," *artist*, " statista," *political economist*, " moralista," *moralist*, " pessimista," *pessimist*, " scrittore," *writer*, "autore," *author*, and "testimonio," *witness*, are applied to men and women alike.

371. Nouns which admit of both genders form the feminine by changing the final vowel into *a*. Ex.

Mio cugino,	my cousin,	mia cugina,	my cousin.
Mio cognato,	my brother-in-law,	mia cognata,	my sister-in-law.
Il mio maestro,	my teacher,	la mia maestra,	my teacher.
Un cameriere,	a valet,	una cameriera,	a lady's-maid.
Un ebreo,	a Jew,	un' ebrea,	a Jewess.
Un vedovo,	a widower,	una vedova,	a widow.

---

372. * The names of some animals, as "un coniglio," *a rabbit*, "un cammello," *a camel*, "una balena," *a whale*, "un' aquila," *an eagle*, serve both for the male and the female, in Italian; so that, to be more explicit, the word "maschio," *male*, or the word "femmina," *female*, is placed after the name of the animal. Ex. " Un coniglio maschio," *a buck rabbit*, "un coniglio femmina," *a doe rabbit*.

373. Words (nouns and adjectives) which are derived from verbs, and end in *ante* and *ente*, as well as those derived from a country or town, ending in *ese*, are the same for both genders. Ex.

Il cantante,	the singer,	la cantante,	the singer.
Il credente,	the believer,	la credente,	the believer.
Un Inglese,	an Englishman,	una Inglese,	an Englishwoman.
Un Francese,*	a Frenchman,	una Francese,	a Frenchwoman.

374. Nouns which have the masculine termination in *tore*, form the feminine in *trice*. Ex.

L'esecutore,	the executor,	l'esecutrice,	the executrix.
L'imperatore,	the emperor,	l'imperatrice,	the empress.
Il traditore,	the traitor,	la traditrice,	the traitress.

375. The following nouns form the feminine in *essa*:

Un abate,	an abbot.	un' abadessa,	an abbess.
Un barone,	a baron,	una baronessa,	a baroness.
Un conte,	a count,	una contessa,	a countess.
Un dottore,	a doctor,	una dottoressa,	a lady doctor.
Un duca,	a duke,	una duchessa,	a duchess.
Un gigante,	a giant.	una gigantessa,	a giantess.
Un leone,	a lion,	una leonessa,	a lioness.
Un oste,	a host,	un'ostessa,	a hostess.
Un poeta,	a poet,	una poetessa,	a poetess.
Un pavone,	a peacock,	una pavonessa,	a pea-hen.
Un principe,	a prince,	una principessa,	a princess.
Un profeta,	a prophet,	una profetessa,	a prophetess.
Un sacerdote,	a priest,	una sacerdotessa,	a priestess.

376. Names of Empires, Kingdoms, Provinces, and Rivers ending in *a* are feminine. Ex. "La Russia," *Russia*, "la Spagna," *Spain*, "la Calabria," *Calabria*, "la Senna," *the Seine*. When they end with any of the other vowels, they are masculine. Ex. "Il Brasile," *Brazil*, "il Tamigi," *the Thames*, "il Portogallo," *Portugal*, "il Perù," *Peru*.

377. Names of Towns ending in *a* or in *e* are feminine. Ex. "La bella Roma," *beautiful Rome*; "La sapiente Atene," *learned Athens*. If they end in any other vowel, they are of either gender.

378. Names of Islands are feminine. Ex. "La Sardegna," *Sardinia*.

379. Names of Lakes are mas. Ex. "Il Ladoga," *lake Ladoga*.

---

* An *s*, dotted thus ṣ, has the soft sound of the *s* in the word *rose*.

380. Names of Trees generally end in *o*, and are masculine. Ex. " Un pero," *a pear-tree;* " un ciriegio," *a cherry-tree.*

Except " una quercia," *an oak;* " un' elce," *a holm-oak;* " una palma," *a palm-tree,* and " una vite," *a vine.*

381. Names of Fruits generally end in *a*, and are feminine. Ex. " Una pesca," *a peach;* " una mela," *an apple;* " una castagna," *a chestnut.*

Except " un pomo," *an apple;* " un fico," *a fig;* "un arancio," *an orange;* " un limone," *a lemon;* " un cedro," *a citron;* " un dattero," *a date;* " un pistacchio," *a pistache nut,* which signify the tree as well as the fruit.

382. Adjectives, Verbs, Adverbs, and Conjunctions, used as nouns, are masculine. Ex. " Il bello," *the beautiful;* " il cantare," *the singing;* " il perchè," *the reason why.*

383. The following nouns must be noticed :—

Un baleno,	a flash of lightning,	una balena,	a whale.
Un colpo,	a blow,	una colpa,	a fault.
Un foglio,	a sheet of paper,	una foglia,	a leaf.
Il porto,	the harbour,	la porta,	the gate, the door.
Il soglio,	the throne,	la soglia,	the threshold.
Il velo,	the veil,	la vela,	the sail.
Il volto,	the face.	la volta,	the arched ceiling.

EXERCISE XL.

His Holiness (368) Pope Leo the tenth (Leone decimo) was a (353) son of the celebrated* Lorenzo de' Medici. There was (154) a sentry at each door of the palace. If he does not act (Pres. Ind.) with prudence, he will soon become the victim of his companions. He has (149) been (277) a widower (354) these four years. Last year I went to Florence with my brother-in-law and my cousin Margaret. The two sentries† were women. When we go to (207) Italy we meet (239) many of our countrywomen.‡ She is French and he is English; they are both good singers.§ The emperor (374) and empress were (Imperf. Ind.) surrounded by princes (375) and princesses, baron and baronesses.

384. * When the word *celebrated* means *famous* it is translated into Italian by " celebre," but when it means *solemnized* it is translated by " celebrato."

385. † The words " sentinella," " recruta," &c., (rule 369) form their plurals by changing the final *a* into an *e*, for men and women alike.

386. ‡ The words " compatriota," " artista," &c., (rule 370) form their plurals by changing the final *a* into an *i* when they refer to men, but by changing the final *a* into an *e* when they refer to women.

387. § The words " cantante," &c., " inglese," &c. (rule 373) form their plurals by changing the final *e* into an *i*, both when they refer to men and women.

DETERMINATION OF THE GENDER OF NOUNS BY THEIR VOWEL ENDINGS, AND FORMATION OF THE PLURAL OF NOUNS.

388. As stated already, nearly all the Italian words end with one of the five vowels, *a, e, i, o, u*,* and the gender and number of nouns is generally indicated by the ending vowel. Therefore, along with the rules for recognising the gender of nouns, will be given the rules for the formation of the plural.

WORDS ENDING IN A.

389. All nouns ending in *a* are feminine, and form their plural by changing the *a* into *e*. Ex.
    La grida,   the edict,   le gride,   the edicts.

390. Of course, names of dignities and professions of men, ending in *a*, are of the masculine gender, and form their plurals in *i*. Ex. "Il papa," *the pope*, "i papi," *the popes;* "il monarca," *the monarch*, "i monarchi," *the monarchs;* "il duca," *the duke*, "i duchi," *the dukes;* "il poeta," *the poet*, "i poeti," *the poets*.

ON THIS POINT THE FOLLOWING OBSERVATIONS ARE NECESSARY:—

391. Feminine nouns ending in *ea* form their plural by changing *ea* into *ee*. Ex.
    La mia idea,   my idea,   le mie idee,   my ideas.

392. Feminine nouns ending in *cia* and *gia may* lose the *i* in the plural. Ex.
    La caccia,   the chase,   le cacce,   the chases.
    La spiaggia,   the shore,   le spiagge,   the shores.

Except in "le bugìe," *the lies;* which is the plural of "la bugìa," *the lie*, because the accent falls upon the *i*.

393. Feminine nouns ending in *ca* and *ga*, in the singular, take an *h* in the plural, and change the *a* into *e*. Ex.
    La bocca,   the mouth,   le bocche,   the mouths.
    La monaca,   the nun,   le monache,   the nuns.
    La strega,   the witch,   le streghe,   the witches.

394. Masculine nouns ending in *ca* and *ga*, in the singular, require an *h* in the plural, and change the *a* into *i*. Ex.
    Il duca,   the duke,   i duchi,   the dukes.
    Il collega,   the colleague,   i colleghi,   the colleagues.

---

395. Un lapis, *a pencil*, "ribes," *currants*, "un diesis," *a semitone*, are almost the only nouns ending with a consonant used in Italian. They do not change in the plural.

396. All nouns ending in "tà" (all "parole tronche")* are feminine and do not change the form in the plural. Ex.

La città,	the town, city,	le città,	the towns, cities.
La carità,	charity,	la sincerità,	sincerity.

397. The following nouns (derived from the Greek language), ending in *a*, are masculine, in Italian, and form their plural by changing the *a* into *i* :—

L'anatema,	the anathema,	gli anatemi,	the anathemas.
L'assioma,	the axiom,	gli assiomi,	the axioms.
Il clima,	the climate,	i climi,	the climates.
Il diadema,	the diadem,	i diademi,	the diadems.
Il diploma,	the diploma,	i diplomi,	the diplomas.
Il dogma,	the dogma,	i dogmi,	the dogmas.
Il dramma,	the drama,	i drammi,	the dramas.
L'emblema,	the emblem,	gli emblemi,	the emblems.
L'enigma,	the enigma,	gli enigmi,	the enigmas.
L'epigramma,	the epigram,	gli epigrammi,	the epigrams.
Il fantasma,	the phantom,	i fantasmi,	the phantoms.
L'idioma,	the idiom,	gl'idiomi,	the idioms.
Il pianeta,	the planet,	i pianeti,	the planets.
Il poema,	the poem,	i poemi,	the poems.
Il problema,	the problem,	i problemi,	the problems.
Il programma,	the programme,	i programmi,	the programmes.
Lo scisma,	the schism,	gli scismi,	the schisms.
Il sistema,	the system,	i sistemi,	the systems.
Il sofisma,	the sophism,	i sofismi,	the sophisms.
Lo stemma,	the coat of arms,	gli stemmi,	the coats of arms.
Lo stratagemma,	the stratagem,	gli stratagemmi,	the stratagems.
Il telegramma,	the telegram,	i telegrammi,	the telegrams.
Il tema,	the theme,	i temi,	the themes.

WORDS ENDING IN E.

398. Nouns ending in *e* are some masculine and some feminine, but for both genders the plural is formed by changing the *e* into *i*. Ex.

Il cane,	the dog,	i cani,	the dogs.
La canzone,	the song,	le canzoni,	the songs.

ON THIS POINT THE FOLLOWING OBSERVATIONS ARE NECESSARY :—

399. Words ending in *ore* (which are very numerous) are all masculine. Ex. " Il fiore," the flower ; " i fiori," the flowers.

---

400. * Notice that the following nouns ending in *à* are masculine, and remain unchanged in the plural : " il sofà," *the sofa,* " i sofà," *the sofas ;* " il falbalà," *the* "*flounce,* i falbalà," *the flounces ;* " il taffetà," *the taffety ;* " il baccalà," *dried cod.*

401. Words ending in *ente* are masculine. Ex. "Il dęnte,"* the tooth; "i denti," the teeth.

Except "la gęnte," *the people,* "le gęnti," *the nations;* "la lęnte," *the lens,* or *lentil,* "le lęnti," *the lenses,* or *lentils;* "la męnte," *the mind,* "le menti," *the minds;* "la corręnte," *the current,* "le corręnti," *the currents;* "la sorgęnte," *the source,* "le sorgęnti," *the sources.*

402. Words ending in *me* are masculine. Ex. "il fiume," the river, "i fiumi," the rivers.

Except "l'arme," *the weapon,* "le armi," *the weapons;* "un' uniforme," *a uniform;* and "la fame," *hunger.*

403. Words ending in *one* are masculine. Ex. "Il balcone," the balcony, "i balconi," the balconies.

Except "la canzone," *the song,* "le canzoni," *the songs,* "la tenzone," *the combat,* "le tenzoni," *the combats.*

404. Concrete nouns (*i.e.,* names of objects) ending in *ione* (about twenty) are masculine. Ex.

L'arcione,	the saddle-bow,	gli arcioni,	the saddle-bows.
Il battaglione,	the battalion,	i battaglioni,	the battalions.
Il bastione,	the bastion,	i bastioni,	the bastions.
Il padiglione,	the pavilion,	i padiglioni,	the pavilions.

405. Abstract nouns (*i.e.,* names of things that have no substance) ending in *ione* (about three hundred) are feminine. Ex.

L'azione,	the action,	le azioni,	the actions.
La conversazione,	the conversation,	le conversazioni,	the conversations.
La discussione,	the discussion,	le discussioni,	the discussions.

406. Nouns ending in *udine* (about twenty) are feminine. Ex.

L'abitudine,	habit,	la solitudine,	solitude.
La mansuętudine,	meekness,	l'incudine,	the anvil.

WORDS ENDING IN I.

407. Nouns ending in *i* are masculine, and do not change form in the plural. Ex. "Il brindisi," *the toast,* "i brindisi," *the toasts;* "il dì," *the day,* "i dì," *the days;* "il lunedì," *the Monday,* "i lunedì," *the Mondays;* "un barbagianni," *an owl.*

Except a few words (about twelve) derived from the Greek, which are feminine. Ex.

La metropoli,	the metropolis,	le metropoli,	the metropolis.
L'analiṣi,†	the analysis,	le analiṣi,	the analysis.
La criṣi,	the crisis,	le criṣi,	the crises.
La dioceṣi,	the diocese,	le dioceṣi,	the diocese.

---

* An *e*, dotted thus ę, has the broad sound of the *a* in the word *gate*.
† An *s*, dotted thus ṣ, has the soft sound of the *s* in the word *rose*.

WORDS ENDING IN O.

408. All words ending in *o* are of the masculine gender, and form their plural by changing the *o* into *i*. Ex.

Il tempo,	the time,	i tempi,	the times.
Il trono,	the throne,	i troni,	the thrones.
Il palazzo,	the palace,	i palazzi,	the palaces.

Except "la mano," *the hand*, "le mani," *the hands*, and "eco,"* *the echo*.

ON THIS POINT THE FOLLOWING OBSERVATIONS ARE NECESSARY:—

409. Nouns ending in *co* and *go* take an *h* in the plural. Ex.

Il bosco,	the wood,	i boschi,	the woods.
Il fuoco,	the fire,	i fuochi,	the fires.
Il manico,	the handle,	i manichi,	the handles.
Il castigo,	the punishment,	i castighi,	the punishments.

410. Notice however that the following words do not require any *h* in their plural form. Ex.

Il Greco,	the Greek,	i Greci,	the Greeks.
Il porco,	the pig,	i porci,	the pigs.
L' amico,	the friend,	gli amici,	the friends.
Il nemico,	the enemy,	i nemici,	the enemies.
Il medico,	the doctor,	i medici,	the doctors.
Il portico,	the portico,	i portici,	the porticoes.
Il mosaico,	the mosaic,	i mosaici,	the mosaics.

411. As a general rule nouns ending in *io* form their plural by merely cutting off the final *o*. Ex.

L' occhio,	the eye,	gli occhi,	the eyes.
Il viaggio,	the voyage,	i viaggi,	the voyages.
Il fornaio,	the baker,	i fornai,†	the bakers.

412. Notice, however, that the following words end with two *ii* in the plural to distinguish them from similar words ending with one *i* only in the plural, and having quite a different meaning:—

I tempii,	the churches,	*to distinguish it from*	i tempi,	the times.
I principii,	the principles,	„ „ „	i principi,	the princes.
I giudicii,	the judgments,	„ „ „	i giudici,	the judges.
Gli omicidii,	the murders,	„ „ „	gli omicidi,	the murderers.
I beneficii,	the benefices,	„ „ „	benefici,	benevolent (plur.).
Gli atrii,	the porches,	„ „ „	atri,	black (plur.).

413. * "Eco" was originally the name of a girl. Some writers make "eco" masculine; in the plural, however, it is always "gli echi," *the echoes*.

414. † Formerly the words ending in *aio* in the singular were made to end in the plural in *aj*, as *fornaj*.

415. Nouns that have an accent over the ì (ìo) in the singular, form their plural by changing the ìo into ii. Ex.

Lo zìo,	the uncle,	gli zii,	the uncles.
Il rìo,	the brook,	i rii,	the brooks.
Il pendìo,	the slope,	i pendii,	the slopes.
Il leggìo,	the reading-desk,	i leggii,	the reading-desks.

WORDS ENDING IN U.

416. There are only a few words in Italian ending in ù; they are feminine and do not change form in the plural. Ex.

La virtù, virtue. le virtù, virtues.

Except "il ragù," *stewed meat*, which is masculine, and has for plural "i ragù," *stewed meats*.

417. The following nouns, indicating parts of the human body, may end in the plural either in *i*, and be masculine, or in *a*, and be feminine.*

Il ciglio,	the eyebrow,	i cigli *or* le ciglia,	the eyebrows.
Il labbro,	the lip,	i labbri *or* le labbra,	the lips.
Il braccio,	the arm,	i bracci *or* le braccia,	the arms.
Il gomito,	the elbow,	i gomiti *or* le gomita,	the elbows.
Il dito,	the finger,	i diti *or* le dita,	the fingers.
Il ginocchio,	the knee,	i ginocchi *or* le ginocchia,	the knees.
Il calcagno,	the heel,	i calcagni *or* le calcagna,	the heels.

EXERCISE XLI.

Chronology (328) and (337) geography are the eyes† (411) of history (328). Spain produces lemons, oranges, and olives in great abundance. Poets (328) compare cheeks (392) to roses, eyes to stars, hands (408) to lilies, and teeth to pearls. One must (307) know (364) mathematics‡ (225) to understand astronomy thoroughly. I admire the theatres (408), fountains, statues, galleries, and gardens of this beautiful city. History proves that (che) philosophers (328) have always been preceded by (269, 270) poets, and (by the) painters. The rose is the queen of flowers, and the emblem of (328) beauty. We have visited the principal cities (396) of Italy. The earth presents on its surface, heights, (137, 389) hollows, precipices, (411) volcanoes, seas, marshes, rivers, (402) forests, and fields. These men are not (125) French; they are German (409); three are sailors (411), the others are workmen.

---

418. * The words "anello," *ring*, "castello," *castle*, "filo," *thread*, "urlo," *howling*, and a few others, may end in the plural either in *i* or in *a*.

† The student is advised to look for the translations of the words in the vocabulary at the end of this grammar before applying the rules bearing on them in the exercises.

419. ‡ Mathematics, statistics, politics, are generally translated into Italian by "La matemàtica, la statìstica, la polìtica."

IRREGULARITIES IN THE GENDER AND NUMBER OF NOUNS.

420. The following nouns have two meanings, and for each meaning there is a different plural:—

IL MEMBRO, the member. I MEMBRI, the members (of a society); and LE MEMBRA, the limbs of the body.

IL GESTO, the gesture. I GESTI, the gestures of an orator, of an actor; and LE GESTA, the exploits of a hero.

IL FRUTTO, the fruit, the result. I FRUTTI, the results; also the fruits of the same plants; and LE FRUTTA, fruits of various kinds (dessert).

IL MURO, the wall. I MURI, the walls of a house, of a garden, of a park; and LE MURA, the walls of a town.

IL CARRO, the chariot, the cart. I CARRI, the chariots; and LE CARRA, the carts, cart-loads.

L'OSSO, the bone. GLI OSSI, the bones (any bones); and LE OSSA, the human bones.

IL CORNO, the horn. I CORNI, the horns (wind instruments); and LE CORNA, the horns of an animal.

IL RISO, the rice, the laugh. I RISI, the rice (an Italian dish); and LE RISA, the plural of laugh.

IL LEGNO, the wood, the carriage, the ship. I LEGNI, the woods, the carriages, the ships; and LE LEGNA, firewood.

IL MAGO, the magician, or the wise man (of the East). I MAGHI, the magicians; and I MAGI, the wise men (of the East).

421. The following nouns in the singular end in *o*, and are masculine, in the plural end in *a*, and are feminine:—

L'uovo,*	the egg,	le uova,	the eggs.
Il miglio,	the mile,	le miglia,	the miles.
Il paio,	the pair,	le paia,	the pairs.
Lo staio,	the bushel,	le staia,	the bushels.
Il grido,	the cry,	le grida,	the cries.
Il centinaio,	the hundred,	le centinaia,	the hundreds.
Il migliaio,	the thousand,	le migliaia,	the thousands.

* Notice that an *o* preceded by a *u* has always the broad sound of the *o* in the word *orphan*.

422. Words ending in *ie** are feminine, and do not change form in the plural. Ex.

La specie,   the species, kind,   le specie,   the species, kinds.
La superficie,   the surface,   le superficie,   the surfaces.

Except "la moglie," *the wife*, which makes in the plural "le mogli."

423. The following nouns are irregular in the plural:—

Dio,   God,   gli dei,   the gods.
L'uomo,   the man,   gli uomini,   the men.
Il bue,   the ox,   i buoi,   the oxen.

424. The following words have two meanings, and two genders:—

"Il tema," means *the exercise;*   "la tema," means *fear.*
"Il fine," means *the aim, scope;*   "la fine," means *the end.*
"Un margine," means *a margin;*   "una margine," means *a scar.*
"Un dramma," means *a drama;*   "una dramma," means *a drachm.*
"Un pianeta," means *a planet;*   "una pianeta," means *a priest's cope.*

425. Observe that the words "la fame," *hunger;* "la sete," *thirst;* "la gioventù," *youth;* "la servitù," *servants, slavery;* "l'udito," *the hearing;* "il miele," *honey;* "il fieno," *hay;* "la stirpe," *race, family,* and the names of virtues, vices, and metals are only used in the singular. Ex. "La probità," *probity,* "la modestia," *modesty,* "la superbia," *pride,* "l'oro," *gold,* "l'acciaio," *steel,* &c., are only used in the singular.

426. The following words are only employed in the plural:—

Gli annali,   the annals.   Le molle,   the tongs.
Le forbici, }   the scissors.   Le stoviglie,   the crockery-ware.
Le cesoie, }   Le spezie,   the spices.
Le nozze,   the wedding.   L'esequie,   the obsequies.

EXERCISE XLII.

The fruit (420) for dessert is (are) on the side-board. The Jupiter of Homer was the first among the gods (88, 423) of mythology. The games (409) and exercises practised by the Greeks, were good for the health of the body, and (for) the strength of the limbs (420). I have bought two pairs (421) of boots, one for Mary, and one for my sister Elizabeth. A friend has sent me (193) a basket of eggs (421). Climate (328, 397) has great influence on the character of (328) men. I have corrected your exercises.

---

427. * Notice that words ending with an accented vowel (see rules 396, 400, and 416), words ending in *i* (see rule 407), and words ending in *ie* (see rule 422) do not, as a rule, change form in the plural. Also that "re," *king* (which was formerly accented) has the same form in the singular and in the plural.

LESSON XXI.

ON ITALIAN AND ENGLISH COMPOUND NOUNS.

On Italian Compound Nouns.

428. The number of Italian compound words is very limited, and the order of the words in them is seldom reversed. *Most* of them are of the masculine gender, and form the plural of the words of which they are composed according to the sense. Ex.

Singular.		Plural.
Un capọlavoro,*	a masterpiece,	dei capilavori.
Un capocaccia,	a chief hunter,	dei capicaccia.
Una ferrovia,	a railway,	delle ferrovie.
Un bassọrilievo,	a bas-relief,	dei bassirilievi.
Un capọgiro,	a fit of giddiness,	dei capọgiri.
Un arcọbaleno,	a rainbow,	degli archibaleno.
Uno spazzacamino,	a chimney-sweeper,	degli spazzacamini.
Madreperla,	mother-of-pearl,	delle madripẹrle.

429. When the first of the two words in a compound noun is Greek or Latin, or has lost the vowel ending, the second word alone is inflected. Ex.

Singular.		Plural.
Un mọnọsillabo,	a monosyllabic word,	dei mọnọsillabi.
Un viceconsolo,	a vice-consul,	dei viceconsoli.
Un cavọlfiore,	a cauliflower,	dei cavọlfiori,

On English Compound Nouns.

430. English Compound Nouns belong to three classes:—

The first class contains such nouns as *straw hat*, *schoolmaster*, *moonlight*, in which one of the two words qualifies the other, with which it has affinity or connection. In translating these compound nouns into Italian, the order of words must be reversed and the preposition "di," only, or (if the article is required, see pages 22, 93) "del," "dello," &c., is placed between the words. Ex.

Un maẹstro di scuola,	a schoolmaster.
Una casa di campagna,	a country-house.
Un mercante di vino,	a wine-merchant.
I raggi del sole,	the sunbeams.
Le stelle della mattina,	the morning-stars.

---

* An *o*, dotted thus ọ, has the broad sound of the *o* in the word *orphan*.

431. The second class of English compound nouns includes such nouns as *writing-paper, dining-room,* in which the first noun expresses the use or destination of the second noun. In translating these compound nouns into Italian, the order of the words must be reversed, and the preposition " da " must be placed between the two words. Ex.

    Carta da scrivere,   writing-paper.
    Una sala da pranzo,   a dining-room.
    Una spazzola da panni, a cloth-brush.
    Una bottiglia da vino,   a wine-bottle.
    Una vesta da camera,   a dressing-gown.

432. The third class of English compound nouns includes such nouns as *steam-boat, wind-mill,* in which the first noun denotes the means by which the object expressed by the first noun acts. In translating these compound nouns, the order of the words is inverted, and the preposition " a " placed between the two words. Ex.

    Un batello a vapore,   a steam-boat.
    Un mulino a vento,   a wind-mill.
    Un bastimento a vela,   a sailing-vessel.

433. No positive rule can be given for the formation of the following expressions, and the like :—

    L' Ufficio della Posta,   the post-office.
    Il mercato del fieno,   the hay-market.
    Bei campi a frumento, beautiful corn-fields.

EXERCISE XLIII.

Do you (122) like my brother's works? I look upon them as master-pieces (428). Give me pen and ink (inkstand), a sheet of writing paper (431), and an envelope. I want (volere) (307) to write to the director of this railway. Last night I met (Past Def.) William at my brother's;† he seemed (Imperf. Ind.) satisfied with (266) the result of his examination. How do you like your new house? I do not like it much; the dining-room (431) is very dark, the bed-rooms are small, and the ground-floor is gloomy. Where did you buy (have you bought) this chimney-piece? (430) I bought it (180, 193) at Johnstone's.† Where have you been? (149, 123) I have been to (the) market, to buy three cart-loads (420) of fire-wood. Where is the pincushion? It is on the work-table, (431) near my sister's leather bag (430). We went to (207) America in a steam-boat (432), and came back in a sailing-vessel.

---

434. † The expressions *at my brother's, at Charles',* meaning *at the house of,* are translated into Italian " da mio fratello," " da Carlo," or " a casa di mio fratello," &c. But expressions such as *at Johnstone's,* are translated into Italian by " nel negozio, *or* nella bottega di Johnstone," when J. keeps a shop for selling goods (linen, furniture, &c.), and by " all' Albergo," *or* " al caffè Johnstone," when J. keeps a hotel, or a *café.*

LESSON XXII.
ON THE ALTERATION IN THE MEANING OF WORDS BY MEANS OF SUFFIXES.

435. The Italians give the names of "Accrescitivi," (*augmentatives*), "Diminutivi," (*diminutives*), and "Peggiorativi," (*depreciatives*), to certain suffixes, which, like the English *ish*, alter or modify the meaning of nouns, adjectives, and even adverbs. The Italian language is very rich in suffixes, which modify in a variety of ways the idea expressed by the primitive term, and are of great use in adding expression to words. Only the principal suffixes will be given here.

"Accrescitivi."

436. The principal Italian "accrescitivi" are "one," "ona," "otto" and "otta."

437. The suffixes "one" and "ona" denote bigness, as well as stoutness. Ex.

    Un libro,   a book,   un librone,   a big book.
    Un uomo,   a man,   un omone,*   a tall, stout man.
    Un cane,   a dog,   un cagnone,†   a large dog.

438. On this point it is to be observed that when a feminine noun takes the suffix *one* it becomes masculine. Ex.

    Una strada, a street,   uno stradone,   a large road.
    Una donna, a woman,   un donnone,   a big, stout woman.

439. But adjectives take both the forms of the suffix, otherwise they might be ambiguous. Ex.

    Una vecchia, an old woman, una vecchiona, a big, old woman.

440. The suffixes "otto," "otta," indicate somewhat of an increase in the ordinary size, as well as vigour. Ex.

    Un ragazzo, a boy,   un ragazzotto, a fine strong lad.

441. The Italian "diminutivi" are divided into two classes:— the "diminutivi-vezzeggiativi," (*endearing*), and the "diminutivi-dispregiativi" (*depreciating*).

"Diminutivi-vezzeggiativi."

442. The principal "diminutivi-vezzeggiativi" are "ino," "ina," "olino," "olina," "etto," "etta," "ello," "ella," "erello," "erella," "icello," "icella," "oncino," and "oncina,"‡ which indicate affection, endearment, as well as smallness. Ex.

    Un fiume,   a river,   un fiumicello,   a nice little river.
    Un pesce,   a fish,   un pesciolino,   a nice little fish.
    Un vecchio, an old man, un vecchierello, a dear little old man.

---

443. * The word "uomo" loses its first letter, *u*, when it takes a suffix.

444. † The word "cane" takes an euphonic *g* before the *n* when it takes a suffix, except before "ino," when the *g* is not inserted. as "un canino," *a nice little dog.*

‡ Discrimination and taste must be had in using the "vezzeggiativi."

445. On this point it is to be observed that many feminine nouns become masculine when they take the suffix " ino." Ex.
Una tavọla, a table, un tavọlino, a nice little table.

446. The suffixes in the following words are often used but cannot be easily classified.
Arboscẹllo* (from " albero," tree), a little tree, a shrub.

" DIMINUTIVI-DISPREGIATIVI."

447. The principal " diminutivi-dispregiativi " are " uccio," " uccia," " uzzo," " uzza," " ọnzolo," " ọnzola," which indicate despicable pettiness. Ex.
Una stanza, a room, una stanzuccia, a small dirty room.

448. On this point it is to be observed that the suffixes " uccio," " uccia," appended to Christian names signify endearment, and *not* contempt. Ex.
Carluccio mio ! My dear little Charley !

" PẸGGIỌRATIVI."

449. The principal Italian " pẹggiọrativi " are " accio," " accia," " azzo," " azza," which signify contempt for worthlessness. Ex.
Uno cappẹllo, a hat, un cappẹllaccio, an ugly, dirty hat.

450. The suffixes " aglia " and "ame," signify plenty but of no value. Ex.
La canaglia (from " cane," dog), the rabble.
Gẹntaglia (from " gẹnte," people), vulgar people.
Ossame (from " ọsso," bone), a heap of bones.

451. The suffixes in the following words are often used but cannot be easily classified.
Un poẹtastro (from " poẹta," poet), a bad poet.
Una casipọla (from " casa," house), a hovel.
Un libẹrcọlo (from " libro," book), a paltry little book.
Una fiẹrucọla (from " fiẹra," fair), an insignificant fair.

452. Sometimes two suffixes are added to one noun. Ex.
Un librẹttino, a nice little book, Un violoncẹllo, a violoncello.
Un ruscẹllettino, a streamlet, Un ọmaccione, a big, nasty man.

453. Some of the above-mentioned suffixes can be added to adjectives. Ex.

Ricco,	rich,	riccone,	very rich.
Fresco,	fresh,	freschetto,	rather fresh.
Rosso,	red,	rossiccio,	reddish.
Amaro,	bitter,	amarastro,	bitterish.

454. Some of the above-mentioned suffixes can be added to adverbs. Ex.

Bẹne,	well,	bẹnone,	very well.
Bẹne,	well,	bẹnino,	pretty well.

† An *e*, dotted thus ẹ, has the broad sound of the *a* in the word *gate*.

ON COLLECTIVE NOUNS.

455. There are two sorts of collective nouns, the *collective general*, and the *collective partitive*.

456. The *collective general* represents the whole collection, as " il pọpolo," *the people*, " l'armata," *the army*, " la flọtta," *the fleet*, " la famiglia," *the family*, &c., and verbs, adjectives, and pronouns referring to it are inflected as if they were used with a noun in the singular. Ex.

Il pọpolo* inglese mantiẹne i suọi diritti politici. — The English people maintain their political rights.

457. The *collective partitive* represents only a portion of the collection, as " un'armata," *an army*, " una moltitudine," *a multitude*, &c., and, as a rule, verbs, adjectives, and pronouns used in the sentence are inflected according to the noun which follows the *collective partitive*.† Ex.

Una piccọla armata di soldati ẹurọpẹi conquistarono le Indie. — A small army of European soldiers conquered India.

EXERCISE XLIV.

Where did you buy (have you bought) that (152) huge book? (437) I bought it at Hachette's (434). I caught (180) this pretty little bird in its nest, in the trunk of a large tree, (437) near your uncle's farm. I am astonished to see you (122, 198) wearing (314) that horrid Spanish hat (177, 449). I wear it because it is light and comfortable. Take‡ (122) these pretty little books, and put them (201) on Elizabeth's little table. This morning we walked (Past Indef.) four miles (421); we went as far as the beautiful little bridge (442) near the village inn. Take away‡ this cur; (444, 447) I hate it. Every evening we take a walk‡ along a small stream, in which a thousand pretty little fishes swim about. How do you do (see page 89) to-day? Very well! (454) I thank you. The committee (456) made a report of the case, and sent it to the king. Under his despotic government the people (456) suffered (Past Def.) many hardships.

---

* See rule 63, to understand the meaning of the letters in the darker type.

458. † Notice, however, that when the Italians employ a collective noun, and want to express the action of the collection, *as a whole*, all words must be inflected as if they were used with a noun in the singular. Ex.

Una fọlla di nẹmici ci apparve all'improvviso, — A crowd of enemies appeared suddenly before us.

459. ‡ *To take* is translated into Italian by " Prẹndere." But *to take*, in the sense of *to lead*, is translated by " condurre," " menare." *To take away*, is translated by " Pọrtar via," " monar via," and *to take off*, by "lẹvare." *To take a portrait* is " Fare un ritratto." *To take a walk*, " Fare una passeggiata."

8

IMPORTANT POETICAL FORMS OF NOUNS.*
(Arranged Alphabetically.)

"Acciaro" is used in poetry for "acciaio," *steel;* "aëre" for "aria," *air;* "aura" and "auretta" for "venticello," *breeze;* "agone" for "combattimento," *combat;* "aita" for "aiuto," *help;* "angue" for "serpente," *serpent;* "albore" for "alba," *dawn;* "albore" and "arbore" for "albero," *tree;* "alma" for "anima," *soul;* "amistà" for "amicizia," *friendship;* "aquilone" for "vento settentrionale," *north-wind;* "ara" for "altare," *altar;* "augei" for "uccelli," *birds;* "austro" for "vento del sud," *south-wind;* "avello" for "sepoltura," *tomb;* "avolo" for "nonno," *grandfather;* "belva" for "fiera," *wild beast;* "beltà" for "bellezza," *beauty;* "borea" for "vento settentrionale," *north-wind;* "brando" for "spada," *sword;* "bufera" for "turbine," *hurricane;* "calle" for "sentiero," *path;* "capei" "chiome" and "crine" for "capelli," *hair;* "cittade" for "città," *city;* "clade" for "strage," *slaughter;* "corsiero" "corridore" "destriero" and "palafreno" for "cavallo," *horse;* "desìo" for "desiderio," *desire;* "delubro" for "tempio," *church;* "die" for "dì," *day;* "diva" for "dea," *goddess;* "dritto" for "diritto," *right;* "dumi" for "spini," *thorns;* "etere" and "etra" for "cielo," *sky;* "euro" for "vento dell'est," *east-wind;* "face" for "fiaccola," *torch;* "favella" for "lingua," *language;* "Filomela" for "rosignolo," *nightingale;* "gaudio" for "allegrezza," *joy;* "gioventude" for "gioventù," *youth;* "gota" for "guancia," *cheek;* "guiderdone" for "ricompensa," *reward;* "imago" for "imagine," *image;* "iri" and "iride," for "arcobaleno," *rainbow;* "labbia" for "labbra," *lips;* "lai" for "lamenti," *laments;* "lari" for "dei," *gods;* "larva" for "spettro," *spectre;* "lemuri" for "spettri," *hobgoblins;* "lena" for "forza," *strength;* "magione" for "casa," *house;* "monile" for "collana," *necklace;* "motto" for "parola," *word;* "nappo" for "tazza," *cup;* "noto" for "vento del sud," *south-wind;* "numi" for "dei," *gods;* "occaso" for "sera," *evening;* "orto" for "mattina," *morning;* "ostello" for "albergo," *abode;* "pelago" for "oceano," *ocean;* "pietà" for "compassione," *pity;* "prence" for "principe," *prince;* "Progne" for "rondine," *swallow;* "quadrello" for "freccia," *arrow;* "rai" for "raggi," *rays;* "rìo" for "ruscello," *brook;* "salma" for "corpo," *body;* "silva" for "foresta," *forest;* "speme" for "speranza," *hope;* "spirto" for "spirito," *spirit;* "stame" for "filo," *thread;* "strale" for "freccia," *arrow;* "stelo" for "gambo," *stem of a plant;* "suora" for "sorella," *sister;* "talamo" for "letto," *bed;* "vallo" for "fortificazione," *fortification;* "veglio" for "vecchio," *old man;* "vespero" for "sera," *evening;* and "vessillo" for "bandiera," *flag.*

---

* The poetical forms of verbs are given on page 92.

LESSON XXIII.
ON QUALIFICATIVE ADJECTIVES.

460. In Italian, qualificative adjectives agree in gender and number with the nouns they qualify; they end either in *o* or in *e*.*

461. Adjectives ending in *o*, become feminine by changing the *o* into *a*. They form their plural by changing the *o* into *i* for the masculine, and by changing the *a* into *e* for the feminine.† Ex.

Il marito è ricco e generoso, e la moglie è bella e modesta.	The husband is rich and generous, and the wife beautiful and modest.
Questi uomini sono ricchi e generosi, e le loro mogli sono belle e modeste.	These men are rich and generous, and their wives are beautiful and modest.

462. Adjectives ending in *e*, serve for both genders. They form their plural by changing the *e* into *i*. Ex.

Il principe è illustre e potente, e la principessa è amabile, ed oltremodo intelligente.	The prince is illustrious and powerful, and the princess is amiable and exceedingly clever.
Questi nobili sono illustri e potenti, e le loro spose sono amabili, ed eleganti.	These noblemen are illustrious and powerful, and their wives are amiable, and elegant.

463. In Italian, when an adjective qualifies two or more nouns, it is put in the plural form, and when the nouns are of different gender, the plural adjective agrees with the masculine. Ex.

Il padre e il figlio sono cattivi ed orgogliosi, mentrechè la madre e la figlia sono buone e cortesi.	The father and son are wicked and proud, whilst the mother and daughter are good and courteous.
Trovammo i contadini e le loro mogli assai industriosi e civili.	We found the peasants and their wives very industrious and civil.

---

464. * "Pari," *equal*, "impari," *unequal*, and "dispari," *unlike, uneven, odd*, are the only Italian adjectives that end in *i*, in the singular; they have only one termination for both genders and numbers. Ex. "Una vostra pari," *such a person as you are*.

465. † Adjectives ending in "co," "go," "ca," "ga," in the singular, *as a rule*, form their plural in "chi," "ghi," "che," "ghe," as "antico," "antichi," "antica," "antiche," *ancient*.

466. Adjectives ending in "io" form their plural by merely cutting off the *o*; as "savio," plural "savi," *wise*. But when the adjective ends in "ìo" the plural ends in "ii"; as "rìo," plural "rii," *wicked*.

467. In Italian there is *no fixed rule* for the position of adjectives; they are placed before or after the nouns they qualify, according to taste, and euphony. Ex.

Un nemico potente, *or* un potente nemico. A powerful enemy.

468. Adjectives denoting colour, shape, taste, physical qualities, or derived from verbs, or names of nations, follow the nouns they qualify. Ex.

Paolo porta un cappello bianco.	Paul wears a white hat.
Le tavole rotonde sono eleganti.	Round tables are elegant.
Mi davano medicine amare.	They gave me bitter medicine.
Un uomo cieco ha l'udito acuto.	A blind man has sharp ears.
Queste sono cose sorprendenti.	These are surprising things.
Leggo un romanzo* francese.	I am reading a French novel.

469. When two adjectives qualify the same noun, if they are short adjectives, they may be placed one before and the other after the noun; but if they are long words, they sound better after the noun. Ex.

Un bel cavallo nero.	A beautiful black horse.
Questa storia è interessante e istruttiva.	This history is interesting and instructive.

470. When there are more than two adjectives, they go after the noun they qualify. Ex.

Un uomo ricco, intelligente e generoso. A rich, intelligent, and generous man.

471. When the adjective is modified by an adverb, both the adverb and the adjective are placed after the noun. Ex.

Sono fanciulli molto intelligenti. They are very intelligent children.

472. Some adjectives vary their significance according as they come before, or after the nouns they qualify; the following are the most important:—

" Un gentiluomo " means *a nobleman*.
" Un uomo gentile " means *a kind man*.
" Un galantuomo " means *a worthy man*.
" Un uomo galante " means *a polite man*.
" Un grand'uomo " means *a great man*.
" Un uomo grande " means *a tall man*.
" Una certa notizia " means *certain news*.
" Una notizia certa " means *news which is authentic*.

---

* A z, dotted thus ẓ, has the soft sound of the *z* in the word *zeal* (50, 53).

ON THE ADJECTIVES "BELLO," "GRANDE," "BUONO," AND "SANTO."

473. The adjective "bello," *beautiful, pretty*, is curtailed of the last syllable, before masculine nouns beginning with a *consonant*, except an *s* "*impure*"; before a vowel it loses the final letter, and takes an apostrophe. The plural of "bello" is "bei," before a word beginning with a *consonant*, and "begli," before a word beginning with a *vowel* or an *s* "*impure*." Ex.

Un bel quadro,	*a fine picture*,	bei quadri,	*fine pictures*.
Un bello scudo,	*a fine shield*,	begli scudi,	*fine shields*.
Un bell'anello,	*a fine ring*,	begli anelli,	*fine rings*.

474. The adjective "grande," *great, tall, large*, loses the final syllable (*de*), before masculine nouns, beginning with a *consonant*, both in the singular and plural.* This elision does not take place before an *s* "*impure*"; before a *vowel*, "grande" drops the final letter and takes in its stead an apostrophe. Ex.

Un gran popolo (21),	*a great people*,	gran popoli,	*great nations*.
Un grande scrigno,	*a large chest*,	grandi scrigni,	*large chests*.
Un grand' elogio,	*a great eulogy*,	grand' elogi.	*great eulogies*.

475. The adjective "buono," *good*, loses the final *o*, before nouns, masculine singular, beginning with a *vowel*, or any *consonant*, except an *s* "*impure*." Ex.

Un buon ammiraglio,	a good admiral.
Un buon temperino,	a good pen-knife.
Un buono scrittoio,	a good writing-desk.

476. "Il santo" means *the saint*, and is a noun.

477. When "santo" means *saint*, and precedes a proper noun of the masculine gender, beginning with any *consonant*, except an *s* "*impure*," it loses the last syllable (*to*). This elision does not take place when "santo" means *holy*. Ex.

Ho veduto la chiesa di San Pietro.	I have seen Saint Peter's.
Il martirio di Santo Stefano.	Saint Stephen's martyrdom.
Ho visitato il santo sepolcro.	I visited the holy sepulchre.

478. * Sometimes "grande" is also curtailed before feminine nouns, both in the singular and plural; as "Una gran disgrazia," *a great misfortune*.

479. A LIST OF IMPORTANT ADJECTIVES.*

Fresco,	fresh, new.	Abile,	clever.
Povero,	poor.	Sordo,	deaf.
Giovine,	young.	Muto,	dumb.
Attempato,	aged.	Idoneo,†	suitable.
Allegro,	cheerful.	Vago,	vague, charming.
Mesto,	sad.	Vezzoso,	} pretty, charming.
Glorioso,	glorious.	Leggiadro,	
Eminente,	eminent.	Brutto,	ugly.
Bravo,	brave, able.	Savio,	wise.
Netto,	clean.	Stolto,	foolish.
Sporco,	dirty.	Oscuro,	dark.
Alto,	high.	Grigio,	grey.
Corto,	short.	Spesso,	thick.
Pieno,	full.	Gentile,	polite.
Vuoto,	empty.	Rozzo,	rude.
Stretto,	narrow.	Cattivo,	bad, wicked.
Largo,	wide, broad.	Forte,	strong.
Pigro,	lazy.	Temerario,	rash.
Leggero,	light, clear.	Avido,	greedy.
Pesante,	heavy.	Rotondo,	round.
Grosso,	large, big.	Ovale,	oval.
Grasso,	fat.	Semplice,	simple.
Magro,	lean.	Finto,	feigned, artificial.

EXERCISE XLV.

Have you seen George's new carriage? Yes, I have (208); it is strong and well made. The glorious productions of the eminent painter Raphael will ever form the delight of mankind. Napoleon I. often wore (Imp. Ind.) a grey (468) coat, and a round hat, with (a) a broad brim. General Garibaldi was riding a beautiful (473, 469) black horse. A great (474) talker is seldom a great speaker. If we had a good (475) telescope we could (304) see the custom-house. A tall man (472) is not always a great man. There is (154) a great difference between a polite (472) man and an honest man. Go (340) and fetch me a jug of warm (468) water. Here it is, (245) on the oval table. Where are you going, Bertha? I am going (179) to Simpson's, (434) to buy some white cotton, and some red wool. I do not like this stair-case; it is dark, and not clean. She writes in a simple (469) and natural style. My aunt has sent me a basket of flowers (348); it contains some red and white (465, 468) pinks, some pretty roses, and several kinds (422) of ferns.

---

* The above List does not contain the adjectives given on the previous pages.

480. † Adjectives ending in *eo* form their feminine by changing the *eo* into *ea*, and their plurals end in *ei* and *ee*. Ex. "Idoneo," "idonea," "idonei," *suitable*.

ON THE WORD "TUTTO."

481. "Tutto," preceded by the definite article, means *the whole*, and is a noun. Ex.

Mi dia il tutto, Signore.	Give me the whole, Sir.

482. "Tutto," meaning *all, every, whole*, is an adjective, variable; it is, *in all cases*, followed by the definite article. Ex.

Tutti gli ufficiali ricevettero la medaglia.	All the officers received the medal.
Tutto il paese era lieto.	The whole country was happy.

483. "Tutto" (or rather "del tutto"), meaning "intieramente," *altogether, quite*, is an adverb. Ex.

Siamo tutto, *or* del tutto convinti.	We are quite convinced.

484. "Tutti quanti," means *the whole of them*. Ex.

Perirono tutti quanti.	The whole of them perished.

ON THE WORD "MEZZO."*

485. "Mezzo" means *middle, way, means*, and is a noun. Ex.

Nel mezzo del giardino.	In the middle of the garden.
Non c'è mezzo di uscire.	There is no way to get out.
Non hanno i mezzi.	They have not the means.

486. When "mezzo" means *half;* it is an adjective, and is variable when it precedes a noun, but remains invariable when it follows it. Ex.

Una mezza libbra di tè.	Half a pound of tea.
Una libbra e mezzo di zucchero.	A pound and a half of sugar.

487. *Half, the half* is translated into Italian by "la metà." Ex.

Me ne dia la metà; il tutto sarebbe troppo.	Give me the half; the whole of it would be too much.
Il terremoto distrusse la metà della città.	The earthquake destroyed half of the city.

ON THE WORD "OGNI."

488. The adjective "ogni" means *each, every;* it is of both genders and can only be used in the singular. Ex.

Ogni paese ha i suoi costumi.	Every country has its own customs.
Ogni signora aveva dei fiori nei capelli.	Every lady had flowers in her hair.

---

* Two *zz*, dotted thus ẓẓ, have the soft sound of the *zz* in the word *muzzle* (52, 53).

ON THE WORD "ALTRO."

489. "Altro," meaning *other*, is an adjective, and agrees in gender and number with the word to which it relates. Ex.

Ho un altra sorella in Italia.   I have another sister in Italy.
Non ha altri libri che questi?   Have you no other books but these?

490. When "altro" is used as a noun, it means *one thing, something else*. Ex.

Altro è il parlar di morte, altro è il morire.   It is one thing to speak of death, but another to die.

491. "Non...altro che" means *nothing else but*. Ex.
Paolo non fa altro che ciarlare.   Paul does nothing but talk.

492. When "altri" is repeated it signifies *some...others*. Ex.

Altri andavano,* altri venivano.   Some were going, others were coming.

493. In the colloquial style "altri" is sometimes used pleonastically after "noi" and "voi." Ex.

Noi altri Italiani amiamo la musica.   We Italians are fond of music.

ON THE WORDS "MOLTO," "TANTO," "ALTRETTANTO," "QUANTO," "TROPPO," AND "POCO."

494. The words, "molto," *much, very;* "tanto," *so much;* "altrettanto," *as much;* "quanto," *how much;* "troppo," *too much;* "poco," *little;* are adjectives, and therefore variable, when they precede a noun. Ex.

V'erano molti uomini e molte donne, ma pochi fanciulli.   There were many men and women, but few children.

495. "Molto," "tanto," "altrettanto," "quanto," "troppo," and "poco," are adverbs when they modify an adjective, a verb or another adverb. Ex.

Queste ragazzine sono molto intelligenti.   These little girls are very intelligent.

496. The expressions "Da quanto tempo," and "Da quanto in qua," mean *How long (up till now).* Ex.

Da quanto tempo studia la lingua italiana? (See rule 277.)   How long have you been studying Italian?

497. The expression "Un poco di," means *A little*. Ex.
Antonio ha un poco di danaro.   Anthony has a little money.

---

* See rule 63, to understand the meaning of the letters in the darker type.

EXERCISE XLVI.

Why do you like the Italian (468) language? I like it because it is sweet and harmonious. The whole (482) country was in a state of agitation. When the clergyman's children saw us, they became (Past Def.) quite (483) cheerful. Let us go into that shop; I have seen there (239, 243) some pretty (473) ribbons and French lace. Here is (245) a pound of good tea; give (122) half (487) of it (240) to your sister. He spent an hour and a half (486) in writing (314) this letter. Louisa does nothing else but (491) sew and embroider. These chickens are large and fat, but the partridges are very lean. My brother has made me a (360) present of some beautiful (473) artificial flowers. How long (496) have you been waiting for (251) us? I have been waiting half (486) an hour. William began again to speak† of his Italian acquaintances.

POETICAL FORMS OF ADJECTIVES.
(Arranged Alphabetically.)

"Algente" is used in poetry for "ghiacciante," *freezing;* "almo" for "che dà animo e vita," *reviving;* "altrice" for "nutrice," *fostering;* "aprico" for "esposto al sole," *sunny;* "boreale" for "settentrionale," *northern;* "arto" for "stretto," *narrow;* "atro" for "nero," *black;* "baldo" for "coraggioso," *courageous;* "corrusco" for "brillantissimo," *very brilliant;* "diro" for "empio," *impious;* "diva" for "come una dea," *godlike;* "eburneo" for "come d'avorio," *like ivory;* "edace" for "divoratore," *devourer;* "ermo" for "solitario," *lonely;* "fedo" for "sporco," *dirty;* "fievole" for "debole," *feeble;* "flavo" for "giallo," *yellow;* "flebile" for "lacrimabile," *tearful;* "ferale" for "funesto," *baneful;* "frale" for "fragile," *fragile;* "immane" for "spietato," *pitiless;* "imo" for "bassissimo," *lowest;* "inulto" for "non vendicato," *unavenged;* "irto" for "irsuto," *shaggy;* "lieve" for "leggiero," *light;* "olezzante" for "profumato," *perfumed;* "prisco" for "primitivo," *primitive;* "protervo" for "arrogante," *arrogant;* "reduce" for "che è di ritorno," *returned from;* "repente" for "subitaneo," *sudden;* "reo" and "rìo" for "colpevole," *guilty;* "romito" for "solitario," *solitary;* "rorido" for "rugiadoso," *dewy;* "truce" for "fiero," *fierce;* "tumido" for "gonfio," *swollen* and *bumptious;* "ultrice" for "vendicatrice," *avenger;* "venusto" for "leggiadro," *charming;* and "vetusto" for "antico," *ancient.*

---

* The poetical forms of verbs and nouns are given on pages 92 and 114.
498. † The expressions *to begin again to speak, to begin again to write,* &c., are translated into Italian by "tornare a parlare," "tornare a scrivere," &c.

LESSON XXIV.

ON THE FORMATION OF ADVERBS FROM ADJECTIVES.

499. Adverbs are invariable and have no fixed place in a sentence, in Italian, but they are generally placed after the verb with which they are connected; when adverbs modify adjectives, or past participles, they precede them. Ex.

Andrea scrive bene.	Andrew writes well.
Matilde parla correttamente.	Matilda speaks correctly.
Questi artisti sono molto bravi.	These artists are very clever.
Filippo era elegantemente vestito.	Philip was elegantly dressed.
Scrive il francese molto bene.	He writes French very well.

500. Some adverbs consist of a single word, as "quando," *when*, "sempre," *always;* others are formed of two or more words, and are commonly called adverbial expressions,† as "all' improvviso," *unexpectedly;* "d'ora in poi," *henceforth.*

501. Many adverbs are formed in Italian by adding "mente" (which means *manner*), to the feminine form of adjectives. Ex.

Generoso,	generous,	generosamente,	generously.
Diligente,	diligent,	diligentemente,	diligently.
Dottissimo,	very learned,	dottissimamente,	very learnedly.

502. When adjectives end in "le" or "re," the *e* must be suppressed in forming adverbs. Ex.

| Facile, | easy, | facilmente, | easily. |
| Particolare, | particular, | particolarmente, | particularly. |

503. The adjectives "chiaro," *clear*, "forte," *hard*, "felice," *happy*, and a few others, are sometimes used as adverbs. Ex.

Parlate chiaro.	Speak clearly.
Egli batte forte.	He strikes hard.
Vivete felice!	Live happily!

504. Adjectives and adverbs may be used in the Positive degree, as "bello," *pretty*, or in the Comparative degree, as "più bello," *prettier*, or in the Superlative degree, as "il più bello," *the prettiest*.

---

* An *s*, dotted thus ṣ, has the soft sound of the *s* in the word *rose*.
† Further on will be found a list of adverbs and adverbial expressions.

COMPARISON OF EQUALITY.

505. Comparisons of equality having reference to adjectives, participles, and adverbs are formed, in Italian, in the following ways:—

First Term.	Second Term.
Così (*or* si), *as* (or *so*)............	come, *as.*
Tanto (*or* altrettanto), *as, as much*........	quanto, *as.* Ex.
Egli è così ricco come mio nipote.	He is as rich as my nephew.
Cesare era tanto valoroso quanto Pompeo.	Cæsar was as brave as Pompey.
Ella scrive così elegantemente come suo fratello.	You write as elegantly as your brother.

506. Comparisons of equality having reference to nouns are formed, in Italian, in the following ways:—

First Term.	Second Term.
Tanta (*or* altrettanta), *as, as much*........	quanta, *as.*
Tanti (*or* altrettanti), Tante (*or* altrettante), } *as many*......	{ quanti, quante, } *as.* Ex.
Non ho tanti amici quanti ne ha mio fratello.	I have not as many friends as my brother has.

507. Comparisons of equality having reference to verbs are formed, in Italian, in the following ways:—

First Term.	Second Term.
Più (*or* quanto più), *the more*.........	più (*or* tanto più), *the more.*
Meno (*or* quanto meno), *the less*.....	meno (*or* tanto meno), *the less.*
Tale, Tali, } *such*............	{ quale, quali, } *as.* Ex.
Più Carlo studia, più desidera di studiare.	The more Charles studies, the more he desires to study.
Ci descrisse la scena tal quale l' aveva veduta.	He described the scene to us such as he had seen it.

508. The first terms "così," "tanto," "tale," may be omitted. Ex.

| Essa non è bella come sua sorella. | She is not so pretty as her sister. |
| Egli non è sapiente quanto lo credevamo. | He is not as learned as we believed him to be. |

509. "Al pari di," *or* "al pari che," *as much as*, and "non meno di," *or* "non meno che," *not less than,* may be used instead of "così...come;" "tanto...quanto." Ex. "Egli fu lodato al par di me." *He was praised as much as I.*

COMPARISONS OF SUPERIORITY AND INFERIORITY.

510. In Italian, the comparative degrees of Superiority and Inferiority are formed by translating the adverbs *more*, by "più"; and *less*, by "meno"; and the conjunction *than*, by "di" or "che."

511. When *more than* and *less than* indicate comparison, and are placed before nouns or adjectives, they are translated either by "più di" *or* "più che," and "meno di," *or* "meno che." Ex.

Carlo è più educato di (che) Pietro.	Charles is more educated than Peter.
Nel decimo quarto secolo l'Italia era più colta di (che) tutte le altre nazioni dell'Europa.	In the fourteenth century Italy was more polished than any other nation of Europe.

512. When *more than* and *less than* indicate comparison, and are placed before personal pronouns, they must be translated by "più di," "meno di," and the personal pronouns must be in the objective form ("me," "te," "lui," &c.). Ex.

Voi siete più ricco di me.	You are richer than I.
Ella è di lunga pezza più dotta di lui.	She is a great deal more learned than he.

513. Notice, however, that when a personal pronoun is followed by a verb (not in the Infinitive) of which it is the subject, *than* is rendered by "che non," "di quel," or "di quello che," and the pronoun is used in the subjective form ("io," "tu," "egli," &c.), as in English. Ex.

Il disegro è più difficile che io non (di quello che) lo credevo.	Drawing is more difficult than I thought.

514. When *more than*, *less than*, do not indicate comparison, they are expressed by "più di," "meno di." Ex.

Egli possiede più di trenta mila lire sterline.	He possesses more than thirty thousand pounds sterling.

515. *Than* must be translated by "che" when the comparison takes place between two verbs in the Infinitive Mood, two nouns, two adjectives, or two adverbs. Ex.

E più difficile saper ascoltare, che saper parlare.	It is more difficult to know how to listen, than to know how to speak.
A New York s'incontrano più Inglesi che Francesi.	In New York one meets more English people than French.
A parer mio, essa è più* vezzosa che bella.	In my opinion, she is rather attractive than beautiful.
È meglio tardi che mai.	It is better late than never.

516. * "Piuttosto" (rather) might be used here instead of "più," thus: "Essa è piuttosto vezzosa che bella." *She is attractive rather than beautiful.*

EXERCISE XLVII.

She is as (505) pretty as her sister, but not so (505) clever. The simplicity of nature is more pleasing than (511) the embellishments of art. Do not (122, 128) walk so fast, walk slower. It is nobler to forgive than (515) to avenge one's self. London has as many (506) inhabitants as Belgium. Shall we go to the Crystal Palace? I think so (271); it is better to go to-day than (515) to-morrow. Give him two guineas; you are richer (512) than I. The twilight in the south is much shorter than in the north. In the first centuries the Romans were more warlike than (515) literary. Wrought iron is much stronger than cast iron; it is less (510) brittle, and much (495) more durable. A feigned peace is more dangerous than open war. It is better to acquit a criminal than (515) to condemn an innocent person.

ON THE SUPERLATIVE DEGREES.

517. Adjectives and adverbs may be raised to the Superlative Relative, or to the Superlative Absolute degree.

ON THE SUPERLATIVE RELATIVE DEGREE.

518. The Superlative Relative is formed by placing "il più," "il meno," before the adjective, or the adverb. Ex.

È il più ricco cittadino di* Londra.
He is the richest citizen in London.

Adolfo è il meno ingegnoso dei tre fratelli.
Adolphus is the least ingenious of the three brothers.

La grazia è la più nobil parte della bellezza.
Grace is the noblest part of beauty.

519. The article may be omitted when "più" and "meno" follow the noun. Ex.

Egli è l'oratore più eloquente dei nostri tempi.
He is the most eloquent orator of our day.

520. The following adjectives form their Comparative, and their Comparative Superlative degrees in two ways:—

Positive.	Comparative.		Superlative Relative.	
Buono, *good*.	Più buono, or migliore,	} *better*.	Il più buono, or il migliore,	} *the best*.
Cattivo, *bad*.	Più cattivo, or peggiore,	} *worse*.	Il più cattivo, or il peggiore,	} *the worst*.
Grande, *great*.	Più grande, or maggiore,	} *greater*.	Il più grande, or il maggiore,	} *the greatest*.

521. * Observe that in Italian after a superlative relative the preposition "di," not "in," is used before names of places.

ON THE DEGREES OF COMPARISON.

Positive.	Comparative.	Superlative Relative.
Piccolo, *small.*	Più piccolo, *or* minore, } *smaller.*	Il più piccolo, *or* il minore,* } *the smallest.*
Alto, *high.*	Più alto, *or* superiore, } *higher.*	Il più alto, *or* il superiore, } *the highest.*
Basso, *low.*	Più basso, *or* inferiore, } *lower.*	Il più basso, *or* il inferiore, } *the lowest.*

Examples.

Il mio libro è più buono, *or* migliore di quello di sua sorella. — My book is better than that of your sister.

È il peggior romanzo ch'io abbia letto. — It is the worst novel I ever read.

522. The following adverbs form the Comparative and Superlative degrees without the help of "più" or "meno."

Positive.	Comparative.	Superlative.
Bene, *well*,	meglio, *better*,	il meglio, *the best.*
Male, *badly*,	peggio, *worse*,	il peggio, *the worst.*
Molto, *much*,	più, *more*,	il più, *the most.*
Poco, *little*,	meno, *less*,	il meno, *the least.*

ON THE SUPERLATIVE ABSOLUTE DEGREE.

523. The Superlative Absolute degree is indicated in several ways in Italian.

524. Adjectives and adverbs can be raised to the superlative absolute degree by changing their final vowel into "issimo," "issima," "issimi," "issime." Ex.

Positive.		Superlative Absolute.	
Buono,	*good*,	bonissimo,	*very good.*
Piccolo,	*little*,	piccolissimo,	*very little.*
Bene,	*well*,	benissimo,	*very well.*
Dottamente,	*learnedly*,	dottissimamente,	*very learnedly.*

525. Adjectives ending in "io" lose these two vowels before the superlative termination "issimo," and those ending in "co" and "go," "ca" and "ga," which take an *h* in the plural also take it before "issimo." Ex.

Savio,	*wise*,	savissimo,	*very wise.*
Ricco,	*rich*,	ricchissimo,	*very rich.*
Largo,	*wide*,	larghissimo,	*very wide.*

526. * In speaking of physical size "più grande," "il più grande;" "più piccolo," "il più piccolo," must be used, and not "maggiore," "il maggiore;" "minore," "il minore." Ex.

La mia casa è più grande che la vostra. — My house is larger than yours.

527. "Maggiore" and "minore" signify also *eldest* and *youngest.* Ex.

Mio fratello maggiore. — My eldest brother.

528. A few adjectives form the superlative absolute in "errimo." Ex.

Misero,	miserable,	miserrimo,	very miserable.
Celebre,	celebrated,	celeberrimo,	very celebrated.
Acre,	bitter,	accerrimo,	very bitter.
Integro,	honest,	integerrimo,	very honest.
Salubre,	salubrious,	saluberrimo,	very salubrious.

529. Sometimes "ottimo," "pessimo," "massimo," "minimo," "sommo," and "infimo," may be employed instead of "bonissimo," "cattivissimo," &c.

530. Adjectives and adverbs can be raised to the superlative absolute degree by translating *very*, or *most*, by the adverbs "molto," "assai," or "oltremodo." Ex.

Egli è molto, assai, *or* oltremodo generoso. He is very generous.

531. Another way of raising adjectives and adverbs to their superlative absolute degree, is to repeat them. Ex.

Ella divenne rossa rossa. She became very red.
Entrarono pian piano. They went very softly.

EXERCISE XLVIII.

This tragedy is very interesting, (471) and very well written. She is taller (512) than you by* three inches. The mosaics (410) of Rome are the most famous (518) in Europe. Write to your brother and tell him (201) to call on me† as soon as possible.‡ I want to go to Paris; all the more so because§ my sister is there also (there is (239) also my sister). She is so kind, amiable, and pretty that|| everybody admires her. My uncle's friend is the richest man in (521) this village. Gold is the purest, the most precious, the most ductile, and after platina, the heaviest of all metals. God's power extends from the lowest (520) abyss of the earth, to the highest (520) parts of the heavens. He is the bravest (518) and ablest general of his time.

---

532. * The English expressions *taller...by, richer...by*, are translated into Italian by "più grande...di," "più ricco...di." Ex. "E più ricco di me, di due mila lire sterline." He is richer than I am, by two thousand pounds.

533. † The expressions *to call on, to go to the house of*, are translated into Italian by "andare da," "passare da." Ex. "Andrò da Giovanni," *I will call on John.*

534. ‡ The expression *as quick as possible* is rendered in Italian by "il più presto possibile."

535. § The expression *all the more so because* is translated into Italian by "tanto più che."

536. || The expressions *so kind that, so amiable that*, &c., are translated into Italian by "così buono che," "talmente buono che," "buono a segno tale che," "amabile a tal segno che," &c. Ex.

E abile a segno tale che fa la mera- He is so exceedingly clever that he ex-
viglia di tutti. cites wonder in everybody.

LESSON XXV.
ON NUMERAL ADJECTIVES.

Cardinal Numbers.		Ordinal Numbers.	
Uno	1.	Primo	1st.
Due	2.	Secondo	2nd.
Tre	3.	Terzo	3rd.
Quattro	4.	Quarto	4th.
Cinque	5.	Quinto	5th.
Sei	6.	Sesto	6th.
Sette	7.	Settimo	7th.
Otto	8.	Ottavo	8th.
Nove	9.	Nono	9th.
Dieci	10.	Decimo	10th.
Undici	11.	Decimo primo‡	11th.
Dodici	12.	Decimo secondo§	12th.
Tredici	13.	Decimo terzo‖	13th.
Quattordici	14.	Decimo quarto	14th.
Quindici	15.	Decimo quinto	15th.
Sedici	16.	Decimo sesto	16th.
Diciassette	17.	Decimo settimo	17th.
Diciotto	18.	Decimo ottavo	18th.
Diciannove	19.	Decimo nono	19th.
Venti	20.	Ventesimo	20th.
Ventuno	21.	Ventesimo primo	21st.
Trenta	30.	Trentesimo	30th.
Quaranta	40.	Quarantesimo	40th.
Cinquanta	50.	Cinquantesimo	50th.
Sessanta	60.	Sessantesimo	60th.
Settanta	70.	Settantesimo	70th.
Ottanta	80.	Ottantesimo	80th.
Novanta	90.	Novantesimo	90th.
Cento*	100.	Centesimo	100th.
Centuno	101.	Centesimo primo	101st.
Mille†	1,000.	Millesimo	1,000th.
Un Milione	1,000,000.	Milionesimo	1,000,000th.

537. * "Cento" does not change in the plural. Ex. "Due cento uomini," *200 men.*
538. † "Mille" does not require the indefinite article before it. Ex. "Mille soldati," *1,000 soldiers,* and is changed into "mila," in the plural. Ex. "Tre mila scudi," *3,000 crowns.*
‡ Or "undecimo." § Or "duodecimo." ‖ Or "Tredicesimo."

ON THE USE OF NUMERAL ADJECTIVES.

539. A nought (*o*) in Italian is translated by "zero;" plural "zeri."

540. The feminine of "uno," *one*, is "una"; but the other cardinal numbers remain invariable. Ex.

Ella ha due libri, ed io ne ho uno.	You have two books, and I have one.

541. "Uno," "una," used as nouns signify *a man, a woman*. Ex.

Ho visto uno che si vanta sempre.	I have seen a man who is always boasting.

542. When the noun is placed after "ventuno," "trentuno," &c., it must be in the singular, as it agrees with "uno;" but when it comes before, it agrees with "venti," and is therefore in the plural. Ex.

"Ventuno* cavallo," *or* "Cavalli ventuno," *twenty-one horses.*

543. In stating the order in which sovereigns, volumes and chapters of books, acts and scenes of plays, follow one another, the *ordinal numbers* (which are variable) are used in Italian as in English, but the article is omitted; and they must agree in gender and number with the noun to which they relate. Ex.

Vittorio Emanuele secondo fu il primo re d' Italia.	Victor Emanuel the second was the first king of Italy.
Scena prima, atto secondo.	Scene the first, act the second.

544. The dates of the month, except the first day, are expressed in Italian by the *cardinal* numbers, preceded by the definite article in the singular or plural; *the first* is expressed by the *ordinal* number. The preposition "di" may be put before the day of the month. Ex.

Quanti ne abbiamo del mese?	What is the day of the month?
Oggi è il primo (di) marzo.	To-day is the first of March.
Colombo scoprì l' America il dodici (di) ottobre, nell'anno, *or simply*, nel mille (e)‡ quattro cento§ novantadue.	Columbus discovered America on (147) the twelfth of October, in the year fourteen hundred and ninety-two.

---

545. * The transposition of the units after the tens is not admissible in Italian; for instance, we never say "due e venti," but "venti due."

546. † *On the second*, &c., are translated into Italian by "i due," or "ai due," or "addì due" (at the day two), &c. Ex. "Londra, addì 20 febbraio, 1892."

‡ The Italians do not usually put the conjunction "e," *and*, between "mille" and "milione" and another number.

547. § *Eleven hundred, twelve hundred*, &c., are rendered in Italian by "mille e cento," "mille e due cento," and *not* by "undici cento," &c.

EXERCISE XLIX.

In the year one (356) thousand and sixty-six, England (330) was conquered by (270) William of Normandy, an (353) event of the greatest (520) importance. I have been reading (179) the "Aristodemo," of Monti, and have learnt by heart scene (543) the fourth, act the first. How old* is your nephew? He will be seventeen on (147) the 5th of next month. How long† will you remain in this city? I shall leave Rome on the 15th (546). Sardinia is (313) one hundred (356) and fifty miles (421) from Italy. Your letter of‡ the the 25th of February (74) reached me on the 1st instant (544). Frederick the second (543) king of Prussia, was a great warrior (474). What is the day (544) of the month? It is the 9th (546).

---

548. Expressions having reference to the hour of the day are rendered in Italian as follows:—

Che ora è? *or* che ora abbiamo?	What o'clock is it?
È un' ora, *or* il tocco.	It is one o'clock.
Sono le due e mezzo.	It is half-past two.
Saranno presto le tre.	It will soon be three o'clock.
A che ora è partito suo fratello?	At what o'clock did your brother leave?
Quando partì erano le undici antimeridiane, ma il suo bastimento non fece vela che alle due pomeridiane.	When he left it was eleven o'clock a.m., but his ship did not set sail before two p.m.
Ora sono le sei meno un quarto, o meno dieci minuti.	Now it wants a quarter, or ten minutes to six.

549. *Ago* is rendered in Italian by "fa;" *this day week*, by "oggi a otto;" *a fortnight*, "quindici giorni;" *this day fortnight*, "oggi a quindici:" *in a month*, "fra un mese," *or* "da qui a un mese." Ex.

Mio fratello lasciò Londra dieci giorni fa, e sarà di ritorno oggi a otto.	My brother left London ten days ago, and will return this day week.
Credo che le elezioni avranno luogo fra un mese.	I think that the elections will take place in a month.

---

550. * The expression *how old is?* is translated into Italian by "quanti anni ha?" or "che età ha?"; and *I am twenty*, &c., by "ho vent'anni," &c.

551. † In speaking of time, *how long* is translated by "quanto tempo."

552. Expressions like *your letter of the 15th instant*, &c., are translated by "La sua (*or* vostra) lettera del quindici corrente."

Distributive and Collective Numbers.

553.
Un terzo,	one third.	Un trimestre,	three months.
La metà,	the half.	Un lustro,	five years.
Il doppio,	the double.	Una volta,	once.
Una coppia,	a couple.	Due volte,	twice.
Una dozzina,*	a dozen.	Ad uno ad uno,	one by one.
Una ventina,*	a score.	A due a due,	two by two.

554. *Both* is translated by "tutti e due," " tutt' e due," " ambo," " ambidue," *or* " ambedue," " entrambo," *or* " entrambi;" and *all three, all four*, &c., are translated by " tutti e tre," " tutti e quattro," &c.; and the substantive which follows them takes the article. Ex.

Tutti e due i fratelli.	Both brothers.
Tutt' e tre le sorelle.	The three sisters.

EXERCISE L.

Send me (201) two dozen (555) of oranges (411), and three dozen of lemons. Neptune, the most (518) distant of the planets (397) takes 164⅔ (164 years and ⅔) (553) years to make its revolution round the sun; Uranus, 84 years and a few (494) days; Saturn, 29½ (486) years; Jupiter, nearly 12 years; Mars, 1 year, 10 months, and 21 days; (542) the Earth, 1 year; Venus, 7 months, and 13 days; Mercury, 2 months, and 27 days. I have just (299) sold my horse for (251) thirty pounds, and ten shillings. What is the height† of this room? It is about twelve feet high,† and seventeen feet long. Out of‡ fifteen thousand inhabitants, there were two thousand (538) killed. We generally breakfast at eight (548), have luncheon at one, and dine at six o'clock. Dante (334), Petrarca (333) and Boccaccio, lived in the fourteenth century,§ they are the most celebrated Italian *trecentisti*.

---

555. * When the words "dozzina," "ventina," "centinaio," "migliaio" (see rule 421), are used in the plural, they are variable. Ex. " Sei dozzine di bicchieri." *Six dozen glasses.*

556. † The expressions *what is the size, height?* &c., are rendered in Italian by " qual' è la grandezza, l'altezza," &c.; and *it is twelve feet high, long*, &c., are translated into " ha dodici piedi di altezza, lunghezza," &c.

557. ‡ *Out of 15,000 men*, &c., is translated by " Di quindici mila uomini," &c.

558. § Instead of " Il decimo quarto," " Il decimo quinto," " Il decimo sesto secolo," *the 14th, 15th, 16th centuries*, the Italians often use the expressions " Il trecento," " il quattrocento," " il cinquecento;" so that a personage who lived in *the fourteenth, fifteenth centuries*, &c., is called "Un trecentista," "un quattrocentista," &c.

LESSON XXVI.

ON POSSESSIVE ADJECTIVES.

559. In Italian the words "mio," "tuo," "suo," "nostro," "vostro," and "loro," are used both as Possessive Adjectives, and as Possessive Pronouns; they are possessive adjectives when they are *used with*, and possessive pronouns when they *stand for*, a noun.

560. In Italian, possessive adjectives agree with the thing possessed, and *not* with the possessor, and are generally preceded by the definite article, as follows:—

SINGULAR.		PLURAL.		
MAS.	FEM.	MAS.	FEM.	
Il mio,	la mia,	i miei,*	le mie,	my.
Il tuo,	la tua,	i tuoi,†	le tue,	thy.
Il suo,	la sua,	i suoi,	le sue,	his, her, its.
Il nostro,	la nostra,	i nostri,	le nostre,	our.
Il vostro,	la vostra,	i vostri,	le vostre,	your.
Il loro,	la loro,	i loro,	le loro,	their.

EXAMPLES.

Il mio amico vuol vendere la sua casa.	My friend wants to sell his house.
I miei vicini hanno perduto il loro cane.	My neighbours have lost their dog.

561. When several nouns follow one another in the same sentence (whether used as subjects or objects), the possessive adjective, as well as the preposition which may accompany it, must be repeated, in Italian, before each of the nouns, if they are already expressed before the first. Ex.

Paolo ha preso i miei colori ed i miei pennelli.‡	Paul has taken my colours and brushes.
Parliamo sempre di voi e delle vostre sorelle.	We always speak of you and your sisters.

---

* Notice that an *e* preceded by an *i* has always the broad sound of the *a* in the word *gate*.

† Notice that an *o* preceded by a *u* has always the broad sound of the *o* in the word *orphan*.

‡ Notice that the *e* in the syllable *ello*, ending nouns and qualificative adjectives, has always the broad sound of the *a* in the word *gate*.

562. When *his*, *her*, do not refer to the subject of the verb, or when there are two nouns of different genders in the same sentence, in order to avoid ambiguity, the pronouns " di lui," *of him*, " di lei," *of her*, *of you*, replace the adjectives " il suo," " la sua." Ex.

Ella bruciò tutte le di lui lettere. — She burnt all his letters.
Egli condusse seco sua sorella e i di lei figli. — He took with him his sister, and her son.

563. The article is omitted before " mio," " tuo," " suo," " nostro," " vostro," (*not* " loro ") when they *immediately* precede nouns of kindred, and rank, in the singular. But when the noun of kindred is in the plural or is preceded by an adjective, or modified by a suffix, the article is prefixed to the possessive abjective. Ex.

Mia madre e le mie sorelle partiranno per Venezia domani. — My mother and sisters will leave for Venice to-morrow.
Furono presentati a Sua Eccellenza* dal Principe. — They were introduced to His Excellency by the Prince.
Il loro padre è in villa. — Their father is in the country.
Fui cortesemente ricevuto dal suo ottimo padre. — I was courteously received by your most excellent father.
Ho dato una cassettina di dolci al vostro fratellino. — I have given a box of sweets to your little brother.

564. The possessive adjectives require the article when they precede the following nouns of kindred :—

Il mio genitore,	*used instead of*		mio padre, *my father.*
La mia genitrice,	,,	,,	mia madre, *my mother.*
Il mio fanciullo, Il mio ragazzo, }	,,	,,	mio figlio, *my son.*
La mia fanciulla, La mia ragazza, }	,,	,,	mia figlia, *my daughter.*
Il tuo germano,	,,	,,	tuo fratello, *your brother.*
La tua germana,	,,	,,	tua sorella, *your sister.*
Il suo sposo, Il suo consorte, }	,,	,,	suo marito, *her husband.*
La vostra sposa, La vostra consorte, }	,,	,,	vostra moglie, *your wife.*

* Notice that the *e* in the termination *enza* has always the broad sound of the *a* in the word *gate*.

565. The possessive adjectives may be placed after the noun, and in this case the article is placed before the noun. Ex.

Se così piace all' Eccellenza vostra.
If it is agreeable to your Excellency.

L' onor mio non permette ciò.
My honour does not permit this.

566. The expressions, *a friend of mine, a sister of yours,* &c., are rendered by "un mio amico," "una vostra sorella," &c., *or* "uno dei miei amici," "una delle vostre sorelle," &c. Ex.

Ho incontrato un vostro amico, sul ponte di Londra.
I met a friend of yours on London Bridge.

567. The relation expressed by the possessive adjectives is elegantly conveyed in Italian by means of the conjunctive pronouns "mi," *to me,* "ti," *to thee,* "gli," *to him,* "le," *to her, or to you.* Ex.

Egli mi è padre (*instead of* Egli è mio padre).
He is my father.

Io non gli sono amico (*instead of* Io non sono suo amico).
I am not his friend.

Io le son figlio (*instead of* Io son suo figlio).
I am her son.

568. When the possessive adjectives *its* and *their* relate to things, and are in the same clause of a sentence with the possessor (noun or pronoun, used as subject), and when they are preceded by any preposition, they are translated into Italian by "il suo," "la sua," "i suoi," "le sue," "il loro," "la loro," "i loro," "le loro." Ex.

Parigi ha le sue bellezze; ammiro lo stile dei suoi pubblici edifizi.
Paris has its beauties; I admire the style of its public edifices.

569. When the possessive adjectives *its* and *their* are *not* in the same clause of a sentence with the possessor, and are *not* preceded by a preposition, they are expressed in Italian by "ne," before the verb, and the article, "il," "lo," "la," &c., before the noun. Ex.

Comprerò questi cavalli, quantunque io non ne conosca la razza, *or* complessione.*
I shall buy these horses, although I do not know their breed (real constitution).

---

570. * "Complessione" means *constitution, physique, temperament. Complexion* is translated into Italian by "carnagione."

EXERCISE LI.

The rose has its (560) beauty, its freshness and its fragrance; but it has also its thorns. The lustre of our ancestors' glory reflects on us, to (225) inspire us (198) to imitate their (560) virtues. One of our horses is so lame (536) that we cannot drive him to-day. That lady is a relation of mine (566). One of my favourite studies is botany. She showed him her (562) splendid picture-gallery, and costly jewels. Cornelia, the mother of the Gracchi, said to her (562) friends as she (mentre) showed them (211) her sons, " These are (245) my jewels." He is a friend of mine, (566) and has just married one of my cousins. I do not like to hear cats mewing* (314) at night. Your sister is prettier (510) than my cousin Jane; she has† fair hair, blue eyes, and a beautiful complexion (570).

---

571. The Italians make use of the definite article, and *not* of the possessive adjective, when the sense *clearly points out* who is the possessor. Ex.

Oggi mi duole il capo.	My head aches to-day.
Diresse le parole alla moltitudine irritata.	He directed his words to the angry multitude.

572. Before a noun indicating mental or physical qualities, or any part of the dress or body, if the action expressed by the verb falls on its subject, the Italians make use of the definite article, and *not* the possessive adjective; and the verb is used reflectively. Ex.

Mi lavo le mani con sapone.	I am washing my hands with soap.
Si è fatto male alla mano destra.	He has hurt his right hand.
Essa si levò subito i guanti.	She took off her gloves at once.
Gaddo mi si gettò piangendo a' piedi. (Dante.)	Gaddo threw himself at my feet weeping.

---

573. * *To mew*, like a cat (gatto), is translated by " Miagolare."
To bark, like a dog (cane) .... " Abbaiare."
To growl, like a dog (cane)..................... " Latrare."
To neigh, like a horse (cavallo) .... " Nitrire."
To bray, like an ass (asino) .... " Ragliare."
To bellow, like an ox (bue) .... " Muggire."
To grunt, like a pig (porcello) .... " Grugnire."
To bleat, like a sheep (pecora) .... " Belare."
To roar, like a lion (leone)..................... " Ruggire."
To howl, like a wolf (lupo)..................... " Urlare."
To crow, like a cock (gallo) .... " Cantare."
To sing, like a nightingale (rosignuolo)...... " Cantare."
To chirp, like a sparrow (passero) .... " Garrire."
To talk, like a parrot (pappagallo) .... " Parlare."
To squeak, like a mouse (sorcio) .... " Squittire."

574. † After the verb " Avere" when particular qualities of the body are mentioned, the definite article is used in Italian. " Ha i capelli biondi." *She has fair hair.*

575. But when the action of the verb is *not* directed to its subject, the English possessive adjective is replaced in Italian by the conjunctive pronouns " mi," *to me*, " ti," *to thee*, " gli," *to him*, " le," *to her*, or *to you*, &c. Ex.

Mi fate sempre male alla mano.   You always hurt my hand.
Il chirurgo gli rimise il braccio, in poco tempo.   The surgeon set his arm, in a very short time.

576. The expression *one's own* is rendered in Italian by " il proprio," " la propria," &c., *or* " il mio proprio," " la mia propria," &c. Ex.

L'ho veduto coi propri, *or* co' miei propri occhi.*   I saw him with my own eyes.

577. In the following cases the definite article is *not* required before the possessive adjectives " mio," " tuo," " suo," &c.

   I. In addressing a person. Ex. " Mio caro." My dear.
   II. In exclamations. Ex. "Oh! miei Signori!" Oh! gentlemen!
   III. In many idiomatic expressions, like the following :—

Ho incontrato una persona di mia conoscenza.   I have met an acquaintance of mine.
Faccio a mio capriccio (voglia *or* senno).   I act according to my whim, (will, or mind).
L'ho salutata da parte vostra.   I gave her your compliments.
E colpa vostra.   It is your fault.
Fabbrico a mie spese.   I am building at my own expense.

ON POSSESSIVE PRONOUNS.

578. The Possessive Pronouns, *mine, thine, his, hers, ours, yours, theirs*, are translated into Italian by the Possessive Pronouns " il mio," " il tuo," &c., " i miei," " i tuoi," &c., which agree in gender and number with the noun to which they relate. Ex.

Mi dia il suo libro, e prenda il mio.   Give me your book, and take mine.
La nostra casa è più grande che la loro.   Our house is larger than theirs.

579. When possessive pronouns are used simply to indicate possession, without limiting the number of persons, or objects, possessed, the article *is not* required before them. Ex.

Questo cavallo è suo.   This horse is his.
Di chi è questo sigillo? È mio.   Whose seal is this? It is mine.
Aspetto vostre lettere.   I expect letters from you.

---

580. * The expressions *to write with one's own hand, to think with one's own mind*, are rendered by " scrivere di propria mano," " pensare di proprio senno."

581. When, in speaking of several persons, animals, or objects, reference is made to something of which each person, animal, or object has *only one*, the Italians always use the name of that thing or object in the singular. Ex.

S'invigoriscono la mente collo studio della filosofia. — They strengthen their minds with the study of philosophy.
Sacrificarono la vita in un' impresa inutile. — They sacrificed their lives in a useless undertaking.

582. The possessive pronouns "il mio," "il tuo," &c., used as nouns, signify *my property, my share*, &c. ; and "i miei," "i tuoi," &c., mean *my friends, relations, supporters, followers*, &c. Ex.

Spendete il vostro, se vi piace. — Spend your own, if you like.
Ho veduto i miei un mese fa. — I have seen my people a month ago.
Lasciò il paese con molti de' suoi. — He left the country with many followers.

EXERCISE LII.

Do you like my (560) books? Yes, I like them (193); they are better (520) than mine. Instead of giving the money to his father, he put (mettersi) it (218) in (572) his own pocket. Your garden is prettier than ours, but our orchard is larger, and better (522) stocked than yours. Henry IV. (543) of France used to play* with his (560) children, carrying them on his (571) back round his royal apartments. Do you buy your clothes ready made?† No; I have them made to order‡ at Johnson's (434). The unfortunate Charles VI. of France passed his (571) time in (278) playing at cards with his attendants. The customs of our ancestors were simpler and healthier than ours (578). The books you have sent to the bookbinder are mine (578) and not yours. He spoils his (572) health by studying too much at night.

---

583. * *To play* (to amuse one's-self) is translated by "Giuocare," *or* "Divertirsi."
To play a game at, by "Giuocare una partita a," *or* "Giuocare a."
To play upon the violin, &c., by "Suonare il violino," &c
To play the part, by "Fare, *or* rappresentare la parte."
To play upon (with guns, &c.), by "Far fuoco su *or* sopra."
To play (speaking of a fountain), by "Zampillare," *or* "Gettare."
To play the fool, by "Fare il pazzo," *or* "Ruzzare."
To play a trick, by "Fare una burla," *or* "celia."
To play on one, by "Prendersi giuoco di." *To play false*, by "Ingannare."

584. † The expressions *ready-made, already written*, &c., are translated into Italian by "bello e fatto," "belli e fatti," "bello e scritto," &c.

585. ‡ *To have a thing done (to order), to have a thing written*, &c., are translated into Italian by "farsi fare," "farsi scrivere," &c.

LESSON XXVII.

ON DEMONSTRATIVE ADJECTIVES.

586. In Italian the words "questo," "cotesto," and "quello," are used both as Demonstrative Adjectives, and Demonstrative Pronouns; they are demonstrative adjectives when they are *used with* a noun, and demonstrative pronouns when they *stand for* a noun.

587. The Demonstrative Adjectives agree in gender and number with the noun with which they are used. They are:—

SINGULAR.		PLURAL.	
Mas. Questo,	} this.	Questi,	} these.
Fem. Questa,		Queste,	
Mas. Cotesto,		Cotesti,	
Fem. Cotesta,		Coteste,	
Mas. { Quello, Quel,	} that.	Quegli, Quei *or* que',	} those.
Fem. Quella,		Quelle,	

588. "Questo," "questa,"* "questi," and "queste,"† precede a noun indicating a person or a thing near the speaker, either with regard to place or time. Ex.

Questo signore e questa signora.   This gentleman and this lady.
Questi scrigni e queste cassette.   These chests and these boxes.

589. "Cotesto," "cotesta," *that*, "cotesti," and "coteste," *those*,‡ precede a noun indicating a person, or an object, near the person spoken to, and distant from the speaker. Ex.

Dove ha ella comprato cotesto bel quadro?   Where have you bought that beautiful picture?
Di chi sono cotesti bei fanciulli?   Whose are those beautiful children?

---

590. * In the colloquial style "stamattina," "stasera," "stanotte," are frequently used instead of "questa mattina," "questa sera," "questa notte."

591. † The poets often use "esto," "esta," "esti," "este," instead of "questo," &c. "Maestro, esti tormenti cresceranno ei dopo la gran sentenza?" (Dante). *Master, will these torments increase after the great judgment?*

592. ‡ "Cotesto," "cotesta," &c., are frequently spelt "codesto," "codesta,' &c.

ON DEMONSTRATIVE ADJECTIVES.

593. "Quello" and "quel," *that*, are used before a noun indicating a person or thing distant from the person who speaks, and also from the person addressed. "Quello" is used before nouns beginning with a vowel,* or an *s* followed by another consonant, and "quel" before nouns beginning with a consonant. Ex.

Quello specchio è rotto in due posti.	That looking-glass is broken in two places.
Quel signore canta bene.	That gentleman sings well.
A quel tempo c'era vino in abbondanza.	At that time wine was plentiful.

594. "Quegli" and "quei" (or "que'") *those*, are used before a noun indicating a person or thing distant from the person who speaks, and also from the person addressed. "Quegli" is used before nouns beginning with a vowel, or an *s* followed by another consonant, and "quei" before nouns beginning with a consonant. Ex.

Quegli uccelli sono di rara bellezza.	Those birds are very beautiful.
Quegli schioppi si fabbricano a Woolwich.	Those guns are manufactured at Woolwich.
Quei ragazzi giuocano tutto il giorno.	Those boys are playing all day long.

595. "Quella" and "quelle" are used before feminine nouns beginning with a consonant; before a vowel they are very often changed into "quell'." Ex.

Quella tela si fabbrica in Irlanda.	That cloth is manufactured in Ireland.
Dove si comprano quelle belle cornici?	Where are those beautiful frames bought?

596. Sometimes the word which ought to follow "questo," "questa," "quello," "quella," is understood. Ex.

In questo (momento) egli arrivò.	At this moment he arrived.
In quella (ora) essa morì.	At that hour she died.

597. Sometimes "questo" and "quello" means *this thing, that thing*, and are nouns. Ex.

Fate questo, vi dico.	Do this, I tell you.

---

598. * Before a vowel, "quello" is very often changed into "quell'." Ex. Quell' arcobaleno è stupendo. That rainbow is magnificent.

599. When several nouns follow one another, in the same sentence (whether used as subjects or objects), the Demonstrative Adjective must be repeated before each of them, when it is expressed before the first. Ex.

Comprerò questi pettini e queste spazzole da capelli.	I will buy these combs and hair-brushes.

EXERCISE LIII.

These (588) cherries and (599) strawberries are ripe, but those (595) pears are not.* Go and (340) fetch me that (593) looking-glass. How much time† did you spend (have you spent) in (to) painting (314) your sister's portrait? I could (sapere) not tell (it) you (198, 218). This money is his (579), and not yours. Give me that (593) thimble, those (594) needles, and that thread. Take off those (589) ugly boots of yours (449, 572); they will lame your feet (572). Have you paid much for (251) these jewels? Yes, I have; I paid (180) two pounds ten shillings for this necklace.

DEMONSTRATIVE PRONOUNS.

600. "Questo,"‡ "cotesto," "quello," "questi," "cotesti," "quelli" (not "quegli," nor "quei"§), are demonstrative pronouns when they are used instead of nouns, and, of course, they agree in gender and number with the noun to which they relate. Ex.

Non voglio il vostro cavallo; voglio questo.	I don't want your horse; I want this one.
Se io fossi in Lei, non comprerei queste carte geografiche; comprerei quelle.	If I were in your place, I would not buy these maps; I would buy those.

601. * When the word *so* is understood in English, it must be translated into Italian by the pronoun *lo*, which always remains invariable.

602. † *Time*, is translated by "tempo." *Time* (of the day), is translated by "ora;" as "A che ora arriva il treno?" *At what time does the train arrive? Time*, meaning *epoch*, is translated by "allora;" as, "Allora era ricco." *Then he was rich. Time*, meaning *season*, is translated by "stagione;" as, "In questa stagione dell'anno." *In this season of the year. Time*, meaning *occasion*, is translated by "volta;" as, "L'ho visto due volte." *I saw him twice.*

603. ‡ The adverbs "qui" and "là" are sometimes put after the demonstrative pronouns, to indicate more forcibly the person or thing referred to. Ex.
 Compri questo qui, e non quello là. Buy this one, and not that one.

604. § "Quei" is however used as a pronoun in expressions like "Quei di Milano." *The men (people) of Milan.* Dante often uses "quei" instead of "colui." Ex.
 E come quei, che con lena affannata. And even as he, who, with panting breath.

605. "Questo" and "quello," "questa" and "quella," "questi" and "quegli," are also used as relative pronouns, meaning *the latter*, and *the former;* "questo" and "quello" should be used with reference *to things;* in speaking of persons "questi" and "quegli" are used, but *only* as subjects, in the masculine singular. Ex.

Ho comprato una grammatica francese e un dizionario tedesco; quella per Filippo, questo per Guglielmo.	I have bought a French grammar and a German dictionary; the former for Philip, the latter for William.
I due più grandi oratori dell' antichità furono Demostene e Cicerone; quegli era greco, questi romano.	The two greatest orators of antiquity were Demosthenes and Cicero; the former was a Greek, the latter a Roman.

ON DEMONSTRATIVE PERSONAL PRONOUNS.

606. THE ITALIAN DEMONSTRATIVE PERSONAL PRONOUNS ARE:—

Costui,	*this man.*	Costei,	*this woman.*	Costoro,	these men. / these women.
Cotestui,* } Colui,	*that man.*	Cotestei, } Colei,	*that woman.*	Cotestoro, } Coloro,	those men. / those women.

607. The above pronouns are used for persons only, and do not refer to any antecedent. When they are used in prose, especially in the colloquial style, they *often* express contempt towards the person or persons alluded to; whilst in poetry they are *often* used in the sense of highest admiration, and even reverence. Ex.

Dimmi, chi è costui?	Tell me who is this man (fellow)?
Sa ella che costoro sono ladri? (Pellico).	Do you know that these fellows are thieves?

"Quando vidi costui (Virgilio) nel gran diserto." (Dante).
  When I beheld him (Virgil) in the great desert.

ON THE INDEFINITE DEMONSTRATIVE PRONOUNS.

608. The demonstrative indefinite pronouns *that* and *this* (meaning *that thing, this thing*), are translated into Italian by "ciò." Ex.

Ciò (69) non mi va a genio.	I do not like that.
Non parliam più di ciò.	Let us speak of that no more.
Da ciò capisco il resto.	From that I understand the rest.

---

609. * There is the same difference in meaning between "costui," "cotestui," and "colui," as there is between "questo," "cotesto," and "quello." (See 587-595).

610. The indefinite pronouns *that, that which, what*, are translated into "ciò che," "quel che," *or* "quello che." Ex.

Ciò che sorprende tutti è l'arrivo del principe.	What surprises everybody is the arrival of the prince.
Quel che dice è vero.	What he says is true.
Tutto quello che* risplende non è oro.	All is not gold that glitters.

611. The indefinite pronoun *what*, meaning *which thing*, is translated into "che," *or* "che cosa." Ex.

Che cosa volete, Francesco?	What do you want, Francis?
A che pensa, Signore?	What are you thinking of, Sir?

EXERCISE LIV.

What (611) do you think of this country?† I like it almost as much as (505, 508) my native country. Of these three horses, this is the one (which)‡ I should prefer. Modesty (328) is to merit, what (610) shadows are to the figures in (di) a painting. We are body and mind; the former (605) should (224, 397) obey, the latter command. That which (610) is superfluous often costs more than that which is necessary. That man, by (con) his (560) extravagance, has not only squandered all his own property, (582) but also that (600) of his wife. I am influenced by (270) love (328) and (by) anger; the former (605) pleads that I should forgive him, the latter that I should punish him. Dante (334) and Shakespeare (333) were two great poets; the former (605) was (Imp. Ind.) an (354) Italian, and the latter an Englishman. I will do all that which (610, 612) depends upon (from) me to obtain that (593) post for you (198). Your sister has just (299) made me a (360) present of this beautiful bunch§ of grapes. That (593) clock is fast,‖ and my (560) watch is ten minutes slow.

---

612. * "Quanto" is often used instead of "tutto quello che." Ex.
  Fa quanto dipende da lui. He does all he can.

613. † *Country* is translated into Italian by "paese" when it means *a territory occupied by a people*. Ex. "L'Italia è un bel paese." *Italy is a fine country*.

614. *Country* is translated into Italian by "campagna," when it means *the country, the fields*. Ex. "Va a passare l'estate alla campagna." *He is going to spend the summer in the country*.

615. *Country* is translated into Italian by "patria," when it means the *fatherland*. Ex. "Amo la mia patria." *I love my native country*.

616. ‡ *The one (which)*, is translated by "quello che," and "quella che."

617. § *A bunch of grapes* is translated by "Un grappolo d'uva;" *a bunch of keys* by "Un mazzo di chiavi;" *a bunch of flowers*, by "Un mazzo di fiori."

618. ‖ In speaking of a clock, or watch, *to be fast* is rendered by "Avanzare," and *to be slow*, by "Star indietro," or "Ritardare."

LESSON XXVIII.

ON RELATIVE PRONOUNS.

619.   THE ITALIAN RELATIVE PRONOUNS ARE:—

SUBJECT.	Che, *or*	il quale, m. s. la quale, f. s. i quali, m. p. le quali, f. p.	*who, which, that.*
DIR. OBJ.	Cui,	*or* il quale, &c.	*whom, which.*
INDIR. OBJ.	Di cui,* A cui, Da cui, Per cui, Con cui, In cui,†	*or* del quale, &c. *or* al quale, &c. *or* dal quale, &c. *or* pel quale, &c. *or* col quale, &c. *or* nel quale, &c.	*of whom, of which, whose.* *to whom, to which.* *from whom, from which.* *for whom, for which.* *with whom, with which.* *in whom, in which.*

620. Both the pronouns "che" ("cui," "di cui," &c.), and "il quale" ("del quale," &c.), are used with reference to persons, animals, and things; but still, when referring to animals or things, "il quale," "del quale," &c., is generally used. Ex.

Il giovine che (*or* il quale) parla.	The young man who is speaking.
Ecco l'albero il quale (*or* che) produsse tanti fiori l'anno passato.	There is the tree which produced so much blossom last year.
Il signore di cui (*or* del quale) le ho parlato.	The gentleman of whom I have spoken to you.
Le farò vedere il fiume dal quale (*or* da cui) tutta questa valle è irrigata.	I will show you the river by which all this valley is watered.

---

621. * When reference is made to things, "di che," "a che," &c., may be used instead of "di cui," "a cui," &c. Ex.

La materia di che parlar dobbiamo è importantissima.	The matter about which we have to speak is most important.

622. † When referring to time "che," instead of "in che," *or* "in cui," is used. Ex.

"Lo dì che (in cui) hanno detto ai dolci amici addio." (Dante).	On the day they said good-bye to their dearest friends.

623. The relative pronoun must always be expressed in Italian, even when it is omitted in English. Ex.

Il ragazzo che vidi non era così grande come mio fratello.	The boy I saw was not so tall as my brother.

624. " Che " as well as " cui " may be used in the accusative ; but when there may be ambiguity between the subject and the object of the phrase, " cui " (which is never used as subject) should be used, and not " che." Ex.

L'individuo cui maltrattò vostro fratello.	The individual whom your brother ill-treated.
L'eroe,* cui tutto il mondo onora.	The hero who is honoured by the whole world.

625. When " di cui " corresponds to *whose*, it is generally placed between the article and the noun with which it is used, and the preposition " di " is omitted. Ex.

La Fiammetta, i cui capelli erano crespi, lunghi e d'oro." (Boccaccio).	Fiammetta, whose hair was crisp, long, and like gold.

626. In poetry, and in the higher style, " onde " is used instead of " di cui," " del quale," &c., " da cui," " dal quale," &c. Ex.

" Amor depose la faretra e l'arco,
Onde (di cui) sempre va carco." (Tasso).
*Love laid down the bow and quiver,
With which he is always armed.*

" Que' begli occhi ond' escon saette." (Petrarca).
Those beautiful eyes whence arrows dart.

627. When referring to persons the " a," of " a cui," is often omitted. Ex.

" Voi, cui (a cui) fortuna ha posto in mano il freno
Delle belle contrade..." (Petrarca).
*You, in whose hands fortune has placed the control
Of the beautiful lands...*

628. When *which, of which, to which*, &c., have for antecedent a clause, or the whole of a foregoing sentence, they are translated by " il che," " del che," " al che," &c. Ex.

Il povero vecchio piangeva amaramente, il che mi commosse oltremodo.	The poor old man was weeping bitterly, which moved me very much.
Lo hanno maltrattato, di che si lagna sempre.	They ill-treated him, of which he always complains.

---

* An *e*, dotted thus ẹ, has the broad sound of the *a* in the word *gate*.

629. The pronouns *he who, she who, the one who, those who, the one that, the one which, those which,* having reference to an antecedent, are relative pronouns, and are expressed by " quello che," " quella che," " quelli che," *or* " quelle che." Ex.

    Ammiro questi giovinetti, specie quello che ha recitato " Il Cinque Maggio" del Manzoni.*
    I admire these youths, particularly the one who recited " The Fifth of May " by Manzoni.

630. But when the words *he who, she who, those who,* do not refer to any antecedent, they are Indefinite Personal Pronouns, and are translated by "colui che" (*or* "il quale"), "colei che" (*or* "la quale"), " coloro che " (" i quali," *or* " le quali "). Ex.

    Colui che le ha detto ciò, si è fatto beffe di Lei.
    He who said that, was making fun of you.

    Coloro che si somigliano si amano.
    Birds of a feather flock together.

631. " Che," " quale," and " quali " are also used as interrogative pronouns ; " che " then means *what,* and " quale," and " quali " mean *which* (of two, or several persons or things). Ex.

    Che lavoro c'è da fare?
    What work is there to do?

    Quale preferite di queste case?
    Which of these houses do you prefer?

632. The exclamations *what! what a!* are translated by "che!" or "quale!" Ex.

    Che bel palazzo! che peccato che non sia abitato.
    What a beautiful palace! what a pity it is not inhabited.

633. The expressions " un non so che," " alcun che," mean *a something or other* (indescribable). Ex.

    Ha "un certo non so che," che mi va a genio.
    There is something or other in him that I like.

634. " Quale " (*or* " quali ")..." quale " (*or* " quali"), mean *one...another, some...others.* Ex.

    Quali andavano, quali venivano, tutti erano affaccendati.
    Some were going, some were returning, all were busy.

635. " Quale " is sometimes used in the sense of *such as.* Ex.

    " E quale è quei che volentieri acquista." (Dante).
    And as he is who willingly acquires.

---

* A z, dotted thus ż, has the soft sound of the *z* in the word *zeal.*

636. When "che" means *that*, it is a conjunction, and is always expressed in Italian, even when it is omitted in English. Ex.

Non credo che abbia alcun diritto di parlare. — I do not think he has any right to speak.

637. "Chè" (whether the accent is marked or not) is often used instead of "perchè," *for, because*. Ex.

"………chè, poder ch' egli abbia,
Non ti torrà lo scender questa roccia." (Dante).
*for, any power that he may have,
Shall not prevent thy going down this crag.*

638. "Che," preceded by a verb used negatively, means *nothing, nothing but, only*. Ex.

Luigi non ha che fare. — Louis has nothing to do.
Non ricevette che lodi; neppure un soldo. — He received nothing but praises; not so much as a half-penny.

639. "Non che," followed by a verb in the Infinitive, is equivalent to the English expression, *not only...but*. Ex.

Non che scrivermi, venne a vedermi due volte. — Not only did he write to me, but he came twice to see me.

640. "Che" is sometimes used instead of "quando," *when*. Ex.

Pietro venne che avevo già finito. — Peter came when I had already finished.

641. "Chè!" *or* "ma chè!" mean the same as *nonsense!* Ex.

Ma chè! non sa neanche leggere. — Nonsense! he cannot even read.

EXERCISE LV.

Which (631) do you like best of those (594) three books? The one that (629) has the illustrations, and is bound in parchment. That lady is Mrs. Trivelli, of whom (619) I spoke (Past Def.) to you yesterday. My sister learns music from the gentleman whom (624) your brother recommended (180) to me (193). The young lady (623) we met last night at Mrs. Jones' (434) has just (299) entered (183) the drawing-room. Which one? (631). The one who (629) spoke French to you. The watch (623) you bought me is broken (rompersi). Not only (639) did he send us the tickets, but he took us to the theatre in his carriage. Historians represent men such as (635) they are poets depict them such as they should be (224).

---

* The straight reading of this sentence is " Non dico che spero trovar perdono; dico che spero trovar anche pietà." *I do not say that I hope to find pardon; I say that I hope to find also pity (sympathy).*

LESSON XXIX.

ON INDEFINITE PRONOUNS.

642. THE PRONOUN "CHI."

Chi,	who, whom, he who, him who.
Di chi,	of whom, whose, of him who.
A chi,	to whom, to him who.
Da chi,	from whom, from him who.
Per chi,	for whom, from him who.
&c.	&c. &c.

643. The pronoun "chi" is both an indefinite and an interrogative pronoun; it is used for persons only, is invariable, and serves for both genders and numbers, it has no need of any antecedent. Verbs employed with "chi" are used in the singular only, except "essere"* which is used in both numbers. Ex.

Chi le ha fatto questo regalo?	Who made you this present?
Chi sono i di lei corrispondenti?	Who are your correspondents?
Sappiamo di chi volete parlare.	We know whom you allude to.
A chi ha dato il biglietto?	To whom did you give the ticket?
Da chi ha ricevuto quest buo‑nat notizia?	From whom did you receive this good news?
Per chi dipinge questo bellissimo quadro?	For whom do you paint this beautiful picture?

644. "Chi"..."chi" mean *one...another, some...others.* Ex.

Chi accorre, chi sguizza tra uomo e uomo, e se la batte. (Manzoni).	One runs up, another sneaks away between man and man, and takes to his heels.

645. "Chi" is often used instead of "colui che," "colei che," "coloro che," especially in proverbial expressions. Ex.

Chi legge, regge.	Knowledge is power.
Chi è in difetto, è in sospetto,	He who is in fault, is in suspicion.
Chi si scusa,‡ si accusa.	He who excuses himself, accuses himself.

---

* See rule 63, to understand the meaning of the letters in the darker type.

† Notice that an *o*, preceded by a *u* has always the broad sound of the *o* in the word *orphan*.

‡ An *s*, dotted thus ṣ, has the soft sound of the *s* in the word *rose*.

"CHIUNQUE," AND "CHICCHESSIA."

646. The Indefinite Pronouns, "chiunque," and "chicchessia" (plural "chicchessiano") mean *whoever*, and can only refer to persons; "chicchessia" is followed by the conjunction "che," and a verb in the Subjunctive Mood. Ex.

Chiunque desiderava parlarle, doveva ottenerne il permesso dal magistrato.
Whoever desired to speak to her, was obliged to get permission from the magistrate.

Ditelo pure a chicchessia che vi piaccia.
Tell it to whomsoever you like.

"CHECCHESSIA."

647. The pronoun "checchessia," means *anything whatever*. Ex.

Datemi checchessia.   Give me anything whatever.

648. "Qualunque," "qualsisia," "qualsivoglia," and their plural forms "qualsisiano," and "qualsivogliano," mean *whatever, whatsoever;* they may refer to things or persons, and are adjectives or pronouns, according as they precede, or stand for a noun. Where they are adjectives they are followed by a verb in the Subjunctive Mood preceded by the conjunction "che." Ex.

Dategli un vestito qualunque.   Give him any coat you like.

Qualunque raccomandazione ch' egli abbia, non* sarà eletto.
Whatever recommendation he may have, he will not be elected.

"ALCUNO."

649. "Alcuno," "alcuna," "alcuni," "alcune," "qualcuno," "qualcheduno," mean *some, any, someone, some people;* "alcuno," &c., are adjectives when they precede a noun, and pronouns when they stand for a noun; "qualcuno" and "qualcheduno" are only pronouns. Ex.

Alcuni poemi italiani sono difficili a tradursi.
Some Italian poems are difficult to translate.

Non ho ancor visto alcuno.   I have not seen anybody yet.

"TALE," AND "COTALE."

650. "Tale" and "tali," "cotale" and "cotali" mean *such a, some one*. These words are adjectives or pronouns, according as they precede or stand for a noun. Ex.

Un tal uomo non è da compiangersi.
Such a man is not to be pitied.

---

* An *o*, dotted thus ọ, has the broad sound of the *o* in the word *orphan*.

"CERTO."

651. "Certo,"* "certa," "certi," and "certe" mean *certain*. These words are adjectives or pronouns, according as they precede or stand for a noun. Ex.

    Ho sentito una certa notizia.   I have heard certain news.

652. "Tale," "tali," and "cotale," "cotali" are also used to begin the second part of a simile, and mean *such, even so*. Ex.

    " Quale colui, che grande inganno ascolta
        Che gli sia fatto, e poi se ne rammarca,
        Tal si fe'Flegias nell'ira accolta." (Dante).
    As one who listens to some great deceit
      Which has been done to him, and then sore resents it,
      Such grew Phegyas in his gathered rage.
    " Cotali uscir dalla schiera ov' è Dido." (Dante).
    So came they from the band where Dido is.

"TALUNO" AND "CERTUNI."

653. "Taluno" and "certuni" are indefinite pronouns; "taluno" means *some one*, and is only used in the singular; "certuni" means *some people*, and is only used in the plural. Ex.

C'è taluno là che non mi va molto a genio.   There is some one there I do not much like.
Certuni hanno idee curiose.   Some people have odd ideas.

EXERCISE LVI.

Who (643) is knocking at the door? My little brother James. To whom (643) have you told the news? To my sister-in-law. The road through which (619) we passed was (Imp. Ind.) very lonely. From whom (643) do you expect a letter? From that lady who (619) spoke to you at my brother's house. Children (328) who (619) obey (to) their parents† deserve to be praised. What (631) is the weight of this shield? It is about ten pounds.‡ For whom are you painting that vase? For my mother-in-law. The pencil with which (619) I was writing (179) is broken. Whose hat is this? It belongs to that little girl (442). What (611) are you thinking of? I was thinking of the advice§ you gave (180) to me.

---

654. * " Un certo tale," "una certa tale" mean *a certain person*. Ex.
    Ho incontrato un certo tale.   I have met a certain person.

655. † *Parents* is translated into Italian by "genitori;" "parenti" means *relations*. The word *acquaintances* is translated by "conoscenti," and "conoscenze."

656. ‡ *Pound*, weight, is translated by "libbra," *pound sterling*, by "lira sterlina." "Lira," alone, means *tenpence*.

657. § *The advice of a friend* is translated by "il consiglio di un amico;" *advice*, in the sense of *opinion*, is rendered by "parere."

"OGNUNO."

658. "Ognuno," "ognuna," mean *any man, any woman, any one;* they are used with or without an antecedent. Ex.

Ognuno che voglia esser membro di quella società deve pagare una ghinea.	Any one who wishes to be a member of that society, must pay one guinea.

"CIASCUNO" AND "CIASCHEDUNO."

659. "Ciascuno," "ciascheduno," and their feminine forms, mean *every, everyone, each*, and are adjectives or pronouns; they are adjectives when they precede a noun, and pronouns when they stand instead of a noun. Ex.

Ciascuno degli officiali ebbe a subire un esame.	Every officer had to pass an examination.
Ricevettero una lira sterlina ciascheduno.*	Each of them received a pound sterling.

"ALTRI."†

660. The indefinite pronoun "altri" means *others, I*. Ex.

Gli altri non parleranno.	The others will not speak.
Altri non agirebbe così.	Another (I) would not act thus.

661. The pronoun "altri" is sometimes used in Italian, when in English the verb may be used in the passive form. Ex.

"Venite a noi parlar, s' altri nol niega." (Dante).
Come and speak to us if it is not forbidden.

"ALTRUI."

662. "Altrui" means *other, others*, and only refers to persons; it is employed both in the singular and plural numbers, as the direct or indirect object of a verb, but never as its subject. The prepositions "di," and "a," before "altrui," are often omitted. Ex.

Egli brama l'altrui.	He covets other people's property.
Vuol sempre aver notizia dei fatti altrui (*or* di altrui).	He always wants to know other people's business.
"La mia vita che è celata altrui." (Petrarca).	My life which is hidden to others.

---

* Instead of "ciascheduno" one could say "per uno," or "a testa." Ex.
Dateci una ghinea a testa. Give us a guinea each.

663. † "Altri"..."altri" mean *one...another, some...others*. Ex.
Altri veniva, altri andava via, &c. One came, another went away, &c.

"L'UN L'ALTRO."

664. The reciprocal pronouns "l'un l'altro," ("l'una l'altra," "gli uni gli altri," &c.) mean *one another;* the second term of these pronouns ("l'altro," "l'altra," &c.) may be preceded by a preposition. Ex.

Si aiutano l'un l'altro.*	They aid one another.
Sparlano l'una dell'altra.	They speak ill of one another.

"L'UNO E L'ALTRO," &c., "AMBO," &c.

665. The collective pronouns "l'uno e l'altro," "l'una e l'altra," "tutti e due," "tutt'e due," "ambo," "ambidue," "entrambi," &c., mean *both;* "gli uni e gli altri," "le une e le altre," mean *all of them.* They are followed by the definite article, when they precede a noun; before a verb the article is omitted. Ex.

L'uno e l'altro de' miei fratelli erano fuori di casa.	Both my brothers were out of doors.

"Ambo le mani per dolor mi morsi." (Dante).
Both my hands in agony I bit.

Gli uni e gli altri furono puniti.	All of them were punished.

"O L'UNO, O L'ALTRO," &c.

666. The pronouns "o l'uno, o l'altro," "o l'una, o l'altra,"† &c., mean *either one, or the other, (or others,) either.* Ex.

Mi mandi l'uno, o l'altro.	Send me either one or the other.

"NÈ L'UNO NÈ L'ALTRO," &c.

667. The relative pronouns "nè l'uno nè l'altro," "nè l'una nè l'altra," &c., mean *neither the one nor the other.* The verb used with these pronouns must be accompanied by the negation "non," and be in the singular or in the plural number, according as the action it expresses may be done by one, or both the persons spoken of, or alluded to. Ex.

Non comprerò nè l'uno nè l'altro.	I shall not buy either of them.
Nè Foscolo nè Monti non è l'autore di questo poema,	Neither Foscolo nor Monti is the author of this poem.
Nè l'una nè l'altra non verranno.	Neither the one nor the other will come.

---

668. * Instead of the reciprocal pronouns "l'un l'altro," &c., the Italians sometimes use the adverbs "scambievolmente," *mutually,* "reciprocamente," *reciprocally.*

669. † The other disjunctives used in Italian instead of "o" are "ovvero," "ossia," "oppure," "odanche."

"NIUNO," "NESSUNO," "VERUNO."

670. "Niuno," "Nessuno," "Veruno," and their feminine forms mean *nobody, no one,* and are adjectives, or pronouns, according as they precede or stand for a noun. When they follow the verb, they must be preceded by the negation "non," but when they precede it, they do *not* require any negation before them. Ex.

Niun uomo è senza difetti.	No man is without his defects.
Non ho parlato a nessuno.	I have not spoken to anyone.
Nessuno è profeta nel proprio paese.	No one is a prophet in his own country.

ON THE WORDS "NIENTE," AND "NULLA."

671. "Niente" and "nulla" used as nouns (preceded by an article) mean *nothing, the slightest thing, a trifle.* Ex.

Rientrerà presto nel nulla dond' è sortito.	He will soon re-enter into the insignificance from whence he arose.
Per un niente si arrabbia.	A trifle makes him enraged.

672. "Niente" and "nulla" are also used as indefinite pronouns, in the sense of *nothing;* when they follow a verb, that verb must be preceded by the negation "non." Ex.

Pareva che nulla si potesse far senza di lui.	It seemed as if they could do nothing without him.
Questi ragazzi non sanno niente.	These boys do not know anything.

673. "Niente" and "nulla" often have the meaning of "qualche cosa," *something, anything.* Ex.

Non vuol nulla oggi?	Do you want anything to-day?

ON THE WORDS "QUANTO," "QUANTUNQUE."

674. "Quanto" is also (494) an adverb, and means *how much;* it is always used with a verb in the subjunctive mood. Ex.

S' ella sapesse quanto io la stimi!	If you knew how much I esteem you!

675. "Quantunque"* is an indefinite pronoun and means *all that which.* Ex.

"Chi vuol veder quantunque può natura." (Petrarca).
Whoever wishes to see all what nature can do.

---

* "Quantunque" is also a conjunction, meaning *although.* See rule 740.

ON THE WORDS "PER QUANTO," AND "PER QUANTI."

676. "Per quanto" is an adverb, and means *however, however much;* it is used with a verb in the subjunctive mood. Ex.

| Per quanto abili siano, non riesciranno nell' impresa. | However able they may be, they will not succeed in the undertaking. |

677. Instead of "per quanto," "per," followed by the conjunction "che" may be used. Ex.

| Per vantaggiose che fossero le sue offerte, non volli accettarle. | However advantageous his proposals might have been, I would not accept them. |

678. "Per quanti" and "per quante" are adjectives and mean *whatever;* they are employed with a verb in the subjunctive mood. Ex.

| Per quante ragioni adducessimo, non ci fu dato di convincerlo. | Whatever reasons we adduced, we were not able to convince him. |

EXERCISE LVII.

They were both (665) students at the University of Oxford. Every one (659) of the pupils of the Royal College of Music and of the Royal Academy of Music received (Past Def.) a ticket of admission to the International Concert. Charity rejoices at the good fortune of others (662). Neither my grandfather nor my aunt (275, 667) have arrived. Neither of them (667) is the owner of the house (623) we have seen. Rich as they are* they will not be admitted to that society. Let them be ever so clever (however clever they may be) (676), they will never succeed (258) in such an undertaking. Some people (649) are never satisfied, however (676) prosperous they may be. I shall buy either (666) this box† or that trunk. How much capital‡ have you entrusted to him? I have entrusted to him about five hundred (537) pounds.

---

679. * The expressions *rich as they are, determined as they were,* &c., may be rendered in Italian by "ricchi quali sono," "risoluti quali erano," &c.

680. † *Box,* if of a good size, is translated into Italian by "cassa;" if a small one, by "cassetta;" and if a very small one, by "scatola."
Snuff-box is translated by "scatola da tabacco."
A box, at the theatre, is translated by "un palco," or "un palchetto."
The box of a carriage, is translated by "il sedile d'una carrozza."
A cartridge-box, is translated by "una giberna."
Box-wood, is translated by "bosso."
A box on the ear, is translated by "uno schiaffo."
To box, is translated by "fare a pugni."

681. ‡ *The capital,* meaning *the funds, money,* is translated by "il capitale."
The capital, meaning *the chief town,* is translated by "la capitale."
The capital of a column, is translated by "il capitello di una colonna."

LESSON XXX.

ON THE INFINITIVE MOOD.

On the use of the Present.

682. The Present of the Infinitive is used in Italian, as in English, to express an action in an indefinite manner, without any reference to time or person. Ex.

Cantare, *or* il cantar troppo a digiuno guasta la voce.
To sing too much before breakfast spoils the voice.

683. The Present of the Infinitive is used in Italian as a noun, both as subject, and object in the sentence, and is generally translated into English by a present participle, or by a noun. Ex.

Lo scrivermi ella così spesso, mi fa molto piacere.
Your writing to me so often, gives me much pleasure.

Non mi piace quel suo parlare enigmatico.*
I do not like his (*or* her) enigmatic way of speaking.

"Non era l'andar suo cosa mortale." (Petrarca).
Her gait was not like that of a mortal being.

684. As already stated in rule 126, the Present of the Infinitive is used in Italian, instead of the second person singular of the Imperative used negatively. Ex.

Non andar giù, Carlino.
Don't go down, Charlie.

On the use of the Past.

685. The Past of the Infinitive is used in Italian as a noun, both as subject, and object in the sentence, and is generally translated into English by the Past Gerund. Ex.

L'avermi ella parlato, è causa di tutta questa gelosia.
Your having spoken to me, is the cause of all this jealousy.

On the use of the Gerund.

686. The English Present Participle, preceded by the prepositions *by, through, with, on,* is translated into Italian by the Gerund, *without* any preposition before it. Ex.

Scrivendogli ogni giorno, lo forzai a rispondermi.
By writing to him every day, I compelled him to reply.

687. Instead of the gerund, the present of the infinitive, preceded by the preposition "con," *with,* and the definite article, may be used. Ex.

Con lo scrivergli ogni giorno lo forzai a rispondermi.
By writing to him every day, I compelled him to reply.

---

* See rule 63, to understand the meaning of the letters in the darker type.

688. The English Present Participle, preceded by the preposition *in*, should be translated into Italian, by the Present of the Infinitive, preceded by "nel" or "nello." Ex.

Nello scriverle, potete palesarle   In writing to her, you can inform
il vostro progetto.   her of your plan.

689. As already stated in rule 200, the Compound of the Gerund is used in Italian as in English; except that in Italian the auxiliary "avendo," or "essendo," is omitted, and the past participle alone is expressed, and is variable, according to the object in the sentence (when "avendo" is omitted), or the subject (when "essendo" is omitted). Ex.

Datoci (avendoci dato) il di-   Having given us the despatch,
spaccio, partì a gambe.   he ran off.
Sedutasi (essendosi seduta) per   Having seated herself on the
terra, si mise a cucire.   ground, she began to sew.

EXERCISE LVIII.

He kept us waiting (683) in the rain till two o'clock (548) in the afternoon. Your having told (685) him frankly that we would wait no longer offended him. Having conducted me (689) into the room destined for (to) me, he wished me a (the) good-night, and went away. Princes (328) who (620) in governing (688) their subjects, are not guided by (270) principles of justice, excite disaffection. Having seated herself (689) on a comfortable arm-chair, she began to narrate the scene (623) she had witnessed. I admire those (594) artists, I saw them painting* some very fine pictures. I should like to have one of those pictures; I saw them being painted.* I often heard him speaking (690) against you, but I never thought‡ (636) he would dare to cause you any loss. Young as he is (679) he knows how to make himself feared.§ I like Miss Williams' voice, I heard her singing (690) last night. The song (623) you have composed is very pretty; I have heard it sung (690) several times. Having dressed (689) themselves in their best clothes, they went out for a walk. I came earlier (510) this morning, because I thought (691) I should have found‖ you at home. I do not like to see horses running (683) so fast.

---

690. * Both the English expressions *I saw them painting*, and *I saw them painted* (being painted), are translated into Italian by "Gli ho veduti dipingere."

691. ‡ *To think*, meaning *to believe*, is translated into Italian by "Credere." The meanings of "Pensare a," and "Pensare di," are given in rule 248.

692. § The expressions *to make himself*, or *herself loved, respected, feared by* are translated into Italian by "farsi amare, rispettare, temere da."

693. ‖ Notice that in Italian the latter of two verbs is *generally* put in the Present of the Infinitive, when both verbs have the same subject. Ex.

Vorrei poter partire subito pel con-   I wish I could start at once for the
tinente.   continent.

LESSON XXXI.
ON THE INDICATIVE MOOD.
On the use of the Present.

694. The Present of the Indicative is used in Italian, as in English, to express an action which always happens, or which is happening at the present time. Ex.

Non lavoriamo per lui.	We do not work for him.
Disegno* un ricamo per mia sorella.	I am making‡ a design which my sister will embroider.
Carolina coglie† fragole per la colazione.	Caroline is gathering strawberries for breakfast.

On the use of the Imperfect.

695. In Italian the Imperfect of the Indicative is used when the verb expresses an action which was still in progress when another action was done. Ex.

Leggevo* quando Giorgio entrò nella mia camera.	When George entered my room, I was reading.‡
Le mie cugine coglievano† fiori nel giardino.	My cousins were gathering‡ flowers in the garden.

696. A verb is also used in the Imperfect of the Indicative when it describes the state or condition of persons and things at a past time, specified or alluded to. Ex.

Quando entrammo, lo specchio era già rotto.	When we entered, the looking-glass was already broken.
A quell' epoca gli Spagnuoli erano un gran popolo.	At that time the Spaniards were a great people.

697. In Italian, the Imperfect Indicative is also used when the verb expresses an action often repeated at a past time. Ex.

Quand' ero a Milano, andavo al teatro tutte le sere.	When I was at Milan, I used to go to the theatre every night.

---

698. * Expressions like these may also be rendered in Italian by the verb "Stare," when the principal verb in the sentence, whilst describing a progressive action, denotes repose, rest. Ex.

Sto disegnando un ricamo per mia sorella.	I am making a design which my sister will embroider.
Stavo leggendo, quando Carlo entrò nella mia camera.	I was reading, when Charles entered my room.

699. † Expressions like these may also be rendered in Italian by the verb "Andare" when the principal verb in the sentence expresses motion and progression. Ex.

La Carolina va cogliendo fragole per la colazione.	Caroline is gathering strawberries for breakfast.
Le mie cugine andavano cogliendo fiori nel giardino.	My cousins were gathering flowers in the garden.

700. ‡ As already stated, the English expressions *I am making*, *I was reading*, *they were gathering*, &c., are translated into Italian as if they were *I make*, *I read*, *they gathered*, &c.

ON THE INDICATIVE MOOD.

701. In Italian, the Imperfect Indicative is also used when the verb denotes the qualities (physical or moral), habits, and customs of persons and nations no longer existing. Ex.

Cesare Borgia aveva il (574) viso pallido, colle guance imfossate, con baffi e barba rossetta. (D'Azeglio.)	Cæsar Borgia had a pale face, sunken cheeks, and a moustache and beard of a reddish colour.
Francesco primo amava la gloria e il potere.	Francis the First loved glory and power.
I Greci coronavano i loro famosi poeti di alloro e di edera.	The Greeks used to crown their famous poets with laurel and ivy.

702. In Italian, the Imperfect Indicative is also used when the verb denotes the qualities (physical or moral), habits, and customs possessed or practised at a past time by persons and nations still existing. Ex.

| Quand'era giovine amava lo studio delle scienze. | When he was young he loved the study of sciences. |
| Altrevolte i Greci coltivavano le arti e le scienze con grandissimo amore. | Formerly the Greeks cultivated the arts and sciences with very great ardour. |

703. Notice that if the time during which the qualities were possessed, the habits and customs were practised, is specified, the verb is put in the Past Definite. Ex.

| Francesco primo amò la gloria durante tutta la sua vita. | Francis the First loved glory during the whole of his life. |
| Gl'italiani fecero gran progressi durante il decimo-terzo secolo (*or* il trecento). | The Italians made great progress during the fourteenth century. |

ON THE USE OF THE PAST DEFINITE.

704. The Past Definite is used whenever the verb expresses an action which was begun and entirely completed at a time entirely past, and specified. Ex.

| Napoleone entrò in Mosca il 24 agosto, 1812. | Napoleon entered Moscow on the 24th of August, 1812. |

705. The Past Definite is also used when the verb expresses an action which was done to a person or thing at a past specified time.* Ex.

| Furono sconfitti una seconda volta, ai venti luglio, dello stesso anno. | They were defeated a second time, on the 20th July, of the same year. |

---

706. * Italian poets often use the Past Definite, instead of the Past Indefinite. Ex.

| Ah! caro Tito, io fui teco ingiusta. (METASTASIO.) | Ah! dear Titus, I have been unjust towards you. |

On the use of the Past Indefinite.

707. The Past Indefinite is used when the verb expresses an action which happened at a time past, but not specified. Ex.

Carlo ha trovato questo libro sulla tavola di mio zio.	Charles found this book on my uncle's table.
Abbiamo viaggiato molto.	We have travelled a great deal.
Ho scritto i miei temi.	I have written my exercises.

708. The Past Indefinite is used when the verb expresses an action which happened at a period of time not entirely past, as "questa mattina," *this morning*, "oggi," *to-day*, "questa settimana," *this week*, &c. Ex.

L'ho incontrato stamattina.	I met him this morning.

On the use of the Pluperfect Indicative.

709. The Pluperfect is used to express an action which had happened, at a time *not specified*, before another action occurred. Ex.

Avevano già distrutto le mura quando arrivai.	They had already destroyed the walls before I arrived.

On the use of the Past Anterior.

710. The Past Anterior is used to express an action which has been done immediately before another action occurred. Ex.

Tosto che avemmo scritto* i nostri temi, uscimmo.	As soon as we had written our exercises, we went out.

711. Notice, however, that if the two actions were habitual, the Pluperfect should be used. Ex.

Tosto che avevamo preso il tè, andavamo a fare un giro.	As soon as we had taken tea, we used to go for a walk.

EXERCISE LIX.

When I was (696) in Paris I often met (697) your American friend. Thomas à Becket was kneeling† (696) before the altar when the knights struck (704) him. At two o'clock we were (696) far from the batteries, and had escaped (709) a great danger. The general assured us that the enemy were (696) not sufficiently numerous to (225) attack us. What (611) did you do (697) in the evening when you were in the country? (614). My brother and I read, and my sisters either sewed, or played upon (583) the piano. Frederick the Great always wore (701) a dark blue uniform. When he entered (183, 704) the room, all the servants were asleep (696). Spain had (696) formerly immense possessions in America.

---

712. * Notice that the Past Anterior is only used after the expressions "tosto che," "appena," "quando," "quanto prima."

713. † *Was kneeling* must be translated by "era inginocchiato." "S'inginocchiava" would mean *was in the action of kneeling*.

FURTHER REMARKS ON MOODS AND TENSES.

On the use of the Present Indicative.

714. When the verb expresses an action or a state which has lasted for some time past, and is still lasting, it must be put in the Present Indicative in one of the two following ways :—

Sto in questa casa da cinque anni. *Or* Sono cinque anni che sto in questa casa.	I have been living in this house these five years.

On the use of the Imperfect Indicative.

715. When the verb expresses an action or a state which had lasted for some time, and was still lasting when a past action occurred, it must be put in the Imperfect Indicative in one of the two following ways :—

Quando Giorgio venne, io lavoravo già da due ore. *Or* Erano* due ore che lavoravo, quando Giorgio venne.	I had already been working for two hours when George came.
Quando Giacomo disse la nuova, io non ne sapevo nulla.	When James told the news, I knew nothing about it.

On the use of the Future.

716. A verb preceded by the adverbs *as soon as*, *when*, &c., indicates a future time, and therefore the future, and *not* the present tense, must be used in Italian. Ex.

Scriverò quando avrò tempo.   I will write when I have time.

717. Sometimes in Italian a verb is used in the Future when it expresses a present action accompanied by an idea of doubt. Ex.

Crederà che sia per indifferenza sui dolori altrui. (Pellico.)   Perhaps you think it is through indifference concerning other people's misfortune.

On the use of the Conditional.

718. In Italian the Conditional is sometimes used instead of the English Present of the Indicative. Ex.

Saprebbe dirmi dove stia di casa il console inglese?   Can you tell me where the English consul lives?
No, non saprei dirglielo.   No, I can't tell you.
Vorrei ch'ella venisse meco.   I wish you would go with me.

719. The Past Conditional is often used in Italian instead of the English Present Conditional. Ex.

Promise che m'avrebbe dato da vivere.   He promised that he would give me wherewith to live.

---

* An *e*, dotted thus ẹ, has the broad sound of the *a* in the word *gate*.

720. The Conditional, instead of the Present Indicative, and the Conditional Past, instead of the Imperfect Indicative, are often used in Italian to express a fact the reality of which depends upon a statement contained in a previous sentence. Ex.

I giornali dicono che una battaglia ha avuto luogo fra le truppe reali ed i ribelli. Aggiungono che mille di questi sarebbero stati uccisi, e due mila sarebbero prigionieri.	The newspapers say that a battle has been fought between the royal troops and the rebels. They add that a thousand of the latter were killed, and two thousand are prisoners.

EXERCISE LX.

Her father was (701) a handsome man, but very proud. Man formerly lived (701) in forests; the meadows were (696) his walks; he had for his food the fruits of the earth, and the chirping (683) of birds delighted (701) his (575) ears. When Crœsus showed (704) to Solon his vast treasures, the latter (605) said: "Sire, if anyone (649) come with better iron than yours, he will be master (146) of this gold." According to the statement of the governor, they escaped (720). My servant behaved (703) very well for the first five years, but afterwards he became (704) very rude, and dishonest. I speak of the Normans, because they were (696) then at the height of their glory. Napoleon commanded (704) the artillery at the siege of Toulon, and gained (704) brilliant victories in Italy, as general-in-chief of the French republic. We met (704) last year at Paris. I had never seen (709) him before. Louis XIV. lived (703) seventy-eight years, and reigned seventy-two. I wrote (708) to him this morning, immediately after breakfast. Dante was born (704) in 1265, and died in exile in 1321 (544). When Tasso was (550, 696) twelve years old he composed (701) very good Greek verses. If (112) I were you, I would not lend him any money. He was (701) very odd; he used to tell the same story so many times, until it was (696) positively painful to hear him. As soon as they reached (710) the top of the mountain, they were killed (705). Ferdinand and Isabella reigned (696) in Spain when Columbus discovered (704) America. In crossing (688) the moor, I saw a flight* of ravens, flying (292) towards the mountains.

---

721. * *A flight of birds* is translated by "uno stormo d'uccelli."
A flock of sheep .... "un gregge di pecore."
A herd of cattle .... "una mandra di bestiame."
A herd of stags .... "un branco di cervi."
A pack of hounds .... "una muta di cani."
A swarm of bees .... "uno sciame di api."
A gang of thieves .... "una banda di ladri."

LESSON XXXII.

ON THE USE OF THE SUBJUNCTIVE MOOD.

722. *The Main Rule is this:* A VERB SHOULD BE USED IN THE SUBJUNCTIVE MOOD WHENEVER THE ACTION IT EXPRESSES IS NOT POSITIVE; therefore a verb is used in the Subjunctive Mood in the following cases:—

723. A verb is used in the Subjunctive Mood, when it is governed by another verb expressing doubt, fear, wish, command, exhortation, &c. Ex.

Dubito ch'ella possa riuscire.	I doubt whether you will succeed.
Temiamo che non* piova.	We are afraid it will rain.
Amo credere ch'ella stia bene.	I hope that you are well.
Voglio che facciate ciò.	I want you to do this.
Ella desidera ch'egli venga.	She desires that he should come.
Mi sorprende che ciò l'adiri.	I am surprised that this should make you angry.

724. A verb is also used in the Subjunctive Mood when it is governed by a verb used interrogatively, negatively,† or interrogatively with a negation.‡ Ex.

Cred'ella ch'egli sia uscito?	Do you think that he has gone out?
Si spera che egli sia eletto?	Do they hope that he will be elected?
Non credo che sia ammalato.	I do not think he is ill.
Non crede che sia arrivato?	Do you not think he has arrived?

---

* The negation in cases like this is explained on pages 174 and 175.

725. Notice that "Dimenticare," *to forget*, "Dissimulare," *to dissimulate*, and "Ignorare," *to ignore*, used negatively, govern a verb in the Indicative, because the two negatives (one inherent, and the other added to the verb) amount to an affirmative. Ex.

Non dimentico che mi ha parlato.	I do not forget that he has spoken to me.
Non ignoro ch'ella ha talento.	I am aware that you have talent.

726. † Notice that a verb may be used negatively, without being accompanied by any negative particle. Ex.

È impossibile che siamo attaccati in questa posizione.	It is impossible that we should be attacked in this position.

727. ‡ Notice that a verb may have an interrogative form or be used interrogatively with a negation, without expressing a real interrogation, and, in that case, it is followed by a verb in the Indicative. Ex.

Dimentica che siamo qui per vegliare agl'interessi della nostra patria?	Do you forget that we are here to watch over the interests of our country?
Non crede che è arrivato?	You do not believe (the fact) that he has arrived?

728. Notice that in many cases instead of the Subjunctive, the Present Infinitive may be elegantly employed, so long as the sense of the sentence remains clear. Ex.

Mi permise di andare a vedere l'Abbazia di Westminster.*	He consented that I should go to see Westminster Abbey.

729. A verb is in the Subjunctive Mood when it is governed by the Impersonal verbs "Sembrare," "Parere," "Essere probabile," "Bisognare," "Essere mestieri,"† &c. Ex.

Sembra ch'egli abbia ragione.	It seems that he is in the right.
Bisogna che me ne vada subito.	I must go away at once.

730. A verb is used in the Subjunctive Mood when it is preceded by one of the following conjunctions, which imply condition, or uncertainty:—

Perchè,	} so that, in order that.	Dato che,	} supposing that.
Affinchè,		Posto che,	
Acciochè,		Supposto che,	
Purchè,	} provided that, on condition that.	Posto il caso che,	
A patto che,		Quand' anche,	even if.
A condizione che,		Solo che,	if but.
Anzi che,	} before that.	Se mai,	if ever.
Innanzi che,		Nel caso che,	in case that.
Avanti che,		Come se,	as if.
Prima che,		A meno che,‡	unless.
Senza che,	without.	Per tema che,	} for fear that, lest.
Checchè,	whatever.	Per paura che,	

EXAMPLES.

Gli parli prima che egli parta.	Speak before he departs.
Purchè agisca a modo mio.	Provided he acts as I like.

731. "Che," when used instead of "perchè," "affinchè," and "acciochè," is followed by a verb in the Subjunctive Mood. Ex.

Venga che (affinchè) parliamo della nostre faccende.	Come so that we may talk about our business.

---

* Instead of "Permise ch'io andassi a vedere l'Abbazia di Westminster."

732. † But such Impersonal verbs as "Essere certo," "Essere evidente," &c., are followed by a verb in the Indicative Mood, because the latter expresses an action in *a positive manner.* Ex.

È certo ch'egli è stato eletto.	It is certain that he has been elected.

733. ‡ Notice that the conjunctions "a meno che," "per tema che," "per paura che," and "che," used instead of "senza che," are followed by the Subjunctive, preceded by "non." Ex.

A meno che Lei non gli parli, egli non lavorerà mai.	Unless you speak to him he will never work.
Si tenea chiuso in castello, per paura che non l'attaccassero.	He kept himself shut up in the castle, for fear of being attacked.
Non fa mai viaggio, che non sia ammalato.	He never travels without getting ill.

ON THE SUBJUNCTIVE MOOD.

734. As stated in rules 674, 676, 677, the Subjunctive Mood is also used after the adverbs " quanto," *how much*, and " per quanto," *or* " per," *however much*. Ex.

L'opera umana, per buona che sia, trova sempre critici. — Human work, be it ever so good, always finds critics.

735. The conjunctions "in maniera che," "in modo che," "talmente che," *in such a manner that*, "finchè," "sinchè," "sino a che," "fintantochè," *until* (in keeping with THE MAIN RULE), are followed by a verb in the Indicative, when the action it expresses is positive, and that is when the tense used is past or present. Ex.

Parlò in maniera che fu udito da tutta l'adunanza. — He spoke in such a manner that he was heard by the whole meeting.

736. But the above conjunctions are followed by the verb in the Subjunctive Mood, when the verb *does not* express a positive action, and that is when it has reference to a future time. Ex.

La prego di parlare in modo tale che sia intesa e capita da tutta l'assemblea* (l'adunanza). — I beg of you to speak in such a manner that you may be heard and understood by the whole assembly.

737. Notice that in many sentences a verb may be in the Indicative or in the Subjunctive Mood, according as the action it expresses is certain or doubtful. Ex.

Andrò in un sito dove sarò quieto. — I shall go to a place where I shall be quiet (*I know* I shall).

Andrò in un sito ove io sia quieto. — I will go to a place where I shall be quiet (*I hope* I shall).

Cerco un uomo che sa la lingua chinese. — I am looking for a man who knows the Chinese language (*I know he does*).

Cerco un uomo che sappia la lingua chinese. — I am looking for a man who knows the Chinese language (*I hope to find one who knows it*).

738. Notice that in many sentences it is necessary to supply the words left out in them, to appreciate correctly the use of the Subjunctive. Ex.

Voglia il cielo ch'ella sia felice! — Heaven grant that you may be happy.

Which means: " Bramo che il cielo voglia ch'ella sia felice ! "

739. Notice that in all the cases hitherto mentioned, the verbs are logically used in the Subjunctive Mood because they *do not express a positive fact;* but the Italians indiscriminately employ the Subjunctive Mood, also, in the following cases:—

---

* Notice that the *e* in *ea*, etc., has always the broad sound of *a* in the word *gate*.

ON THE SUBJUNCTIVE MOOD.

740. The Italians put a verb in the Subjunctive Mood, also, when it is preceded by the conjunctions "benchè,"* "ancorchè," "sebbene," "contuttochè," "quantunque," "avvegnachè," and "nonostantechè," *although*. Ex.

Voglio andare a ballare, quan-   I want to go to dance, although
tunque non mi senta bene.   I do not feel well.

"Italia mia, benchè 'l parlar sia indarno." (PETRARCA).
My Italy, although speaking may be in vain.

741. The verb is put in the Subjunctive Mood, also, when it is preceded by the indefinite pronoun "niente," *nothing*, or the adjectives "solo,"† *only*, "primo," *first*, "ultimo," *last*, "unico," *only one*, "pochi" "poche," *few*, or any adjective in the superlative-relative degree; as "il più grande," *the greatest*, "il migliore," *the best*, &c., *followed by a relative pronoun*. Ex.

Non c'è niente che mi spiaccia   There is nothing I dislike so
come l'ipocrisia.   much as hypocrisy.
Il cane è il solo animale la cui   The dog is the only animal
fedeltà sia provata.   whose fidelity has been proved.

742. But when "solo," "il più grande," &c., are followed by an indirect object, the verb is used in the Indicative. Ex.

Londra è la più grande delle   London is the largest of the
città che ho vedute.   towns I have seen.

EXERCISE LXI.

Do you hope that he will be elected (724) a (354) member of Parliament? I wish he may succeed (723) in his undertaking. It is possible that I may have been (729) imprudent, but I have not been criminal. I do not like you to go out (724) with that good-for-nothing fellow. I do not think you have acted (724, 636) prudently. I take so much care with (of) your education, in the hope that you will profit (723) by it (240). I do not forget that you have invested (725) much capital (681) in that speculation. Tell the servant to awake (723, 728) me early to-morrow morning. Stop with me until I receive (730) assistance, I beg of you.

---

743. * Notice that, according to THE MAIN RULE, as stated at the beginning of this lesson, the verb which follows "benchè," "ancorchè," &c., should be used in the Subjunctive Mood *only when the action it expresses is not positive;* so in the first example given above Petrarca rightly uses "essere" in the Subjunctive Mood, because its action is *not positive*, but in the second example the Subjunctive is illogically used, because the verb "sentire" expresses *a most positive fact*. There are, however, many examples of the Indicative Mood being used by the best Italian authors, after the above-mentioned conjunction. For instance, Tasso in the second canto (stanza xxv.) of the "Gerusalemme Liberata," says :—

"Benchè nè furto è il mio, nè ladra sono."
Although my deed is not a theft, nor am I a thief.

744. † The above remark holds good with regard to "solo," "il più grande," &c.

Rules for the Concord between the Tenses of the Governing Verb and the Governed Verb.

745. The use of the four tenses of the Subjunctive Mood depends upon the tense of the governing verb in the Indicative Mood.

746. When the governing verb is in the Present or in the Future (Indicative), the governed verb is put in the Present of the Subjunctive, to express a present or a future action, or state, and in the Imperfect, or in the Past Subjunctive, to express a past action, or state; in the Imperfect, if the action or state is alluded to as having been incomplete at a past time; in the Past, if it is alluded to as complete. Ex.

Non credo che Giuseppe lavori adesso.	I do not think that Joseph is working now.
Pagherò, purchè io abbia denaro.	I will pay, if I have money.
Non credo che lavorasse quando siamo venuti.	I do not think that he was working when we came.
Dubito che abbia ricevuto la lettera di suo padre.	I doubt whether he has received his father's letter.

747. Notice that the Imperfect, instead of the Present Subjunctive, and the Pluperfect, instead of the Past Subjunctive are used when some conditional expression follows the verb in the subjunctive. Ex.

Dubito ch' ella studiasse, se non ci fosse costretta.	I doubt that you would study, if you were not compelled to do so.

748. When the governing verb is in one of the past tenses (Indicative), or in the Conditional, the governed verb is put in the Imperfect Subjunctive to express a present action, or state, but in the Pluperfect Subjunctive to express a past action, or state. Ex.

Non sapevo che Carlo dimorasse qui.	I did not know that Charles was living here.
Vorrei ch'ella venisse da me domani.	I wish you would call on me to-morrow.

749. Notice that when the governing verb is in the Past Indefinite, followed by "*perchè*," "*affinchè*," "*benchè*," "*quantunque*," &c., the governed verb is put in the Present Subjunctive, to express a present, or a future action, or state. Ex.

Vi ho dato il denaro perchè possiate andare a vedere i vostri.	I gave you the money so that you may go to see your friends.

750. Notice finally that when the governing verb is in the Past Indefinite, it is customary to use the Past, instead of the Pluperfect Subjunctive. Ex.

Non ho mai conosciuto un uomo che abbia tanto lavorato.	I have never known a man who has worked so hard.

ON THE CONJUNCTION "SE," IF.

751. When "se" is a real Conditional Conjunction, it is followed in Italian either by a verb in the Indicative or in the Subjunctive Mood, according to the following rules:—

752. "Se" is followed by a verb in the Present Indicative, if the condition refers to a future time, not far off. Ex.

| Se mio zio viene ditegli di aspettarmi. | If my uncle comes tell him to wait for me. |
| Se fa bel tempo domani, andremo alla campagna. | If it is fine to-morrow, we shall go into the country. |

753. "Se" is followed by a verb in the Future, if the condition refers to a future time, far off. Ex.

| Se mi pagheranno alla fine dell' anno, vi darò una ghinea. | If they pay me at the end of the year, I will give you a guinea. |

754. "Se" is followed by a verb in the Imperfect Subjunctive, if the condition refers to the present time. Ex.

| Se avessi denaro comprerei questo oriuolo. | If I had money I would buy this watch. |
| Se io fossi in Lei non gli scriverei questa sera. | If I were you I would not write to him this evening |

755. "Se"* is followed by a verb in the Pluperfect Subjunctive, if the condition refers to a time past. Ex.

| Se avessi conosciuto le sue intenzioni, non gli avrei parlato. | Had I known his intentions, I should not have spoken to him. |

756. But when "se" is *not a real Conditional Conjunction*, when it means, in fact, *whether*, *as*, or *when*, it requires after it the verb in the same mood and tense as the English conjunction *if*. Ex.

| Essi non sanno se ritorneremo qui, o no. | They do not know if (whether) we shall return here, or not. |
| Se aveva bisogno di me, era amabilissimo. | If (when) he needed my help, he was very amiable. |

757. A verb is used in the Subjunctive Mood after "quando," "ove," and "qualora," when these words are used instead of "se," meaning *in case that*. Ex.

| Quando (*or* ove) le piaccia, andremo al teatro questa sera. | If you like we will go to the theatre this evening. |

758. A verb is put in the Subjunctive Mood after "che" used instead of repeating "se." Ex.

| Se è ricca e che voglia aver amici, sia buona e generosa. | If you are rich and wish to have friends, be good and generous. |

---

759. * In poetry, by a turn of the phrase, "se," *if*, is often omitted. Ex. "Almeno Tito trovar potessi." (METASTASIO). *If, at least, I could find Titus.*

EXERCISE LXII.

Unless you invite (733) him yourself, he will not come. The elephant never attacks, unless he is provoked. I do not think he was working (724, 746) when I rang the bell. It was necessary (704) that two of our squadrons* should advance (729), and force the enemy's line. Learn your lessons for to-morrow, lest your master punish (733) you. If Mr. John comes (752) before dinner, tell him to wait for (251, 728) me, until I come back (736). I wish (718) you would (748) play this piece of music slowly and with expression.† He wishes (desiderare) that I should reflect (723) on that proposal. I wrote (707) to him by post, so that (730) he might learn the news in time. That man has given me a fearful blow with a stick.‡ If (754) I had some paper, I would write to him. Whatever he undertakes (730) to do, he does it diligently. Your father will pay all your debts, on condition that (730) you will execute his orders faithfully. I do not know where little William is (724). There are few men whose character is (741) better known (365) than his. It is the most interesting book I ever read (741). However ingenious the Greeks and Romans were (734), still they did not discover the art of printing books. It seems as if (che) nothing could (729, 746) save him. I find it§ difficult to learn poetry by heart (imparare a mente).

760. * *A squadron* (of cavalry), is translated by "uno squadrone."
A squadron (of ships), is translated by "una squadra."

761. † "Adagio" is the technical expression for *slow and with expression*.

Ad libitum=*at the performer's pleasure.*
Affettuoso=*with tenderness.*
Allegro=*quick, lively.*
Allegretto=*not so quick as* Allegro.
Al segno=*return to the sign.*
Amoroso=*softly, tenderly.*
Andante=*slow and distinct.*
Andantino=*not so slow as* Andante.
Bis=*twice.*
Calando=*gradually slower and softer.*
Con brio=*with spirit and brilliancy.*
Crescendo=*gradually louder.*
Da capo=*repeat from the beginning.*
Decrescendo *or* Diminuendo=*gradually softer.*
Dolce=*soft;* dolcissimo=*very soft.*
Forte=*loud;* fortissimo=*very loud.*
Gorgheggi=*trills.*
Legato=*smoothly.*
Maestoso=*majestic.*
Moderato=*moderately quick.*
Piano=*soft;* pianissimo=*very soft.*
Presto=*quick;* prestissimo=*very quick.*
Sostenuto=*sustain the sound.*
Volti subito=*turn over quickly.*
Vivace *or* Con vivacità=*with vivacity.*

762. ‡ The suffix "ata" signifies *a blow from*, &c.; hence "una bastonata," means *a blow from a stick,* "una boccata," *a mouthful,* or *a bite,* "un'occhiata," *a glance of the eye.*

763. § The pronoun *it* is not translated into Italian in sentences like this.

LESSON XXXIII.

ON THE FORM AND USE OF PASSIVE VERBS.

764. There are three ways of expressing the Passive Form of verbs, in Italian.

765. The first way is to use the verb " Ęssere " as an auxiliary, followed by the Past Participle of any active transitive verb. Ex.

Egli è stimato da tutti.	He is esteemed by everybody.
Ed iọ dico che gli Egiziani furono sconfitti dai Francęsi alla battaglia delle Piramidi.	And I say that the Egyptians were defeated by the French at the battle of the Pyramids.

766. A verb is rendered passive in the way indicated above only when one desires *to lay a stress* on the result of the action.

767. Many English sentences are best rendered into Italian by giving them an active turn, and this is done by changing the indirect object in the sentence into the subject, and the subject into the direct object Ex.

Ognuno dẹsidera le ricchezze.	Riches are desired by everybody.
La sua cattiva condotta mi ruinò.	I was ruined by his bad conduct.
Gli fecero regalo di un anẹllo.	They presented him with a ring.
I Francęsi sconfissero gli Egiziani alla battaglia delle Piramidi.	The Egyptians were defeated by the French at the battle of the Pyramids.

768. The second way is by using the verb " Venire,"* instead of " Ęssere " as an auxiliary. Ex.

Venni chiamato agli ęsami.	I was called to the examination.
Vennero dichiarati innọcęnti.	They were declared innocent.
Sono sicuro che verrà ęlętto dẹputato.	I am sure he will be elected a deputy.

---

769. * Notice that the verb "Venire" is used instead of "Ęssere" only in the simple tenses of passive verbs; for instance, it would be wrong to say, " Ęrano venuti dichiarati innocenti." *They had been declared innocent.* The right form is " Ęrano stati dichiarati innocenti."

770. The verb "andare" is also used in some cases instead of " ęssere " in the passive forms of verbs. Ex.

La cọsa va fatta cọsì.	The thing is done in this way.
Il vero mẹrito va sempre congiunto alla mọdẹstia.	True merit is always accompanied by modesty.

771. The third way of forming a Passive Verb—the way most congenial to the Italian language—is to employ the word "si,"* followed by a verb in the third person singular, or plural, according as the noun in the sentence is in the singular, or plural. Ex.

Si dice che la Regina partirà domani.	It is said that the Queen will depart to-morrow.
Il buon vino si vende a caro prezzo in Inghilterra.	Good wine is sold very dear in England.
I libri si stampano a buon mercato in Germania.	Books are printed cheaply in Germany.
Vi si parlano tutte le lingue europee.	All the European languages are spoken there.
Se ne parla dapertutto.	It is talked of everywhere.

772. The expressions, *I am asked, He is promised, They are ordered*, &c., are translated by "Mi si† dice," *or* " Mi si domanda," " Gli si promette," " Si comandò loro," &c. Ex.

Mi si disse di parlare.	I was told to speak.
Si permise loro di uscire.	They were allowed to go out.

773. Sometimes, and more especially when the verb is in the reflective form, "l'uomo," "uno," "alcuni," or "la gente," is used, instead of "si," before the verb. Ex.

Uno si avvezza facilmente alla pigrizia.	We easily accustom ourselves to idleness.

774. Whenever "si" would cause any ambiguity in the sense of the phrase, the passive verb must be formed with "essere," or "venire," as explained above. Ex.

Gli uomini virtuosi sono ammirati (*not* si ammirano, which might mean *they admire themselves*). } Wise men are admired.

---

775. * Notice that the word "si," which translates the English words *one, they, we, people,* has all the appearance of *always* being an indefinite pronoun, the same as the French word "on," but it is not so; the proof of this assertion is that the verb used with "si" must agree in number with the noun in the sentence. Nor is "si," as it has often been wrongly stated, a mere reflective pronoun; for it would be a very weak way of expressing, to say, for instance, *It says itself that the Queen will start to-morrow*. "Si dice che la Regina, &c.," "I libri si stampano, &c.," are really passive sentences, in which the word "uomo" (which does the action expressed by the verb) is understood; thus "Si dice (dall' uomo) che la Regina partirà domani." "I libri si stampano (dall' uomo) a buon mercato in Germania." This shows that verbs in the passive form are used nearly as often in Italian as in English.

776. † In this case, when "si" is used with an indirect complement (see rule 196), it is an indefinite pronoun, like the French word "on."

EXERCISE LXIII.

He is greatly loved (765) by (270) his parents. He has been long considered (714, 765) the best poet of the age. They were ordered (772) to keep themselves ready, in case of a sudden attack. The Austrians were defeated (767) by the Prussians at the battle of Sadowa. We went (699, 704) wandering all night through the forest. It is generally believed (771) that Rome was founded (723, 765) by Romulus, though there are no proofs in support of the tradition. Is it true that your cousin John has married (727) a Spanish lady? I think so (271); they speak of it (771) everywhere in town. I have heard* the report of a gun. I am requested (772) to tell you not to go away without leave. They were allowed (772) to enter the church after Divine Service. These pictures have been admired (765), but I am sure (636) they will not be sold (771). It is reported† that he will be made (769) Minister for Foreign Affairs. I have heard it said‡ that lions can be trained (771) to perform like dogs. I have not heard from§ my brother-in-law since the 15th (546) of January. At country fairs‖ one sees very curious people.¶ It is said (771) that popular songs reveal (723) the character of a people. They were advised (767) by the judge to confess their crime. The barbarous sport of the bull fight was introduced (765) into Spain by the Arabs, amongst whom it was celebrated (771) with great pomp. They were promised (772) two pounds each (659).

---

777. * *To hear* is translated into Italian either by "Udire," *or* by "Sentire." Ex. Ho udito (*or* sentito) la voce di mio fratello. I have heard my brother's voice.

778. "Sentire" means also *to feel*. Ex. "Non mi sento bene." *I do not feel well.*

779. † *It is said that, it is reported that, people will have it that*, are elegantly translated into "corre la voce che," "corre fama che," "si vuole che."

780. ‡ *I have heard it said that*, is translated into "ho sentito dire che."

781. § *To hear from*, in the sense of *to receive news from*, is translated into "ricevere lettere da," "ricevere notizie da."

782. ‖ *A fair*, meaning a market, is translated into Italian by "una fiera."
A fair lady, is translated by "una bella signora."
A fair complexion, is translated by "una carnagione bianca."
A fair price, is translated by "un prezzo giusto."

783. ¶ *The people*, meaning the inhabitants of a country, is translated by "il popolo." (21). *People*, meaning persons, is translated by "la gente." Ex.
"E che gent'è che par nel duol sì vinta?" (Dante).
What folk is this which seems by pain so vanquished?

LESSON XXXIV.

ON "VOLERE," "DOVERE," "POTERE," AND "SAPERE."

784. When *do, did, will, shall, would, should, may, might, can, could,* and *let*, are employed as auxiliary verbs, they are *not* translated into Italian; but when they are used as distinct verbs of themselves, each of them has its corresponding Italian verb.

785. When *do* and *did* are not mere auxiliaries, they are translated by "Fare." Ex.

Ho* fatto il mio lavoro.	I have done my work.

786. When *will, would,* and *shall* are not mere auxiliaries, they are translated by "Volere" or "Dovere," according as *will* or *duty* is to be expressed. Ex.

Voglio parlargli io stesso.	I will speak to him myself.
Voleva sempre parlare.	He would always speak.
Dovrà lavorare.	He shall (he will have to) work.

787. The expressions *will you have? will he have?* &c., meaning *do you wish? do you like?* or *do you choose to have?* &c., are translated by the corresponding tenses of the verb "Volere." Ex.

Vuole un biglietto per il concerto di mia sorella?	Would you like to have a ticket for my sister's concert?
Quale vuole dei due?	Which do you choose of the two?

788. The expressions *will you have the kindness? will you have the goodness? will you do me the favour to?* are translated into Italian by "Vuol' avere la bontà di," or "Vuol farmi il piacere di." Ex.

Vuol' avere la bontà di tradurmi questa lettera in italiano?	Will you have the kindness to translate this letter into Italian for me?

789. The expressions *I will have him, you would have me, I want him,* are translated into Italian by "Volere," followed by "che," and the verb in the Subjunctive Mood. Ex.

Voglio che stia a casa finchè sia guarito.	I will have him stay at home until he is quite well.
Vorrebbe che lavorassimo dalla mattina alla sera.	He would have us work from morning till night.

---

* An *o*, dotted thus o, has the broad sound of the *o* in the word *orphan*.

790. The verb *to have to* (*to be obliged to, to think it right to*), is translated into Italian by "Dovere." Ex.

Debbo essere al mio posto a mezzogiorno. — I am to be at my post at noon.

791. The verbs *I ought, you ought, I ought to have*, &c., *I should, you should, I should have*, &c., are also translated by the Conditional, or the Conditional Past, of "Dovere." Ex.

Dovrei andare da mio cognato. — I ought to call on my brother-in-law.
Dovrebbe scrivere a suo padre. — You ought to write to your father.
Avrebbero dovuto pagarmi prima di lasciar Londra. — They ought to have paid me before they left London.

792. The verb *I must, you must*, &c. (*I am expected to, I am to*, &c.), is also translated by "Dovere." Ex.

Debbo parlare al presidente del comitato. — I must speak to the chairman of the committee.

793. The verb "Dovere" is sometimes used to express *probability* that the action expressed by the chief verb in the sentence will happen (is expected). Ex.

Il mio viaggio deve durare cinque giorni. — My journey is to last five days.
Si sapeva che doveva un giorno governare la Francia. — It was known that he was likely one day to govern France.

794. When the verbs *can* and *could, may* and *might*, are not mere auxiliaries, they are translated by "Potere." Ex.

Posso rendervi questo servizio. — I can render you this service.
Potrei andare a Parigi. — I could go to Paris.
Potete venir meco. — You may come with me.
Avreste potuto venir prima d'ora. — You might have come before now.

795. When *can* and *could* are used in the sense of *to know how*, they are translated into Italian by "Sapere." Ex.

Sa ella parlar francese? — Can you speak French?
Sapeva disegnare, ma non sapeva dipingere. — He could draw, but he could not paint.
Sapreste insegnarmi la via che conduce al ponte di Londra? — Could you tell me the way to London Bridge?

796. When *to let* is a verb by itself it is translated by "Lasciare." Ex.

Lasciatemi andar fuori. — Let me go out.

---

* Two *zz*, dotted thus ẓẓ, have the soft sound of the *zz* in the word *muzzle* (52, 53).

EXERCISE LXIV.

I would like (718, 786) to speak to you on (298) a matter of importance. They are to be (790) here this afternoon at three o'clock. I ought to (791) write to my mother. My essay must be (792) ready for the next issue of the magazine. Will you have (787) a steel pen, or a quill? I prefer a quill, if you have one (144). Will you be so good as (788) to tell me where you buy your gloves? With the greatest (520) pleasure; I buy them at Johnstone's (434). Our cousin Charles is expected (793) to visit us to-morrow, or the day after to-morrow. The Queen is expected (793) to leave London this week. We should (791) encourage the beautiful, (336) because the useful is sure to be sought after. They say (771) that the procession is (792) to pass through Piccadilly. It ought to have passed (791) through Oxford Street. Am I to do (792) all this work for nothing? No, you will be paid. She is to write (792) to him three times a (the) week. Will you go (305) with me, or not? I want you (789) to make up your mind.* I am sorry, but I cannot; I have to be at my father's office before five o'clock (548). You should have told me (786) that last night; I could have asked Charles to come. Do not let (796) him bring those (594) flowers in your bedroom (431).

LESSON XXXV.

ON THE NEGATION.

797. The Italian negatives are "No," "Non," "Nè."

798. "No" has the same meaning in Italian as in English.

799. "Non" means *not*, and always precedes the verb. Ex.

Egli non parla bene.   He does not speak well.

800. "Nè...nè" mean *neither...nor*, and are used when there is no verb before *neither...nor*. Ex.

Nè leggo, nè scrivo.   I neither read nor write.

801. But when there is a verb before *neither...nor*, they are translated by "Non...nè...nè." (See rule 667). Ex.

Non ha nè danaro nè amici.   He has neither money nor friends.

802. "Non...che," "non...altro che," mean *nothing but, only.* Ex.

Paolo non fa che parlare.   Paul does nothing but talk.
Non avevo che un cavallo.   I had but one horse.

---

803. * The expression *to make up one's mind* is translated into Italian by "prendere il suo partito." Ex.

Ha preso il suo partito.   *He has made up his mind.*

804. "No, mai" and "non...mai" (in answer to a question), mean *never*. Ex.

L'ha mai veduto? No, mai.	Have you ever seen him? Never.
Non l'ho mai veduto.	I have never seen him.

805. The words "mica," "punto," "neppure," and "già," add strength to the negation "non." Ex.

Non ho mica danaro.	I have no money at all.
Non credo punto quel che dice.	I do not believe a word that he says.
Non ho neppure un soldo.	I have not even a half-penny.
Non crediate già ch'io voglia sapere i vostri affari.	You must not think that I care to know your affairs.

806. The negation "non" is *always* required after the verbs "impedire," *to prevent*, "evitare," *to avoid*, "badare" (followed by a verb in the Subjunctive Mood), *mind lest*, "guardarsi di," *to beware of*. Ex.

La neve impedì che non venisse.	The snow prevented his coming.
Badi* che il cane non le scappi.	Mind the dog does not escape you.
Gli dica che si guardi di non credere la notizia.	Tell him to beware of believing the news.

807. The negation "non" is *always* required after the compound conjunctions "a meno che," *unless*, "per paura che," "per tema che," *for fear that, lest*, and "che," used instead of "senza che." Ex.

Verrà per certo, a meno che non sia partito.	He will certainly come unless he has departed.
Me ne vado per paura che non m'insulti.	I go away for fear that he should insult me.

808. The verbs "temere" and "aver paura," *to fear, to apprehend*, require after them the negation "non" when they are used affirmatively, and *the realisation* of the action expressed by the verbs they govern is feared. Ex.

Temo† che Carlo non venga.	I fear that Charles will come.

"E temo che non sia già sì smarrito." (Dante).
And I fear that he is already so far bewildered.

---

809. * Observe that "bada che," "badi che," and "badate che," followed by a verb in the Indicative Mood, means *notice that*. Ex.

Badate che non ha fatto il suo dovere.	Notice that he has not done his duty.

810. † The use of the negation in all the cases mentioned in this lesson can be justified on the ground that the "non" does *not* negative the verb expressed, but a verb left out (because of the excited state of the mind under fear, &c.), whose meaning is the reverse of the meaning of the verb expressed. For instance, in the example cited above, "Temo che Carlo non venga," the full meaning of the sentence is "Temo che Carlo non (rimanga dov'è, ma che) venga," *I fear that Charles will not remain where he is, but that he will come.*

811. The verbs "temere," and "aver paura," *to fear, to apprehend*, require "non...mica" "non...punto" when they are used affirmatively, and we fear the *non-realization* of the action expressed by the verbs they govern. Ex.

Temo ch'ei non venga mica. I fear that he will not come.

812. But when "temere," and "aver paura," are used negatively, they do not require the negative after them. Ex.

Non temo che vengano. I do not fear they will come.

813. The negation "non" is also required after the noun "altro," *another thing*, the adjectives "migliore," *better*, "peggiore," *worse*, "più grande," *greater*, &c., and the adverbs "altrimenti," *otherwise*, "meglio," *better*, "peggio," *worse*, "meno," *less*, and "più," *more*, when the verb which precedes them is used affirmatively. Ex.

Questo terreno è migliore ch'io non lo credevo. This soil is better than I thought.

Egli era più ricco che voi non siete. He was richer than you are now.

Parlano altrimenti che non agiscono. They speak otherwise than they act.

814. But when the verbs preceding the above-mentioned adjectives and adverbs are used negatively, no negative is required after them. Ex.

Non parlano altrimenti che agiscono. They do not speak otherwise than they act.

815. Many authors put the negation "non" after the verbs "negare," *to deny*, and "dubitare," *to doubt*, when they are used negatively, or interrogatively with a negation. Ex.

Non nego che non* sia un uomo abile. I do not deny his being an able man.

EXERCISE LXV.

Can (795) that boy write? No, he can neither (801) write nor read. My brother has (802) only one horse, but it is a good one. They could (794) not deny the accusation we brought against them. Mind (806) they do not come here; if (752) they do, I shall never come to see you again.† I recognised him, although (740) I had never (804) seen him before. He can (802) only do mathematics (419). It was they who prevented us from writing (to write.) Unless you speak to them, they will always prevent us coming. I apprehend (808) that he will succeed; I wish (748) he would not.‡ I do not deny (815) his being extremely clever, but he is too conceited. I am afraid (808) that Frederick will not succeed (258); I wish he would.‡ I have no fear (812) of her speaking.

816. * It would be very difficult to justify the negation in such cases as this.
817. † *Any more, never* (verb) *again*, are translated into "non (verb) più."
‡ Add *succeed*.

LESSON XXXVI.
ON THE PAST PARTICIPLE.

818. The Past Participle is a word which partakes of the nature of a verb and an adjective; it is conjugated either with "Avere,"* or "Essere,"† used as auxiliaries. When a Participle is conjugated with "Avere," it is a verb; but when it is conjugated with "Essere," it may be regarded as an adjective.

819. The following rules are adhered to by most Italians at the present time.

ON THE PARTICIPLE PRECEDED BY "AVERE."

820. The Past Participle of an Active Transitive verb (see rule 159) is conjugated with "Avere," and remains invariable, that is to say ends in *o*, when the Direct Object (see rule 195) in the sentence follows it.‡ Ex.

Abbiamo comprato tre libri.   We have bought three books.

821. But when the Direct Object precedes the Past Participle, the latter is variable. Ex.

Ecco qui i libri che ho comprati questa mattina. — Here are the books I bought this morning.
Li ho comprati a buon mercato. — I bought them cheap.
Le ho vedute ballare. — I have seen them dancing.
Ho scritto a mia madre, e l'ho pregata di venir qui. — I have written to my mother, and asked her to come here.

822. The Past Participles "potuto," "creduto," "dovuto," and "desiderato," are often invariable because the Direct Object in the sentence, which ought to follow them, is left understood. Ex.

Gli ho reso tutti i servizi che ho potuto (rendergli). — I did him all the services I was able to.

---

823. * All the Active Verbs—both Transitive and Intransitive (see rules 159 and 160)—and most Neuter verbs (see rule 274), are conjugated with "Avere."

824. † "Essere" is used to form the compound tenses—(a) of Passive Verbs (see rule 765)—(b) of eighteen Neuter Verbs, (see rule 275)—(c) of Reflective Verbs (see rule 280).

825. ‡ There are cases when the Past Participle, conjugated with "Avere," *does not* express an action, but expresses a quality of the Object in the sentence; when this is the case the Participle agrees with the noun it qualifies. Ex.

"Un altro, che forata avea la gola." (Dante).
Another one, who had his throat pierced through.

826. The Past Participle of Active Intransitive Verbs (see rule 160) always remains invariable. Ex.

Ci hanno parlato stamattina.   They spoke to us this morning.

827. The Past Participle of most Neuter Verbs is preceded by "Avere" (see rule 274), and remains invariable. Ex.

Abbiamo passeggiato tutta la mattina.   We have been walking about all the morning.

828. With regard to the Impersonal Verbs, the Past Participle of those which, like "Piọvere,"* can be conjugated either with "Ẹssere" or "Avere" (see rule 283), always remains invariable. Ex.

È *or* ha piọvuto tutta la nọtte.   It rained all night.

829. But the Past Participle of those Impersonal Verbs which are conjugated like "Bastare" (see rule 283), and have "Ẹssere" for an auxiliary, is variable. Ex.

I suọi libri gli sono bastati.   His books have been sufficient for him.

ON THE PARTICIPLE PRECEDED BY "ẸSSERE."

830. The Participle conjugated with "Ẹssere" (or "Venire," see rule 768) always agrees with the Subject in the sentence, whether it belongs to an active verb, used passively, or to one of the eighteen neuter verbs conjugated with "Ẹssere," as explained in rule 275. Ex.

Ella è stimata da tutti.   She is esteemed by everybody.
Essi sono caduti nella rete.   They have fallen into the trap.

831. Notice that sometimes the auxiliary is not expressed, but understood, in that case the ellipsis must be supplied, and then the participle will be found to follow the rules given above. Ex.

Oh! quante case (sono state) distrutte!   Oh! how many houses (have been) destroyed!
Le battaglie (che sono state) vinte dagl' Inglesi.   The battles (which have been) won by the English.

832. Instead of "Quand' ẹbbi veduto," *when,* or *as soon as I had seen,* "Quand'ẹbbe sentito," *when,* or *as soon as he had heard,* "Quando fui arrivato," *when,* or *as soon as I had arrived,* "Quando fu scọperto," *when,* or *as soon as he was discovered,* &c., the more elegant expressions "Veduto che ẹbbe," "Sentito che ẹbbe," "Arrivato che fu," "Scọperti che furono," &c., are used. Ex.

Veduto che ẹbbi il palazzo, mi venne l'idẹa di comprarlo.   As soon as I saw the palace, I had the idea of buying it.

---

* See rule 63, to understand the meaning of the letters in the darker type.

833. In the following cases, and in scores of a similar nature, the Past Participle in Italian is illogically inflected for the sake of euphony:—

Egli ci ha mandati* a cercare.	He sent for us.
Questi quadri mi vanno a genio; li ho veduti† dipingere.	I like these pictures very much; I saw them being painted.
Figliuoli, vi siete dimenticate‡ le mie parole.	Children, you have forgotten my words.
Non mi date più fragole; ne ho mangiate§ abbastanza.	Do not give me any more strawberries; I have eaten enough.

EXERCISE LXVI.

Have you finished (820) the letter (636) I gave you to (310) write? The heavy rains, which we had (704) in the spring, have been the cause of many diseases. We have not slept (827) for the last forty-eight hours. The painter Caracci having been plundered by some robbers, drew their likenesses so well that they were discovered (704, 830). The hostile army being routed (689), their camp plundered, their baggage carried away, their ammunition taken, the French re-entered triumphant. A noble but confused thought is a diamond covered with (831, 348) dust. The high mountains of (330) Switzerland are always covered with snow and ice. King Harold and his two brothers were killed (704, 830) at the battle of Hastings. Demetrius, on hearing‖ that the Athenians had overturned (833) his statues, remarked, "They have not overturned the virtues which erected (821) them to me." (218). Look, I have bought this box (680) to put my clothes in (198, 238); do you think it is large enough? Yes, I think so (271). As soon as he had received (832) his money, he started for America. Before (730) men possessed the art of writing, all deeds worthy of being preserved were transmitted (701, 769, 830) to posterity in verse (verses).

---

* "Mandati" should be "mandato," because "ci," is governed by "cercare," and not by "mandati;" but "mandato," near to "ci," would sound inharmonious.

† "Veduti" should be "veduto," because "li," is governed by "dipingere," and not by "veduti;" but "veduto," near to "li," would sound inharmonious.

‡ "Dimenticate" should be "dimenticato" because "le mie parole" is the direct object of "dimenticato;" but "dimenticato" would make the sentence sound inharmonious.

§ "Mangiate" should be "mangiato," because this participle is not preceded by a direct object; but "mangiato" would make the sentence sound inharmonious.

834. ‖ In English when there are two or more verbs, in the same sentence, denoting actions done by the same subject, the verb expressing the action which was done first, is often employed in the Present Participle, but in Italian it must be used in the compound of the Gerund (as explained in rule 689) thus: "Demetrio, udito che gli Ateniesi avevano," &c.

LESSON XXXVII.

ON THE VERB "AVERE," USED IDIOMATICALLY.

835. "Avere" is used idiomatically to translate the English expressions, *What is the matter with you? What is the matter with him?* &c. Ex.

<table>
<tr><td>Non so che cosa abbiano questi fanciulli; sembrano, molto addolorati.</td><td>I do not know what is the matter with these children; they seem very grieved.</td></tr>
</table>

836. "Avere," followed by a noun, is used in Italian in the following idiomatical expressions, instead of the verb *to be,* followed by an adjective, as in English:—

(a) Aver caldo, *to be warm.*
(b) Aver freddo, *to be cold.*
(c) Aver fame, *to be hungry.*
(d) Aver sete, *to be thirsty.*
(e) Aver sonno, *to be sleepy.*
(f) Aver ragione, *to be in the right.*
(g) Aver torto, *to be in the wrong.*
(h) Aver paura, *to be afraid.*
(i) Aver fretta, *to be in a hurry.*
(j) Aver piacere, caro, *to be glad.*
(k) Aver cura di, *to be careful of.*
(l) Aver giudizio, *to act sensibly.*

EXERCISE LXVII.

Are you (122) warm, (a) Charles? Yes, I thank you; when I came in I was very cold (b). When these men came in (705) they were (695) very hungry (c) and thirsty (d). The children are very sleepy (e). Do you think (691) that Margaret is in the right (f) (724)? Yes, and that you are in the wrong (g). I never thought (691) that you would be so wicked as* to offend her. These little children (442) are afraid (h) of that big dog (437). Do (126, 128) not detain me, because I am in a hurry (i). I am very glad (j) to hear that your brother is going to Florence. Shut that window; I feel very cold (b). Those who (630) think they are always in the right (f) are often wrong. They were very happy (j) to be again with us. I think you should be (791) more careful of (k) your health. If (754) he would act sensibly, (l) he would be liked by (270) everybody. If he were wise, (l) he would be rich.

---

837. * The expressions *to be so good as, to be so wicked as,* &c., are translated into Italian by "essere abbastanza buono per," "essere abbastanza cattivo per."

ON THE VERB "AVERE" USED IDIOMATICALLY.

838. "Avere" is used idiomatically in the following expressions:—

(a) Aver buona cera, *to look well*.
(b) Aver cattiva cera, *to look ill*.
(c) Aver male a, *to feel a pain in*.
(d) Avere a mano, *or* in pronto, *to have a thing ready*.
(e) Aver bisogno di, *to need*.
(f) Aver l'intenzione di, *to intend*.
(g) Aver voglia di, *to have a wish*.
(h) Aver vaghezza di, *to have a great desire to*.
(i) Aver di mira, *to aim at*.
(j) Aver luogo, *to take place*.
(k) Aver un bel dire, un bel fare, &c., *to speak in vain, to act in vain*, &c.
(l) Aver voce in capitolo, *to have much influence*.
(m) Aver il capo ai grilli, *to be out of temper*.
(n) Aver della ruggine con, *to bear a grudge to*.
(o) Averla con,* *to be angry with*.
(p) Aversela a† male, *to take offence*.

EXERCISE LXVIII.

Your brother looked very well (a) when I saw him a few days ago. You do not look well (b); what (611) is the matter with you (835)? I feel a pain in (c) my head, and in my right arm. She has the money ready (d) to pay him if (752) he comes. I intend (f) to buy a copy of Tennyson's poems for you (213). He has a wish (g) to eat some French strawberries. She had a great desire to (h) see the Tower of London. They aim at (i) making money. Now I will tell you what took place (j) at my brother's house (434). He may say what he likes (k), he may do what he likes (k), he will not succeed (258). Do not pay attention to (216) what (610) he says; he has no influence (l). Your brother Louis is always out of temper (m). I am afraid (808) he bears you a grudge (n); I do not know why. He is angry with (o) me because I sold (707) the horse without telling him anything. Charles is easily offended (p). It is true that‡ I intend (f) to go to Florence and remain there (239) for (311) five or six months, but I cannot make up my mind (803) thus in a moment.§

---

839. * "Averla con" is conjugated as follows :—
L'ho con, *I am angry with*.
L'hai con, *thou art angry with*.
L'ha con, *he is angry with*.

† "Aversela a male" is conjugated as follows :—
Me l'ho a male, *I am offended*.
Te l'hai a male, *thou art offended*.
Se l'ha a male, *he is offended*.

840. ‡ The expression *It is true that* is rendered in Italian by putting "ben" or "bensì" after the first verb in the sentence. Ex.
Ho ben l'intenzione di viaggiare ma non adesso. It is true that I intend to travel, but not now.

841. § The expressions *in a moment, on the spur of the moment*, are rendered in Italian by "su due piedi," or "in quel subito."

ON THE VERB "ESSERE" USED IDIOMATICALLY.

842. "ESSERE" IS USED IDIOMATICALLY IN THE FOLLOWING EXPRESSIONS:—

(a) Essere necessario di, essere d'uopo di, essere mestieri di, esser forza di,* *to be necessary*, or *I, you, one, we, they must*, or *I have to*, &c.
(b) Essere prezzo dell'opera, *to be worth while.*
(c) Essere in grado di, *to have it in one's power.*
(d) Esser pago, *or* soddisfatto di, *to be satisfied with.*
(e) Essere all'ordine, *or* pronto, *to be ready.*
(f) Essere in ritardo, *to be late.*
(g) Essere d'accordo, *to agree.*
(h) Essere un poco di buono, *to be a good for nothing.*
(i) Essere da poco, *to be worth little.*
(j) Essere da più di, *to be worth more than.*
(k) Essere a mal termine, *to be in a critical position.*
(l) Essere sul punto di, essere in procinto di, essere per, essere lì lì per, *to be on the point of.*
(m) Essere in buon concetto, *to bear a good character.*
(n) Essere vago di, *to desire.*

EXERCISE LXIX.

It is necessary (a) to make all (482) preparations for the Prince of Wales, who will arrive at two o'clock, with the Princess of Wales and the Prince of Naples. I must (a) make a speech on behalf of our College. It is worth while (b) to go to (make) some expense on (650) such an occasion. They have it in their power (c) to do a great deal of good to the institution. I hope our director will be satisfied with (d) our endeavours. I am sure he will (208). Well, boys, are you ready (e)? Yes, we are quite ready, except Mary; she is always late (f). Those two boys never agree (g). To (225) say the truth, that little fellow there, is a good for nothing (h). When I caught hold of him, he was (695) on the point of (l) throwing a stone at my window. Does that man (606) bear a good character? (m). No, he does not (208). I should be very glad (n) to know who that lady is. I have had (dovere)† to grant him all (610) he asked me. I have had (dovere)‡ to come alone. He has not been able (potere)† to sleep. He has not been able (potere)‡ to succeed. They would (volere)† (707) not walk. They would (volere)‡ (707) not live in (with) dishonour.

---

* Rule 287 holds good with these verbs.

843. † When the verbs "dovere," "potere," and "volere" are followed by verbs, which, in their compound tenses, are conjugated with "avere," they ("dovere," "potere," and "volere") are also conjugated with "avere."

844. ‡ When the verbs "dovere," "potere," and "volere" are followed by verbs, which, in their compound tenses are conjugated with "essere," they ("dovere," "potere," and "volere") are conjugated with "essere."

ON THE VERB "ANDARE," USED IDIOMATICALLY.

845. "Andare" is used Idiomatically in the following expressions:—

(a) Andare a genio a, *to like.*
(b) Andare a piede, *to go on foot.*
(c) Andare in carrozza, *or* in legno, *to ride in a carriage.*
(d) Andare a cavallo, *to ride.*
(e) Andare in collera, *to get into a passion.*
(f) Andare in estasi, *to fall into ecstasies.*
(g) Andare altiero di, *to be proud of.*
(h) Andare a vele gonfie, *to prosper.*
(i) Andar di bene in meglio, *to get better and better.*
(j) Andar di male in peggio, *to get worse and worse.*
(k) Andare a vuoto, *to fail.*
(l) Andare a fondo, *to sink.*
(m) Andar dietro a, *to follow.*
(n) Andar per la mente, *to be in one's mind.*
(o) Andare alle corte, *to come to a decision.*
(p) Andare alla lunga, *to go on slowly.*
(q) Andar di mezzo, *to suffer from.*
(r) Andarsene,* *to go away.*
(s) Andare a prova, a gara, *to vie.*

EXERCISE LXX.

I do not like (a) to go on foot (b). My sisters are very fond of riding in a carriage (c); they very seldom walk (b). Elizabeth rides (d) every morning to the top† of the hill with her brother. Why do you get into a passion (e) for nothing? The sound of this instrument is so (536) melodious that it makes me fall into ecstasies (f). He is very proud of (g) his (560) riches; and she is very proud of her beauty. His affairs are very prosperous (h). His business is getting better and better (i). Their condition is getting worse and worse (j). The scheme has failed (k); I am afraid (808) he is ruined. I do not think so (271). The ship sank (l) near the harbour, at three o'clock p.m. (548). His dog followed him (m) (697) wherever he went. Some of his verses are really beautiful, they are always in my mind (n). Let us come to a decision (o) at once; I am tired of arguing (683). He was so slow (p) in making up his mind (803) that I lost my patience. I do not want to suffer from it (q) (240). I am going (r) now; goodbye.

---

846. * "Andarsene" is conjugated thus: "me ne vo," "te ne vai," "se ne va," &c.

847. † *Top* (of a mountain, hill) is translated by "sommità," "sommo." *Top* (of a house, wall), "comignolo," "vetta." *Top* (of a tree), "cima." *Top* (of a table), "coperchio." *A top*, "un paleo."

ON THE VERB "DARE," USED IDIOMATICALLY.

848. "Dare"*is used idiomatically in the following expressions:—

(a) Dare ad intendere a, *to make believe.*
(b) Dar fede a, *to believe.*
(c) Dar retta a, *to mind, to listen.*
(d) Dar del (*or* di) tu a, *to address one in the second person singular.*
(e) Dar del (*or* di) voi a, *to address one in the second person plural.*
(f) Dar del (*or* di) lei a, *to address one in the third per. sing. (fem.)*
(g) Dar parola a, *to promise.*
(h) Dar fuoco a, *to set on fire to*
(i) Dar mano a, *to begin.*
(j) Dar una mano a, *to give some help, to give a coat of* (paint, varnish, &c.).
(k) Dar conto di, *to account for.*
(l) Dar nel rosso, *to border on red.*
(m) Dar del furfante a, *to call one a rascal.*
(n) Dare sfogo a, *to give vent to.*
(o) Dar d'occhio a, *to look at.*
(p) Dare udienza a, *to receive.*
(q) Dar di piglio a, *to seize.*
(r) Dar ragione a, *to agree that someone is in the right.*
(s) Dar torto a, *to say that someone is in the wrong.*
(t) Dar lo sfratto a, *to expel.*
(u) Dar volta, *to turn back.*
(v) Dar carico a, *to accuse.*
(w) Dar bene *(a pen), to write well.*

EXERCISE LXXI.

He would make me believe (a) that he was rich. I never believe (b) flatterers. He does (784) not repent of (184) having listened to (c) his bad companions. He always addresses everybody in the second person singular (d). Italian ladies and gentlemen address their inferiors in the second person plural (e). I always address him in the third person singular (f), respectfully. He gave me his word (g) that he would be here again in a week (549). It is said (771) that he set fire to (h) his house. Why do you not begin (i) your poem? You had better help me a little (j). They were obliged to account for (k) their (560) conduct. This cloth borders on red (l). I wish I could† give vent to (n) my feelings. They looked at me (o) two or three times. The President received him (p) this morning. He seized (q) a stick, and began to strike me. He agrees that you are in the right (r). This pen writes well (w).

---

849. * The verb "Dare," used unipersonally, with the pronoun "si," means *to be probable.* Ex.
 Può darsi che non vengano.   It is probable that they will not come.
850. † The expressions *I wish I could speak, I wish I could have written,* &c., are translated into Italian by "Vorrei poter parlare," "Vorrei aver potuto scrivere," &c.

ON THE VERB "DARE," USED IDIOMATICALLY.

851. "Dare" is used Idiomatically in the following expressions:—

(a) Dare alla luce, *to publish.*
(b) Dar nella rete, *to fall into a snare.*
(c) Dar l' animo a di, *to be bold enough to.*
(d) Dar luogo a, *to give rise to.*
(e) Dar la burla, *or* la baia, *to make fun of.*
(f) Dar la colpa a, *to throw the blame on.*
(g) Dare in ismanie, *to show a great deal of irritation.*
(h) Dare in uno scoppio di risa, *to burst out laughing.*
(i) Dare in uno scoppio di lagrime, *to burst out crying.*
(j) Dare in prestito a, *to lend.*
(k) Dar di naso da per tutto, *to meddle with everything.*
(l) Darsi la mano *to wed.*
(m) Darsi vanto di, *to boast.*
(n) Darsi allo studio, *to apply one's-self to study.*
(o) Darsi bel tempo, *or* Darsi al dolce far niente, *to live in idleness.*
(p) Darsi a conoscere per, *to make one's-self known as.*
(q) Darsi briga di, *to meddle with.*
(r) Darsi pensiero di, *to worry one's-self about.*
(s) Darsi pace, *to be contented.*
(t) Darsela a gambe,* *to run away.*
(u) Poter darsi, *to be possible.*

EXERCISE LXXII.

He has published (a) a good translation of Molière's Comedies. He fell (704) into the snare (b) like an idiot. I am bold enough (c) to send him a challenge. His election gave rise to (d) (704) a very warm discussion. They are making fun of you (e). Mary always throws the blame on (f) her sister. When we accused him, he showed a great deal of irritation (g). When I told him the news, he burst out laughing (h). I advise you not to lend her (j) your parasol. That busybody meddles with everything (k). They are leading a life of idleness (o). He would not make himself known as (p) the author of the comedy. I wish that she would not (723) meddle with (q) my affairs. My dear friend, do not worry yourself about (r) trifles, be contented (s). The thief ran away (t) directly. It is possible (u) that Frederick and his friends will arrive (Pres. Subj.) this afternoon.

---

852. * The verb "Darsela a gambe" is conjugated as follows:—

Me la do a gambe,	*I run away.*	Ce la diamo a gambe,	*we run away.*
Te la dai a gambe,	*thou runnest away.*	Ve la date a gambe,	*you run away.*
Se la dà a gambe,	*he runs away.*	Se la danno a gambe,	*they run away.*

ON THE VERB "FARE," USED IDIOMATICALLY.

853. "Fare" is used Idiomatically in the following expressions :——

(a) Far bel tempo, *to be fine weather.*
(b) Far cattivo tempo, *to be bad weather.*
(c) Far freddo, *to be cold.*
(d) Far caldo, *to be warm.*
(e) Far umido, *to be damp.*
(f) Far colazione, *to breakfast.*
(g) Far merenda, *to have luncheon.*
(h) Far animo, *to encourage.*
(i) Far pompa di, *to boast.*
(j) Far ala a, *to make room for.*
(k) Far alto, *to halt.*
(l) Fare il grugno a, *to sulk.*
(m) Far mestieri di, *or* far d'uopo di, *to be necessary.*
(n) Far vela, *to set sail.*
(o) Far naufragio, *to be shipwrecked.*
(p) Far vista, *or* mostra di, *to pretend.*
(q) Far piacere a, *to please.*
(r) Far le veci di, ⎫
(s) Far le parti di, ⎬ *to act as.*
(t) Far da, ⎭
(u) Far brindisi a, *to drink the health of.*
(v) Far il dottore, *to lay down the law.*

EXERCISE LXXIII.

It was fine weather (a) (704) during the whole month we remained at Brighton. The weather is very bad (b) just now; we cannot go out. Sometimes it is very cold (c) in (207) Paris, I assure you. In summer it is very warm (d) in Italy; perhaps too warm. In the western part of Ireland the weather is very damp (e). At home we breakfast (f) at seven o'clock (548) in (328) summer, and eight o'clock in winter. We shall have luncheon (g) before we go out. I encouraged him (h) by promising (686) that I would take him with me. He was always boasting (i) (701) of his ancestors. The crowd made room for (j) her. They halted (k) during the night. He is sulking (l) with me, because I would not lend him my horse. The ship set sail (n) for America three days ago; she had three hundred passengers on board. They were shipwrecked (o) off the coast of Cornwall. He pretended (p) to give the money to his father, but instead of that, he put it in his pocket (572). He played another tune to please (q) the officers of the staff.* On (298) that occasion he acted as (r) chaplain. He acted as (s) a father to her. They drank the chairman's health (u). He is always laying down the law (v).

854. * *Staff* (military), is translated by "Stato Maggiore." *Staff* (of a newspaper), "redazione." *Staff* (stick), "bastone." *Pilgrim's staff,* "bordone."

ON THE VERB "FARE," USED IDIOMATICALLY

855. "Fare" is used Idiomatically in the following expressions:—

(a) Fare i conti di, *to intend.*
(b) Fare una visita, *to pay a visit.*
(c) Fare una passeggiata, *to take a walk.*
(d) Fare un bagno, *to take a bath.*
(e) Far l'orecchio del mercante, *to turn a deaf ear.*
(f) Far vedere a, *to show.*
(g) Far male a, *to hurt.*
(h) Fare attenzione, *to pay attention.*
(i) Far parola di, *to mention.*
(j) Far prova di coraggio, *to give proofs of courage.*
(k) Far capolino, *to peep in.*
(l) Far fare, *to have made.*
(m) Far risaltare, *to fetch out.*
(n) Farsi fare, *to have made for one's-self.*
(o) Farsi animo, *to take courage.*
(p) Farsi nuovo di, *to pretend to be ignorant of.*
(q) Farsi beffe di, *to ridicule.*
(r) Farsi innanzi, *to put one's-self forward.*
(s) Farsi in qua, *to draw near.*
(t) Farsi in là, *or* indietro, *to draw back.*
(u) Far tanto di cappello a, *to bow most respectfully to.*
(v) Sul far del giorno, *at the break of day.*
(w) Sul far della notte, *at sunset.*

EXERCISE LXXIV.

I intend (a) to pay him a visit (b). We shall take a walk (c) this evening after tea. I take a bath (d) every morning before breakfast. I asked him to lend me his gun, but he turned a deaf ear (e). I want to show him (f) that I am not easily frightened. Do not (126) hurt him (g) with that big stick. You never pay attention (h) to what I tell you. Remember that you have promised me not to mention it (i) to my brother. He gave proofs of great courage (j) in the last war. We were busy preparing the exhibition* when my father peeped in (k). I have had two tables made (l) for the garden. He had a letter written (l) to me by his secretary. This dark tint fetches out (m) the colours of the flowers. Take courage, (o) my dear friend. He pretended to be ignorant of (p) all that (610) had happened. They ridicule (q) everybody. You should not be afraid; you should put yourself forward (r). If you draw near (s), you will see the effect. Draw back (t) a little; I cannot see the game. When they meet, they bow to one another most respectfully (u). He always gets up to work (225) at the break of day (v), and comes home at sunset (w).

---

856. * *Exhibition* is translated by "esposizione." "Un'esibizione" means *an offer.*

ON THE VERB "FARE" USED IDIOMATICALLY.

857. "Fare" is used idiomatically in the following expressions:—

(a) Far caso di, *to value.*
(b) Far specie a, *to be astonished.*
(c) Far meno di, far a meno di, *to help it,* or *to do without.*
(d) Far senno, *to become serious.*
(e) Fare spalla, *to back.*
(f) Fare una domanda, *to ask a question.*
(g) Far l'indiano, *to look as if butter would not melt in one's mouth.*
(h) Fare il bell'umore, fare il gallo, *to be impertinent.*
(i) Fare il bravo, *to brag.*
(j) Far rigar dritto, far stare a segno, *to take down a peg or two.*
(k) Fare il sarto, *to be a tailor.*
(l) Far crocchio, *to form groups.*
(m) Far festa a, *to greet.*
(n) Farsi mallevadore, *to stand guaranty.*
(o) Non fa niente, *never mind.*
(p) Come si fa? *what will you do?*
(q) E un uomo così fatto, *that is his character.*
(r) C'è un bel da fare, *there is plenty to do.*

EXERCISE LXXV.

He does not value (a) your friendship; so much the worse* for him. I was astonished (b) to see him dressed in mufti. I could not help it (c). He promised to become serious (d), and I backed him (e) with all my means. I asked his parents (655) some questions (f). When I caught the pickpocket, at first he looked as if butter would not melt in his mouth (g), and then he began to be impertinent (h). The policeman told him that it was useless to brag (i), and that he would take him down a peg or two (j). What do these men do? This one is a tailor (k) and that one a carpenter. The procession broke up (704) and the people began to form groups (l). They greeted us (m) warmly. He has promised my father to stand guaranty (m) for me. Never mind (o), he will be compelled to speak. What will you do (p)? I know him; that is his character (q). There is plenty to do (r), the members of the Commission are coming here to dine. This time the secretary will have something to do for his salary.†

---

858. * The expressions *so much the better, so much the worse,* are translated into Italian by "tanto meglio," "tanto peggio."

859. † *The salary of a secretary* is translated by "lo stipendio di un secretario."
The wages of a servant..................... "il salario di un servo."
The wages of a workman .... "la paga di un operaio."

ON THE VERB "STARE" USED IDIOMATICALLY.

860. "Stare" is used idiomatically in the following expressions:—

(a) Stare (di salute), *to be (in health)*.
(b) Stare di casa, *to reside*.
(c) Stare a sedere, *to be seated*.
(d) Stare in piedi, *to stand*.
(e) Stare a sentire, *to listen*.
(f) Stare all'erta, *to be on one's guard*.
(g) Stare in orecchi, *to prick up one's ears*.
(h) Star per, *to be on the point of*.
(i) Star in agguato, *to lie in wait*.
(j) Star sull' avviso, *to be prepared*.
(k) Star in forse, *or* Star tra il sì e il no, *to hesitate*.
(l) Star quieto, fermo, *to be quiet*.
(m) Star allegro, *to be merry*.
(n) Stare zitto, cheto, *to be silent*.
(o) Sta a me di,* *it is my turn*.
(p) Stare a galla, *to float*.
(q) Star con le mani a cintola, *to stand idle*.
(r) Star fresco, *to be in a pickle*.
(s) Non istar bene, *to be wrong*.

EXERCISE LXXVI.

How are (a) you to-day? I am very well, I thank you. Do you reside (b) in this neighbourhood? No, I am staying† with my sister. The ladies were allowed to sit down (c), but the gentlemen had (790) to stand (d) all the time. When you came in I was listening (e) to (698) a very interesting conversation. Be on your guard (f); for he might (794) escape. I saw that the stranger was pricking up his ears (g) when you were speaking to my partner. Lions and tigers lie in wait (i) for their prey near streams and brooks. He wanted to (786, 307) surprise us, but we were prepared (j). I hesitated (k) whether I was to go (756) to Paris. Be quiet (l), John. Let us be merry, (m) children; to-day it is little Charlie's (448) birthday. His being (683) silent (n) gave great advantage to his enemies. Now it is his turn (o) to speak. Light substances float (q) on water. Write this exercise, instead of standing idle (q). Elizabeth, we have missed our train; we are in a pickle (r) now. It is wrong (s) to gamble.

---

861. * The expressions "tocca a me di," "a voi di," &c., are frequently used instead of "sta a me di," &c.; but "tocca a me di," &c., has more force; it often means *it is my duty, it is my right*.

862. † The Italian for *to stay with*, is "essere in visita da."

863. ‡ In speaking of dresses, "Star bene" means *to suit, to become*, and "Star male," *to be unsuitable, to be unbecoming*. Ex.

Cotest'abito non le sta bene.   That coat does not suit you.

IDIOMS FORMED WITH "SAPERE," "TENERE," "VOLERE," AND "VENIRE."

864. Idioms with "Sapere."

(a) Sapere a mente, *or* a memoria, *to know by heart.*
(b) Saper male, *to be sorry for.*
(c) Saper di buono, *to have a good taste*, or *smell.*
(d) Saper di cattivo, *to have a bad taste*, or *smell.*
(e) Saper di poco, *to have little taste*, or *smell.*
(f) Saper di niente, *to have not any taste*, or *smell.*
(g) Saper di muschio, *to smell of musk.*
(h) Saper di pesce, *to smell of fish.*

865. Idioms with "Tenere."

(i) Tenere a bada, *to trifle with.*
(j) Tenere a battesimo, *to be godfather*, or *godmother.*
(k) Tenere da uno, *to side with one.*
(l) Tener le lagrime, *or* le risa, *to keep from weeping*, or *laughing.*
(m) Tener uno per galantuomo, *to believe one an honest man.*

866. Idioms with "Volere."

(n) Voler bene a, *to be fond of.*
(o) Voler dire, *to mean.*

867. Idioms with "Venire."

(p) Venir meno, *to faint.*
(q) Venire in mente a, *to remember.*
(r) Venir voglia a, *to take a fancy.*
(s) Venir fatto a, *to succeed.*

EXERCISE LXXVII.

My brother knows by heart (a) many Italian sonnets. I am sorry (b) to see you afflicted; I hope that* you have not received any bad news. These apples have a good smell (c). I am sure that he is trifling with (i) you. She has been godmother (j) to all my children. I side with (k) you because you are in the right (836, f). Camelias are very beautiful flowers, but they have not any smell (f). All her clothes smell of musk (g). We could not help weeping (l). I always believed (707) him to be (m) an honest man. William is very fond of (n) your cousin Elizabeth. If I had known what he meant (o), I should have spoken to him. When she heard the news, she fainted (p) in her mother's arms. I remember (q) that I promised to meet her at my mother's house, at three o'clock this afternoon. I took a fancy (r) to go and (340) see the exhibition (856). He succeeded (s) (693) in obtaining the post.

---

868. * The expressions *I hope that*, *we hope that*, &c., when referring to a present or past time, are translated by "Amo credere che," "ci piace credere che," &c. (followed by a verb in the Subjunctive). To hope for a thing *that is*, or *has been*, is illogical.

LESSON XXXVIII.

ADVERBS.

869. The rules for the formation of adverbs from adjectives, and the mode of forming the degrees of comparison are given in pages 122, and following.

870. Adverbs are divided into classes, according to their signification.

871. THE PRINCIPAL ADVERBS OF AFFIRMATION.

Sì,	yes.	Già,	⎫
Certo,	certainly.	Appunto,	⎬ exactly so.
Sicuramente,	surely.	Per l'appunto,	⎭
Indubitatamente,	⎫	Infatti,	
Senza dubbio,	⎬ undoubtedly.	Davvero,	really.
Senz' altro,	⎭	Sia così,	be it so.

872. In giving an answer containing the verbs "credere," "sperare," "dubitare," and "temere," the idioms "di sì," and "di no," are used instead of "sì" and "no." Ex.

È in casa mio zio? Credo di sì. Is my uncle at home? I think so.

873. THE PRINCIPAL ADVERBS OF NEGATION.

No,	no.	Niente affatto,	⎫ by no means.
Non (verb),	not, no.	In nessun modo,	⎭
Non (verb) mica,	⎫ not at all.	Non (verb) mai,	⎫ never.
Non (verb) punto,	⎭	Non (verb) giammai,	⎭

874. The negation *not* is translated into Italian by "non," and is always placed before the verb. Ex.

Non vi ho chiamato, Enrico. I did not call you, Henry.

875. THE PRINCIPAL ADVERBS OF ORDER.

Prima,	⎫	Dopo,	after.
In prima,	⎪ first.	Poi,† poscia,	⎫ then.
Dapprima,	⎬ firstly.	Indi, quindi,	⎭ next.
Primieramente,	⎭ to begin with.	Gradualmente,	gradually.
Secondariamente,	secondly.	Successivamente,	successively.
In terzo luogo,	in the third place.	Finalmente,	finally.

876. † "Poi," also means *besides*. Ex. "Aveva poi un modo di vestire tutto suo." *Besides, he had a very peculiar way of dressing himself.*

877. THE PRINCIPAL ADVERBS OF PLACE.

Qui, qua, ci,	here.	In su,	upwards.
Costì, costà,	⎫	In giù,	downwards.
Lì, là, colà, vi, ivi,	⎬ there.	Su e giù,	up and down
	⎭	Vicino,*	near.
Ove, dove,	where.	Lontano,*	far.
Onde, donde, di dove,	} whence.	Altrove,	elsewhere.
		Da banda,	⎫ aside.
Quassù,	up here.	Da parte,	⎭
Quaggiù,	down here.	A mano destra,	⎫ on the right.
Lassù,	up there.	A destra, diritta,	⎭
Laggiù,	down there.	A sinistra, manca,	on the left.
Di sopra,	{ above, upstairs	Avanti,* innanzi,*	forward.
		Da per tutto,	⎫
Di sotto,	{ below,	Ovunque,	⎬ everywhere.
Da basso,	{ downstairs	Ognidove,	⎭

878. "Qui," "qua," and "ci" (*here*), are used to indicate the place in which the speaker is; "costì," "costà" (*there*), the place occupied by the person addressed; "Lì," "là," "colà," "ivi," and "vi" (*there*), mark a place distant alike from the speaker and the person addressed. "Qui" and "costì" are generally used with verbs expressing state, whereas "qua" and "costà" are always connected with verbs expressing movement.

879. "Ci," "vi," and "ivi," can only be used when the place to which these adverbs refer has been already mentioned in the sentence. Ex.

Ora che sono in questo posto ci voglio rimanere.   Now that I am in this place I will remain in it.

880. ADVERBS WHICH CAN BE USED INTERROGATIVELY.

Quando?	when?	Ove?	⎫ where?
Quanto?	how much?	Dove?	⎭
Mai?†	⎫ ever?	Donde?	whence?
Giammai?	⎭	Perchè?	why?
Come?	how?	Fin dove?	how far?
Da quando in qua? since when?		Fino a quando?	until when?

881. "Mai" and "giammai," employed without being preceded by "non," have the signification of *ever;* but when they are employed with "non," or "no," they mean *never.* Ex.

Ha ella mai visto il duomo di Milano? No, mai.   Have you ever seen the cathedral of Milan? No, I have not.

---

* "Vicino," "lontano," "avanti," and "innanzi" can also be used as prepositions.
882. † "Unqua" is often used in poetry instead of "mai."

883. SENTENCES CONTAINING ADVERBS OF TIME.
(To be learnt by heart.)

Giuseppe andò al passeggio ieri, ed io v'andrò oggi e domani.
Joseph went for a walk yesterday, and I shall go to-day, and to-morrow.

Vidi i miei avantieri (a), e li vedrò ancora fra poco (b).
I saw my family the day before yesterday, and I shall see them again very soon.

È difficile di fare utili scoperte al giorno d'oggi (c).
Now-a-days it is difficult to make useful discoveries.

Che faremo ora? (d). Non faremo niente fino a posdomani (e).
What shall we do now? We shall do nothing till the day after to-morrow.

Pel momento (f) non posso dar risposta, ma deciderò al più presto possibile.
For the present I cannot give an answer, but I will decide as soon as possible.

Finora (g) egli ha fatto a modo suo; ormai mi obbedirà.
Hitherto he has done what he likes; now he will obey me.

L'ho visto due ore fa, e lo rivedrò oggi a otto.
I saw him two hours ago, and I shall see him again to-day week.

È ancora (i) prigioniero, ma sarà liberato fra (j) un mese.
He is still a prisoner, but he will be liberated in a month.

Incontrai Carlo poc'anzi (k).
I have just met Charles.

Non l'ho veduto da due mesi in qua.
I have not seen him for the last two months.

Pel passato lo vedevo raramente, (l) ma d'ora in avanti (m) lo vedrò sovente (n).
In past time I seldom saw him, but henceforth I shall see him often.

Quando partiremo? Subito* (o); ho già preparato i miei bauli.
When shall we start? At once; I have already prepared my trunks.

Egli si decise su due piedi (p).
He made up his mind in a moment.

Per l'avvenire verrò a trovarla di quando in quando (q).
For the future I shall come to see you now and then.

Non mancherò di scrivergli subito che (r) arriverò a Parigi.
I shall not fail to write to him as soon as I arrive in Paris.

(a) *Or* ieri l'altro.
(b) *Or* tosto, fra breve, quanto prima.
(c) *Or* oggidì, oggimai.
(d) *Or* adesso.
(e) *Or* domani l'altro.
(f) *Or* per ora, per adesso.
(g) *Or* infino ad ora.
(i) *Or* tuttora, tuttavia.
(j) *Or* da qui a un mese.
(k) *Or* pur dianzi, pur mo, pur ora, poco fa, testè.
(l) *Or* di rado.
(m) *Or* d'ora innanzi, da qui in avanti, da qui innanzi, d'ora in poi, d'oggi in poi.
(n) *Or* spesso.
(o) *Or* a momenti, immediatamente.
(p) *Or* in un attimo, in un batter d'occhio, in men che non si dice.
(q) *Or* di tempo in tempo, di tratto in tratto.
(r) *Or* tosto che, appena, come prima.

884. * "Ratto" is sometimes used in poetry instead of "subito."

Non l'ho vista d'allora in poi (a).	I have never seen her since then.
Altre volte era ricca, ma in questi ultimi tempi (b) divenne povera.	Formerly she was rich, but of late she became poor.
Vi prego di venire per tempo, (c) allorquando (d) volete parlarmi.	I beg of you to come early, whenever you wish to speak to me.
Roberto viene sempre (e) a seccarmi, ora (f) per una cosa, ora per l'altra.	Robert always comes to bother me, now for one thing, then for another.
Allora Carlo arrivava per lo più prima di me.	Then Charles generally arrived before me.
Andiamo, si fa tardi; siamo sempre in ritardo; ciò non va bene.	Let us go, it is getting late; we are always late; that is not right.
Era fin d'allora all'apice della sua gloria.	He was even then at the very height of his glory.
Lo vidi circa sei giorni fa.	I saw him about six days ago.
Qualche volta (g) restava per molto tempo scioperato.	Sometimes he remained for a long while idle.
All'indomani era di gran lunga innanzi dei suoi competitori.	On the morrow he was far ahead of his competitors.
Verrete da me qualora vi piaccia (h).	You will come to me whenever you like.
Agguantò l'agnello addirittura, e, senz'altro, se lo divorò.	He seized the lamb, and without more ado, devoured it.

EXERCISE LXXVIII.

What are you doing here, Mrs. Vincenzi? I am spending an hour in the fresh air; I come here almost every morning. Where have you been? (123) I do not know from whence I came; we lost our way after (185) crossing the little green bridge, near Mr. Prati's house. We went up and down I do not know for how long; but at last we have arrived here safe and sound. Will you go with me to see the pictures in the National Gallery? Yes, if you will permit me to take my sister with me. With the greatest pleasure. No doubt you have seen Mascagni's new opera? No, not yet; I have no time at all, just now. Now we will begin this work; we shall finish it before midnight. If I were in your place, I would remain in Nice during the winter. I often meet your cousin, Mrs. Alberti; sometimes in the park, sometimes in the Reading Room of the British Museum.

(a) *Or* d'allora in qua.
(b) *Or* recentemente, non ha guari.
(c) *Or* di buon ora.
(d) *Or* ogniqualvolta.
(e) *Or* ognora.
(f) *Or* quando...quando.
(g) *Or* talora.
(h) *Or* quando che sia.

885. SENTENCES CONTAINING ADVERBS OF QUALITY AND MANNER.

(To be learnt by heart.)

Ella parla bene, ma parlerebbe meglio (a) se parlasse più adagio.
You speak well, but you would speak better if you spoke slower.

Il suo sarto lavora male (b) perchè lavora in fretta.
Your tailor works badly because he works in a hurry.

Credo di no; il fatto sta che lavora malvolentieri (c).
I do not think so; the fact is he works unwillingly.

Davvero lavora alla carlona (d); di male in peggio (a) ogni giorno.
Really he works carelessly, worse and worse every day.

Si direbbe che lo fa apposta (e), o per burla (f), per mettervi in collera.
One would say that he does it on purpose, or for fun, to make you cross.

Vorrei parlarle a quattr'occhi (g); ho qualcosa da dirle a bocca (h).
I would like to see you privately; I have something to tell you by word of mouth.

Volentieri (i), eccomi qui, dite presto, sotto voce ma senz' ambagi.
Willingly, here I am, be quick, in a whisper but to the point.

Tutta la casa è a soqquadro (j) e sua moglie piange dirrottamente (k).
The whole house is in confusion; and your wife is weeping bitterly.

Parlate sul serio (l); non son cose da dirsi alla pazza.
Speak seriously; they are not things to be said wantonly.

Vendeva i suoi quadri di mano in mano che li finiva.
He sold his pictures as fast as he finished them.

Lo passò da parte a parte (m), ad onta della (n) maglia che portava.
He pierced him through and through, in spite of the coat of mail he wore.

Tutt'a un tratto (o) si rimisero a lavorare con amore.
All at once they began again to work in good earnest.

Me ne vivo quietamente in questo castello, mercè la bontà del governatore.
I live quietly in this castle, thanks to the kindness of the governor.

Agirò comunque ei voglia.
I shall act just as he wishes.

(a) The adverbs "meglio" and "peggio" are the comparative forms of "bene" and "male." Their superlative forms are "ottimamente," "pessimamente."
(b) *Or* malamente.
(c) *Or* a malincuore.
(d) *Or* alla buona.
(e) *Or* a bello studio.
(f) *Or* per ischerzo.
(g) *Or* da solo a solo.
(h) *Or* a voce, viva voce.
(i) *Or* buona voglia.
(j) *Or* sottosopra.
(k) *Or* a dirotte lagrime.
(l) *Or* da senno.
(m) *Or* da banda a banda.
(n) *Or* malgrado.
(o) *Or* all'improvviso, di repente.

Lavorarono siffattamente (a), che dappoi il terreno produce fromento a dovizie (b).	They worked in such a manner that since then the soil has produced corn in abundance.
In somma (c) volete leggere ad alta voce (or voce alta) o no?	In short, will you or will you not read louder?
Sicuro, comincerò da capo.	Certainly, I shall begin over again.
Dove debbo cominciare? a capo di riga? Sicuro (d).	Where shall I begin from? at the head of the line? Certainly.
Mi chiamò da parte (h) e mi raccontò tutto sotto voce.	He called me aside and whispered to me all that had happened.
La tratto alla buona (i) cioè (j) come vorrei ch'ella trattasse me.	I treat you without compliments, that is as I would like you to treat me.
Uscì diverse volte al buio (k) e di soppiatto, (l) ma coll'andar del tempo fu acchiappato.	He went out several times in the dark and by stealth, but at length he was caught.
Guadagna più vendendo all'ingrosso che vendendo a minuto.	He gains more by selling wholesale than by retail.
Io sto sempre alla larga (h) quando veggo barruffe.	I always keep aloof when I see disturbances.
Egli si veste sempre alla moda, per lo più all'inglese.	He always dresses in the fashion, generally in the English style.
Fa sempre al rovescio di quel che gli si dice.	He always does the reverse of what he is told.
Egli va sempre a zonzo, scioperato.	He is always sauntering about, wasting his time.
Invece di (m) lì colle mani a cintola, venite ad aiutarmi.	Instead of staying there idle, come and help me.
Vorrei morire, piuttosto (n) che servire un tal tiranno.	I would sooner die than serve such a tyrant.
Inoltre, non agì bene.	Besides, he did not act well.
Forse arriveranno questa sera, ma non si sa per certo.	Perhaps they will arrive this evening, but it is not certain.
A che ora arriva il treno? Non saprei precisamente; circa alle cinque.	At what time does the train arrive? I could not tell you exactly; at about five o'clock.
È così bravo che, per poco che studiasse, farebbe facilmente il suo esame.	He is so clever that, if he studied ever so little, he would easily pass his examination.

(a) *Or* per modo che.
(b) *Or* a bizzeffe.
(c) *Or* in fine, in breve.
(d) *Or* sicuramente, già.
(h) *Or* in disparte.
(i) *Or* senza complimenti.
(j) *Or* cioè a dire, vale a dire.
(k) *Or* all'oscuro.
(l) *Or* di nascosto.
(m) *Or* in luogo di.
(n) *Or* prima che, avanti che, innanzi che.

REMARKS ON "ONDE,"* "BENE," AND "PURE."

886. The adverb "Onde" is used especially in the higher style and in poetry instead of "di cui," "del quale," &c., "da cui," "dal quale," &c., "per cui," "pel quale," &c. Ex.
"Di quei sospiri ond' io nutriva il core." (Petrarca).
Of those sighs with which I nourished my heart.

887. "Onde" and "donde" have also the meaning of *good reason for*. Ex.
"Oimè, bene il conosco ed ho ben donde." (Tasso).
Alas, I know him well and I have good reasons for it.

888. "Onde" has also the meaning of *therefore*. Ex.

Si fa buio, onde è meglio andarsene.	It is getting dark, therefore we had better go.

889. "Onde" has also the meaning of *in order to*. Ex.

Egli riparò qui, onde salvarsi.	He repaired here, to save himself.

890. "Onde" has also the meaning of *from whence*. Ex.

Onde venite, così tardi?	Whence do you come so late?

891. "Bensì" ("bene sì") means *it is true*. Ex.

Sempre mi prometteva bene† (*or* bensì) del danaro, ma non me ne dava mai.	It is true that he always promises me money, but he never gives me any.

892. "Ben altro" means *quite another matter*. Ex.

Ben altro udrai fra poco.	You will soon hear more important news.

893. "Pure" is sometimes used for "solamente," *only*. Ex.

Ciò accadde non pure una volta, ma cento.	That happened not only once, but a hundred times.

894. "Pure" is sometimes used to give strength to an expression. Ex.

A che pur pensa?	What are you still thinking of?
Dite pure quel che volete.	You may say what you like.

895. "E pure," or "eppure," means *and yet*. Ex.

"E pur si move!" (Galileo).	It moves though!

896. "Nè pure," or "neppure" means *not even*. Ex.

Non avevo neppure un soldo.	I had not even a half-penny.

897. "Pur troppo" means *alas too well, alas too true*. Ex.

È vero che Carlo è fuggito? Pur troppo!	Is it true that Charles has fled? It is but too true!

---

* The word "onde," as a noun, means *waves*.

898. † "Bene" and "bensì" may be put before the verb. Ex. "Bene (*or* Bensì) mi prometteva sempre del danaro, ma," etc.

899. SENTENCES CONTAINING ADVERBS OF QUANTITY.

(To be learnt by heart.)

Ho speso a bastanza (a) danaro; più (b) di voi; non voglio spender di più.	I have spent enough money; more than you; I will not spend any more.
Studiano poco; meno (b) di noi; non più di tre ore ogni giorno.	They study little; less than we do; not more than three hours a day.
Ho veduto solamente (c) tre elefanti in vita mia.	I have only seen three elephants in my life.
Non avevo che (d) cento lire sterline, eppure furono abbastanza.	I had only a hundred pounds, and yet it was enough.
Era alquanto (e) spiacente di non essere stato eletto, ma non molto.	He was somewhat displeased at not having been elected, but not much.
Fu quasi (f) ucciso in quella zuffa; erano tre contr'uno.	He was almost killed in that quarrel; they were three to one.
Non pensò guari, e poi mi domandò un poco (g) di danaro in prestito.	He did not think much, and then asked me for a little money as a loan.
V'erano molti soldati alla rivista? A un dipresso (h) ventimila.	Were there many soldiers at the review? About twenty thousand.

EXERCISE LXXIX.

At what o'clock must they depart? At half past seven. Then, I shall lay the cloth at once. The dinner will be ready in half an hour. Walk slowly, my daughter, I have a pain in my foot; I cannot walk quickly. Do what I tell you, otherwise I shall dismiss you. Do you speak in earnest? Certainly. Why did you break my penknife? I did not do it (209) on purpose; it was a mere accident. I tell you frankly that you ought to apologise to him, at once. He started up suddenly (885, o) and gave Francis a fearful blow. The most beautiful flowers last but (802) a short time. The compass was not invented (799) by a mariner, nor (800) the telescope by an astronomer, nor the microscope by a philosopher, nor printing by a man of letters, nor gunpowder by a soldier. The loadstone always points towards the north.

(a) *Or* a sufficienza.
(b) The adverbs "più" and "meno" are the comparative forms of "molto" and "poco."
(c) *Or* soltanto.
(d) When *only* means *but*, it is translated into Italian by "non (verb) che."
(e) *Or* un tantino.
(f) *Or* presso che.
(g) "Poco" is the only adverb followed by "di."
(h) *Or* presso a poco.

LESSON XXXIX.

ON PREPOSITIONS.

900. The Principal Prepositions are :—

Di,	of.	Accanto a,	beside.
A,	to, at.	Vicino a,*	near.
In,	in within.	Presso a,	
Per,	for, through, in order to.	Intorno a,	about, around, near.
		D'intorno a,	
Con,	with.	Attorno a,	
Fra, *or* tra,	between.	Lontano da,*	far.
Infra, *or* intra,		Lungi da,	
In mezzo a,		Lungo,	along, alongside.
Entro,		Lunghesso,	
Su, *or*	on, upon.	Stante,	according to.
Sopra,		Secondo,	
		A seconda di,	
Sotto,	under, underneath.	Durante,	during.
Di sotto di,			
Dentro,	in, within.	Eccetto,	except.
Di dentro di,		Salvo,	
Fuori di,	outside.	Mediante,	by means of, concerning.
Di fuori di,		Rispetto a,	
Prima di,	before.	Tranne,	excepting.
Avanti di,*		Senza,	without.
Davanti a,		Contro,	against.
Innanzi di,*		Contra,	
Dinanzi di,		In vece di,	instead of.
Dietro a,	behind.	Oltre,	beyond.
Di dietro a,		Verso,	towards.
In faccia a,	opposite.	Alla volta di,	
Rimpetto a,		Malgrado,	in spite of, notwithstanding.
Di rimpetto a,		Nonostante,	
Dopo,	after.	Ad onta di,	

* "Avanti," "innanzi," "vicino," and "lontano" can also be used as adverbs.

THE PREPOSITION "DI," *OF*.

901. The preposition "di" is used to denote relation of property, affinity, and connection between one word and another. Ex.

Il padrone di questa casa.	The master of this house.
Una casa di campagna.	A country-house.
Il libro di mio fratello.	My brother's book.
La Divina Commedia di Dante.	Dante's Divine Comedy.
Il regno di Spagna.	The kingdom of Spain.
Il duomo di Milano.	The cathedral of Milan.
Un abito d'inverno.	A winter coat.
Questo signore è di Napoli.	This gentleman is from Naples.

902. The Preposition "di" is also used to connect two nouns when the second of them is the name of the material which the object indicated by the first noun is "made of," "full of," or "deals in." Ex.

Un cappello di paglia.	A straw hat.
Un bicchiere di vino.	A glass of wine.
Mercanti di tè.	Tea merchants.

903. The Preposition "di" is also used after an adjective, or a past participle preceded by a verb, expressing any idea of rest, or state. Ex.

Il mio cavallo era coperto di fango.	My horse was covered with mud.
Egli era carico di onori.	He was loaded with honours.
Ella è dotata di bonissimo ingegno.	She is endowed with very great intelligence.
Parve contento di vedermi.	He appeared pleased at seeing me.
Sono felice di proporle cosa di tanta utilità.	I am happy to propose to you a thing so useful.
Mio padre mi ha promesso di condurmi a Milano.	My father has promised to take me to Milan.
Ho dimenticato di mandare queste lettere alla posta.	I have forgotten to send these letters to the post.

904. The Preposition "di" is also used in the phrases:—

Viaggiar di giorno,* di notte, *to travel by day, by night.*
Vivere di frutti, di legumi, &c., *to live on fruit, on vegetables, &c.*

---

* That is to say "in tempo di giorno."

THE PREPOSITION "A" *TO, AT.*

905. The preposition "a" is used to indicate the end or object to which the action of the verb is directed. Ex.

Ho parlato a Carlo.	I have spoken to Charles.
Vado sovente a Parigi.	I often go to Paris.

906. The preposition "a" is also used to denote a state. Ex.

Mia sorella è a scuola.	My sister is at school.
Mio padre è a casa di Paolo.	My father is at Paul's.
Mio fratello è ancora a Venezia.	My brother is still in Venice.

907. The preposition "a" is also used to connect two nouns, the first of which denotes the means by which the object expressed by the first noun acts. Ex.

Un battello a vapore.	A steam-boat.
Un mulino a vento.	A windmill.
Un bastimento a vela.	A sailing-vessel.

908. The preposition "a" is also used to indicate the form in which an object is made. Ex.

Un abito a coda di rondine.	A swallow-tail coat.

909. The preposition "a" is also used in the sense of "with." Ex.

Un campo a luppoli.	A hop-field.
Un cappello a larghe falde.	A hat with a broad brim.
Lucia portava un bel busto di broccato a fiori.	Lucy wore a pretty bodice of flowered brocade.

910. The preposition "a" is also used in the following phrases:—

Tagliare a fette.	To cut in slices.
Stare a bocca aperta.	To remain open-mouthed.
Stare a occhi bassi.	To remain with downcast eyes.
Cantare a meraviglia.	To sing wonderfully well.
Darsi a conoscere.	To make one's-self known.
Morire a centinaia.	To die by hundreds.
Andare a due a due, &c.	To go two by two, &c.
Un cannone carico a mitraglia.*	A cannon loaded with grapeshot.

---

* Besides the phrases given above, the preposition "a" is used in the verbal expressions "andare a gara," *to vie,* "stare a galla," *to float,* "tener a bada," *to trifle with,* &c., which have been already given.

911. The preposition "a" is also used in the adverbial expressions "alla francese," *in the French fashion*, "alla rinfusa," *in a confusion*, &c., already given, rule 885.

912. The preposition "a" is also used before a verb in the Infinitive mood, preceded by another verb expressing motion. Ex.

Venga a trovarmi domani.	Come to see me to-morrow.
Andate ad impostare queste lettere.	Go to post these letters.
Venga a pranzo con me.	Come and* dine with me.

THE PREPOSITION "DA," *FROM, BY, &c.*

913. The preposition "da" is used in the sense of "from." Ex.

Arrivai ieri da Vienna.	I arrived yesterday from Vienna.
Ho ricevuto regali da lui.	I have received presents from him.
Rafaello da Urbino morì all'età di trentasette anni.	Raphael (from) Urbino died at the age of thirty-seven.
Rimase prigioniero da maggio fino a novembre.	He remained a prisoner from May to November.

914. The preposition "da" is also used in the sense of "by," "near," "in the direction of," "through." Ex.

Andando a Costantinopoli passai da Atene.	In going to Constantinople I passed by Athens.
Nell'andare a scuola passai da Strada della Croce.	In going to school I went through Cross Street.

915. The preposition "da" is also used in the sense of "by" when preceded by a past participle. Ex.

Egli è stimato da tutti.	He is esteemed by everybody.
Ho comprato un bellissimo quadro dipinto da Landseer.	I have bought a beautiful picture painted by Landseer.

916. The preposition "da" sometimes means "by myself," "by my own will," &c., "by yourself," "by your own will," &c. Ex.

L'ha fatto da sè.	He did it by himself.
Da me non venni.	I did not come by my own will.

---

* As already stated, the preposition "a" is used in Italian instead of the English conjunction *and*, after a verb expressing motion. Ex.
Andate a prendermi il mio cappello. Go and fetch my hat.

917. The preposition "da"* is also used to connect two nouns, the first of which expresses the use or destination of the second. Ex.

Carta da scrivere.	Writing paper.
Una bottiglia da vino.	A wine bottle.
Una veste da camera.	A dressing-gown.
Un istrumento da fiato.	A wind instrument.
Un cavallo da corsa.	A race-horse.

918. The preposition "da" is also used in the sense of "to," "towards." Ex.

Ecco là i vostri amici, andate da loro.	There are your friends, go to them.

919. The preposition "da" is also used in the sense of "at the house of."* Ex.

Passerò da Lei domani, o pos-domani.	I will call on you to-morrow, or the day after to-morrow.

920. The preposition "da" is also used in the sense of "wherewith." Ex.

Questo povero vecchio non ha da mangiare.	This poor old man has nothing to eat.
Datemi da scrivere; voglio scrivere a mio fratello.	Give me something to write with; I want to write to my brother.

921. The preposition "da" is also used in the sense of "fit for." Ex.

Vi assicuro che non è cosa da ridere.	I assure you it is no laughing matter.
Mi ha fatto un azione da mariuolo.	He played me a knavish trick.

922. The preposition "da" is also used in the sense of "like a." Ex.

Egli combattè da eroe, e morì da Cristiano.	He fought like a hero, and died like a Christian.
L'ho sempre trattato da amico.	I always treated him as a friend.
Vi parlo da padrone, e voi dovreste ubbidirmi da servo.	I speak to you as a master, and you should obey me as a servant.

923. The preposition "da" is also used in the sense of "on." Ex.

Da una parte c'era un bel praticello, dall'altra un vigneto.	On one side there was a pretty little meadow, on the other a vineyard.

924. * The expressions "da me," "da te," &c., must not be used instead of "a casa mia," &c., when ambiguity may be incurred; for instance, *I am going home*, must be translated by "vado a casa," and not "vado da me."

THE PREPOSITION "IN," *IN, INTO.*

925. The Italian preposition "in" has generally the same meaning as the English preposition *in, into.* Ex.

Sua moglie è in Swizzera.	His wife is in Switzerland.
L'ho tradotto in francese.	I translated it into French.

926. In Italian the preposition "in" does not require the definite article after it in sentences like the following:—

Era in giardino con Giovanni.	He was in the garden with John.
Non vado mai in cucina.	I never go into the kitchen.
Carlo è in cantina a mettere vino in bottiglia.	Charles is in the cellar bottling some wine.
Aveva un bastone in mano.	He had a stick in his hand.
Essi discutono in istrada.	They are discussing in the street.

927. In sentences like the following the preposition "in" is not translated literally into English:—

Non posso stare in piedi.	I cannot stand on my feet.
Tien e il cappello in testa.	He keeps his hat on his head.
Aveva in dito un anello d'oro.	He had a gold ring on his finger.
Il pranzo era già in tavola.	The dinner was already served.
Lingua toscana in bocca romana.	The Tuscan language as it is spoken by the Romans.
Mi piace molto andare in barca.	I am very fond of rowing on the river.
Va in chiesa ogni domenica.	She goes to church every Sunday.
Andò in Austria un mese fa.	He went to Austria a month ago.
Scriverò la mia lettera in un'ora.	It will take me an hour to write my letter.

THE PREPOSITION "PER," *FOR, THROUGH, IN ORDER TO.*

928. The preposition "per" is also used in the sense of "for." Ex.

L'ho dipinto apposta per Lei.	I painted it on purpose for you.

929. The preposition "per" is also used in the sense of "in order to." Ex.

Ritornerò presto per compiacervi.	I will return soon to please you.

930. The preposition "per"* is also used in the sense of *because, on account of.* Ex.

Fu espulso per aver osato mettere in caricatura il suo maestro.	He was expelled because he caricatured his master.

---

* In this case "per" is used instead of "per causa di," *because, on account of.*

931. The preposition "per" is also used in the expressions "per uno," *each*, and "per tempo," *early*. Ex.

Ricevettero uno scellino per uno, perchè vennero per tempo.
They received a shilling each, because they came early.

932. The prepositions "su per" are used together to express graphically an upward progress. Ex.

Andammo su per la collina.
We went up the hill.

THE PREPOSITION "CON," *WITH*.

933. The preposition "con" has *generally* the same meaning as the English preposition *with*. Ex.

Oggi ho pranzato con un vecchio amico di scuola.
To-day I dined with an old schoolfellow.

Dipingo sempre con colori francesi.
I always paint with French colours.

"FRA," AND "TRA," *BETWEEN, AMONGST*.

934. "Fra" and "tra," besides meaning "between," "amongst," "in the midst of," are used in the sense of "after the space of," "hence." Ex.

Scriverò la mia lettera fra un' ora.
I shall write my letter in an hour (in an hour hence).

Carlo ritornerà fra (*or* da qui a) due mesi.
Charles will return in two months (two months hence).

935. "Parlare tra sè" means *to speak to one's self*. Ex.

Egli soleva passeggiar soletto e parlare tra sè ad alta voce.
He used to walk alone speaking aloud to himself.

THE PREPOSITIONS "SU," "SOPRA," "SOVRA,"* ON, UPON.

936. The prepositions "su," and "sopra," have generally the same meaning and are used in the same way as the English preposition *on, upon*. In the following sentences, however, "su" and "sopra" are translated by other prepositions than *on* or *upon*:—

Egli abitava una villa a venti miglia sopra Firenze.
He inhabited a villa twenty miles beyond Florence.

Partimmo in sull' alba, e ritornammo sulla sera.
We started at break of day, and returned at dusk.

Ordinarono un grandissimo esercito per andare sopra i nemici. (Boccaccio).
They organized a very numerous army to go against the enemy.

---

* The other prepositions given on page 198 do not require any explanation.

LESSON XL.

ON THE COMPLEMENTS OF VERBS.

One of the most difficult things for English people learning Italian, is the proper use of the complements of verbs, that is to say, the proper use of the prepositions which ought to follow verbs to complete their meaning. In some cases the English and Italian languages agree on this point, but in many instances there is a remarkable difference between them, as will be shown in the seven following exercises.

937. VERBS WHICH DO NOT REQUIRE ANY PREPOSITION IN ITALIAN, ALTHOUGH THEY REQUIRE ONE AFTER THEM IN ENGLISH.

EXERCISE LXXX.

Do not listen to (a) him; if he begins to* talk, he will not stop all day. I am waiting for (b) (251) my brother. I have been looking (714) for (c) some red ink this half hour. I have bought (to buy for) (d) these steel pens for sixpence a dozen. Charles is well acquainted with (e) our affairs. We look upon (f) him as your best friend. She wished for (g) her mother's return. He puts off (h) his decision from (di) day to day; I do not like that (608). I have asked (to ask for) (i) him for some matches† several times (602). They were (695) ignorant of (j) what we intended to do. I never met with (I have never met with) (k) a man so witty. Martial music inspires (inspire with) (l) soldiers with courage and confidence. She set off (m) yesterday morning by (per) the first train. I cannot bear with (n) his nonsense any longer (817). He sold (to sell for) (o) his house for two hundred pounds (656).

(a) Ascoltare.
(b) Aspettare.
(c) Cercare.
(d) Comprare.
(e) Conoscere.
(f) Considerare.
(g) Desiderare.
(h) Differire.
(i) Domandare a.
(j) Ignorare.
(k) Incontrare.
(l) Inspirare a.
(m) Partire.
(n) Soffrire.
(o) Vendere.

938. * The expressions *to begin to*, *to set about to*, are rendered in Italian by " Mettersi a," " Cominciare a."

939. † *Match*, " zolfanello." *Match* (in artillery), " miccia." *Match* (marriage), " matrimonio." *To match*, " assortire."

940. Verbs which do not require any preposition in English, although they require one after them in Italian.

EXERCISE LXXXI.

He wants (a) money to (225) furnish his house. He was told to mind (b) the horses while we were dining. They mocked (c) him, because he was poor. I ordered (d) him to leave the house, but he would not. I distrust (e) him. They displease (f) everybody. You will be punished, because you disobeyed (707) (g) your father. We asked (h) him to take (459) us to the opera. She doubted (i) the truth of his assertion. Every time (636) he entered (j) (697) the drawing-room, he bowed to the company. For many years we enjoyed (k) (704) the advantages of his friendship. She taught us (707) (l) the art of painting upon china. She understands (m) the fine arts. He would not hurt (n) my reputation.

EXERCISE LXXXII.

He was punished, because he would not obey (o) the king's order. I am sure (636) she will never pardon him for (p) (184) having broken her (562) watch. They permitted (q) him to make sketches of the castle. I persuaded (r) him to buy the pictures. It pleased (s) them to make me a (360) present of this pencil-case. He resisted (t) all the entreaties of his poor parents. Those who are not able to resist (t) temptations, ought (791) to avoid them. He had to (790) renounce (u) his bad companions. They used (707) (v) cement for the foundation of that building. I am sure that he will outlive (w) his nephew. He slanders (x) everybody. He ordered (d) the waiter to bring him a glass of wine, and a bottle of soda-water. The rivulet entered (j) a dark cavern on the western side of the hill.

(a) Abbisognare di.
(b) Aver cura di.
(c) Burlarsi di.
(d) Comandare a...di.
(e) Diffidarsi di.
(f) Dispiacere a.
(g) Disubbidire a.
(h) Domandare a...di.
(i) Dubitare di.
(j) Entrare in.
(k) Godere di.
(l) Insegnare a.
(m) Intendersi di.
(n) Nuocere a.
(o) Obbedire a.
(p) Perdonare a...di
(q) Permettere a...di.
(r) Persuadere a...di.
(s) Piacere a.
(t) Resistere a.
(u) Rinunciare a.
(v) Servirsi di.
(w) Sopravvivere a.
(x) Sparlare di.

941. Verbs which require one Preposition in Italian, and a different one in English.

EXERCISE LXXXIII.

The garden was embellished with (a) beautiful marble statues. This country abounds with (b) corn. His sword was adorned with (c) jewels. He grieved at (d) the loss of his property. He was satisfied with (e) (696) the little he had earned. They were burning with (f) indignation. When his deceit was (768) discovered, he blushed with (g) shame. I blame him for (h) having fled (685). The ship was laden with (i) provisions for the besieged fortress. All the guns were loaded with (j) balls. They loaded him with (k) kindness. He could (767, 695) not be consoled for (l) the loss of his child. They all agree (842, g) that it is a poem to be (921) greatly admired.

EXERCISE LXXXIV.

They could (704) not agree about (m) the price. All the furniture was (696) covered with (n) dust. I took possession of the room destined for (o) me. Everything depends upon (p) what he is going to say. He parted with (q) (704) his vicious horse as soon as he could. He was (702) endowed with (r) the finest (518) gifts that nature can give. They had filled (with) (s) the rooms with the old furniture they had taken from the castle. He was presented with (t) a beautiful gold watch (346). I congratulated him upon (u) the success he has obtained. He glories in (v) the mischief he does. She wore a beautiful white satin dress trimmed with (w) pearls. He seized upon (x) our goods.

(a) Abbellire di.*	(i) Caricare di.	(q) Disfarsi di.
(b) Abbondare di.	(j) Caricare a.	(r) Dotare di.
(c) Adornare di.	(k) Colmare di.	(s) Empire di.*
(d) Affliggersi di.	(l) Consolare di.	(t) Far regalo a…di.
(e) Appagarsi di.	(m) Convenire di.†	(u) Felicitare di.
(f) **Ardere** di.	(n) Coprire di.‡	(v) Glorificarsi di.
(g) Arrossire di.*	(o) Destinare a.	(w) Guarnire di.*
(h) Biasimare di.	(p) Dipendere da.	(x) Impadronirsi di.*

* This verb is conjugated like "Finire."

942. † "Convenire" (irregular) besides the above meaning of *to agree on*, or *about*, and the meaning of *to be obliged*, or *compelled*, explained in rule 136, it has also the meaning of *to meet by appointment*. Ex.
    Convennero nel Teatro della Scala.   They met in the Teatro della Scala.

‡ This verb is conjugated like "Servire."

943. Verbs which require one Preposition in Italian, and a different one in English.

EXERCISE LXXXV.

He was inflamed with (a) rage, on hearing (686) the losses he had sustained. He inquired about (b) the state of the country. The table was (696) covered with (c) books and papers. He fell in love with (d) my cousin. He languished from (703) (e) hunger for (311) three days, and then died. He praised them for (f) their honesty. She wondered at (g) the sudden return of my brother. He was threatened with (h) (767) death if he would not confess the truth. He meddles with (i) everybody's business. His mind was stored with (j) useful knowledge. The theft was concealed a long time from (k) everybody. He was fed on (l) (703) fish and fruit for three weeks. They were oppressed with (m) taxes. I shall call upon (n) you this evening.

EXERCISE LXXXVI.

What were you thinking of (o) when I met you? They wept for (p) joy when they heard that their father had arrived. They profited by (q) the ruin of their friend. He was punished for (r) the crime he had committed. They were speaking about (of) politics (419) till midnight. They rejoiced at (s) the good news. He laughed at (t) the misfortune of my brother. He returned thanks for (u) the favour he had received. He will have (790) to answer for (v) his bad conduct. They were surfeited with (w) food. In consequence of his behaviour at the last election he has (is) decreased in (x) popularity. He used (697) to take (y) the money from his sister. He triumphed over (z) his enemies at last. He lives upon (aa) a pension granted to him by the king.

(a) Infiammare di.	(j) Munire di.*	(s) Rallegrarsi di.
(b) Informarsi di.	(k) Nascondere a.	(t) Ridersi di.
(c) Ingombrare di.	(l) Nutrire di.	(u) Ringraziare di.
(d) Innamorarsi di.	(m) Opprimere di.	(v) Rispondere di.
(e) Languire di.*	(n) Passare da.	(w) Satollarsi di.
(f) Lodare di.	(o) Pensare a.	(x) Scemare di.
(g) Maravigliarsi di.	(p) Piangere di.	(y) Togliere a.
(h) Minacciare di.	(q) Profittare di.	(z) Trionfare di.
(i) Ingerirsi in.*	(r) Punire di.*	(aa) Vivere di.

* This verb is conjugated like "Finire."

LESSON XLI.

ON CONJUNCTIONS AND INTERJECTIONS.

§ 1. On Conjunctions.

944. The Italian conjunctions are followed by verbs either in the Indicative, the Subjunctive, or the Infinitive Mood.

945. The following Conjunctions govern the Verb in the Indicative Mood.

E,	and.	Pure,	⎫
E pure, eppure,*	and yet.	Tuttavia,	⎪
O,	or.	Tuttavolta,	⎪ yet,
O......o,	⎫	Nonostante,	⎬ for all that,
Ovvero...ovvero,	⎬ either...or.	Nondimeno,	⎪ nevertheless.
Ossia...ossia,	⎭	Nulladimeno,	⎪
Non (verb) nè...nè,	neither...nor.	Ciononpertanto,	⎪
Ma,	but.	Con tutto ciò,	⎭
Però,	⎫	Anche,	⎫ also,
Pertanto,	⎬ however.	Altresì,	⎬ moreover.
Perchè,	⎫	Eziandìo,	⎭
Perocchè,	⎪	In fine,	⎫ in fact.
Perciocchè,	⎪ because,	In somma,	⎭
Conciossiachè,	⎬ since, in as	Se non che,	⎫
Poichè,	⎪ much as.	Salvo che,	⎬ except that.
Giacchè,	⎪	Eccetto che,	⎪
Stantechè,	⎭	Tranne che,	⎭
Quindi,	⎫	Secondo che,	according as.
Laonde,	⎬ therefore.	Cioè,	⎫
Così,	⎭	Cioè a dire,	⎬ that is to say.
Anzi,	⎫ nay, more,	Vale a dire,	⎭
Che dico,	⎭ on the contrary.	Stante,	referring to.
Di più,	⎫	Tanto più che,	{ so much the more so that.
Inoltre,	⎪		
D'altronde,	⎬ besides.	Quand'è così,	in that case.
Oltracchè,	⎪	Quand'ecco,	when, behold.
Oltracciò,	⎭	Ecco perchè,	that is why.

946. The conjunction "anzi" is very expressive, it means *on the contrary, further, nay, rather.* Ex.

Egli venne a vederci, anzi pranzò con noi.   He came to see us, nay more, he dined with us.

"Anzi impediva tanto 'l mio cammino."   (Dante).
Nay, rather did impede so much my way.

---

* "E pure" has been illustrated in rule 891.

947. NOTE.—As the Conjunctions which govern verbs in the Subjunctive Mood were given in rule 730 (page 162) and rule 740 (page 164), they will not be repeated here.

948. THE FOLLOWING CONJUNCTIONS GOVERN THE VERB IN THE INFINITIVE MOOD :—

A fine di,	in order to.	Per tema di, }	for fear of.
Avanti di	before.	Per paura di, }	
A condizione di, }	on condition of.	A meno di,	unless.
Con patto di, }		Lungi dal,	far from.

§ 2. ON INTERJECTIONS.

949. Besides the interjections ah! oh! which in Italian, as in most languages, indicate almost any sudden emotion of the mind, the following are the principal Italian interjections :—

950. ADMIRATION.
Buono!		good!
Capperi!	Affè!	I say!
Bene!	Bravo!	well done!
Bis!		encore!
Viva!	Evviva!	hurrah!

951. ENCOURAGEMENT.
Su! Via!	Suvvia!	come now!
Animo!	Coraggio!	courage!

952. ENTREATY.
Deh! Di grazia!	pray!
Mercè!	mercy!

953. WARNING.
Guai a voi!	woe to you!
Badate!	take care!
Piano! Adagio!	softly!

954. GRIEF AND SURPRISE.
Ahi! Ahi lasso!	ay! oh dear!
Aimè! Oimè!	oh me!
Lasso! Lasso me!	alas!
Che peccato!	what a pity!
Povero me!	poor me!
O cielo!	O heavens!

955. AVERSION AND INDIGNATION.
Ma che!	nonsense!
Le zucche!	twice! not I!
Via! Oibò!	pshaw! fie!
Vergogna!	for shame!

956. CALLING AND SILENCING.
Ehi! Olà! St!	oh hey! st!
Silenzio!	silence!
Zitto! Cheto!	hush! be still!
Basta! Basta così!	enough!

957. * The interjection "O...!" is only used, before a noun, in the lofty style: it expresses different emotions of the mind. Ex.

O crudel destino! O cruel destiny! O patria mia! O my country!

EXERCISE LXXXVII.

The eagle rises above the clouds. The wise man acts according to (900) the dictates of reason. He has gone to America in spite of (900) the advice of his best friends. The fleet cannot sail on account of (930) contrary winds. On (298) that occasion he acted like a (925) hero. You were playing, instead of (900) studying. When I went out, I saw* her leaning against the window. Here is Mrs. Pettegola; she comes to propose an arrangement between us two. What a bore! Why does she not mind her own affairs; she has nothing to do with this matter.† Margaret wrote me a line‡ the day before yesterday, informing me of her intended departure for Venice, in a week (549), or ten days.

EXERCISE LXXXVIII.

"About that time I walked out into the fields towards Bow. Here§ I met a poor man walking on the bank of the river." "On the fifteenth of May they were ten miles from Pekin. They had now‖ been travelling for six months." The immediate loss of Constantinople may be ascribed (771) to the bullet, or arrow, which pierced the gauntlet of John Giustiniani. "Into the ecclesiastic federation our Saxon ancestors were admitted.¶ A regular communication was opened between our shores and that part of Europe in which the traces of ancient power and policy were yet discernible." Courage! (951) soldiers, fear nothing (672). For shame! (955) said he, to insult a poor old man. Softly (953), do not fly into a passion. Pray! (952) do not make such a noise. We have arrived at the end of the grammar. Hurrah!

---

958. * After the verbs "vedere," to see, and "scorgere," to perceive, the Past Participle is employed to describe a person or thing in a state. Ex.
L'ho veduta appoggiata alla finestra. I saw her leaning against the window.

959. † The expressions *to concern, to have something to do with the matter,* are translated into Italian by the verb "entrare" and the adverb "ci," thus: "Io c'entro," "tu c'entri," "egli c'entra," "noi c'entriamo," &c. *It concerns me, &c.*

960. ‡ *A line* in writing is translated by "una riga;" *a line* made with a pencil, or a pen, by "una linea;" and *a line* of poetry, by "un verso."

961. § When *here* is used in English instead of *there*, it must be translated into Italian by "là," *there.*

962. ‖ When *now* is used in English instead of *then*, it must be translated into Italian by "allora," *then.*

963. ¶ In a case like this, when, in English there are several sentences containing verbs in the passive form, in Italian, each sentence should be given a different turn. In this particular case the first phrase should be translated as if it was, "Our Saxon ancestors were admitted into," &c. The second should be translated as if it was, "One opened (or established) a regular communication," &c. The third must be translated so as to introduce "si," followed by the verb in the singular, or plural, according to rule 771.

TRANSPOSITION OF WORDS IN ITALIAN SENTENCES.

964. In Italian poetry, words are constantly transposed so as to add force, and impart harmony to the verses, but in modern Italian prose the words in sentences preserve, as a rule, the most simple and direct order, and are arranged in accordance with the rules explained in this grammar.* In some cases, however, clearness, force, and fluency of diction are obtained by inverting the order of words.† The following examples may be interesting and instructive to the student:—

I. "Salirono la scala Don Michele e Boscherino, e vennero alla camera dov'era il duca," (D'Azeglio) *instead of* " Don Michele e Boscherino salirono la scala, &c.," *Don Michele and Boscherino mounted the stairs, and entered the room where the duke was.*

II. "Ventitrè o ventiquattro giorni stettero i nostri fuggitivi nel castello, in mezzo a un movimento continuo," (Manzoni) *instead of* "I nostri fuggitivi stettero nel castello ventitrè o ventiquattro giorni, in mezzo a un movimento continuo," *Our fugitives remained twenty-three or twenty-four days in the castle, in the midst of a general movement.*

III. "Egli solo delle vostre ragioni e della mia fede potrà esser giudice," (Monti) *instead of* " Egli solo potrà esser giudice, &c.," *He alone can be the judge of your reasons, and of my fidelity.*

IV. "Alle premure reiterate ed autorevoli, Caterina rispose sempre con un rifiuto," (Tommaseo) *instead of* " Caterina rispose sempre con un rifiuto alle premure reiterate ed autorevoli," *Catherine always answered with a refusal to the often repeated and authoritative entreaties.*

V. "Ma a nessuno (dei forni) la gente accorse in numero tale da poter intraprender tutto," (Manzoni) *instead of* " Ma la gente non accorse a nessuno, &c.," *But to none (of the bakers' shops) did the people rush in sufficient numbers to be able to undertake everything.*

VI. "Fin qui può correre il mio servigio," (Monti) *instead of* " Il mio servigio può correre fin qui," *Thus far my services may extend.*

VII. "La fantasìa si rifugiò fredda nella mia memoria," (Foscolo) *instead of* " La fredda fantasia si rifugiò nella mia memoria," *My fancy (imagination) shrank cold into my memory.*

---

* In Manzoni's celebrated novel "I Promessi Sposi," which is the best written book in modern Italian, upwards of ninety sentences out of every hundred are written in direct syntax, entirely in harmony with modern thoughts and feelings.

† This matter belongs rather to rhetoric than to grammar, nevertheless it may be acceptable not to leave it wholly unnoticed here.

IDIOMS AND SAYINGS.

1. Non veggo l'ora di parlargli. — I long to speak to him.
2. Costui è nato vestito. — That fellow was born with a silver spoon in his mouth.
3. Egli vuol salvar la capra e i cavoli. — He wants to run with the hare and hunt with the hounds.
4. Sfido io! sa ben condurre la sua barca. — I rather think so; he can paddle his own canoe.
5. Oramai siamo a buon porto. — We are now out of danger.
6. Non si può fare un buco nell' acqua. — There's no washing the black-a-moor white.
7. Questo ragazzo ha il cuore in bocca. — This boy is very sincere.
8. Suo fratello non ha sale in zucca. — His brother is weak-minded.
9. Gli è venuto il grillo di viaggiare. — He has taken a fancy to travel.
10. È come portar acqua al mare. — It is like carrying coals to Newcastle.
11. Egli ha perduto la tramontana (*or* la bussola). — He is quite bewildered (*or* at his wit's end).
12. Ei cerca sempre il pelo nell' ovo. — He is always very particular.
13. Costui si compra brighe a denari contanti. — This man wants to get into trouble.
14. Parlate sul serio o per ischerzo? — Do you speak in earnest or in jest?
15. Fare un viaggio e due servizi. — To kill two birds with one stone.
16. Questo c'entra come il cavolo a merenda. — This is entirely beside the question.

LITERAL TRANSLATION.

1. I do not see the hour of speaking to him.
2. That fellow was born dressed.
3. He wishes to save the goat and the cabbages.
4. I challenge (any one to do better); he knows how to steer his boat.
5. Now we are in a good harbour.
6. One cannot make a hole in the water.
7. This boy has his heart in his mouth.
8. His brother has no salt in his pumpkin (head).
9. The grasshopper (whim) has come to him to travel.
11. He has lost the point marking north (*or* the mariner's compass).
12. He always looks for a hair in the egg.
13. This man buys troubles with cash.
16. This enters in it like the cabbage in a picnic.

IDIOMS AND SAYINGS.

1.	Ma sapete che ne va la vita?	But do you know that life is at stake?
2.	Colui fa la gatta morta, ma è molto astuto.	That fellow looks as if butter would not melt in his mouth, but he is very astute.
3.	Promette mari e monti, per tenermi a bocca dolce.	He is very prodigal of promises with me, in order to keep me quiet.
4.	Egli vuol vendere lucciole per lanterne.	He wants to make one believe that the moon is made of green cheese.
5.	Non posso trovare il bandolo della matassa.	I cannot find the proper way.
6.	I paperi vogliono menar a ber le oche.	The goslings try to teach the ganders how to swim.
7.	Camminavano a braccetto.	They were walking arm-in-arm.
8.	Non so cosa abbia nome.	I don't know what his name is.
9.	La mia finestra dà sur un bellissimo giardino.	My window looks upon a beautiful garden.
10.	La collera ha la meglio della sua ragione.	Passion prevails over his reason.
11.	Non li posso soffrire perchè lavorano sempre sott' acqua.	I cannot bear them because they always act in an underhand manner.
12.	Essa rende sempre pane per focaccia.	She always gives tit for tat.
13.	Il bosco si estende oltre il tiro dell' occhio.	The wood extends further than the eye can see.
14.	Egli s' intende di libri.	He is a good judge of books.
15.	Ma perchè la prende con me?	Why do you find fault with me?
16.	Auguro a tutti felicissime feste e buon capo d' anno.	I wish you all a merry Christmas and a happy new year.

LITERAL TRANSLATION.

1. But do you know that for it goes life (life is risked).
2. That fellow shams the dead cat, but he is very astute.
3. He promises seas and mountains to keep my mouth sweet.
4. He wishes to sell glow-worms for lanterns.
5. I cannot find the end of the skein.
6. The goslings wish to lead the ganders to drink.
10. Anger has the better over his reason
11. "Sott' acqua" literally means *under water*.
12. She always gives bread for bun.
13. The wood extends beyond the reach of the eye.
14. He understands books.
15. But why do you take (up) the matter with me?
16. I wish to all very happy feasts, and a good head of the year.

ITALIAN PROVERBS.

1. Volere, è potere. — Where there's a will, there's a way.
2. A chi ha testa, non manca cappello. — A good head is never in want of a hat.
3. Acqua cheta rovina i ponti. — Still waters run deep.
4. Batti il ferro quand'è caldo. — Make hay while the sun shines.
5. Buon principio è la metà dell' opera. — Well begun is half-done.
6. Chi è in difetto, è in sospetto. — He that is in fault, is in suspicion.
7. Chi la dura, la vince. — A mouse in time may cut a cable.
8. Chi parla, semina, chi tace, raccoglie. — The talker sows, the listener reaps.
9. Chi troppo abbraccia, nulla stringe. — Grasp all, lose all.
10. Chi va piano, va sano. — Slow and sure wins the race.
11. Dal detto al fatto vi è gran tratto. — Easier said than done.
12. Dimmi con chi vai, e ti dirò chi sei. — Birds of a feather flock together.
13. E meglio piegare che rompere. — Better bend than break.
14. Meglio è fringuello in man, che tordo in frasca. — A bird in the hand is worth two in the bush.
15. L'abito non fa il monaco. — It is not the cowl that makes the friar.
16. La bella gabbia non nutre l'uccello. — The fine cage won't feed the bird.
17. Oro non è tutto quel che risplende. — All is not gold that glitters.
18. Non v'è rosa senza spina. — No rose without a thorn.
19. Pietra mossa non fa musco. — A rolling stone gathers no moss.
20. Povertà non ha parenti. — Poverty has no kin.
21. Patti chiari, amici cari. — Short reckonings make long friends.
22. La fine corona l'opera. — All's well that ends well.

LITERAL TRANSLATION.

2. He who has a (good) head, is never short of a hat.
3. Quiet water ruins bridges.
7. He who persists, conquers.
8. He who speaks, sows, he who listens, reaps.
9. He who embraces (grasps) too much, grasps nothing.
10. He who goes slow, goes safe.
11. From the said to the done there is a great distance.
12. Tell me whom you go with, and I will tell you who you are.
14. It is better a chaffinch in the hand, than a thrush on the branch.
21. Clear arrangements, dear friends.

ENGLISH-ITALIAN DIALOGUES.
(To be learnt by heart.)

Good morning, how do you do?	Buon giorno, come sta?*
Very well, thank you, madam, and how are you?	Benissimo, signora, a' suoi comandi, e come sta lei?
Pretty well; I have had a slight cold in my chest, but I am better now.	Benino; ho avuto una lieve infreddatura di petto, ma oggi sto meglio.
I am glad to see you well again.	Godo di vederla ristabilita in salute.
How is your brother?	Come sta il suo signor fratello?
He has been ill for some days; he has to keep his room.	Da qualche giorno è ammalato; deve rimanere in camera.
I am very sorry for that; I hope it is not anything serious.	Me ne rincresce assai; amo credere che non sia cosa seria.
I do not think so; it is only a slight illness.	Credo di no, la è una leggera indisposizione.
Pray take a seat; you are not in a hurry, are you?	S'accomodi, la prego, non ha fretta, è vero?
Oh no; I have nothing to do to-day, but to make a few calls.	Oh no; non ho altra occupazione oggi che da fare alcune visite.
Then you had better stay and have luncheon with me.	Quand'è così, farà meglio di rimanere a fare una seconda colazione con me.
I do not usually take luncheon so early; however to keep you company, I will eat a little.	Non son solito di fare una seconda colazione così per tempo; però per farle compagnia, mangerò un boccone.
Let us go into the dining room.	Andiamo nella sala da pranzo.
Pray be seated.	Si segga qui, la prego.
May I offer you some oysters?	Posso offrirle delle ostriche?
I will trouble you for a few.	Ne accetterò qualcuna.
Allow me to pour you out a glass of white wine.	Lasci che le mesca un bicchiere di vino bianco.
Give me very little, I am not accustomed to drink wine.	Me ne dia ben poco non ho l'abitudine di ber vino.
Will you take a mutton chop, or some fowl?	Preferisce una costoletta di castrato o del pollo?
Thank you, I will take the wing or the leg of a fowl.	La ringrazio, mi favorisca un' ala od una coscia di pollo.

---

* These Dialogues are intended as *a beginning* to speak Italian. They are all in the third person singular, because, as explained in rule 120 (page 19), of this grammar, that is the mode of address between people not intimately acquainted, wishing to show respect to each other.

Will you have any fruit?	Vuol prendere un po' di frutta?
No, thank you; I would rather have a small piece of cheese.	No, la ringrazio; preferirei un bocconcino di formaggio (*or* cacio).
Do you take tea or coffee?	Beve tè o caffè?
I do not take either in the middle of the day.	Non bevo nè dell'uno nè dell' altro durante la giornata.
Well do as you like.	Ebbene faccia a suo genio.
Now if you like we will go out together.	Adesso se vuole usciremo insieme.
Very well, let us go.	Benissimo, usciamo.

Shall we go on foot or drive?	Andremo a piedi o in vettura?
I should like to walk a little way, and then take a cab.	Amerei camminare un pochino e poi prendere un calessino.
We can do that.	Ebbene si farà così.
It is cold to-day, is it not?	Fa freddo oggi, non è vero?
Yes, it is rather cold, but the sky is clear.	Anzi che no, ma però il cielo è sereno.
I prefer dry cold to damp unhealthy weather.	Preferisco un freddo secco ad un tempo umido e malsano.
So do I; I hate rain, snow, and fog.	Ed io pure; detesto la pioggia, la neve e la nebbia.
I like when there is a hard frost, because I am very fond of skating.	Amo quando c'è ghiaccio sull' acqua, perchè mi piace molto pattinare.
At what time must you be back to your hotel?	A che ora deve ritornare al suo albergo?
I should like to be in a little before dinner, so as to have time to dress.	M'aggradirebbe d'esser di ritorno un po' prima dell'ora del pranzo, per aver tempo di cambiar vestito.
Then we had better take a cab.	In questo caso sarà meglio di prendere un cabriolet.
I say, cabman, are you engaged?	Ehi! cocchiere siete impegnato?
No, sir.	No, signore.
Very well, then; drive us to 43, St. John's Street.	Va bene; guidate (portateci) Via San Giovanni, No. 43.

How well you speak Italian, Miss Field; have you studied it long?	Come parla bene l'italiano, Signorina Field; è molto tempo che lo studia?
I do not know exactly, I think about two years.	Non me ne rammento precisamente; da circa due anni.

Have you ever been to Italy?	È ella mai stata in Italia?
No, I have never been there.	No, non vi sono mai stata.
Really? I have been there three times, and yet I cannot speak Italian as correctly as you do.	Davvero? Io vi sono stata tre volte, eppure non so parlare italiano così correttamente come lei.
That is because you do not study it; you cannot learn a foreign language without studying it.	Ciò è perchè non lo studia; non si può imparare una lingua straniera senza studiarla sul serio.
Have you taken many lessons?	Ha prese molte lezioni?
Yes, I take two lessons regularly every week.	Sì, ho lezione regolarmente due volte la settimana.
Have you read many Italian books?	Ha ella letti molti libri italiani?
Yes; I have read three novels, about half of the "Divina Commedia," also "Saul," by Alfieri, several comedies, and the lyrics of Leopardi.	Sì; ho letto tre romanzi, la metà della "Divina Commedia," anche "il Saul," dell'Alfieri, parecchie commedie, e le liriche del Leopardi.
Which is the most interesting of the Italian books you have read?	Qual'è il più interessante dei libri italiani che ha letti?
Dante, of course; and of modern books, "I Promessi Sposi" is the one I care most for.	Dante, non occorre dirlo; e dei libri moderni preferisco "I Promessi Sposi" a tutti gli altri.
Do you intend to visit Italy?	Ha l'intenzione di veder l'Italia?
Indeed I do; I intend to go there next spring.	Altrochè! faccio i conti di andarvi la primavera prossima.
I wish you would allow me to accompany you.	Vorrei ch'ella mi permettesse d'accompagnarvela.
I shall be very pleased; we will start together next March, if all goes well.	Ne sarò contentissima; partiremo insieme il prossimo marzo, se non accadon disgrazie.
Very well, that is settled; goodbye.	Benissimo, siamo d'accordo; addio.

Well, did you go to Mr. Well's concert, last night?	Ebbene, andò ella al concerto del Signor Well, ieri sera?
Yes, I did; and I liked it very much.	Sì, v'andai; e mi piacque assai.
Were there many people?	C'erano molte persone?
Yes; the place was crowded.	Sì; un vero formicolaio.
Who were the performers?	Chi vi si produsse?

There were many *artistes*, but the most distinguished was the celebrated pianist Brook.	C'erano molti virtuosi; ma il più distinto era il celebre pianista Brook.
Well, is the *artiste* really deserving of his great reputation?	Or bene, questo virtuoso merita veramente la grande riputazione che gode?
Yes, I think so. He can draw from the piano the most exquisite sounds, and his execution is full of expression and grace.	Credo di sì. Egli sa cavare dal pianoforte suoni tali che incantano, e la sua esecuzione è oltre modo espressiva e graziosa.
Did the performance consist of instrumental music only?	Fu eseguita soltanto musica strumentale?
Oh no; there was plenty of vocal music.	Oh no; la musica vocale non venne dimenticata.
Miss Moretti sang a beautiful duet with Mr. Barnott.	La Signorina Moretti cantò un bel duetto col Signor Barnott.
What sort of voices have they?	Che voce hanno?
Miss Moretti has a powerful and thrilling soprano voice, and she can make it very soft and melodious.	La Signorina Moretti ha una voce di soprano, forte e vibrata, e sa renderla dolcissima ed armoniosa.
Mr. Barnott has a fine tenor voice, I have heard him several times; he is our best tenor.	Il Signor Barnott ha una bellissima voce di tenore; l'ho sentito cantare parecchie volte, è il miglior tenore che abbiamo.
His voice is not very powerful, but it is clear and very sympathic.	La sua voce non è molto forte, ma è chiara e assai simpatica.
Was the orchestra well managed?	Era ben condotta l'orchestra?
As well as it could be; let it suffice to say that it was conducted by Mr. Warbling.	Non si poteva meglio; basti dire che ne era conduttore il Signor Warbling.
I see that you are, like myself, passionately fond of music.	Veggo che lei, al par di me, è amantissima della musica.
I am indeed; I think it the best recreation we can enjoy.	Lo sono davvero; credo che sia il miglior divertimento che ci sia dato di godere.

What o'clock is it, Mr. Trench?	Che ora è, Signor Trench?
It is a quarter past eight.	Sono le otto e un quarto.
Have you had your breakfast?	Ha fatto colazione?
No; I have only just got up.	No; mi sono appena alzato.
When do you take your meals?	A che ora fa i suoi pasti?

We breakfast at nine, luncheon at half past one, and dine at six o'clock.	Facciamo colazione alle nove, la seconda colazione a un'ora e mezzo, e pranziamo alle sei.
What are you going to do before breakfast?	Di che cosa si occuperà prima di far colazione?
I am going to write a letter to my uncle.	Voglio scrivere una lettera a mio zio.
Do you write with steel pens or quills?	Scrive con penne metalliche, o con penne d'oca?
I always write with steel pens, I am so accustomed to write with them that I can scarcely write with any others.	Scrivo sempre con penne metalliche, ho tant'abitudine di servirmene, che con altre penne non so quasi più scrivere.
Have you got a sheet of blotting paper to lend me?	Avrebbe un foglio di carta sugante da prestarmi?
Yes, here is some, but it is not of very good quality.	Sì; eccogliene, ma non è di eccellente qualità.
To complete my obligation to you, sell me a postage-stamp.	Perchè le sia vieppiù obbligato, mi venda un francobollo.
Here it is, I give it to you, but will not sell it to you.	Eccogliene uno, glielo do, ma non voglio venderglielo.
Waiter, run and take this letter to the post.	Garzone, correte presto ad impostare questa lettera.

Do you draw, Miss Barretti?	Ella disegna, Signorina Barretti?
Yes, a little; I am only a beginner; but I am very fond of it.	Sì, un pochino; sono una principiante sa; ma mi piace tanto.
Do you draw from copies or from nature?	Copia da modelli o dalla natura?
As yet I only draw from copies, but I long to copy from nature.	Finora copio soltanto da modelli; ma non veggo l'ora di poter ritrarre dalla natura.
Have you been to the Royal Academy, this year?	È ella stata a vedere l'esposizione dei quadri all'Accademia Reale, quest'anno?
Yes, I went there last Monday.	Sì, v'andai lunedì scorso.
Well, what do you think of it?	Ebbene, che gliene pare?
It is a very fine exhibition; much more interesting than that of last year.	E una bellissima esposizione; molto più interessante che quella dell'anno scorso.
Have you seen the New Gallery in Regent Street?	Ha visitata la Galleria Nuova nella strada del Reggente?
Yes, I have; I think it excellent.	Sì, l'ho visitata; mi pare eccellente.

As you take an interest in art, allow me, Miss Barretti, to introduce to you an intimate friend of mine, Mr. Trivelli.	Siccome ella si occupa di belle arti, mi permetta, Signorina Barretti, di presentarle un mio intimo amico, il Signor Trivelli.
How do you do, I am very happy to make your acquaintance.	La riverisco, ho molto caro di fare la sua conoscenza.
You are very kind.	Ella è molto cortese.
Is this the first time you have been in England?	E questa la prima volta che viene in Inghilterra?
No; I came here in 1891, to see the Naval Exhibition.	No; ci venni nel 1891, per vedere l'Esposizione Navale.
How do you like England?	Come le piace l'Inghilterra?
I like it very much, except the climate however, which at times is really very bad.	Mi piace moltissimo, ma non il clima, però, che qualche volta è veramente cattivo.

How happy I am to see you, Miss Vestri; where have you been all this time?	Oh come sono lieta di vederla Signorina Vestri; dov'è ella stata dacchè non l'ho veduta?
I have been out of town with my family; we have been to the sea-side.	Sono stata fuori di città con tutti i miei; siamo stati ai bagni di mare.
You look very well; and how are you all?	Che bella cera ha; e come stanno tutti i suoi?
We are all very well, thank you, except Mary; she sprained her ankle, just before we left Folkestone.	Stiamo tutti in ottima salute, la ringrazio, tranne Maria che si è slogato un piede, appunto quando si lasciava Folkestone.
Oh that is where you have been; it is a pretty place, is it not?	Oh sono stati là; è un bel sito, non è vero?
Beautiful; the air is very good, and the place has not become common yet.	Bellissimo; l'aria è saluberrima, e quel paese non è ancora divenuto volgare.
I am very glad to hear that, because we ourselves intend to go there next month.	Son ben contenta d'udir ciò, perchè noi abbiamo l'intenzione d'andarvi il mese prossimo.
Oh, if that is the case, you had better call on me one day next week, and then I will tell you all about the place.	Oh, quand'è così venga da me qualche giorno della settimana prossima, e allora le dirò quanto mi sappia del luogo.
Very well, I will; let us say on Thursday. Goodbye, for the present.	Benissimo non mancherò di venirci; sia deciso per giovedì. Per ora, Addio.

TITLES AND EXPRESSIONS USED IN WRITING LETTERS IN ITALIAN.

IN WRITING TO MINISTERS, (MINISTRI DI STATO) AMBASSADORS, (AMBASCIATORI) GENERALS, (GENERALI D'ARMATA) AND CHIEF MAGISTRATES :—

Commence—*Illustrissimo ed Eccellentissimo Signore*, or *Eccellenza.*
In the body of the letter—*Illustrissimo ed Eccellentissimo Signore*, or *Vostra Eccellenza.*
Conclude—*Coi sensi del più profondo ossequio sono*—
Or *Desiderando occasioni per poterle dar prova della mia devozione, ho l'onore di protestarmi*—
Or *Pregandola di conservarmi la di Lei grazia, mi dico,*
    Di Vostra Eccellenza,
      umilissimo e devotissimo servitore—*
Address—*All' Illustrissimo ed Eccellentissimo Signore, il Signor, &c.*

IN WRITING TO MARQUESSES, (MARCHESI) COUNTS, (CONTI) BARONS, (BARONI), KNIGHTS OF ALL ORDERS, (CAVALIERI) AND JUDGES :—

Commence—*Illustrissimo Signore.*
In the body of the letter—*Illustrissimo Signore*, or *Vossignoria illustrissima.*
Conclude—*Colla massima stima ho l'onore di segnarmi*—
Or *Ossequiandola distintamente, ho l'onore d' essere,*
    Di Vossignoria illustrissima,
      umilissimo e devotissimo servo —
Address—*All' Illustrissimo Signore,*
    il Signor Marchese, &c.

IN WRITING TO DOCTORS, (DOTTORI, MEDICI) PROFESSORS, (PROFESSORI) AND ESQUIRES (SIGNORI) :—

Commence—*Pregiatissimo*, or *Stimatissimo*, or *Ornatissimo Signore.*
In the body of the letter—*Pregiatissimo*, or *Stimatissimo*, or *Ornatissimo Signore.*
Conclude—*Sono e sarò sempre, con tutto l'animo, suo devotissimo ed obbligatissimo servitore* —
Or *Coi sensi del più profondo rispetto (or della più profonda stima) sono di Lei devotissimo servo*—
Or *Mi creda sempre, come sono e sarò di cuore, suo affezionatissimo amico* -
Or *Mi offro a servirla e mi ripeto di tutto cuore suo affezionatissimo servitore ed amico*—
Or *Gradisca i miei affetuosi saluti e mi creda suo devotissimo servo*—
Or *Facendole i miei cordiali saluti, me Le dico devotissimo servo ed amico*—
Address—*Al Riveritissimo*, or *Pregiatissimo Signor, &c.*

---

* In Italian, the address of the writer and the date of a letter were formerly always written at the end of a letter, except in commercial letters, and sometimes in letters to familiar friends; but now-a-days many people write address and date at the top or at the end of letters, as they like.

IN WRITING TO FRIENDS OF ALL RANKS:

Commence—*Caro*, or *Carissimo amico* (or the name of the person, or his title).
In the body of the letter—*Ella, voi,* or *tu.*
Conclude—*E salutandola affettuosamente con sincera stima, sono suo devotissimo amico*—
Or *Vogliatemi bene e credetemi il vostro affezionatissimo amico*—
Or *Salutatemi caramente N. N.; e se mi volete bene, abbiate cara sopra tutto alla vostra salute. Addio, addio di tutto cuore*—
Or *Salutandoti di cuore sono tuo vero amico.*
Address—*Allo Stimatissimo,* or *Ornatissimo Signor, &c.**

N.B.—In writing to ladies the same regard must be paid to rank as is paid towards gentlemen.

ECCLESIASTICAL DIGNITARIES.

IN WRITING TO ARCHBISHOPS (ARCIVESCOVI), AND BISHOPS (VESCOVI):—

Commence—*Monsignore Illustrissimo e Reverendissimo.*†
In the body of the letter—*Monsignore Illustrissimo e Reverendissimo.*
Conclude—*Ossequiandola rispettosamente, Le bacio la mano.*
    Di Vossignoria Illustrissima e Reverendissima,
        umilissimo e devotissimo servitore—
Address—*All' Illustrissimo e Reverendissimo Signore,* or *Monsignore, &c.*

IN WRITING TO DEANS (DECANI), AND ARCHDEACONS (ARCIPRETI).

Commence—*Reverendissimo Signore.*
In the body of the letter—*Vossignoria Reverendissima.*
Conclude—*Sono colla massima stima,*
    Di Vossignoria Reverendissima,
      ubbidientissimo servitore—
Address—*Al Reverendissimo signore, &c.*

TO CLERGYMEN.

Commence—*Molto Reverendo Signore.*
In the body of the letter—*Vossignoria Reverenda,* or *Molto Reverenda.*
Conclude—*Sono col più profondo rispetto,*
    Di Vossignoria Reverenda,
      ubbidientissimo servitore, &c.
Address—*Al Molto Reverendo Padre,* or *Signore il Signor, &c.*

---

* In addressing persons who have distinguished themselves in their professions or arts, often instead of *Pregiatissimo, Stimabilissimo,* &c., the titles, *Egregio, Esimio, Chiarissimo,* are used.

† *Illmo, Illu^{mo}, Rev^{mo}, Rev^{mo}, V.S., Pregiat^{mo}, Stimat^{mo}, Ornat^{mo}, Umil^{mo}, Dev^{mo}, Obblig^{mo}, Sig. Sig^a*, are written instead of *Illustrissimo, Reverendissimo, Pregiatissimo, Vossignoria,* or *Vostra Signoria,* &c.; but to write the title in full is an additional mark of respect.

A GUIDE TO ITALIAN COMPOSITION.

Note.—The translations of the words occurring in these extracts, not given in the foot notes, are to be found in the English-Italian Vocabulary, beginning at page 246 of this grammar.

THE CONJUGATING DUTCHMAN.*

Two Italian (468) gentlemen once stepped (entered) into a coffee-house in (di) Paris, where they observed a tall, odd-looking (a) man, who appeared not to be a native (b), sitting (seated) at one of the tables, and looking around with the most stone-like gravity of countenance upon every object (c). Soon after the two Italians had entered (832), one of them told the other that a celebrated dwarf had arrived in (207) Paris. At this (d), the grave-looking personage above mentioned (e) opened his mouth (705) and said :

"I arrive, thou arrivest, he arrives; we arrive, you arrive, they arrive."

The Italian, whose (625) remark (word) seemed to have suggested this mysterious speech, stepped up to (f) the stranger and asked, "Did you speak (do you speak) to me (210), sir?"

"I speak," replied the stranger, "thou speakest, he speaks; we speak, you speak, they speak."

"How is this?" (g) said the Italian much astonished; "do you mean (h) to insult me?"

The other replied, "I insult, thou insultest, he insults; we insult, you insult, they insult."

---

* "L' Olandese smanioso di coniugare."

(a) di strano aspetto.
(b) che pareva straniero.
(c) "and looking..." e che guardava ogni oggetto colla massima impassibilità.
(d) All' udir ciò.
(e) prefato.
(f) si mosse verso.
(g) "Che vuoi dir ciò?"
(h) " avreste l' intenzione" (rule 119).

"This is too much!" (a) said the enraged Italian. "I will have satisfaction! (b). If you have any spirit with your rudeness (c), come along (come) with me."

To this defiance the stranger replied, "I come, thou comest, he comes; we come, you come, they come;" and thereupon (d) he rose with great coolness (calm), and followed his challenger (e).

In those days, when every gentleman wore (the) a sword, duels were speedily despatched (771) (f). They went into a neighbouring alley, and the Italian, unsheathing (834) his weapon, said to his antagonist, "Now, sir, you must fight me" (g).

"I fight," replied the other, "thou fightest, he fights; we fight (here he made a thrust) (h), you fight, they fight" (and here he disarmed his antagonist).

"Well," said the Italian, "you have the best of it (i), and I hope (868, 636) you are satisfied."

"I am satisfied," said the original, "thou art satisfied, he is satisfied; we are satisfied, you are satisfied, they are satisfied."

"I am glad (836, j) everybody is satisfied," said the Italian; "but pray leave off quizzing me (j) in this strange manner, and tell me what is your object, if you have any, in doing it" (k).

The grave gentleman now, for the first time, became intelligible.

"I am a (354) Dutchman," said he, "and am learning your language. I find it (763) very difficult to remember the peculiarities of the verbs; and my tutor has advised me, in order to fix them in my mind (l), to conjugate every Italian verb that I hear spoken (m). This I have made it a rule to do (n). I don't like to have my plans broken in upon (o) while they are in operation, or I would have told you this before."

(a) " Ciò è troppo."
(b) "Me ne darete ragione."
(c) " Se avete cuore che basti alla vostra rozzezza."
(d) così dicendo.
(e) colui che l' avea sfidato.
(f) si decidevano presto.
(g) " bisogna battersi in duello meco."
(h) lanciò una botta.
(i) " mi do per vinto."
(j) " non si faccia più beffe di me, la prego." (rule 120).
(k) " what is your..." " a quale scopo, se pur ne ha uno, agisce così."
(l) se voglio fissarmeli bene in mente.
(m) che sento pronunciare (rule 690)
(n) " a questa regola aderisco sempre."
(o) Non amo che si contravenga ai miei disegni."

The Italians laughed heartily at this explanation (p) and invited the conjugating Dutchman to dine with them.

"I will dine," replied he, "thou wilt dine, he will dine; we will dine, you will dine, they will dine, we will all dine together."

This they accordingly did (q), and it (r) was difficult to say whether the Dutchman ate or conjugated with more perseverance (s). (* * *)

A CLEVER RETORT.*

A friend of Dean Swift one day sent him (193) a turbot, as a present (a), by a servant lad (b) who had frequently been on similar errands (c), but who had never received the most trifling mark (d) of the Dean's generosity. Having gained admission (e), he opened (704) the door of the study, and abruptly putting down the fish, cried, very rudely, "Master has sent you (sends you) (120) a turbot." "Young man," said the Dean, rising from his easy chair, "is that the way you deliver your message? (f). Let me teach you better manners (g): sit down in my chair; we will change situations (character), and I will show you (118, 197) how to behave in future" (h). The boy sat down, and the Dean, going (834) to the door, came up to the table at a respectful pace, and making a low bow (i), said, "Sir, my master (146) presents his kind compliments (j), hopes (868) you are well, and requests your acceptance of (k) a small present." "Does he?" (l) replied the boy; "return him my best (m) thanks, and there's (n) half-a-crown for yourself." The Dean, thus drawn (o) into an act of generosity, laughed heartily, and gave the boy a crown for his wit. (* * *)

(p) "The Italians laughed..." Sentito lo schiarimento, gl' Italiani scoppiarono nelle risa.
(q) Il che fecero.
(r) "it," in cases like this, is not translated.
(s) "whether the Dutchman ate or conjugated..." se l'Olandese fosse più perseverante nel coniugare o nel mangiare.

* "Arguta Risposta."
(a) "as a present," in regalo.
(b) ragazzotto.
(c) che aveva sovente eseguito simili ordini.
(d) la minima prova.
(e) Tosto che si trovò nella casa.
(f) è così che eseguisci gli ordini che ti son dati?
(g) Ti fo veder subito come si agisce meno villanamente.
(h) come dovresti comportarti all'avvenire.
(i) profondo inchino.
(j) "presents his..." la saluta caramente.
(k) la piega di accettare.
(l) "Davvero?"
(m) ringrazialo pure da parte mia.
(n) ecco. (o) spinto.

THE DERVIS.*

A Dervis, travelling through (a) Tartary, having arrived (689) at the town of Balk, went (704) into the king's palace by mistake, thinking it to be (b) a public inn or caravansary. Having looked about him for (311) some time, he entered into (c) a long gallery, where he laid down his wallet and spread his carpet, in order to (932) repose himself upon it (d), after the manner of (e) the Eastern nations (468). He had not been long (f) in this posture before he was (g) discovered by some of the guards, who asked him what was his business (h) in that place? The Dervis told them (636) he intended (838, f) to take up his night's lodging (i) in that caravansary. The guards let him know (j), in a very angry manner (k), that the house he was in (l) was not a caravansary, but (m) the king's palace. It happened (n) that the king himself passed through the gallery during this debate (o), and smiling at (p) the mistake of the Dervis, asked him how he could possibly be so dull as (q) not to distinguish a palace from a caravansary? "Sire," said the Dervis, "give me leave to ask your majesty (r) a question (306) or two. Who were the persons that lodged in this house when it was first built?" The king replied "My ancestors." "And who," said the Dervis, "was the last person that lodged here?" (s) The king replied, "My father." "And who is it," said the Dervis, "that lodges here at present?" The king told him that it was he himself (t). "And who," said the Dervis, "will be here after you (your Majesty) (563)?" The king answered, "The young prince, my son." Ah! Sire," said the Dervis, "a house that changes its inhabitants so often (u) and receives such a perpetual succession of guests, is not a palace, but (m) a caravansary."—ADDISON.

---

* "Il Dervigio."
(a) che viaggiava in.
(b) credendolo.
(c) infilò.
(d) "upon it" is not translated.
(e) alla moda di.
(f) Non era stato guari.
(g) "before he was," allorquando fu.
(h) ciò che venisse fare.
(i) d'alloggiarsi per la notte.
(j) gli fecero sapere.
(k) con gran collera.
(l) in cui si trovava.
(m) ma bensì.
(n) il caso volle.
(o) discussione.
(p) See p. 208, note (t).
(q) abbastanza stupido per.
(r) mi sia permesso di fare a Vostra Maestà.
(s) "E chi fu l'ultimo che vi ebbe alloggio?"
(t) che vi alloggiava egli stesso.
(u) che cambia così spesso di abitanti.

RABELAIS A TRAITOR.*

This celebrated wit (a) was once at a great distance from Paris, and without money to bear his expenses thither (b). The ingenious author being sharp set (c), got together (d) a convenient quantity of brickdust, and having disposed of it (e) into several papers (f), wrote upon one, *Poison for Monsieur* (g); upon a second, *Poison for the Dauphin* (h); and on a third, *Poison for the King*. Having made this provision for (i) the royal family of France, he laid his papers so that (j) the landlord, who was an inquisitive man and a good (faithful) subject, might get a sight of them (k). The plot succeeded as he desired (l); the host gave immediate intelligence to (m) the secretary of state. The secretary presently sent down (n) a special messenger, who brought up the traitor to court, and provided him, at the king's expense, with proper accommodation on the road (o). As soon as he appeared, he was known to be (p) the celebrated Rabelais, and his powder, upon examination, (q) being found very innocent, the jest was only laughed at (r); for which a less eminent droll would have been sent to the galleys.—
BUDGELL.

THE CUNNING CUTLER.*

There is (154) in London, at a place called Charing Cross, a very fine statue in bronze of Charles the First (543) on horseback (a). After the revolution and the decapitation of that monarch, the statue was taken down (b) and sold to a cutler who undertook to demolish it. He immediately manufactured great numbers

---

* "Rabelais Colpevole di Lesa Maestà."

(a) bell' ingegno.
(b) "to bear his..." pagar le sue spese, fin là.
(c) ridotto all' ultima risorsa.
(d) raccolse.
(e) messala (rule 689).
(f) "papers," involtini.
(g) A title given to the eldest of the brothers of the kings o France.

(h) A title given to the eldest son of the king of France.
(i) Avendo provveduto così a' bisogni di.
(j) in modo tale che.
(k) potesse vederli.
(l) come lo desiderava (notice the pronoun "lo" referring to plot).
(m) ne avvertì immediatamente.
(n) spedì subito.

(o) "and provided him..." facendogli dare sulla via, a spese del re, alloggio e vitto.
(p) riconobbero esser lui.
(q) analisi fatta.
(r) non si fece che ridere della burla.

* "Il Sagace Coltellinaio."

(a) a cavallo.
(b) si tirò giù la statua.

(quantity) of knives and forks with bronze handles, and exposed them (c) in his shop as the produce of the statue which was supposed (771) to have been melted. They were so rapidly bought, (d) both by (e) the friends and the enemies of the late monarch, that the cutler soon made a (360) fortune and retired from business.

Soon after the restoration it was proposed (771) to erect a new statue to the memory of the unfortunate king; the cutler hearing of this, (834) informed the government that he could spare them (456) the trouble and expense of casting a statue, as the old one (f) was yet in his possession, and that he would sell it to them (456) at a moderate price. The bargain (affair) was concluded (771), and the statue, which he had secretly preserved, was re-elevated (705) (g) on the pedestal at Charing Cross, where it now stands (h). (* * *)

THE MONKEY AND THE TWO CATS.*

Two cats, having stolen some cheese, could not agree (842, g) about dividing their prize (a). In order, therefore, to settle the dispute (b), they consented to refer the matter (c) to a monkey. The proposed arbitrator very readily (d) accepted the office, and, producing (taking) a balance, put a part (bit) into each scale. " Let me see," said he, " ay! this lump outweighs (e) the other; " and immediately he bit off a considerable piece (f) " in order to reduce it," he observed, " to an equilibrium" (g). The opposite scale had now become the heavier, which (628) afforded our conscientious judge an additional (other) reason for a second mouthful. " Hold! hold!" (h) said the two cats, who began to be alarmed for the result (i), " give us our respective shares (j) and

c) li mişe in mostra nella sua bottega dicendoli fatti col bronzo.
(d) ębbero tale şmercio.
(e) "by" is translated by "e."
(f) stante che la vecchia.
(g) posta di bel nuovo.
(h) si vede tuttora.

* "La Scimia e i due Gatti."
(a) quanto al modo di dividere il bottino.
(b) "In order..." Quindi per decidere la lite.
(c) sottomettere il caso.
(d) con gran premura.

(e) pęsa più che.
(f) ne lęvò co'dęnti un buon boccone.
(g) "in order..." per istabilire, disse, l'equilibrio.
(h) basta! basta!
(i) temerne il risultato.
(j) dacci la nostra parte.

we are satisfied." " If you are satisfied," returned (j) the monkey, justice is not (k); a case of this intricate nature is by no means (l) so soon determined." Upon this (m) he continued to nibble first at one piece and then the other, till the poor cats, seeing (834) their cheese gradually diminishing (314), entreated him to give himself no further trouble, but deliver (restore) to them what remained. " Not so fast, I beseech you, friends," replied the monkey ; " we owe justice to ourselves as well as (n) to you : what remains is due to me in right of my office." Upon which (m) he crammed the whole into his mouth, (o) (572) and with great gravity dismissed the court (p).—DODSLEY.

CURIOUS EXPEDIENT.*

Two Irishmen, blacksmiths by trade (857, k) went to Jamaica. Finding soon after their arrival, that they could do nothing without money to begin with (a), but that, with sixty or seventy pounds and industry, they might be able to do some business, they hit upon (b) the following ingenious expedient.

One of them made the other black (blackened) from head to foot. This being done (c), he took him to one of the negro-dealers, who, after viewing (834) and approving his stout, athletic appearance, made a bargain (d) to pay eighty pounds for (251) him and prided himself on (845, g) the purchase, supposing him to be (e) one of the finest negroes on the island. The same evening this newly manufactured negro (f) made off to (g) his countryman, washed himself clean, and resumed his former appearance. Rewards were in vain offered in hand bills (h), pursuit was eluded, and discovery, by care and caution, was made impossible (i).

(j) rispose.
(k) non lo è.
(l) " by no..." punto.
(m) Detto ciò.
(n) non meno che.
(o) si ficcò il resto.
(p) finì l' udienza.

* " Curioso Spediente."
(a) per cominciare.
(b) immaginarono.
(c) Ciò fatto.
(d) convenne.
(e) credendo che fosse.
(f) negro improvvisato.

(g) scappò e andò dal.
(h) avvisi al pubblico.
(i) Turn " pursuit..."
" they eluded pursuit, and with care and caution made it impossible that any one should discover them."

The two Irishmen with the money commenced business (j), and succeeded (258) so well, that they returned to England with a fortune of several thousand (migliaia di) pounds (656). Previous however to their departure from the island (k), they went to the gentleman from whom they had received the money, recalled the circumstances of the negro to his recollection (l), and made amends, both for principal and interest, with thanks (m). (* * *)

NAPOLEON AND THE BRITISH SAILOR.*

Whilst the French troops were encamped at Boulogne, public attention was much excited by (270) the daring attempt at escape (a) made by an English sailor. This person (man) having escaped (689) from the depôt and gained (b) the borders of the sea, the woods near which served him for concealment (c), constructed, (704), with no other instrument than a knife, a boat entirely of the bark of trees. When the weather was fair (853), he mounted (d) (697) a tree and looked out for (e) the English flag; and having at last observed (discovered) (689) a British cruiser, he ran to the shore with his boat on his back, and was about (842, p) to trust himself in his frail vessel to the waves, when he was (705) pursued, arrested, and loaded with chains. Everybody in the army was anxious (desired) (300) to see the boat; and Napoleon, having at length heard of the affair (f), sent for (g) the sailor and interrogated him. "You must" (h), said Napoleon, "have had a great desire

---

(j) si misero a negoziare.
(k) "Previous..." Però prima di lasciar l'isola."
(l) " recalled..." " gli rammentarono l'affare del negro."
(m) Turn "made amends ..." "thanked him, paying him capital and interest."
* " Napoleone e il Marinaro Inglese."
(a) audace tentativo di evadersi. (b) pervenuto.
(c) servivano di nascondiglio. (d) Add " su di."
(e) guardava se potesse vedere.
(f) " having..." sentito parlare dell'accaduto.
(g) mandò a chiamare.
(h) Dovete, ne son certo.

to see your country again, since you could resolve (i) to trust yourself on the open (full) sea in so frail a bark. I suppose you have left a sweetheart there?" (239) "No," said the sailor, "but a poor infirm mother, whom I was (695) anxious (I desired) to see." "And you shall see her," said Napoleon, giving at the same time orders to set him at (j) liberty, and to bestow upon him (k) a considerable sum of money for his mother, observing that "she must be a good mother who had so good a (such a) son." (* * *)

DESCRIPTION OF ENGLAND.*

Few countries exhibit a greater variety of surface than England, or have been more highly favoured by (270) nature. "Although," says Dr. Aikin, "its features are moulded on a comparatively minute scale (a), they are marked with all the agreeable interchange (varieties) which constitute picturesque beauty. In some parts, plains clothed in (covered of) the richest verdure, watered by copious streams, and pasturing innumerable cattle, extend as far as the eye can reach (b); in others (c) gently rising hills (d) and bending vales (e), fertile in corn (f), waving with woods (g), and interspersed with (266) flowery meadows, offer the most delightful landscapes of rural opulence and beauty. Some tracts furnish (offer) prospects of the more romantic and impressive kind; lofty mountains, craggy rocks, deep dells, narrow ravines, and tumbling (precipitous) torrents: nor are there wanting, as a contrast to (h) those scenes in which every variety of nature is a different charm, the vicissitude of (i) black barren moors and wide inanimate heaths." Such is (j) a vivid description of the general appearance of England. But the beauty and fertility of the country are not the only things to excite (which excite) admiration. The mild-

---

(i) v'è bastato il cuore.
(j) metterlo in.
(k) e di dargli.
  * "Descrizione dell' Inghilterra."
(a) "its features.." le sue prospettive non siano relativamente che di piccola proporzione.
(b) fin dove può giunger l'occhio.
(c) altrove.
(d) collinette a dolce clivo.
(e) valloncelli tortuosi.
(f) che producono frumento in abbondanza.
(g) coperti di boschi ondeggianti.
(h) "nor are there..." nè mancavi, come per far risaltare.
(i) l'aspetto vicendevole di.
(j) Ecco.

ness of the climate, removed alike from the extremes of heat and cold (j); the multitude of rivers, their (560) depth, and the facility they afford to internal navigation; the vast beds of coal and other valuable minerals hid under the surface (k); the abundance and excellence of the fish in the rivers and surrounding seas; the extent of sea-coast; the number, capaciousness (l), and safety of the ports and bays; and the favourable situation of the country for commerce; give (m) England (330) advantages that are not enjoyed in an equal degree by any other nation (n).—Dr. AIKEN and J. R. M'CULLOCH.

CHARACTER OF RICHARD I.

This renowned prince was (701) tall, strong, straight and well-proportioned. His arms were remarkably long, (574) his eyes blue, and full of vivacity; his hair was of a yellowish colour; his complexion fair (782), his countenance comely, and his air majestic. He was endowed with good natural understanding; his penetration was uncommon; he possessed a fund of manly eloquence; his conversation was spirited, and he was admired for his talents of repartee (a); as for his courage and ability in war, both Europe and Asia resound with his praise. The Saracens stilled their children with the terror of his name; and Saladine, who was an accomplished prince, admired his valour to such a degree of enthusiasm, that immediately after Richard had defeated (710) him on the plains of Joppa, he sent him a couple of fine Arabian horses, in token of his esteem; a (342) polite compliment, which Richard returned with magnificent presents. These are the shining parts (b) of his character, which, however, cannot dazzle the judicious observer so much, but that he may perceive a number of blemishes, which no historian has been able (c) to efface from the memory of this celebrated monarch. His ingratitude and want of filial affection are unpardonable. He was proud, haughty, ambitious, choleric, cruel, vindictive, and vicious; nothing could (794)

(j) " removed alike..." nè troppo freddo, nè troppo caldo.
(k) che il suolo nasconde.
(l) grandezza.
(m) tutto ciò dà.

(n) " that are not..." di cui nessun altra nazione gode al medesimo grado.

(a) " for his talents of repartee," per la sua arguzia.

(b) qualità ammirabili.
(c) "the judicious observer ..." un osservatore di senno al punto di nascondergli i tanti difetti, che niuno storico ha saputo.

equal his rapaciousness but his profusion, and, indeed, the one was the effect of the other; he was a tyrant to (d) his wife, as well as (e) to his people (456), who groaned under his taxations to such a degree, that (f) even the glory of his victories did not exempt him from their execrations: in a word, he has been aptly compared to a lion, a species of animal which he resembled not only in courage, but likewise in ferocity.—SMOLLETT.

WILLIAM PITT, EARL OF CHATHAM.

On the stage, Pitt would have been the finest Brutus or Coriolanus ever seen (a)...His figure when (b) he first appeared in Parliment, was strikingly graceful and commanding; (c) his features high and noble; his eye full of fire. His voice, even when it sank to a whisper (d), was heard (771) to the remotest benches; and when he strained it to his full extent (e), the sound rose like the swell of the organ (f) of a great cathedral—shook the house with its peal (g) —and was heard through lobbies (h) and down staircases, to the Court of Requests and the precincts (i) of Westminster Hall. He cultivated all these eminent advantages with the most assiduous care. His action is described by a very malignant observer (j) as equal to that of Garrick. His play of countenance (k) was wonderful; he frequently disconcerted a hostile orator by a single glance of indignation or scorn. Every tone, from the impassioned cry (l) to the thrilling aside, was perfectly at his command. It is by no means improbable (m) that the pains which he took to improve his great personal advantages had in some respects a prejudicial operation, and tended to nourish in him that passion for theatrical effect which, as we have already remarked (n), was one of the most conspicuous blemishes (defects) in his character.—MACAULAY.

(d) verso.
(e) come pure.
(f) a segno tale che.

(a) che si vedesse mai.
(b) Turn, "When he first appeared...his..."
(c) imponente.
(d) " even " persino quando parlava sotto voce.

(e) " he strained it..." quando se ne serviva a più non posso.
(f) " like the swell of the organ," come quello dell' organo.
(g) ne faceva tremare la sala del senato.
(h) gallerie. (i) circuito.
(j) critico ostile.

(k) l'espressione del suo volto.
(l) " Every tone..." Tenevo in freno completo ogni emozione dell' animo ; dal grido della passione, fino all' aparte commovente.
(m) Egli è probabile.
(n) Come si è già fatto osservare.

ITALIAN POETRY.

VERSES* AND SYLLABLES.

Italian "versi"* consist of a fixed number of syllables; and their expression and harmony depend on the words they contain, and the manner in which these words are arranged.

In Italian a syllable in poetry is not exactly the same as a syllable in prose; often a syllable in a verse consists of two prose syllables pronounced together so as to require but one emission of the voice; for instance, the following verse, which contains seven prose syllables, is counted as a verse of five syllables:

Metrical Syllables   1   2   3   4   5
"Già il cielo indora" † (Zeno).
Prose Syllables   1   2   3   4   5   6   7

Italian verses have different names given them, according to the number of the syllables they contain.

VERSI QUINARI.

Verses of five (metrical) syllables ‡ are called "versi quinari." They have generally two rhythmical accents; one on the first, or second, and one (essential) on the fourth syllable.

LA MELANCONÌA.

Fonti e colline§	Gli onor che sono?
Chiesi agli dei:	Che val ricchezza?
M'udìro al fine,‖	Di miglior dono
Pago io vivrò:	Vommene altier:¶
Nè mai quel fonte	D'un' alma pura,
Co' desir miei,	Che la bellezza
Nè mai quel monte	Della Natura
Trapasserò.	Gusta e del Ver.

---

* In these pages the word *verses* is used in the sense of *lines in poetry*. In Italian the word "versi" means *lines* of poetry.

† "It (the dawn) already gilds the sky."

‡ There are Italian verses of four syllables, called "versi quadrisillabi," which, though not musical, when used alone, have a very pretty effect when they are judiciously mixed with verses of eight syllables. (See "Riso di Bella Donna," page 241.) There are also verses of three, or even two syllables, but these are very seldom used, except to versify short trifles; they are utterly unmusical.

§ For translation see Italian-English Vocabulary (page 260).

‖ "Udìro," poetical form for "udirono," *they heard me* (see rule 261).

¶ Vommene "="me ne vo," *I am* (see rule 194, and rules 218 and 845 r).

Nè può di tempre*
  Cangiar mio fato;
  Dipinto sempre
  Il ciel sarà;
    Ritorneranno
      I fior nel prato
      Sin che a me l'anno
      Ritornerà.

Melanconia,
  Ninfa gentile
  La vita mia
  Consegno a te:
    I tuoi piaceri
    Chi tiene a vile
    Ai piacer veri
    Nato non è.

PINDEMONTE (1753-1828).

VERSI SENARI.

Verses of six syllables are called "versi senari." They have two rhythmical accents; one on the second and the other (essential) on the fifth syllable.

A IMELDA.

Nell'ora pietosa
  Che assonna ogni cura,
  L'affanno sol dura
  Che amore destò.

Solingo, scorato,
  Disotto al verone
  D'Imelda si pone
  Sprezzato amator.

Mentr'ella tornata
  Nell'erma stanzetta
  Le vesti s'affretta
  Del ballo a spogliar.

E a lei che disdegna
  D'amor la parola
  Al suon di mandola
  Ei dice così:

Nell'ora pietosa
  Che addorme ogni cura,
  La pena sol dura
  Che amore destò.

La notte serena
  Che al sonno ti chiama,
  Del giovin che t'ama
  Raddoppia il sospir.

Ah! solo un istante
  M'ascolta, ben mio,
  Alonzo son io,
  Che il core perdè.

E tu che il rapivi,
  Ô Imelda crudele,
  D'Alonzo fedele
  Non senti pietà!

I. RICCIARDA CAPECELATRO (1800-1860?).

The student is again desired to read over rules 5, 9, 48, 53, and 63, in order to thoroughly understand the directions for the double pronunciation of the letters "E," "O," "S" and "Z," and the meaning of the letters in darker type.

VERSI SETTENARI.

Verses of seven syllables are called "versi settenari." They have two or three rhythmical accents. When they have two accents, the first can be on any of the first four syllables, and the other (essential) on the sixth syllable; when they have three accents, one is on the first or second syllable, the other on the fourth, and the last (essential) on the sixth syllable.

IL CINQUE MAGGIO.*

Ei fu. Siccome immobile,†
  Dato il mortal sospiro,
  Stette la spoglia immemore
  Orba di tanto spiro,
  Così percossa, attonita,
  La terra al nunzio sta,‡

Muta pensando all' ultima
  Ora dell' uom fatale;§
  Nè sa quando una simile
  Orma di piè mortale
  La sua cruenta polvere
  A calpestar verrà.

Lui sfolgorante in solio
  Vide il mio genio e tacque;
  Quando, con vece assidua,‖
  Cadde, risorse e giacque,
  Di mille voci al sonito
  Mista la sua non ha:

Vergin di servo encomio¶
  E di codardo oltraggio,
  Sorge or commosso al subito
  Sparir di tanto raggio;
  E scioglie all' urna un cantico,
  Che forse non morrà.

---

* This sublime ode, the best Italian lyric of modern times, was written by Manzoni in commemoration of the 5th of May, 1821, the day on which Napoleon I. died at St. Helena, where he had been kept a prisoner for six years. Manzoni, who had always kept aloof alike from the detractors and the flatterers of the great man, takes a rapid survey of the hero's life, but leaves it to posterity to judge; and, like a true Chrstian poet, kneels down at the death-bed of the dying penitent, and prays.

† Notice that this line consists of eight metrical syllables, because it ends with a " parola sdrucciola " (see rule 60), but still it is reckoned as a " verso settenario," for the reason that the last (essential) rhythmical accent falls upon the sixth syllable.

‡ Notice that this line consists of six metrical syllables only, because it ends with a " parola tronca " (see rule 62), but still it is reckoned as a " verso settenario," for the reason that the last (essential) rhythmical accent falls upon the sixth syllable.

§ " Fatale," *marked by fate.* ‖ " Vece assidua," *rapid vicissitudes (changes).*

¶ " Vergin di servo encomio," *pure from servile flattery (praise).*

Dall' Alpi alle Piramidi,
  Dal Mansanare al Reno,*
  Di quel securo il fulmine
  Tenea dietro al baleno;†
  Scoppiò da Scilla al Tanai,‡
  Dall' uno all' altro mar.

Fu vera gloria? Ai posteri
  L'ardua sentenza: nui §
  Chiniam la fronte al Massimo
  Fattor, che volle in lui
  Del creator suo spirto
  Più vasta orma stampar.

La procellosa e trepida
  Gioia d'un gran disegno,
  L'ansia d'un cor che indocile
  Ferve, pensando al regno,
  E il giunge, e ottiene un premio
  Ch'era follia sperar;

Tutto ei provò: la gloria
  Maggior dopo il periglio,
  La fuga e la vittoria,
  La reggia e il tristo esiglio:
  Due volte nella polvere,‖
  Due volte sull' altar.

Ei si nomò: due secoli
  L'un contro l'altro armato,
  Sommessi a lui si volsero
  Come aspettando il fato;
  Ei fe' silenzio, ed arbitro
  S'assise in mezzo a lor.

Ei sparve, e i dì nell'ozio
  Chiuse in sì breve sponda,¶
  Segno d'immensa invidia,
  E di pietà profonda,
  D'inestinguibil odio
  E d'indomato amor.

Come sul capo al naufrago
  L'onda s'avvolve e pesa,
  L'onda, su cui del misero,
  Alta pur dianzi e tesa,
  Scorrea la vista a scernere
  Prode remote invan;

Tal su quell' alma il cumulo
  Delle memorie scese!
  Oh! quante volte ai posteri
  Narrar sè stesso imprese,
  E sull'eterne pagine
  Cadde la stanca man!

---

* *From the Mansanare* (a small river near Madrid) to the Rhine.
† This bold image means: "The thunderbolt (fulmine) of that fearless man (Napoleon) followed quickly its flash (baleno)"; *i.e.*, He no sooner appeared on the battle-field than he smote down his enemies.
‡ *From Scylla* (a famous rock in the Strait of Messina) to the River Don.
§ "Nui" is used, as a poetical licence, instead of "noi."
‖ "Due volte...," an allusion to Napoleon's exile at Elba, and at St. Helena.
¶ "In sì breve sponda," *on so narrow a shore* (St. Helena).

Oh quante volte al tacito
   Morir di un giorno inerte,
   Chinati i rai fulminei,
   Le braccia al sen conserte,
   Stette, e dei dì che furono
   L'assalse il sovvenir!

E ripensò le mobili
   Tende, e i percossi valli,
   E il lampo de' manipoli
   E l'onda dei cavalli,
   E il concitato imperio,
   E il celere obbedir.

Ahi! forse a tanto strazio
   Cadde lo spirto anelo,
   E disperò; ma valida
   Venne una man dal cielo,
   E in più spirabil aere
   Pietosa il trasportò;

E l'avviò pei floridi
   Sentier della speranza,
   Ai campi eterni, al premio
   Che i desideri avanza,*
   Dov'è silenzio e tenebre
   La gloria che passò.

Bella immortal! benefica
   Fede ai trionfi avvezza!
   Scrivi ancor questo, allegrati;
   Chè più superba altezza
   Al disonor del Golgota†
   Giammai non si chinò.

Tu dalle stanche ceneri
   Sperdi ogni ria parola:
   Il Dio che atterra e suscita,
   Che affanna e che consola,
   Sulla deserta coltrice
   Accanto a lui posò.

                   MANZONI (1785-1873).

IL POTERE DI DIO.

DOVUNQUE il guardo io giro,
   Immenso Dio ti vedo:
   Nell' opre tue t'ammiro,
   Ti riconosco in me.

La terra, il mar, le sfere
   Parlan del tuo potere:
   Tu sei per tutto, e noi
   Tutti viviamo in te.

LA GRATITUDINE.

Benchè di senso privo,
   Fin l'arboscello è grato
   A quell'amico rivo,
   Da cui riceve umor;

Per lui di fronde ornato,
   Bella mercè gli rende,
   Quando dal sol difende
   Il suo benefattor.

                   METASTASIO (1698-1782).

---

   * *Exceeds all desires.*
   † "Al disonor del Golgota," *to the disgrace of Calvary*, which by Christ's death became a sign of salvation: an allusion to the Crucifix which Napoleon held in his hand on his death-bed.

VERSI OTTONARI.

Verses of eight syllables are called "versi ottonari." They can have only two accents; one on the third and the other (essential) on the seventh syllable.

LA RONDINELLA.

RONDINELLA pellegrina
  Che ti posi in sul verone,
  Ricantando ogni mattina
  Quella flebile canzone,
  Che vuoi dirmi in tua favella,
  Pellegrina rondinella?

Solitaria nell'oblio,
  Dal tuo sposo abbandonata,
  Piangi forse al pianto mio
  Vedovetta sconsolata?
  Piangi, piangi in tua favella,
  Pellegrina rondinella.

Pur di me manco infelice
  Tu alle penne almen t'affidi,
  Scorri il lago e la pendice,
  Empi l'aria de' tuoi gridi,
  Tutto il giorno in tua favella
  Lui chiamando, ò rondinella.

Oh se anch'io!...Ma lo contende
  Questa bassa, angusta volta,
  Dove sole non risplende,
  Dove l'aria ancor m'è tolta,
  Donde a te la mia favella
  Giunge appena, o rondinella.

Il settembre innanzi viene,
  E a lasciarmi ti prepari:
  Tu vedrai lontane arene,
  Nuovi monti, nuovi mari
  Salutando in tua favella,
  Pellegrina rondinella:

Ed io tutte le mattine
  Riaprendo gli occhi al pianto,
  Fra le nevi e fra le brine
  Crederò d'udir quel canto,
  Onde par che in tua favella
  Mi compianga, ò rondinella.

Una croce a primavera
  Troverai su questo suolo:
  Rondinella, in sulla sera
  Sovra lei raccogli il volo:
  Dimmi pace in tua favella,
  Pellegrina rondinella.

---

* This very pretty song, a masterpiece of harmony and elegance, is taken from "Marco Visconti," a fine novel by Grossi (1800-1850). It is very popular in Italy, and has been set to music by several celebrated composers.

RISO DI BELLA DONNA.

Se bel rio, se bell'auretta
    Tra l'erbetta
Sul mattin mormorando erra;
Se di fiori un praticello
    Si fa bello,
Noi diciam: ride la terra.

Quando avvien che un zeffiretto
    Per diletto
Bagni il piè nell'onde chiare,
Sicchè l'acqua in sull'arena
    Scherzi appena,
Noi diciam che ride il mare.

Se giammai tra fior vermigli,
    Se tra gigli
Veste l'alba un aureo velo,
E su rote di zaffiro
    Move in giro,
Noi diciam che ride il cielo.

Ben è ver, quand'è giocondo
    Ride il mondo;
Ride il ciel quand'è gioioso;
Ben è ver; ma non san poi,
    Come voi,
Fare un riso grazïoso.

                      CHIABRERA (1552-1637).

VERSI NOVENARI.

Verses of nine syllables are called "versi novenari;" but, as they are seldom used, they need not be illustrated.

VERSI DECASILLABI.

Verses of ten syllables are called "versi decasillabi." They have three rhythmical accents; one on the third, one on the sixth, and the last (essential) on the ninth syllable.

LA BATTAGLIA DI MACLODIO.*

S'ode a destra uno squillo di tromba;
  A sinistra risponde uno squillo;
  D'ambo i lati calpesto rimbomba
  Da cavalli e da fanti il terren.
  Quinci spunta per l'aria un vessillo;
  Quindi un altro s'avanza spiegato:
  Ecco appare un drappello schierato;
  Ecco un altro che incontro gli vien.

---

* This masterly lyric is a part of the chorus in "Il Conte di Carmagnola," a fine tragedy by Manzoni. The great poet deplores the intestine warfare which desolated Italy in the Middle Ages, and, with words breathing the greatest humanity and purest patriotism, conjures his countrymen to keep friendly and united.

Già di mezzo sparito è il terreno;
  Già le spade respingon le spade;
  L'un dell'altro le immerge nel seno;
  Gronda il sangue, raddoppia il ferir.
  Chi son essi?   Alle belle contrade
  Qual ne venne straniero a far guerra?
  Qual è quei che ha giurato la terra
  Dove nacque far salva, o morir?

D'una terra son tutti; un linguaggio
  Parlan tutti; fratelli li dice
  Lo straniero: il comune lignaggio
  A ognun d'essi dal volto traspar.
  Questa terra fu a tutti nudrice,
  Questa terra di sangue ora intrisa,
  Che natura dall'altre ha divisa,
  E recinta coll'Alpe e col mar.

Ahi! qual d'essi il sacrilego brando
  Trasse il primo il fratello a ferire?
  O terror! del conflitto esecrando
  La cagione esecranda qual'è?—
  Non la sanno: a dar morte, a morire
  Qui senz'ira ognun d'essi è venuto;
  E venduto ad un duce venduto,
  Con lui pugna, e non chiede il perchè.

Ahi sventura! Ma spose non hanno,
  Non han madri gli stolti guerrieri?
  Perchè tutti i lor cari non vanno
  Dall'ignobile campo a strappar?
  E i vegliardi, che ai casti pensieri
  Della tomba già schiudon la mente,
  Chè non tentan la turba furente
  Con prudenti parole placar?

. . . .

MANZONI (1783-1873).

I very much regret to have no space here to print the whole of this splendid chorus, but I intend to republish it, in full, in my "Italian Reader." The poetry of Manzoni should be cherished by all who value heartfelt, religious, and patriotic sentiments expressed by a great poet.

MESSINA.

Chi non vide a marina Messina,
  Mal può dir ch'egli vide beltà:
  Di Triquetra è la figlia, è conchiglia,
  E la perla che pari non ha!

Sei pur vaga supina, ò Messina,
  Sul guancial di tue rose odorose,
  Cinta ognor dal monile d'Aprile,
  Circonfusa d'aroma e fulgor!

Mattutina, sei cara, ò Messina,
  Se l'aurora ti bacia e colora,
  Se in te cada, e t'imperli rugiada,
  S'hai nel grembo un bel nembo di fior!

Sei divina al meriggio, ò Messina,
  Tra palmeti, bei fonti e laureti,
  Tra gli aurati ed olenti cedrati,
  Con torrenti di luce e d'ardor!

Vespertina sei maga, ò Messina,
  S'hai pacato, sereno stellato:
  Sei portento s'hai luna d'argento,
  Danze, suoni e canzoni d'amor!

Sei regina, ò azzurrina Messina,
  Per giardini di fate beate,
  Per convalli sott'onda in coralli,
  Coronata Sirena del mar!

Chi non vide a marina Messina,
  Mal può dir ch'egli vide brillar
  Le beltà che rinserra la terra,
  Chiude il flutto, ed il ciel sa versar!
                PEPOLI (1801-1881).

VERSI ENDECASILLABI.

Verses of eleven syllables are called "versi endecasillabi," or "versi eroici." They are the principal Italian verses and the best wherewith to express great and noble thoughts. These verses may have two, three, four, and even five (rhythmical) accents, arranged in almost every conceivable manner.

BEATRICE.

Tanto gentile e tanto onesta pare
   La donna mia, quand ella altrui saluta,
   Ch' ogni lingua divien tremando muta,
   E gli occhi non ardiscon di guardare.

Ella sen va sentendosi laudare, *
   Benignamente d' umiltà vestuta ; †
   E par che sia una cosa venuta
   Di cielo in terra a miracol mostrare.

Mostrasi sì piacente a chi la mira,
   Che dà per gli occhi una dolcezza al core,
   Che intender non la può chi non la prova.

E par che dalle sue labbia si mova ‡
   Uno spirto soave e pien d' amore,
   Che va dicendo all' anima : sospira.
                         DANTE (1265-1321).

LAURA.

Erano i capei d' oro all' aura sparsi,
   Che 'n mille dolci nodi gli avvolgea ;
   E 'l vago lume oltra misura ardea
   Di quei begli occhi, ch' or ne son sì scarsi ;

E 'l viso di pietosi color farsi,
   Non so se vero o falso mi parea :
   I' che l' esca amorosa al petto avea,
   Qual maraviglia se di subit' arsi ?

Non era l' andar suo cosa mortale,
   Ma d' angelica forma ; e le parole
   Suonavan altro che pur voce umana.

Uno spirto celeste, un vivo sole
   Fu quel ch' i' vidi : e se non fosse or tale,
   Piaga per allentar d' arco non sana. §
                         PETRARCA (1304-1374).

---

* In order to understand " sen va," see rule 845, r.
† " vestuta," for " vestita," *clothed, full of.* ‡ " labbia," for " labbra," *lips.*
§ " Piaga per allentar d' arco non sana," means : " A wound (piaga) does not get healed (non sana) when the bow (arco) relaxes." After the words " the bow," the words " from which the arrow which inflicted the wound came," are understood. This pretty " concetto " of Petrarca, one of the earliest in the Italian language, is now used as a proverb.

SOPRA LA MORTE.

Morte, che se' tu mai? Primo dei danni
   L'alma vile e la rea ti crede e teme;
   E vendetta del ciel scendi ai tiranni,
   Che il vigile tuo braccio incalza e preme.

Ma l'infelice, a cui de' lunghi affanni
   Grave è l'incarco, e morta in cuor la speme,
   Quel ferro implora troncator degli anni,
   E ride all'appressar dell'ore estreme.

Fra la polve di Marte e le vicende
   Ti sfida il forte, che ne' rischi indura;
   E il saggio senza impallidir ti attende.

Morte, che se' tu dunque? Un' ombra oscura,
   Un bene, un male, che diversa prende
   Dagli affetti dell'uom forma e natura.

                              MONTI (1754-1828).

VERSI DODECASILLABI.

Verses of twelve syllables are called "versi dodecasillabi." They have four accents; one on the third, one on the fifth, one on the eighth, and the other (essential) on the eleventh syllable.

UN POPOLO DEGRADATO.

Dai guardi dubbiosi, dai pavidi volti,
   Qual raggio di sole da nuvoli folti,
   Traluce de' padri la fiera virtù:
   Ne' guardi, ne' volti confuso ed incerto
   Si mesce e discorda lo spregio sofferto
   Col misero orgoglio d'un tempo che fu.

                             MANZONI (1785-1873).

Blank verses are called in Italian "versi sciolti."

I regret also to have no space here for more than these few lines taken from one of the two beautiful choruses in the other excellent tragedy by Manzoni, "Adelchi," but this also I intend to republish in full in my "Italian Reader."

VOCABULARY.

PART I.

ENGLISH—ITALIAN.

NOTE.—*Nouns ending in* o *are masculine, and those in* a, *as a rule, feminine. The gender of nouns ending in* e *is given.*

A

A, an, un, uno, una.
Abandon, v. a. abbandonare.
Ability, abilità.
Able, abile.
About, circa.
Above, al di sopra.—mentioned, suddetto.
Abruptly, bruscamente.
Abundance, abbondanza.
Abyss, golfo, abisso.
Academy, accademia.
Accent, accento.
Accept, v. a. accettare.
Accident, accidente.
Accompany, v. a. accompagnare.
Accomplish, v. a. compire.
Accomplished, compito.
According, secondo.
Accusation, accusa.
Accuse, v. a. accusare.
Acquaintance, conoscenza, (friend), conoscente.
Acquit, v. a. assolvere.
Act, atto.
Act, v. a. agire.
Action, azione, f.
Address, indirizzo.
Admiration, ammirazione, f.
Admire, v. a. ammirare.
Admission, entrata.
Admit, v. a. ammettere.
Adorn, v. a. adornare.
Advance, v. a. avanzarsi.
Advantage, vantaggio.
Advice, consiglio.
Advise, v. a. consigliare.
Affair, affare, m.
Affection, affetto.
Afflicted, afflitto.
Afford, v. a. dare, procurare.
After, dopo.
Afternoon, dopo pranzo.
Afterwards, dopo.
Again, ancora, di nuovo.
Against, contro.
Age, età, secolo.
Agitation, agitazione.
Ago, fa.
Agreeable, piacevole.
Air, aria.
Album, album.
All, tutto, tutti.
Allege, v. a. addurre.
Alley, chiasso.
Allow, v. a. permettere.
Almost, quasi.
Alone, solo.
Along, lungo.
Alps, Alpi, f.
Already, già.
Also, anche, ancora, altresì, eziandio.
Altar, altare, m.
Although, benchè, sebbene.
Always, sempre.
Ambitious, ambizioso.
America, America.
American, Americano.
Amiable, amabile.
Ammunition, munizione, f.
Among, amongst, fra, tra.
Ancestors, antenati, predecessori.
Ancient, antico.
And, e, ed.
Anger, collera.
Animal, animale.
Another, un'altra.
Answer, v. n. rispondere.
Antagonist, avversario, rivale.
Any, del, dello, &c., alcuno, &c.
Any, chiunque, ognuno, qualunque.— one, alcuno.—thing, qualche cosa.
Anyone, alcuno.
Apartment, appartamento.
Apologise, v. a. far delle scuse a.
Appear, v. n. apparire.
Appearance, apparenza.
Apple, mela, pomo.
Apprehend, v. a. temere.
Approve, v. a. approvare.
Aptly, attamente.
Arab, Arabian, Arabo.
Arabia, Arabia.
Arbitrator, arbitro.
Architect, architetto.
Argue, v. n. argomentare, discorrere, ragionare.
Arm, braccio.
Army, esercito, armata.
Arrangement, accomodamento.
Arrest, v. a. arrestare.
Arrival, arrivo.
Arrive, v. n. arrivare.
Arrow, freccia.
Art, arte, f.
Artificial, artificiale, finto.
Artillery, artiglieria.
Artist, artista, m., rule 370.
As, mentre, come.
As far as, fino a.
As if, come se.
As soon as, tosto che.
Ascribe, v. a. attribuire.

Asia, Asia.
Ask, v. a. chiedere, domandare.
Asleep, addormentato.
Assembly, adunanza.
Assertion, asserzione, f.
Assiduous, assiduo.
Assistance, aiuto.
Assure, v. a. assicurare.
Astonished, attonito.
Astronomer, astronomo.
Astronomy, astronomìa.
At, a,—all, punto.—last, finalmente. — once, subito.—present, ora, adesso.
Athenian, Ateniese.
Athletic, d'atleta.
Attack, attacco, assalto.
Attack, v. a. attaccare.
Attend, v. a. accudire a (like Finire).
Attendant, servo.
Attention, attenzione, f.
Aunt, zia.
Austrian, Austrìaco.
Author, autore.
Autumn, autunno.
Avenge,(one's-self), v. r. vendicarsi.
Avoid, v. a. evitare.
Awake, v. a. svegliare.
Awfully, terribilmente.

B

Back, dosso, schiena.
Bad, cattivo.
Bag, sacco.
Baggage, bagaglio.
Balance, bilancia.
Ball, palla, (dancing) ballo.
Bank, riva.
Banker, banchiere.
Barbarous, barbaro.
Bark (boat), barca.
Baron, barone.
Baroness, baronessa.
Barren, sterile.
Basket, canestro, paniere.
Battery, batterìa.
Battle, battaglia.
Bay, baia.
Be, v. n. and auxiliary, essere.—able, potere.— afraid, temere.—born, nascere. — due, appartenere a.- -obliged, dovere. — necessary, abbisognare. — sorry, rincrescere. — willing, volere, esser disposto.
Beat, v. a. battere.—down, buttar giù.
Beautiful, bello, leggiadro.
Beauty, bellezza.
Because, perchè, per causa di.
Become, v. n. divenire.
Bed, letto.—room, camera da letto. Bed (of coal), strato.
Before (prep. of time), avanti, prima di,(prep. of place), davanti.
Beg, v. a. pregare.
Begin, v. n. principiare.
Behave, v. n. comportarsi.
Behaviour, condotta.
Behind, indietro, (adv.) dietro di, (prep.)
Belgium, Belgio.
Believe, v. n. credere.
Bell, campanello.
Belong, v. n. appartenere.
Bench, scranno.
Bertha, Berta.
Beseech, v. a. pregare.
Besiege, v. a. assediare.
Best, migliore.
Betray, v. a. tradire (like Finire).
Better, meglio, migliore.
Between, betwixt, fra, tra.
Big, grosso, grande.
Bind, v. a. legare.
Bird, uccello.
Birthday, giorno di nascita.
Bit, pezzo.
Black, nero.
Blacksmith, fabbroferraio.
Blame, v. a. biasimare.
Blotting-paper, carta sugante.
Blow, colpo, botta.
Blue, turchino, azzurro.
Board, asse, f. on—, a bordo di.
Boat, barca, battello.
Body, corpo.
Bonnet, cappellino.
Book, libro.—binder, legatore di libri.
Boot, stivale, m.
Border, margine, m. orlo, spiaggia.
Bore, seccatura.
Botany, botanica.
Both, tutti e due, e...e.
Bottle, bottiglia.
Boulogne, Bologna.
Bow, v. a. fare un inchino a.
Box, scatola, cassetta.
Boy, ragazzo, fanciullo.
Branch, ramo.
Brandy, acquavite.
Brass, lottone.
Brave, bravo, animoso.
Bravely, bravamente.
Bread, pane, m.
Breadth, larghezza.
Break, v. a. rompere.—up, separarsi.
Breakfast, colazione, f.
Breakfast,v.a. far colazione.
Brick-dust, polvere di mattoni.
Bridge, ponte.
Brilliant, brillante.
Brim (of a hat), le falde (di un cappello).
Bring, v. a. portare.—up, menare.
British, Brittanico.
Brittle, fragile.
Broad, ampio, largo.
Bronze, bronzo.
Brook, ruscello.
Brother, fratello.—in-law, cognato.
Browse, v. a. pascersi.
Brutus, Bruto.
Build, v. a. fabbricare.
Building, edifizio, fabbricato.
Bullet, palla di fucile.
Bull-fight, combattimento fra uomini a piedi o a cavallo con un toro.
Burn, v. a. abbruciare.
Business, affare, affari.
Busy, affaccendato.
Busybody, affannone.
But, ma.—still, però, eppure.
Buy, v. a. comprare.

C

Cabbage, cavolo.
Cage, gabbia.
Cairo, Cairo.
Call, v. a. chiamare.
Calm, calma.
Cambric, cambrìa.
Camelia, camelia.

Camp, campo.
Can, I can, posso; we can, possiamo.
Cannon, cannone.
Canto, canto.
Capital (of a country) la capitale; (funds) il capitale.
Captain, capitano.
Caravansary, caravanseraglio.
Card, carta.
Care, pensiero, cura.
Carpenter, falegname.
Carpet, tappeto.
Carriage, carrozza, vettura.
Carry, v. a. portare.—away, portar via.
Cart-load, carro, plur., carra.
Case, caso, soggetto.
Cast, v. a. gettare.
Castle, castello.
Cat, gatto.
Catch, acchiappare.—hold of, afferrare.
Cathedral, cattedrale.
Cattle, bestiame.
Cause, causa, cagione.
Cause, v. a. cagionare.
Caution, cautela.
Cavern, caverna.
Celebrate, v. a. celebrare.
Celebrated, (famous), celebre.
Celebrity, celebrità.
Cement, cemento.
Century, secolo.
Certainly, certamente.
Chain, catena.
Chair, sedia, seggiola. Arm —, seggiola a braccioli. Easy —, sedia d'appoggio.
Chairman, presidente.
Challenge, sfida.
Chance, caso, ventura.
Change, v. a. cambiare.
Chaplain, cappellano.
Character, carattere, m.
Charity, carità.
Charles, Carlo.
Charlotte, Carlotta.
Charm, incanto.
Cheek, guancia, gota.
Cheerful, allegro.
Cheese, cacio, formaggio.
Cherry, ciriegia.

Chicken, pollastro.
Child, fanciullo.
Chimney-piece, quadro di camino.
China, porcellana.
Chirp, v. n. cantare.
Choleric, collerico.
Choose, v. a. scegliere.
Christmas, Natale.
Chronology, cronologìa.
Church, chiesa.
Circumstance, circostanza.
City, città.
Clean, netto, pulito.
Clergyman, parroco, pievano.
Clever, abile, destro.
Climate, clima.
Clock, pendola, orologio. O'clock (see rule 548).
Cloth (of linen, or cotton) tela, (of wool) panno.
Clothes, panni.
Cloud, nube, nuvola.
Coal, carbon fossile.
Coast, costa, spiaggia
Coat, vestito, abito.
Coffee and coffee-house, caffè.
College, collegio.
Colonel, colonnello.
Colour, colore.
Columbus, Colombo.
Come, v. n. venire.—back, ritornare.—in, entrare.
Comedy, commedia.
Comely, piacevole, vago, avvenente.
Comfortable, confortevole, comodo.
Command, comando.
Command, v. a. comandare.
Commerce, commercio.
Commercial, commerciale.
Commission, commissione.
Commit, v. a. commettere.
Committee, comitato.
Communication, comunicazione.
Companion, compagno.
Company, compagnìa.
Compare, v. a. paragonare.
Compass, bussola.
Compel, v. a. forzare.
Complexion, carnagione, f.
Compliment, complimento.
Compose, v. a. comporre.
Conceited, vanitoso.

Concert, concerto.
Conclude, v. a. conchiudere.
Condemn, v. a. condannare.
Condition, condizione, f.
Conduct, v. a. condurre.
Conduct, condotta.
Confess, v. a. confessare.
Confidence, confidenza.
Confused, confuso.
Conjugate, v. a. coniugare.
Conquer, v. a. conquistare.
Conscientious, coscienzioso.
Consequence, conseguenza.
Consider, v. a. considerare.
Considerable, considerabile.
Conspicuous, cospicuo.
Constitute, v. a. costituire (like Finire).
Construct, v. a. costruire, (like Finire).
Contain, v. a. contenere.
Continue, v. a. continuare.
Contrary, contrario.
Contribute, v. a. contribuire (like Finire).
Convenient, conveniente.
Conversation, conversazione, f.
Copious, abbondante.
Copper, rame.
Copy, copia.
Coriolanus, Coriolano.
Corn, frumento.
Cornelia, Cornelia.
Correct, v. a. correggere.
Cost. v. n. costare.
Costly, dispendioso.
Cottage, capanna.
Cotton, cotone, m.
Countenance, viso, aspetto, carnagione, f.
Country, (in a general sense) paese, (out of town), in campagna, (in opposition to the capital) provincia. — house, casa di campagna. — man, paesano, compatriota.
Couple, coppia, paio.
Courage, coraggio.
Course, corso.
Court, corte, f. cortile, m.
Cousin, cugino, cugina.
Cover, v. a. coprire (like Servire).
Craggy, scosceso, diroccato.

Crime, delitto.
Criminal, criminale.
Crœsus, Creso.
Cross, v. a. attraversare.
Crowd, calca, folla.
Crown, corona.
Cruel, crudele.
Cruiser, vascello di corso.
Cry, v. a. gridare.
Crystal, cristallo.
Cultivate, v. a. coltivare.
Cur, cagnuccio.
Curious, curioso.
Custom-house, dogana.

D

Danger, pericolo.
Dangerous, pericoloso.
Dare, v. a. ardire, (like Finire).
Dark, oscuro, tenebroso.
Daughter, figlia.
Day, giorno, dì.
Day after-to-morrow, posdomani, m.
Dazzle, v. a. abbagliare.
Dean, decano.
Dear, caro.
Death, morte, f.
Debt, debito.
Decapitation, decapitazione, f.
Deceit, frode, f.
Decide, v. a. decidere.
Decision, decisione, f.
Deed, azione, f. fatto.
Deep, profondo.
Defeat, v. a. sconfiggere.
Defect, difetto.
Defiance, sfida.
Defray, v. a. pagare.
Degree, grado, segno.
Delight, delizia.
Delight, v. a. dilettare.
Delightful, dilettevole.
Dell, valle, f. vallone, m.
Demetrius, Demetrio.
Demolish, v. a. demolire (like Finire).
Deny, v. a. negare.
Depart, v. n. partire (like Servire).
Departure, partenza.
Depend, v. n. dipendere.
Depict, v. a. dipingere.
Dépôt, dépôt.
Depth, profondità.
Describe, v. a. descrivere.

Description, descrizione, f.
Deserve, v. n. meritare.
Desire, desiderio.
Desire, v. a. desiderare, pregare ; see rule 300.
Despise, v. a. disprezzare.
Despotic, despotico.
Dessert, dopopasto.
Destine, v. a. destinare.
Detain, v. a. ritenere.
Determine, v. a. determinare.
Diamond, diamante, m.
Dictates, precetti.
Dictionary, dizionario.
Die, v. n. morire.
Difference, differenza.
Different, differente.
Difficult, difficile.
Diligently, diligentemente.
Diminish, v. n. diminuire (like Finire).
Dine, v. n. pranzare.
Dining-room, sala da pranzo.
Dinner, pranzo.
Directly, in un subito.
Director, direttore.
Disaffection, scontento.
Disarm, v. a. disarmare.
Discernible, potevansi vedere.
Disconcert, v. a. sconcertare.
Discover, v. a. scoprire (like Servire).
Discovery, scoperta.
Discussion, discussione, f.
Disease, malattìa.
Disguise, travestimento.
Dishonest, disonesto.
Dishonour, disonore.
Dismiss, v. a. dar licenza.
Displease, v. a. dispiacere a.
Distance, distanza.
Distant, distante.
Distinguish, v. a. discernere.
Divine, divino.
Do, v. a. fare.—How do you do ? come sta ? or come state ?
Doctor, dottore.
Dog, cane.
Door, porta.
Down, giù.
Dozen, dozzina.
Draw, v. a. disegnare.

Drawing, disegno.
Dress, abito, veste.
Dress, v. a. vestire.—one'sself, vestirsi (like Servire).
Drink, v. a. bere.
Drinking, il bere.
Drive, v. a. guidare.
Droll, originale.
Ductile, duttile.
Duel, duello.
Durable, durabile.
During, durante.
Dust, polvere, f.
Duty, dovere, m.
Dwarf, nano.

E

Each, ogni.
Eagle, aquila.
Ear, orecchio.
Early, per tempo.
Earn, v. a. guadagnare.
Earnest, in earnest, sul serio, con amore.
Earth, terra.
Easily, facilmente.
Eastern, orientale.
Easy-chair, poltrona.
Eat, v. a. mangiare.
Eating, il mangiare.
Ecclesiastic, ecclesiastico.
Education, educazione, f.
Edward, Odoardo.
Efface, v. a. cancellare.
Effect, effetto.
Egg, uovo.
Egypt, Egitto.
Eight, otto.
Eighty, ottanta.
Either, o...o, ovvero...ovvero.
Elect, v. a. eleggere.
Election, elezione, f.
Elephant, elefante.
Elizabeth, Elisabetta.
Eloquence, eloquenza.
Elude, v. a. sfuggire.
Embark, v. n. imbarcarsi.
Embellishment, abbellimento.
Emblem, emblema, m.
Embroider, v. a. ricamare.
Eminent, eminente.
Emperor, imperatore.
Empress, imperatrice.
Encamp, v. n. accamparsi.

ENGLISH-ITALIAN VOCABULARY.

Encourage, v. a. incoraggiare.
End (termination), fine, f.
Endeavour, sforzo,
Endow, v. a. dotare.
Enemy, nemico.
England, Inghilterra. English and Englishman, Inglese.
Enjoy, v. a. godere.
Enough, abbastanza.
Enraged, arrabbiato.
Enrich, v. a. arricchire (like Finire).
Enter, v. n. entrare.
Enthusiasm, entusiasmo.
Entirely, intieramente.
Entreat, v. a. supplicare.
Entreaty, preghiera.
Entrenchments, fortificazioni, f.
Equal, eguale, simile.
Equal, v. a. pareggiare.
Erect, v. a. erigere, innalzare.
Escape, fuga.
Escape, v. n. scappare, fuggire (like Servire).
Essay, saggio.
Establish, v. a. stabilire (like Finire).
Esteem, stima.
Esteem, v. a. stimare.
Europe, Europa.
Even, persino.
Evening, sera.
Event, evento.
Ever, mai, sempre.
Every, ogni. —one, ognuno. —thing, tutto. —body, tutti.
Everywhere, da per tutto.
Examination, esame, m.
Excellence, eccellenza.
Except, eccetto, tranne.
Excite, v. a. eccitare.
Excuse, scusa.
Execration, esecrazione, f.
Execute, v. a. eseguire (like Finire).
Exempt, v. a. esentare.
Exercise, esercizio, tema.
Exhibition, esposizione, f.
Exile, esiglio
Expect, v. a. aspettare.
Expense, spesa.
Explain, v. a. spiegare.
Exploit, gesto (rule 420)

Extend, v. a. stendere.
Extent, ampiezza.
Extraordinary, straordinario.
Extravagance, stravaganza.
Extremely, estremamente.
Eye, occhio.

F
Facility, facilità.
Fair, biondo, bello.
Faithful, fedele.
Faithfully, fedelmente.
Family, famiglia.
Famous, famoso.
Far, lontano.
Farm, podere, m.
Farther, più lontano.
Fashion, moda, guisa. In the —, alla moda.
Fast, presto.
Fat, grasso.
Father, padre. — in law, suocero.
Fault (mistake), sbaglio, (error), errore.
Favour, favore.
Favour, v. a. favorire (like Finire).
Favourable, favorevole.
Favourite, favorito.
Fear, timore.
Fear, v. n. temere.
Fearful, terribile.
Features, fattezze.
February, febbraio.
Federation, federazione.
Feeling, sentimento.
Feigned, finto.
Fellow, compagno. —little, birichino.
Ferdinand, Ferdinando.
Fern, felce, f.
Ferocity, ferocità.
Fertility, fertilita.
Fetch, v. n. andare a cercare.
Few, pochi, poche.
Field, campo.
Fifteen, quindici.
Fifth, quinto.
Fifty, cinquanta.
Fight, v. n. combattere.
Figure, figura.
Filial, filiale.
Find, v. a. trovare.
Fine, bello, fino.
Finish, v. a. finire.

Fire, fuoco.—wood, legna.
First, primo.
Fish, pesce.
Five, cinque.
Flag, bandiera.
Flatterer, lusingatori.
Fleet, flotta.
Florence, Firenze.
Flower, fiore, m.
Flowery, fiorito.
Fly, v. n. volare, fuggire (like Servire).—into a passion, andare in collera.
Follow, v. a. seguire.
Following, seguente.
Food, cibo, vivanda.
Foot, piede, m.
For, per.
Force, v. a. forzare.
Foreigner, straniero.
Forest, foresta.
Forget, v. n. scordarsi di.
Forgive, v. a. perdonare.
Fork, forchetta.
Form, v. a. formare.
Former, d'altrevolte.
Formerly, altre volte.
Fortress, fortezza.
Fortune, fortuna.
Forty, quaranta.
Found, v. a. fondare.
Foundation, fondamento.
Fountain, fontana.
Four, quattro.
Fourteen, quattordici.
Fourteenth, decimo quarto.
Fourth, quarto.
Fragrance, fragranza.
Frail, fragile.
Frame, cornice, f.
France, Francia.
Francis, Francesco.
Frankly, francamente.
Frederick, Federico.
Freeze, v. n. gelare.
French, Francese.
Frequently, sovente.
Freshness, freschezza.
Friday, venerdì.
Friend, amico.
Friendship, amicizia.
From, da.
Fruit, frutto.
Fulfil, v. a. adempire.
Full, pieno.
Fund, fondo.
Furnish, v. a. ammobigliare.
Furniture, mobili.

G

Gain, v. a. guadagnare.
Gallery, gallerìa.
Galley, galera.
Gamble, v. a. biscazzare.
Game, giuoco.
Garden, giardino.
Gardener, giardiniere.
Gather, v. a. cogliere.
Gauntlet, guanto ferrato.
General, generale. —in chief, generalissimo.
Generally, generalmente.
Generosity, generosità.
Gentleman, Signore.
Geography, geografia.
George, Giorgio.
German, Tedesco.
Get, v. a. guadagnare, ottenere.—dark, v. i. annottare.
Gift, dono, regalo.
Girl, fanciulla, ragazza.
Give, v. a. dare.
Glance, occhiata.
Glass, bicchiere.
Gloomy, buio, d'apparenza melanconica.
Glorious, glorioso,
Glory, gloria.
Glove, guanto.
Go, v. n. andare.—out, uscire. —away, andar via.
Goat, capra.
God, Dio, Iddio.
Gold, oro.
Good, buono.
Good-bye, addio.
Good-for-nothing fellow, buono a niente.
Goods, beni, roba.
Govern, v. a. governare.
Government, governo.
Governor, governatore.
Graceful, grazioso.
Gradually, più e più, gradualmente.
Grammar, grammatica.
Grandfather, nonno, avo.
Grant, v. a. accordare.
Grapes, uva.
Grave, grave.
Gravity, gravità.
Great, grande.—A great deal, moltissimo.
Greatly, moltissimo.
Greek, Greco.

Green, verde.
Grey, grigio.
Groan, v. n. gemere.
Ground-floor, pianterreno.
Guard, guardia.
Guess, v. n. indovinare.
Guest, convitato.
Guide, v. a. guidare.
Guinea, ghinea; pl. ghinee.
Guitar, chitarra.
Gun, cannone, fucile. - powder, polvere da cannone.

H

Hair, capelli.
Half, (noun) metà a. (adjective) mezzo.—a crown, mezza corona.
Hall, sala.
Hand, mano, f.
Handle, manico.
Handsome, bello, vezzoso.
Happen, v. n. accadere.
Happy, felice.
Harbour, porto.
Hardship, privazione.
Harmonious, armonioso.
Harold, Aroldo.
Hat, cappello.
Hate, v. a. odiare.
Haughty, altiero.
Have, v. a. avere.
He, egli, esso.
Head, testa, capo.
Health, salute, f.
Hear, v. a., intendere, sentire (like Servire).
Heart, by heart, a mente.
Heartily, di cuore.
Heaven, cielo.
Heavy, pesante.
Height, altezza. at the—, all' apice.
Help, v. a. aiutare.
Henry, Enrico.
Her, lei, essa.
Here, qui, qua.
Here is, ecco qui.
Here it is, eccolo, eccola.
Here they are, eccoli, eccole.
Hero, eroe.
Hide, v. a. nascondere.
High, alto, pronunciato.
Highly, generosamente.
Hill, collina.
Him, lui, lo.

Himself, egli stesso.
His, il suo, la sua.
Historian, storico.
History, storia.
Hollow, cavità.
Home, dimora.
Homer, Omero.
Honest, onesto.
Honesty, onestà.
Hope, v. a. sperare.
Horse, cavallo.
Host, oste.
Hostile, ostile, nemico.
Hour, ora.
House, casa.
How ? come ? — many ? quanti ? — much, quanto.
However, però, nulladimeno.
Hundred, cento.
Hunger, fame, f.
Hurrah ! Evviva !

I

I, io.
Ice, ghiaccio.
Idiot, idiota, sciocco.
If, se. If you please, per piacere.
Ignorance, ignoranza.
Illustration, disegno.
Imitate, v. a. imitare.
Immediate, immediato.
Immediately, immediatemente.
Immense, immenso.
Importance, importanza.
Impossible, impossibile.
Impressive, impressivo.
Improve, v. n. migliorare.
Imprudence, imprudenza.
Imprudent, imprudente.
In, in, (hence), fra.
Inanimated, inanimato.
Inch, dito.
Indeed, in verità.
Indignation, indignazione, f.
Induce, v. a. indurre.
Industry, industria.
Inferior, inferiore.
Infirm, infermo.
Influence, influenza.
Influence, v. a. influenzare.
Inform, v. a. istruire (like Finire).
Ingenious, ingegnoso.

Ingratitude, ingratitudine, f.
Inhabitant, abitante.
Ink, inchiostro. — stand, calamaio.
Inn, albergo.
Innocent, innocente.
Innumerable, innumerabile.
In order to, per, onde.
Inquisitive, curioso.
Inspire, v. a. inspirare.
Instead of, in luogo di, in vece di.
Institution, istituzione, f.
Instrument, istrumento.
Insult, v. a. insultare.
Intelligible, intelligibile.
Intend, v. a. aver l'intenzione, fare i conti.
Interest, interesse.
Interesting, interessante.
Internal, interno.
International, internazionale.
Interrogate, v. interrogare.
Intersperse, v. a. framescolare.
Into, in.
Intricate, imbrogliato.
Introduce, v. a. introdurre.
Invent, v. a. inventare.
Invention, invenzione, f.
Invest, v. a. investire (like Servire).
Invitation, invito.
Invite, v. a. invitare.
Irishman, Irlandese.
Iron, ferro. Wrought —, ferro battuto. Cast —, ghisa.
Isabella, Isabella.
Island, isola.
Issue, successo, impressione, f.
It, esso, lo, la.
Italian, Italiano.
Italy, Italia.

J

Jamaica, Giamaica.
James, Giacomo.
Jane, Giovanna.
January, gennaio.
Jewel, gioia.
John, Giovanni.
Joppa, Giappa.
Journey, viaggio.
Joy, gioia.
Judge, giudice.
Jug, boccale, m.
Jump, v. n. saltare.
Jupiter, Giove.
Just, adj. giusto, adv. (just now) questo momento, *or* appunto.
Justice, giustizia.

K

Keep, v. a. tenere. —waiting, far aspettare.
Kill, v. a. uccidere.
Kind, buono.
Kind, qualtità, sorte, f.
Kindness, bontà.
King, re.
Kneel v. n. inginocchiarsi.
Knife, coltello.
Knight, cavaliere.
Knock, v. a. picchiare, bussare.
Know, sapere, conoscere.
Knowledge, conoscenze, sapere.

L

Lace, merletto.
Lady, Signora.—Young—signorina.
Lake, lago.
Lame, v. a. storpiare.
Landlord, proprietario, padrone.
Landscape, paesaggio.
Language, lingua.
Large, grande, grosso.
Last, passato.—night (yesterday evening) ierisera. Last-night, meaning till this morning, is translated by "La notte scorsa."
Late, defunto.
Latter, questo, questi.
Laugh, v. n. ridere.
Law, legge, f.
Lay, v. a. mettere.—down, deporre.— the cloth, mettere la tovaglia.
Lean, magro.
Learn, v. a. imparare.— by heart, imparare a mente.
Learning, sapere.
Leather, cuoio.
Leave, permissione, f.
Leave, v. a. lasciare.
Lecture, discorso, lettura.
Lemon, limone, m.
Lend, v. a. prestare.
Length, lunghezza. At— finalmente.
Less, meno.
Lesson, lezione, f.
Lest, per paura che (see rule 733).
Letter, lettera.
Liberty, libertà.
Life, vita.
Light, leggero.
Light, v. a accendere.
Like, come, simile.
Like, v. a. amare, andare a genio.
Likeness, ritratto.
Likewise, parimente, anche.
Lily, giglio.
Limb, membro.
Line, linea, riga (of writing or print).
Lion, leone.
Listen, v. n. ascoltare.
Literary, letterario, letterato.
Little, piccolo.
Live, v. n. vivere.
Load, v. a. caricare.
Loadstone, calamita.
Lodge, v. n. alloggiare.
Lofty, alto, sublime.
London, Londra.
Lonely, isolato.
Long, lungo.
Look, v. a. guardare.— upon, considerare.— out, cercar degli occhi.
Looking-glass, specchio.
Lord, conte, marchese.
Lose, v. a. perdere.
Loss, perdita.
Louis, Luigi.
Louisa, Luigia.
Love, amore, m.
Love, v. a. amare.
Lowest, infimo.
Luncheon, la seconda colazione, merenda.
Lustre, lustro.

M

Madeline, Maddalena.
Magazine, rivista, magazzino.
Magnificent, magnifico.

ENGLISH-ITALIAN VOCABULARY. 253

Majestic, maestoso.
Majesty, maestà.
Make, v. a. fare.—haste, affrettarsi.—up one's mind, decidersi.
Man, uomo. — of letters, letterato.
Mankind, genere umano.
Manly, virile.
Manner, maniera, usanza.
Manufacture, v. a. fabbricare.
Many, molti.
Marble, marmo.
Margaret, Margherita.
Mariner, marinaro.
Mark, pegno.
Mark, v. a. marcare.
Market, mercato.
Marry, v. a. sposare.
Mars, Marte.
Marsh, palude, f.
Martial, marziale.
Mary, Maria.
Master, maestro, padrone, (see rule 146)—piece, capo-lavoro.
Match, zolfanello.
Mathematics, matematica.
Matter, materia.
May, maggio.
Me, mi, me, a me.
Meadow, prato.
Means, mezzo.
Measure, misura.
Meet, or meet with, v. a. incontrare.
Meeting, riunione.
Melodious, melodioso.
Melt, v. a. fondere.
Member, membro, pl. membri, *or* membra (rule 420).
Memory, memoria.
Mercury, Mercurio.
Mere, puro, mero.
Merit, merito.
Messenger, messaggiero.
Metal, metallo.
Microscope, microscopio.
Midnight, mezzanotte.
Mildness, dolcezza.
Mile, miglio, plur. miglia.
Milk jug, boccale da latte.
Mind, spirito, mente, f.
Mind, v. a. badare a.
Mine, il mio, la mia, &c.
Mineral, minerale, m.

Minister, ministro. — for Foreign Affairs, Ministro degli Affari Esteri.
Minute, minuto.
Mischief, male.
Misfortune, disgrazia.
Miss, v. a. mancare.
Mistake, sbaglio.
Moderate, moderato.
Modesty, modestia.
Moment, momento.
Monarch, monarca.
Monday, lunedì.
Money, danaro, soldi.
Monkey, scimia.
Month, mese, m.
Moor, landa, brughiera.
Moralist, moralista.
More, più.
Morning, mattina.
Mosaic, mosaico (rule 410).
Most, il più.
Mother, madre. — in-law, suocera.
Motive, motivo.
Mountain, montagna.
Mouth, bocca.
Mouthful, boccata.
Mr., Signore.
Mrs., Signora.
Much, molto.
Mufti, alla borghese.
Multitude, moltitudine, f.
Municipal, municipale.
Museum, musèo.
Music, musica.
Must.—I must, debbo.—we must, dobbiamo, &c.
My, il mio, la mia, i miei.
Mysterious, misterioso.
Mythology, mitologia.

N

Name, nome.
Naples, Napoli.
Napoleon, Napoleone.
Narrate, v. a. raccontare.
Narrow, stretto.
Nation, nazione.
National, nazionale.
Natural, naturale.
Nature, natura.
Navigation, navigazione.
Navigator, navigatore.
Near, vicino.
Nearly, quasi.
Necessary, necessario.
Necessity, necessità.

Necklace, monile, vezzo.
Needle, ago.
Negro, negro. — dealer, mercante di schiavi.
Neighbourhood, vicinato.
Neighbouring, nel vicinato.
Neither, nè.
Nephew, nipote.
Neptune, Nettuno.
Nest, nido.
Never, non...mai, no, mai.
New, nuovo.—born, pur mo' nato.
News, nuova, notizie.— paper, giornale.
Next, prossimo.
Nibble, v. a. morsecchiare.
Nice, Nizza.
Night, notte, f.
Nine, nove.
Ninth, nono.
No, no.—body, nessuno.— doubt, senza dubbio, senz'altro. — longer, non...più.
Noble, nobile.
Noise, rumore, strepito.
Nonsense, sciocchezze, spropositi.
Noon, mezzogiorno.
Nor, nè.
Norman, Normanno.
Normandy, Normandia.
North, tramontana, settentrione.
Not, non.
Nothing, niente, nulla.
Nourish, nutrire.
Now, adesso, ora.
Number, numero.
Numerous, numeroso.

O

Occasion, occasione.
O'clock, dell' orologio. Six—alle sei (see rule 548).
October, ottobre.
Obey, v. a. ubbidire (like Finire).
Observe, v. a. osservare.
Obtain, v. a. ottenere.
Odd, singolare, bizzarro.
Of, di.
Off, in vista di.
Offend, v. a. offendere.
Offer, v. a. offrire (like Servire).

ENGLISH-ITALIAN VOCABULARY.

Office, carica, officio.
Officer, ufficiale.
Often, sovente, spesso.
Old, vecchio.
Olive, uliva.—tree, ulivo.
On, su, sopra. —behalf of, in favore di.
Once, una volta. At—, subito.
One, uno, una.
Only, solo, solamente, non ...che.
Open, aperto.
Open, v. a. aprire (like Servire).
Opera, opera.
Operation, operazione, f.
Opposite, opposta.
Opulence, opulenza
Or, o, ovvero, ossia.
Orange and orange-tree, a-rancio.
Orator, oratore.
Orchard, pometo.
Order, ordine, m.
Order, v. a. commandare.
Origin, origine, f.
Original, originale.
Other, altro.
Otherwise, altrimenti.
Our, il nostro, &c.
Ourselves, noi stessi.
Oval, ovale.
Over, sopra, di sopra.
Overturn, sovvertere, rovesciare.
Owe, v. n. dovere.
Own, proprio.

P

Pace, passo.
Pain, male, dolore, m.
Painful, doloroso.
Paint, v. a. dipingere.
Paint brush, pennello.
Painter, pittore.
Painting, pittura, quadro.
Pair, paio, coppia.
Palace, palazzo.
Paper, carta.
Parasol, ombrellino.
Parchment, pergamena, carta pecora.
Pardon, v. a. perdonare a.
Parent, padre, madre, genitore.
Paris, Parigi.
Park, parco.

Parliament (member of), deputato al parlamento.
Parlour, salotto.
Part, parte, f., porzione, f.
Partner, socio.
Partridge, pernice, f.
Pass, v. n. passare.
Passenger, passaggero.
Passion, passione, f.
Past, passato.
Pasture, v. a. pasturare.
Patience, pazienza.
Paul, Paolo.
Pay, v. a. pagare.—attention to, badare a.
Peace, pace, f.
Pear, pera.
Pearl, perla.
Peculiarities, singolarità.
Pedestal, piedestallo.
Pekin, Pechino.
Pen, penna.
Pencil, lapis, m., matita.—case, porta-lapis.
Penetration, acume.
Penknife, temperino.
Penny, due soldi.
Pension, pensione, f.
People, popolo, gente.
Perfectly, perfettamente.
Perform, v. a. (to fulfil), adempire. To perform, (to play) prodursi.
Perhaps, forse.
Perpetual, perpetuo.
Perseverance, perseveranza.
Person, persona.
Personage, personaggio.
Personal, personale.
Philosopher, filosofo.
Piano, pianoforte.
Pickpocket, borsaiuolo.
Picture, quadro, pittura.
Picturesque, pittoresco.
Piece, pezzo.
Pierce, v. a. forare.
Pincushion, cuscinetto per le spille.
Pink, garofano.
Place, luogo, sito, posto.
Place, v. a. porre.
Plain, pianura, chiaro.
Planet, pianeta, m.
Platina, platino.
Play, v. a. giuocare.—on an instrument, suonare.
Plead, piatire (like Finire).
Pleasing, piacevole.

Pleasure, piacere.
Plot, congiura, trama.
Plunder, v. a. (persons) svaligiare; (habitations), saccheggiare.
Pocket, tasca, scarsella.
Poem, poema, m.
Poet, poeta.
Poetry, poesìa.
Point, v. a. indicare.
Poison, veleno.
Policeman, agente di polizìa, sbirro.
Policy, politica.
Polite, civile, cortese.
Politics, polìtica.
Pomp, pompa.
Poor, povero.
Pope, papa.
Popular, popolare.
Popularity, popolarità.
Port, porto.
Portrait, ritratto.
Positively, positivamente.
Possess, v. a. possedere.
Possession, possessione, f.
Possible, possibile.
Post (for letters), posta; (place), posto.
Postage-stamp, francobollo.
Posterity, posterità.
Posture, posizione, f.
Pound, libbra, lira (see rule 656).
Poverty, povertà.
Powder, polvere, f.
Power, potere, m.
Practise, v. a. practicare, esercitarsi.
Praise, lode.
Praise, v. a. lodare.
Precede, precedere.
Precious, prezioso.
Precipice, precipizio.
Precipitous, precipitoso.
Prefer, preferire, v. a. (like Finire).
Prejudicial, pregiudicativo.
Preparation, preparativo.
Prepare, v. a. preparare.
Present, dono, regalo.
Present, v. a. presentare.
Preserve, v. a. preservare.
President, presidente.
Pretty, bello, vago.
Prevent, v. a. evitare, impedire (like Finire).
Previous, prima di.

ENGLISH-ITALIAN VOCABULARY.

Prey, preda.
Price, prezzo, valore.
Pride one's-self, v. r. inorgoglirsi.
Prince, principe.
Princess, principessa.
Principal, principale.
Principle, principio.
Print, v. a. stampare.
Printing, stampa.
Prison, prigione, f.
Probably, probabilmente.
Procession, processione, f.
Produce, prodotto.
Produce, v. a. produrre.
Production, produzione, f.
Profit, v. n. profittare.
Profusion, profusione, f.
Progress, progresso.
Promise, v. a. promettere.
Proof, prova.
Property, proprietà, beni.
Proportioned, proporzionato.
Proposal, proposizione, f.
Propose, v. a. proporre.
Prospect, prospettiva, vista.
Prosperous, prospero.
Proud, orgoglioso.
Prove, v. a. provare.
Provision, provvisione, f.
Provoke, v. a. provocare.
Prudence, prudenza.
Prudently, prudentemente.
Prussia, Prussia.
Prussian, Prussiano.
Public, pubblico.
Punish, v. a. punire (like Finire).
Pupil, scolare, allievo.
Purchase, compra.
Pure, puro, semplice.
Purpose, intenzione. On—, a disegno.
Pursue, v. a. inseguire.
Pursuit, incalzo.
Put, v. a. mettere.—off, v. n. indugiare.

Q

Quantity, quantità.
Queen, regina.
Question (see rule 306).
Quickly, presto.
Quietly, tranquillamente.
Quill, penna d'oca.
Quire, quinterno di carta.
Quite, affatto, interamente.

R

Rage, rabbia.
Rain, pioggia.
Rain, v. i. piovere.
Rapaciousness, rapacità.
Raphael, Raffaello.
Raven, corvo.
Ravine, burrone, m.
Reach, v. a. giungere.
Read, v. a. leggere.
Reading-room, sala di lettura.
Ready, pronto.
Really, realmente.
Reason, ragione, f. senno.
Recall, v. a. richiamare.
Receive, v. a. ricevere.
Recognise, v. a. riconoscere.
Recommend, v. a. raccomandare.
Red, rosso.
Re-enter, v. n. rientrare.
Reflect, v. a. riflettere.
Regular, regolare.
Reign, v. a. regnare.
Reindeer, cervo (della Lapponia).
Rejoice, v. a. rallegrarsi.
Relation, parente, m.
Religion, religione, f.
Remain, v. n. rimanere, restare.
Remark, v. a. far osservare, dire.
Remarkably, notevolmente.
Remember, v. n. ricordarsi.
Remote, rimoto.
Renowned, rinomato.
Repent, v. n. pentirsi.
Reply, v. a. rispondere.
Report, rapporto. — of a gun, lo strepito d'un cannone.
Repose, v. r. riposarsi.
Represent, v. a. rappresentare.
Republic, repubblica.
Reputation, riputazione.
Request, richiesta, domanda.
Request, v. a. domandare.
Resemble, v. a. somigliare.
Resist, v. a. resistere.
Resolve, v. a. risolvere.
Resound, v. a. risuonare, rimbombare.
Respect, rispetto.
Respectful, rispettoso.

Respectfully, rispettosamente.
Respective, rispettiva.
Restoration, restaurazione.
Restore, v. a. rendere.
Result, risultamento.
Resume, v. a. ripigliare.
Retire, v. n. ritirarsi.
Return, ritorno.
Return, v. n. ritornare, scambiare, rispondere.
Reveal, v. a. rivelare.
Review, rivista.
Revolution, rivoluzione, f.
Reward, ricompensa, taglia.
Ribbon, nastro, fettuccia.
Rich, ricco.
Richard, Riccardo.
Riches, ricchezze.
Ride, v. n. cavalcare, andare a cavallo.
Right, diritto.
Ring, anello.
Ring. v. a. and n. suonare.
Ripe, maturo.
Rise, v. n. levarsi.
River, fiume, m. riviera.
Rivulet, ruscellino.
Road, strada, cammino.
Robber, ladro.
Rock, roccia, rupe, balza.
Roman, Romano.
Romantic, romantico.
Rome, Roma.
Romulus, Romolo.
Room, camera, stanza. Drawing—, salone.
Rose, rosa.
Round, adj. rotondo, prep. attorno, intorno.
Rout, v. a. sfrattare.
Royal, reale, regale.
Rude, grossolano, zotico, impertinente.
Rudely, rozzamente.
Ruin, rovina.
Ruin, v. a. rovinare.
Rule, regola.
Run, v. n. correre.
Rural, campestre.

S

Sack, v. a. saccheggiare.
Safe, adj. sano.
Safety, sicurezza.
Sail, v. a. far vela.
Sailing-vessel, bastimento a vela.

ENGLISH-ITALIAN VOCABULARY.

Sailor, marinaio.
Saladin, Saladino.
Salary, stipendio.
Same, medesimo, stesso.
Saracen, Saraceno.
Sardinia, Sardegna.
Satin, raso.
Satisfied, soddisfatto, contento.
Satisfy, v. a. soddisfare.
Saturday, sabato.
Saturn, Saturno.
Save, v. a. salvare.
Saxon, Sassone.
Scale, bilancia, guscio.
Scene, scena, teatro.
Scheme, progetto.
School, scuola.
Science, scienza.
Scorn, disprezzo.
Scotland, Scozia.
Sculptor, scultore.
Sculpture, scultura.
Sea, mare.—coast, spiaggia del mare.
Season, stagione, f.
Seat-one's-self, v. n. sedersi.
Second, secondo.
Secretary, secretario.
Secretly, segretamente.
See, v. a. vedere.—again, rivedere.
Seek, or seek for, v. a. cercare.—after, ricercare.
Seem, v. n. parere, sembrare.
Seldom, di rado, raramente.
Sell, v. a. vendere.
Send, v. a. mandare.
Sentry, sentinella, m. and f.
Separate, v. a. disgiungere.
Servant, servo.
Service, servizio.
Seven, sette.—Seventeen, diciassette.—Seventy, settanta.
Several, molti, parecchi.
Severely, severamente.
Sew, v. a. cucire.—again, ricucire.
Shadow, ombra.
Shame, vergogna.
Share, parte, f.
She, ella, essa.
Sheep, pecora.
Sheet, foglio.
Shield, scudo.
Shilling, scellino.

Ship, nave, f. vascello.
Shop, bottega.
Shore, spiaggia, lido.
Short, corto.
Show, v. a. mostrare.
Shudder, v. n. tremare.
Shut, shut up, v. a. chiudere.
Side, parte, f.
Side-board, credenza.
Siege, assedio.
Sight, vista, prospettiva. By—, di vista.
Silver, argento.
Simple, semplice.
Simplicity, semplicità.
Since, di poi, da, poichè. —since that, dacchè.
Sing, v. a. cantare.
Singer, cantante.
Single, solo, semplice.
Sir, Signore.
Sire, Sire.
Sister, sorella.
Sister-in-law, cognata.
Sit, v. n. sedere, sedersi.
Situation, situazione, f.
Six, sei.
Sixth, sesto.
Sixty, sessanta.
Sketch, schizzo.
Skip about, v. n. saltellare.
Slate, lavagna.
Sleep, v. n. dormire (like Servire).
Slow, slowly, adagio.
Small, piccolo.
Smile, v. n. ridere.
Snow, neve.
Snow, v. i. nevicare.
So, così.
Society, società.
Soldier, soldato.
Solon, Solone.
Some, del, dello, &c., alcuno, &c., qualche, poco (po').
Something, qualche cosa.
Sometimes, qualche volta.
Son, figlio.
Song, canzone, f.
Sonnet, sonetto.
Soon, tosto, presto.
Sound, suono, rimbombo.
Source, sorgente, f.
South, mezzogiorno.
Spain, Spagna.
Spanish, spagnuolo.

Spare, v. a. risparmiare.
Speak, v. a. parlare.
Speaker, oratore.
Special, speciale.
Species, spezie.
Speculation, speculazione, f.
Speech, discorso.
Spend, v. a. spendere.
Spirited, animato.
Spite, rancore, m.—Inspite of, ad onta di.
Splendid, magnifico.
Spoil, v. a. guastare.
Sport, divertimento.
Spread, v. a. distendere.
Spring (season), primavera. (source), fonte, sorgente.
Squander, v. a. scialacquare.
Stage, scena, teatro.
Staircase, scala.
Star, stella.
Start, v. n. partire.—up, saltar su.
State, stato.
Statement, dichiarazione, f.
Statue, statua.
Steal, v. a. rubare.
Steam-boat, battello a vapore.
Steel, acciaio.
Steward, castaldo.
Stick, bastone, m.
Still, v. a. quietare.
Still, adv. eppure.
Stock, v. a. fornire.
Stone, pietra, sasso.
Stop, v. a. and n. fermare, fermarsi.
Story, storiella.
Stout, grosso.
Straight, diritto.
Strange, strano, bizzarro.
Stranger, forestiero.
Strawberry, fragola.
Stream, ruscello, riviera.
Street, strada, via.
Strength, robustezza, forza, fortezza, potere, m.
Strike, sciopero.
Strike, v. a. battere, ferire (like Finire).
Strikingly, sorprendentemente.
Strong, forte, potente.
Student, scolare, alunno.
Study, studio.

Study, v. a. studiare.
Style, stile, m.
Subject (of a monarch), suddito.
Substance, materia.
Succeed, v. n. riuscire, succedere (see rule 258).
Success, successo, esito.
Succession, successione, f.
Such, tale.—a, un tale.—as, tale quale.
Sudden, improvviso.
Suddenly, all'improvviso.
Suffer, v. n. soffrire (like Servire), patire (like Finire).
Sufficiently, abbastanza.
Suggest, v. a. suggerire (like Finire).
Sum, somma.
Summer, estate, f.
Sun, sole, m.
Superfluous, superfluo.
Superstition, superstizione.
Support, in support, per corroborare.
Support, v. a. sostenere, sopportare.
Suppose, v. a. supporre.
Sure, sicuro, certo.
Surface, superficie, f.
Surprise, v. a. sorprendere.
Surround, v. a. circondare.
Surrounding, circonvicino.
Sustain, v. n. subire (like Finire).
Sweet, dolce.
Sweetheart, amante.
Swim (about), v. n. guizzare.
Switzerland, Svizzera.
Sword, spada.

T
Table, tavola.
Take, v. a. prendere.—a walk, fare una passeggiata. — away, condur via.—care, aver cura.—off, levare, or levarsi.
Talent, talento.
Talk, v. a. chiacchierare.
Talker, parlatore, ciarlone.
Tall, grande, alto.
Tartary, Tartaria.
Tax, taxation, tassa.
Tea, tè.—cup, tazza da tè.
Teach, v. a. insegnare.

Telescope, cannocchiale, m.
Tell, v. a. dire.
Temptation, tentazione, f.
Ten, dieci.
Tend, v. n. inclinare.
Terror, spavento.
Than, che.
Thank, v. a. ringraziare.
That, quello, quel, quella, che.
The, il, lo, la, &c.
Theatre, teatro.
Theatrical, teatrale.
Theft, ladrocinio.
Their, il loro, la loro, &c.
Them, loro, essi, esse.
Then (at that time), allora.
Then (therefore), dunque.
There, là, lì.
There is, c'è, or v'è.—There are, ci sono, or vi sono, &c.
These, questi, queste.
They, eglino, elleno, essi.
Thief, ladro.
Thimble, ditale, m.
Thing, cosa.
Think (of), v. n. pensare a, credere.
Third, terzo.
Thirteen, tredici.
Thirty, trenta.
This, questo, questa.
Thomas, Tommaso.
Thorn, spina.
Thoroughly, completamente.
Those, quelli, quei, quelle.
Thou, tu.
Though, quantunque, sebbene.
Thought, pensiero.
Thousand, mille, migliaio.
Thread, filo.
Three, tre.
Through, per, a traverso.
Throw, v. a. gettare.
Thunder, tuono.
Thursday, giovedì.
Thy, il tuo, la tua, i tuoi, le tue.
Ticket, biglietto.
Tiger, tigre, f.
Till, fino, infino.
Time, tempo, volta (see rule 602).
Tint, tinta, colore, m.
Tired, stanco.

Title, titolo.
To, prep. a or onde (see rule 225).
To, a verbal prefix, is not translated (see rules 226 and 227).
To-day, oggi.
Together, insieme.
Token, segno.
To-morrow, domani. — after, posdomani.
Too, anche.—Too (meaning too much), troppo.
Tooth, dente.
Top, sommità, vetta.
Torrent, torrente.
Toulon, Tolone.
Towards, verso.
Tower, torre, f.
Town, città.
Trace, traccia.
Tract, tratto.
Trade, mestiere, m. commercio. By —, di mestiere.
Tradition, tradizione, f.
Tragedy, tragedia.
Train, treno, traino.
Train, v. a. allevare, istruire.
Traitor, traditore.
Translate, v. a. tradurre.
Translation, traduzione, f.
Transmit, v. a. trasmettere.
Travel, v. n. viaggiare.
Treasure, tesoro.
Tree, albero.
Trifles, coserelle.
Triumphant, trionfante.
Troops, truppe, esercito.
Trouble, fatica.
Troy, Troia.
True, vero.
Trunk, tronco, baule.
Trust, v. a. confidare. — one's-self, confidarsi.
Truth, verità.
Tune, aria.
Turbot, rombo.
Turk, Turkish, Turco.
Turmoil, fracasso.
Tutor, precettore, maestro.
Twelve, dodici.
Twenty, venti.
Twice, due volte.
Twilight, crepuscolo.
Two, due.
Tyrant, tiranno.

ENGLISH-ITALIAN VOCABULARY.

U

Ugly, brutto.
Umbrella, ombrello.
Uncle, zio.
Uncommon, straordinario.
Under, sotto.
Understand, v. a. capire (like Finire).
Understanding, ingegno.
Undertake, v. a. intraprendere.
Undertaking, impresa.
Unfortunate, sfortunato.
Unfortunately, sfortunatamente.
Uniform, uniforme, m.
Universal, universale.
University, università.
Unless, a meno che.
Unpardonable, imperdonabile.
Unsheath, v. a. sguainare.
Until, fino.
Up, upon, su, sopra.—up and down, su e giù.
Uranus, Urano.
Us, noi.
Use (to be accustomed), v. n. solere.—To use (to make use of), v. a. servirsi di.—To use (to wear out), v. a. usare.
Useful, utile.
Useless, inutile.

V

Vain, vano, inutile. In—, invano.
Valour, valore, m.
Valuable, prezioso.
Variety, varietà.
Vase, vaso.
Vast, vasto.
Venice, Venezia.
Venus, Venere.
Verb, verbo.
Verdure, verdura.
Verse, verso, poesìa. Blank—, verso sciolto.
Very, molto, assai.—much, moltissimo. — soon, presto, fra poco.
Vessel, vascello, nave, f.
Vice, vizio.
Vicious, vizioso.
Victim, vittima.
Victory, vittoria.
View, vista prospettiva.— v. a. esaminare.
Village, villaggio.
Vinditive, vindicativo.
Virtue, virtù, f.
Visit, v. a. visitare.
Vivacity, vivacità.
Vivid, vivido, allegro.
Voice, voce, f.
Volcano, vulcano.
Vote, v. a. votare.

W

Waistcoat, panciotto, sottoveste, gilè.
Wait, v. n. aspettare.
Waiter, garzone.
Wales, Gallia.
Walk, passeggiata.
Walk, v. n. camminare.
Wall, muro.
Wallet, valigia.
Wander, v. a. vagare.
Want, mancanza.
Want, v. n. abbisognare di.
War, guerra.
Warble, v. a. cantare.
Warlike, bellicoso.
Warm, caldo, ardente.
Warmly, affezionatamente.
Warrior, guerriero.
Wash (one's-self), v. r. lavarsi.
Watch, oriuolo.
Water, v. a. annaffiare.
Water, acqua. Soda—, acqua di seltz.
Wave, onda.
Way, strada, modo, maniera.
We, noi.
Weapon, arma.
Wear, v. a. portare.
Weather, tempo.
Wednesday, mercoledì.
Week, settimana.
Weight, peso.
Well, bene.
Well ! Ebbene !
Western, occidentale.
What, che, che cosa, quale, ciò che.
Whatever, checchè.
When, quando.
Whence, donde.
Where, dove.
Wherever, ovunque.
Whether, se.
Which, che, quale.
While, whilst, mentre.
White, bianco.
Who, he who, chi.
Whole, tutto.
Whom, cui, quale, &c.
Whose, di che, del quale, &c. (see rule 619).
Why ? perchè ?
Wide, largo.
Widower, vedovo.
Wife, moglie.
William, Guglielmo.
Wind, vento.
Window, finestra
Wine, vino.
Winter, inverno.
Wise, saggio, savio.
Wisely, saviamente.
Wish (to desire), v. a. bramare, desiderare.—To wish (to somebody else), v. a. augurare.
Wit, ingegno, spirito, bell' ingegno.
With, con.
Without, senza, fuori.
Witness, v. a. assistere a.
Witty, spiritoso.
Woman, donna.
Wonderful, meraviglioso.
Wood, bosco.
Wool, lana.
Word, parola.
Work, lavoro.
Work, v. a. lavorare.
Workman, operaio.
World, mondo.
Worst, peggiore.
Worthy, degno.
Wound, ferita.
Write, v. a. scrivere
Writing-desk, scrittoio.
Writing-paper, carta da scrivere.

Y

Yard, braccio.
Year, anno.
Yellowish, giallognolo.
Yes, sì.
Yesterday, ieri.
Yet, ancora.
Yield, v. a. cedere.
You, voi, ella.
Young, giovane. — man, giovinotto.
Your, vostro. — self, voi, voi medesimo.

VOCABULARY.

PART II.

ITALIAN—ENGLISH.

A

A, to, at.
Abbandonata, abandoned.
Accanto, at the side of.
Acqua, water.
Addorme, v. a. lulls to sleep.
Aëre, air (see page 114).
Affanna, he afflicts.
Affanno, affanni, sorrow, sorrows.
Affetti, affections.
Affidi, you trust.
Affretta, she hastens.
Ahi! alas!
Al, all', alle, ai, to the.
Alba, dawn.
Allegrati, rejoice.
Alma, soul, mind (see page 114).
Almen, at least.
Alpe, Alpi, Alps.
Alta, high.
Altar, altar.
Altezza, height.
Altier, proud.
Altro, other, another.—che, more than.
Altrui, others.
Ama, he loves.
Amator, lover.
Ambo, ambe, both.
Amico, friendly.
Ammiro, I admire.
Amor, amore, love.
Amorosa, love inspiring.
Anche, anch', also.
Ancor, also.
Andar, gait.
Anelo, breathless.
Angelica, angelic.
Angusta, narrow.
Anima, soul.
Anno, anni, year, years.
Ansia, anxiety.
Appare, it appears.
Appena, scarcely.
Appressar, approaching.
Aprile, April, spring.
Arbitro, judge.
Arboscello, shrub.
Ardea, it was burning.
Ardiscon, they dare.
Ardor, warmth.
Ardua, difficult.
Arena, arene, sands, shores.
Argento, silver.
Aria, air.
Armato, armed.
Aroma, fragrance.
Arsi, I burnt.
Ascolta, listen.
Aspettando, awaiting.
Assalse, it assailed.
Assise (si), placed himself.
Assonna, it lulls to sleep.
Attende, he awaits.
Atterra, he prostrates.
Attonita, astonished.
Aura, breeze (see page 114).
Aurati, golden.
Aureo, golden.
Auretta, gentle breeze (see page 114).
Aurora, dawn.
Avanza, it advances.
Avea, I had.
Avvezza, accustomed.
Avvien, it happens.
Avviò, it sent him.
Avvolgea, twisted.
Avvolve (s') coils up.
Azzurrina, azure.

B

Bacia, it kisses.
Bagni, it bathes.
Ballo, ball, dance.
Basso, low.
Battaglia, battle.
Beate, happy.
Bel, bello, bella, bell', bei, begli, beautiful.
Bellezza, beauty.
Beltà, beauty, beauties (see page 114).
Ben, love.
Benchè, although.
Bene, blessing.
Ben è ver, it is quite true.
Benefattor, benefactor.
Benefica, beneficent.
Benignamente, kindly.
Braccio, braccia, arm, arms.
Brando, sword.
Brillar, to shine.
Brine, hoar-frosts.

C

Cada, it falls.
Cadde, he, it fell.
Cagione, cause.
Calpestar, to trample on.
Calpesto, trodden upon.
Campo, campi, field, fields.
Cangiar, to change.
Cantico, song.
Canto, song.
Canzone, canzoni, song, songs.
Capei, hair (see page 114).
Capo, head.

ITALIAN-ENGLISH VOCABULARY.

Caro, cari, dear.
Casti, chaste, pure.
Cavalli, horses.
Cedrati, citron trees.
Celere, rapid.
Celeste, heavenly.
Ceneri, ashes.
Che, ch', who, that, what, which, so that.
Chè, for, why.
Chi, who, he who, whom.
Chiama, he, it calls.
Chiamando, calling.
Chiare, clear.
Chiede, he asks.
Chiesi, I asked.
Chinati, bent down.
Chiniam, we bend low.
Chinò (si), it bent itself.
Chiude, it encircles.
Chiuse, he ended, finished.
Cielo, ciel, sky, heavens.
Cinta, girt.
Circonfusa, bathed.
Codardo, cowardly.
Col, coll', co', with the.
Colline, hills.
Color, colours.
Colora, it colours.
Coltrice, bed (lit. coverlet).
Come, how, as if, like.
Commosso, moved.
Compianga, you sympathise with.
Comune, common.
Con, with.
Conchiglia, sea shell.
Concitato, rapid.
Conflitto, conflict.
Confuso, confused, intermingled.
Consegno, I consign.
Conserte, crossed.
Consola, gives consolation.
Contende, it objects.
Contrade, countries.
Contro, against.
Convalli, valleys.
Coralli, corals.
Core, cor, heart.
Coronata, crowned.
Cosa, thing, being.
Così, thus, even so.
Creator, creating.
Crede, it believes.
Crederò, I shall think.
Croce, cross.
Crudele, cruel.

Cruenta, blood-stained.
Cui, whom, which.
Cumulo, heap.
Cuor, cuore, heart.
Cura, care.

D

Da, from, by.
Dà, she gives.
Dal, dall' dai, dagli, from the.
Danni, ills, woes.
Danze, dances.
Dar, to give.
Dato, (having) given.
Degradato, degraded.
Dei, gods.
Del, della, dell', dei, de', degli, of the.
Deserta, deserted.
Desir, desires.
Destò, it kindled.
Destra, right.
Di, d', of.
Dì, day, days.
Dice, he, she says, names.
Dicendo, saying.
Diciam, we say.
Difende, it defends.
Diletto, delight, pleasure.
Dimmi, tell me, bid me.
Dio, God.
Dipinto, painted.
Dir, v. a. to say.
Dirmi, to tell me.
Discorda, it is out of harmony.
Disdegna, she disdains.
Disegno, design.
Disotto, under.
Disperò, he lost hope.
Diversa, different.
Divien, it becomes.
Divina, heavenly.
Divisa, divided.
Dolcezza, sweetness.
Dolci, sweet.
Donde, whence.
Donna, woman, lady.
Dono, gift.
Dopo, after.
Dov', dove, where.
Dovunque, wherever.
Drappello, troop of soldiers.
Dubbiosi, anxious.
Duc, duke, leader.
Due, two.
Dunque, then.

Dura, it lasts.

E

E, ed, and.
È, he, she, it is.
Ecco, behold.
Egli, he.
Ella, she.
Empi, you fill.
Era, it was.
Erano, they were.
Erbetta, grass.
Erma, secluded.
Erra, it wanders.
Esca, food, bait.
Esecrando, esecranda, execrable.
Esiglio, exile.
Essi, they.
Estreme, last.
Eterne, eterni, eternal.

F

Fa, makes. Si fa, it makes itself.
Falso, false.
Fanti, foot-soldiers.
Fare, far, to make, to do.
Farsi, to make itself.
Fate, fairies.
Fato, fate, destiny.
Fattor, maker.
Favella, language.
Fe', he did.
Fede, faith, belief.
Fedele, faithful.
Ferire, ferir, to wound, wounding.
Ferro, weapon.
Ferve, it is fervent, boils.
Fiera, fierce, brave.
Figlia, daughter.
Fin, even.
Fine, end.
Fior, fiori, flowers.
Flebile, doleful.
Floridi, blooming.
Flutto, waves, sea.
Follìa, folly.
Folti, thick.
Fonte, fonti, fountain, fountains, springs.
Forma, form.
Forse, perhaps.
Forte, brave man.
Fosse, he was.
Fra, between, amongst.
Fratelli, brothers.

ITALIAN-ENGLISH VOCABULARY.

Fronde, leaves, branches.
Fronte, brow.
Fu, he, it was.
Fuga, flight.
Fulgor, splendour.
Fulmine, thunderbolt.
Fulminei, beaming.
Furente, maddened.
Furono, they were, they have gone.

G

Genio, genius.
Gentile, gentle.
Già, already.
Giacque, he laid down, he lay low.
Giammai, ever. But when "giammai" is used with a negation, it is translated by *never*.
Giardini, gardens.
Gigli, lilies.
Giocondo, pleasant.
Gioia, joy.
Gioioso, happy.
Giorno, day.
Giovin, youth.
Giro (noun) turn. In giro, around. Move in giro, spans the heavens.
Giro, I turn.
Giunge, it arrives at it.
Giurato, sworn.
Gli, the, to him, to it, to them.
Gloria, glory.
Gran, great.
Gratitudine, gratitude.
Grato, grateful.
Grave, heavy.
Grazioso, graceful.
Grembo, lap.
Gridammo, we cried.
Grido, gridi, cry, cries.
Gronda, pours down.
Guancial, pillow.
Guardando, looking.
Guardare, to look.
Guardo, guardi, look, looks.
Guerra, war.
Guerrieri, warriors.
Gusta, it enjoys.

H

Ha, he, it has.
Hai, you have.
Hanno, they have.

I

I, the.
Ignobile, ignoble.
Il, the, it.
Immemore, unconscious, uncared for.
Immenso, immense.
Immerge, he plunges.
Immobile, motionless.
Immortal, immortal.
Impalidir, becoming pale.
Imperio, command.
Imperli, it decks with pearls.
Implora, he implores.
Imprese, he undertook.
In, on.
Incalza, pursue hotly.
Incarco, burden.
Incerto, uncertain.
Incontro, against.
Indocile, unchecked.
Indomato, unabated.
Indura, he hardens himself.
Inerte, idle.
Inestinguibil, unquenched, unassuaged.
Infelice, unhappy.
Innanzi, forward.
Intender, to understand.
Intrisa, soaked.
Invan, in vain.
Invidia, jealousy.
Io, i', I.
Ira, anger.
Istante, instant.

L

La, le, l', the, her, it.
Lago, lake.
Lampo, lightning.
Lasciarmi, to leave me.
Lati, sides.
Laudare, v. a. to praise.
Laureti, laurel groves.
Le, the, from her.
Lei, her, it.
Li, them.
Lignaggio, race, lineage.
Lingua, tongue.
Linguaggio, language.
Lo, the, him, it.
Lontana, distant.
Lor, them, their.
Luce, light.
Lui, him, he, it.
Lume, light, brilliancy.
Luna, moon.
Lunghi, long.

M

Ma, but.
Madri, mothers.
Maga, enchantress.
Maggior, greater.
Mai, ever.
Mal, badly.
Male, ill, woe.
Man, hand.
Manco, less.
Mandola, mandoline.
Manipoli, battalions.
Mar, mari, sea, seas.
Maraviglia, wander.
Marina, sea-shore. A—by the sea-shore.
Marte, mars, war.
Massimo, greatest.
Mattin, morning.
Mattine, mornings.
Mattutina, in the morning.
Me, m', me, from me.
Melanconia, melancholy.
Memorie, recollection.
Mente, mind, memory.
Mentr', whilst.
Mercè, reward.
Meriggio, mid-day.
Mesce, it mixes itself.
Mezzo, middle.
Mi, in', me, to me.
Miei, my.
Miglior, better.
Mille, a thousand.
Mio, mia, my, mine.
Mira, he looks.
Miracol, miracle.
Misero, miserable.
Mista, mingled.
Misura, measures.
Mobili, changing.
Mondo, world.
Monile, necklace.
Montagna, mountain.
Monte, monti, hill, hills.
Morir, morire, to die.
Mormorando, murmuring.
Morrà, he, it will die.
Morta, dead.
Mortal, mortale, mortal.
Mortalmente, mortally.
Morte, death.
Mostrare, to show.
Mostrasi, she shows herself.
Mova (si), there moves.
Move, it moves.
Muta, dumb-struck.

ITALIAN-ENGLISH VOCABULARY.

N
Nacque, he was born.
Narrar, to relate.
Nato, born.
Natura, nature.
Naufrago, shipwrecked.
Ne, of it, to us.
Nè, nor.
Nel, nella, nell', nei, ne', in the.
Nembo, cloud, shower.
Nevi, snows.
Ninfa, nymph.
Nodi, curls.
Noi, we.
Nomò (si), he named himself.
Non, not.
Notte, night.
Nudrice, mother.
Nunzio, announcement.
Nuovi, new.
Nuvoli, clouds.

O
O, or, either.
O, O!
Obbedir, to obey.
Oblìo, oblivion, neglect.
Occhi, eyes.
Ode, s'ode, one hears.
Odio, hatred.
Odorose, perfumed.
Ogni, each, every.
Ognor, always.
Ognun, each one.
Olenti, sweet scented.
Oltra, beyond.
Oltraggio, outrage.
Ombra, shade.
Ombroso, shady.
Onda, onde, wave, waves.
Onde, by which.
Onesta, honest, modest.
Onor, honours.
Onorava, he honoured.
Opre, works.
Or, ora, now.
Ora, ore, hour, hours.
Orba, bereaved.
Orgoglio, pride.
Orma, mark, foot-print.
Ornato, adorned.
Oro, gold.
Oscura, dark.
Ottiene, he, it obtains.
Ozio, idleness.

P
Pacato, calm.
Pace, peace.
Padri, fathers.
Pagine, pages.
Pago, satisfied.
Palmeti, palm groves.
Par, pare, it appears.
Parea, it appeared.
Pari, equal.
Parlan, they speak.
Parola, parole, word, words.
Passò, it passed away.
Pavidi, terrified.
Pel, pei, for the, through the.
Pellegrina, wandering.
Pena, pain.
Pendice, brow of the hill.
Penne, feathers, wings.
Pensando, thinking.
Pensieri, thoughts.
Per, for, through, in order to, on account of.
Perchè, why.
Percossa, struck.
Perdè, he lost.
Periglio (poet. for pericolo), danger.
Perla, pearl.
Pesa, it weighs.
Petto, breast.
Piacente, charming.
Piacer, piaceri, pleasures.
Piangi, weep.
Pianto, weeping.
Piè, foot.
Pien, full.
Pietà, pity, sympathy.
Pietosa, solemn.
Pietosi, compassionate.
Piramidi, Pyramids.
Più, more, il più, the most.
Placar, to pacify.
Poi, then, after.
Polve (poet.), polvere, dust.
Pone, he places himself.
Popolo, people.
Portento, miracle.
Posi, you rest.
Posò, he rested.
Posteri, posterity.
Potere, power.
Praticello, meadow.
Preme, weighs you down.
Premio, reward.
Prende, it takes.
Preparazione, preparation.
Prepari (ti), you prepare yourself.
Primavera, spring.
Primo, first.
Privo, deprived.
Procellosa, stormy.
Prode, shores.
Profonda, profound.
Prova, he experiences.
Provò, he experienced.
Prudenti, prudent.
Pugna, he fights.
Può, he, it can.
Pur, yet, merely, really.
Pura, pure.
Pur dianzi, just now.

Q
Qual, quale, who, which, what, like.
Quando, when.
Quante, how many.
Quei, those, he who.
Quel, quella, quell', that.
Questo, questa, this.
Qui, here.
Quinci, on this side.
Quindi, on that side.

R
Raccogli, stay.
Raddoppia, redoubles.
Raggio, ray.
Rai, rays (see page 114).
Rapivi, you stole.
Rea, wicked (see page 121).
Recinta, surrounded, girt.
Reggia, royal abode.
Regina, queen.
Regno, reign, power.
Remote, distant.
Rende, it gives.
Respingon, clash against.
Ria, insulting.
Riaprendo, re-opening.
Ricantando, singing over again.
Ricchezza, riches.
Riceve, it receives.
Riconosco, I recognise.
Ride, he, it smiles.
Rimbomba, re-echoes.
Rinserra, it contains.
Rio, brook.
Ripensò, he thought again.
Rischi, risks, perils.
Riso, smile.
Risorse, he rose again.

ITALIAN-ENGLISH VOCABULARY.

Risplende, it shines.
Risponde, it answers.
Ritornerà, it will return.
Ritorneranno, they will return.
Rivo, brook.
Rondinella, swallow.
Rose, roses.
Rote, wheels.
Rugiada, dew.

S

Sa, it knows how to, it can.
Sacrilego, sacrilegious.
Saggio, wise man.
Saluta, she greets, salutes.
Salutando, greeting.
Salva, safe, free.
San, they know.
Sangue, blood.
Sanno, they know.
Sarà, it will be.
Scarsi, scarce, bereft.
Scendi, you descend.
Scernere, to perceive.
Scese, it descended.
Scherzi, it may sport, it may ripple.
Schierato, in battle array.
Schiudon, they open.
Scioglie, it bestows.
Sconsolata, disconsolate.
Scoppiò, it burst out.
Scorato, discouraged.
Scorrea, it was looking.
Scorri, you cross over.
Scrivi, write.
Se, s', if.
Sè stesso, himself.
Secoli, centuries.
Securo, secure, fearless.
Segno, sign, mark.
Sei, se', you are.
Sempre, always.
Sen, seno, breast.
Senso, sense, sentiment.
Sentendosi, hearing herself.
Sentenza, decision.
Senti, you feel.
Sentier, paths.
Senz', senza, without.
Sera, evening.
Sereno, serena, cloudless.
Serve, he serves.
Settembre, September.
Sfere, spheres.
Sfida, he defies.

Sfolgorante, shining.
Si, s', himself, herself, itself, themselves.
Sì, so much.
Sia, she may be.
Sicchè, in such a manner that.
Siccome, just as.
Silenzio, silence.
Simile, similar.
Sin che, so long as.
Sinistra, left.
Sirena, syren.
So, I know.
Sofferto, suffered.
Soglio, throne.
Sogno, dream.
Sol, solo.
Sola, alone, only.
Sole, sun.
Solingo, lonely.
Solitaria, solitary.
Sommessi, humbly.
Son, I am.
Sonito, sound, din.
Sonno, sleep.
Sono, I am, they are.
Sopra, on, concerning.
Sorge, it rises.
Sospir, sospiro, sigh.
Sospira, sigh.
Sott' onda, submarine.
Sovra, upon.
Sovvenir, remembrance.
Spade, swords.
Sparir, disappearing.
Sparito, disappeared.
Sparsi, dishevelled.
Sparve, he disappeared.
Speme, hope (see page 114).
Speranza, hope.
Sperar, to hope.
Sperdi, do thou divert.
Spiegato, unfurled.
Spirabil, breathing.
Spiro, spirit.
Spirito, spirto (see page 114), spirit.
Spoglia, corpse.
Spogliar, to take off.
Spose, wives.
Sposo, husband, mate.
Spregio, contempt, thraldom.
Sprezzato, despised.
Spunta, it appears, looms in the distance.
Squillo, blast of a trumpet.

Sta, it remains.
Stampar, to mark.
Stanca, fatigued.
Stanche, fatigued.
Stanzetta, little room.
Stellato, starry sky.
Stesso, himself.
Stette, he, it stood.
Stolti, foolish.
Straniero, foreigner.
Strappar, to snatch away.
Strazio, torture.
Su, upon, on.
Subit', di subit', at once.
Subito, sudden.
Sul, sulla, sull', on the, in the.
Suo, sua, sue, his, hers, its.
Suolo, soil.
Suon, suoni, sound, sounds.
Suonavan, they sounded.
Superba, proud.
Supina, languid.
Suscita, it raises up.
Sventura, misfortune.

T

Tacito, silent.
Tacque, it was silent.
Tale, tal, such, even so.
Tanto, so great.
Te, t', you, to you.
Teme, it fears.
Tempo, time.
Tempre, quality.
Tenea dietro, it followed.
Tenebre, darkness.
Tende, tents.
Terra, earth, land.
Terreno, terren, ground.
Terror, terror.
Tesa, extended, intent.
Ti, t', you, yourself.
Tiene, he holds.
Tiranni, tyrants.
Tolta, taken away.
Tomba, tomb.
Tornata, having returned (see rule 200).
Torrenti, torrents.
Tra, amongst, between.
Traluce, appears, shines.
Trapasserò, I shall outpass.
Traspar, appears.
Trasportò, it transported.
Trasse, unsheathed.
Tremando, trembling.
Trepida, anxious.

Trionfi, triumphs.
Triquetra, ancient name for Sicilia, Sicily.
Tristo, sad.
Tromba, trumpet.
Troverai, you will find.
Troncator, abbreviator
Tu, thou.
Tua, tue, thy.
Tuo, thy.
Tuoi, thy, your.
Turba, crowd.
Tutte, tutti, all.
Tutto, tutta, all, everything.

U

Ubbidir, v. n. to obey.
Udir, v. a. to hear.
Ultima, last.
Umana, human.
Umiltà, humility.
Umor, moisture.
Un, uno, una, un', one, an, a.
Uomo, uom, man.
Urna, urn.

V

Va, he, she, it goes.
Vago, vaga, beautiful, lovely.

Val, it is worth.
Valida, helping.
Valli, bulwarks.
Vanno, they go.
Vasta, vast, wide.
Vedo, I see.
Vedovetta, little widow.
Vedrai, you will see.
Vegliardi (poet. for "vecchi,") old men.
Velo, veil.
Vendetta, vengeance.
Venduto, sold.
Venga, he comes.
Venne, nevenne, he, it came.
Venuto, venuta, come.
Ver, truth.
Vera, true.
Veri, true.
Vermigli, red.
Verone, verandah.
Verrà, it will come.
Versar, to pour down, to bestow.
Verso, towards.
Vespertina, in the evening.
Vessillo, standard.
Veste, it clothes.
Vesti, clothes.

Vicende, events.
Vide, he, it saw.
Vidi, I saw.
Viene, vien, it comes.
Vigile, vigilant.
Vile, vile. A—, in contempt.
Virtù, virtue, valour.
Viso, face.
Vista, sight, view.
Vita, life.
Vittoria, victory.
Viviamo, we live.
Vivo, lively, brilliant.
Vivrò, I shall live.
Voce, voice.
Voi, you.
Volle, he willed.
Volo, flight.
Volsero, they turned themselves.
Volta, vault, dungeon.
Volte, times.
Volto, volti, face, faces.
Vuoi? will you?

Z

Zaffiro, sapphire.
Zeffiretto, zephyr, breeze.

WORKS BY PROFESSOR N. PERINI.

PUBLISHED BY
MESSRS. HACHETTE & CO., 18, KING WILLIAM STREET,
CHARING CROSS, LONDON, W.C.

"**La Vita Nuova,**" by Dante Alighieri, with Notes and Comments in English. Imperial 16mo, cloth lettered, 2s. 6d.

"**A First Italian Reading Book,**" containing Prose and Poetry, with Rules for the Pronunciation of the Italian Language, with Notes, Hints on Italian Versification, and a Complete Vocabulary of all the words contained in the Text, in which the "tonic accent" is marked in darker type, and the proper pronunciations of the Letters "E," "O," "S," and "Z" are indicated. Cloth gilt, 2s. 6d.

The First Chapters of "I Promessi Sposi," by Manzoni, followed by a repetition of the text, with an English Interlinear Translation. Cloth gilt, 2s. 6d.

"**La Clemenza di Tito,**" by Metastasio, followed by a repetition of the text of the First Act, with an English Interlinear Translation, and numbers indicating the position of the words in the Text. Cloth gilt, 2s. 6d.

Questions and Exercises on the Grammar and Idioms of the French Language; with answers to the most Important Questions, and a Repetition of all the Questions, for the purpose of Class, or Self-Examination. Ninth edition. Price 2s.

The above work, now in the hands of all Candidates preparing for all the Competitive Examinations, contains all the most important questions on the Grammar and Idioms of the French Language.

Each question is followed by a blank for the answer thereto.

"**The Bridge,**" or Exercises on Useful English Words, Phrases and Proverbs, for translation into other languages. On the same plan as the above-mentioned work. Second edition. Price 9d.

Extracts in English Prose, from the Best Authors; arranged progressively for translation into other languages. The extracts are divided into numbered sections, to facilitate translation at sight, in class. Third edition. Price 2s.

Five-and-Twenty Exercises on French Verbs, with an Index for Examination. Large 8vo, 24 pages, in paper cover. Eighth edition. Price 6d.

A "**Key**" to this work, sold to Teachers only. Price 1s.

The above work is intended to meet a want long felt in English Schools. The plan of the book is very simple, and yet it goes thoroughly into the subject. It possesses, moreover, the great advantage of entirely relieving the teacher of the tiresome and laborious task of setting verbs to conjugate.

Genealogical and Chronological Tables of the Kings and Princes of France. Price 1s.

LIBRAIRIE HACHETTE & CIE.,

LONDON: 18, KING WILLIAM STREET, CHARING CROSS.

The Catalogue of the firm, containing a complete list of their Classical and Prize Books will be sent free by book-post on application.

THE PUBLIC SCHOOL GERMAN GRAMMAR

With Exercises for Translation, Composition and Conversation,

BY

A. L. MEISSNER, M.A., Ph.D., D.Lit.,

LIBRARIAN AND PROFESSOR OF MODERN LANGUAGES IN QUEEN'S COLLEGE, BELFAST,

Mitglied der Gesellschaft, fur das Studium der neueren Sprachen zu Berlin,

1 Vol. small 8vo, 384 pages, cloth. Price 3s. 6d.

Teachers and Students of German are to be congratulated upon such an acquisition as Professor Meissner's PUBLIC SCHOOL GERMAN GRAMMAR. It is as thoroughly well done as the name of its author would lead one to expect.

LONDON. HENRY ATTWELL.

Die Anlage und Ausstattung gefallen mir sehr.

The Reverend A. L. BECKER.

The general plan of the book is so good that it is pretty sure to have a wide circulation.

LIVERPOOL. E. L. NAFTEL.

A new and improved method of learning the German language grammatically and conversationally, if simple and comprehensive, is certain to be welcomed and widely used, and we have no hesitation in saying that this is the best work of the kind we have met with. A look at the preface will fully explain Dr. Meissner's system—it could scarcely fail to be successful. Practice in conversation commences once the first principles are mastered, and the first "conversation lessons are intended to furnish the pupil with the most necessary travel talk for a journey up the Rhine and into Switzerland;" anyone who has travelled being totally ignorant of the language will appreciate this. The new official spelling has been adopted throughout the book, but it has been sufficiently compared with the old in an introductory chapter to enable the student to read the books printed in the old spelling.

The Dublin Evening News.

LE MIE PRIGIONI,

BY

SILVIO PELLICO.

Adapted for English Schools, with Grammatical and Explanatory Notes,

BY

REV. A. C. CLAPIN, M.A.

CLOTH, 1s. 6d.

www.ingramcontent.com/pod-product-compliance
Lightning Source LLC
Chambersburg PA
CBHW031942230426
43672CB00010B/2018